ASP.NET MVC 5

How to build a Membership Website

Contents

1. Introduction 1
   Introduction 1
      Other titles by the author 1
         MVC 5 - How to build a Membership Website 1
         C# for Beginners: The tactical guidebook 2
      Source code and bonus materials 2
      Disclaimer – Who is this book for? 3
      Rights 3
      About the author 3
2. Entity Framework 5
   Introduction 5
      Technologies used in this chapter 5
   The use case 5
      A brief description of the tables 6
   Creating the membership solution 7
   Enable Migrations 8
      Enable database migrations 9
   What's in the database? 10
      User and login tables 12
      Subscription tables 12
      Product tables 12
      Content tables 13
   Creating the database 13
      Changing the database name 14

ASP.NET MVC 5 - How to build a Membership Website

Enabling Data Annotations 14
    Data Annotation Attributes 15
The Section class 16
    Adding the table 17
    The dbContext 18
    Adding a DbSet for the Section class 18
    Create and inspect the database 19
The Part class 21
    Adding the table 21
The ItemType class 22
    Adding the table 23
The Item class 24
    Adding the table 26
The Product class 28
    Adding the table 29
The ProductType class 31
    Adding the table 32
The ProductLinkText class 33
    Adding the table 34
The Subscription class 35
    Adding the table 36
The ProductItem class 37
    Adding the table 39
The SubscriptionProduct class 40
    Adding the table 42
The UserSubscription class 43

- Adding the table 44
- Modifying the AspNetUser class 45
  - Modifying the table 46
- The ApplicationDbContext class 46
- What's Next? 47

3. Create the Admin area & Menu 49
- Introduction 49
  - Technologies used in this chapter 49
- The use case 49
  - The different views 50
  - A brief recap of the different tables 50
- The Admin area 51
- The Admin menu 52
  - Creating the _AdminMenuPartial partial view 54
  - Adding the Admin menu to the navigation bars 55
    - Adding the Admin menu to the main project's navigation bar 56
    - Adding the Admin menu to the Admin area navigation bar 56
  - Adding menu items to the Admin menu 57
  - JavaScript Hover functionality 59
    - Adding the AdminMenu JavaScript file 60
    - Adding the admin bundle for the JavaScript files 61

4. Adding UIs for the Minor Entities 63
- Introduction 63
  - Technologies used in this chapter 63
- The use case 63
- Scaffold the Section controller and views 64

- The Create View 71
  - Change the Create button color 71
  - Create the _BackToListButtonPartial view 71
- The Edit View 74
  - Change the Save button color 74
  - Change the Back to List link to a button 74
- The Details View 76
  - Change the Back to List link to a button 77
  - Create the _EditButtonPartial view 77
- The Delete View 79
  - Change the Delete button color 80
  - Change the Back to List link to a button 80
- The Index View 81
  - Styling the table 82
  - Styling the Create New link 82
  - The SmallButtonModel class 83
  - Creating a generic reusable partial view button 86
  - Create the partial view _TableButtonsPartial 87
  - Add the partial view _TableButtonsPartial to the Index view 90
- Scaffold the Part controller and views 92
- Scaffold the ItemType controller and views 94
- Scaffold the ProductType controller and views 95
- Scaffold the ProductLinkText controller and views 97

5. Adding UIs for the Major Entities 99
- Introduction 99
  - Technologies used in this chapter 99

The use case 99
Scaffold the Item controller and views 100
    The Create Action (HttpGet) 101
    The Create View 102
        Fixing the dropdown labels 103
        Creating the GetPropertyValue extension method 104
        Creating the ToSelectListitem extension method 105
        Fixing the dropdowns 107
    The Edit View 109
        Modifying the Edit controller action (HttpGet) 111
        Replacing the textboxes with dropdowns in the view 111
        Styling the Edit view 112
    The Details View 113
    The Delete View 115
    The Index View 116
        Replacing the Create New link with a button 117
Scaffold the Product controller and views 119
    Adding necessary data 120
    Adding the ProductModel 120
    Adding the ProductController and views 123
    Altering the Index view 124
        Creating the asynchronous Convert extension method 125
        Altering the ProductController's Index action 126
        Altering the Index view 127
    Altering the Create view 129
        Altering the Create action in the ProductController class 132

- Altering the Details view 132
  - Altering the view 133
  - Adding the asynchronous Convert extension method 134
  - Changing the Details action in the ProductController 137
- Altering the Delete view 138
  - Altering the Delete view 139
  - Altering the Delete action in the ProductController 140
- Altering the Edit view 141
  - Altering the Edit view 142
  - Altering the Edit action in the ProductController 143
- Scaffold the Subscription controller and views 144
  - Scaffold the controller and views 144
  - The Index View 145
  - The Create View 148
  - The Edit View 150
  - The Details View 152
  - The Delete View 153

6. Adding UIs for the Connecting Entities 155
- Introduction 155
  - Technologies used in this chapter 155
- The use case 155
- Scaffold the ProductItem controller and views 156
  - Adding the ProductItemModel 157
  - The Create View 158
    - Change @model and add @using 160
    - Changing the label descriptions and the textboxes 160

- Changing the Create controller action (HttpGet) 162
- Styling the Create button and the Back to List link 163
- The Index view 164
  - Modify the table 165
  - Changing the links to buttons 166
  - Modify the Index action and create a Convert method 167
- The Edit View 168
  - The Edit View - Display data (HttpGet) 169
  - Modifying the Edit view 170
  - Modifying the Edit controller action (HttpGet) 172
  - The Edit View - Update data (HttpPost) 175
  - Adding the CanChange method 177
  - Adding the Change method 178
  - Modifying the Edit controller action (HttpPost) 180
- The Details View 181
  - The Details controller action 182
  - Altering the Convert method 183
  - Creating the _EditButtonDetailsPartial partial view 184
  - Creating the EditButonModel class 185
  - Modifying the Details view 187
- The Delete view 188
  - Modifying the view 190
  - Modifying the Delete controller action (HttpGet) 191
  - Modifying the DeleteConfirmed controller action (HttpPost) 192
- Adding UI for the SubscriptionProduct Table 192
  - Generating the SubscriptionProduct Controller and its views 193

Create the SubscriptionProductModel class 194

Copy and alter the Convert method which return a list... 195

Copy and alter the Convert method which return a single item............................ 196

Copy and alter the CanChange method 197

Copy and alter the Change method 198

The Index view... 201

    Modify the Index view... 202

    Modify the Index controller action.. 202

The Create view... 203

    Modify the Create controller action (HttpGet) 206

The Edit view... 207

    Modify the Edit controller action (HttpGet)... 209

    The GetSubscriptionProduct method... 211

    Modify the Edit controller action (HttpPost).. 212

The Details View... 213

    Modify the Details view.. 214

    Modify the Details controller action 215

The Delete View.. 216

    Modify the Delete view 217

    Modify the HttpGet Delete controller action.. 218

    Modify the DeleteConfirmed controller action.. 219

7. Adding transactions to the DeleteConfirmed actions 221

Introduction.. 221

    Technologies used in this chapter 221

Adding a transaction to the Item's DeleteConfirmed action 221

Adding a transaction to the Product's DeleteConfirmed action 223

Adding a transaction to the Subscription's DeleteConfirmed action 225

Adding the delete check to the DeleteConfirmed actions 226

8. Users & Subscriptions 231

Introduction 231

    Technologies used in this chapter 231

User Registration 231

    Alter the RegisterViewModel 232

    Alter the Register action 232

    Alter the Register view 233

    The Admin role 234

    Restict access to the Admin menu and its controllers 235

Modify user information 237

    Create the UserViewModel class 237

    Create the extension methods 239

        Adding the IdentityExtension class 240

        Adding the GetUserFirstName extension method 240

        Adding the GetUsers extension method 241

    Adding the Index view 242

    Adding the Index action 244

    Styling the Index view 245

        Modifying the SmallButtonModel 246

        Modifying the _TableButtonsPartial view 246

        Adding the _TableButtonsPartial view to the Index view 248

    Adding the Create view 248

    Adding the Create actions 251

        The HttpGet Create action 251

- The HttpPost Create action 252
- Adding the Edit view 255
- Adding the Edit actions 259
  - The HttpGet Edit action 259
  - The HttpPost Edit action 261
- Adding the Delete view 263
- Adding the Delete actions 266
  - The HttpGet Delete action 266
  - The HttpPost Delete action 268
- Adding subscriptions to a user 269
  - Adding the UserSubscriptionModel class 270
  - Adding the UserSubscriptionViewModel class 271
  - Adding the Subscriptions view 272
    - Displaying subscriptions in a dropdown 273
    - Displaying a user's subscriptions in a table 275
  - Adding the Subscriptions actions 278
    - Adding the HttpGet Subscriptions action 278
    - Adding the HttpPost Subscriptions action 281
    - Adding the RemoveUserSubscription action 284

9. Application Layout 287
- Introduction 287
  - Technologies used in this chapter 287
- Use case 287
- Alter the navigation bar 287
  - Adding the navbar.css file 288
  - The navigation bar 288

The navigation links	290
Adding a Logo	291
Adding the logo image	292
Styling the menu items	294
Fonts	295
Alter the layout of the Index view	295
10. Display products	**299**
Introduction	299
Adding a subscription	301
Adding a product link text	301
Adding the Product Type	301
Adding the products	302
Adding the subscription	302
Adding a subscription	303
Adding a product to the subscription	303
Adding a subscription to a user	303
Creating thumbnails	304
Adding the ThumbnailModel class	305
Adding the ThumbnailAreaModel class	306
Adding the thumbnails.css style sheet	307
Adding the _ThumbnailAreaPartial partial view	307
Style the _ThumbnailAreaPartial view heading	311
Fetch the user id with Owin Context	312
The GetSubscriptionIdsAsync method	315
Add a ThumbnailEqualityComparer	318
Fetch the thumbnails from the database	319

Modify the Index action 322

Modify the Index view 324

Display data in the _ThumbnailAreaPartial view 325

Add the labels 328

Styling the thumbnail labels 330

Animating the thumbnail image and labels 333

    Animating the lower label 333

    Add a shadow around the thumbnail 334

    Rotate and zoom the image 334

11. Display Product Page 337

Introduction 337

Adding the ProductContent controller 338

Adding the model classes 340

    The ProductItemRow class 340

    The ProductSection class 341

    The ProductSectionEqualityComparer class 341

    The ProductSectionModel class 343

Adding the Index view for the ProductContent controller 343

Adding the GetProductSectionsAsync extension method 346

Altering the Index action 348

Styling the Index view 349

Adding the _ProductSection partial view 351

Styling the carret symbol 355

    The gly-rotate-90 selector 355

    Alligning the carret to the top of the header text 356

    Rotating the carret 356

  The JavaScript 356

 Adding the GetProductItemRowsAsync extension method 357

 Altering the GetProductSectionsAsync extension method 360

 Adding the _ProductItemRow partial view 362

 Altering the _ProductSectionPartial view 366

 Styling the _ProductItemRowPartial view 368

12. Show Content 371

 Introduction 371

 JW Player 371

  Create a JW Player cloud player URL 371

  Adding the necessary JavaScript to play a video 372

 Register a ProductContent route 373

 The ContentViewModel class 373

 The GetContentAsync extension method 374

 Adding the Content Action 375

 Adding the Content view 376

  Adding the Content view 377

  Adding the title and header section 377

  Displaying HTML conent 378

  Displaying Video conent 378

  Styling the Video element 380

  Styling the article HTML markup 380

13. Register Subscription Code 381

 Introduction 381

 Adding the _RegisterCodePartial view 382

 Adding the Register Code panel content 383

Styling the Register Code panel 385

Adding the Register Code panel to the Index view 386

The GetSubscriptionIdByRegistrationCode extension method 386

The Register extension method 388

The RegisterUserSubscriptionCode method 390

The RegisterCode controller 391

    Adding the RegisterCode Controller 392

    Adding the Register action method 392

The JavaScript functions 393

14. Register User 397

Introduction 397

    Technologies used in this chapter 397

Use case 398

Adding the RegisterUserModel 399

    Add the RegisterUserModel 399

Authentication check and calling the partial view 401

Add the _RegisterUserPartial view 402

    Add the partial view 403

    Add the panel to the view 404

Adding controls to the Register User panel 404

    Adding the controls 405

    Styling the panel and the controls 408

        Styling the validation error summary 408

        Removing the rounded corners 409

        Adding space between the textboxes 409

        Styling the icons 409

Styling the button 409

Adding the RegisterUserAsync action 410

   The AddUserErrors method 411

   The Register action 412

Adding JavaScript click events 414

   Add the JavaScript file 415

   Wire up the checkbox click event function 415

   Adding the Ajax action call 416

      Wire up the button click event function 416

15. Login 421

Introduction 421

The GlyphLink extension method 422

Adding the login styles heet and JavaScript files 424

Altering the _LoginPartial view 424

Styling the Log off link 427

Adding the _LoginPanelPartial view 428

   Creating the view 429

   Adding the login panel 429

   Adding JavaScript and CSS to display the login panel 433

   Adding JavaScript to close the login panel 434

Styling the login panel 435

   The panel 435

   The panel heading and body 436

   The textboxes 437

   The Log in button 438

   The checkbox 439

The LoginAsync action 439

The Log in button JavaScript 442

16. Forgot Password 447

Introduction 447

Sending email 448

Web.Config 449

The Send extension method 449

The Account controller 451

The SendAsync method 452

The modal reset password form 453

Adding the CSS and Javbascript files 454

Modifying the GlyphLink extension method 454

Adding the password link 456

Building the modal form 457

Adding the _ForgotPasswordPanelPartial view 458

Adding the modal dialog to the view 458

Styling the modal dialog 461

Adding JavaScript to the modal dialog 462

The Forgot Password Confirmation view 464

The Reset Password email 464

The Reset Passsword view 465

17. Useful Tools & Links 467

Tools 467

Microsoft Web Platform Installer 5.0 467

Bootstrap 467

CodeLens 467

ASP.NET MVC 5 - How to build a Membership Website

Web Essentials	467
Browser link	468
SideWaffle	468
Plunker	468
Visual Studio Code	468
Atom	469
TypeScript	469
Angular	470
Grunt	470
Gulp	471
ECMAScript 6 (JavaScript)	471
Entity Framework (EF Core)	471
Microsoft ASP.NET MVC Documentation	472

1. Introduction

Introduction
This course is primarily aimed at developers who have some prior experience with MVC 5 and are proficient in C#, since the language won't be explained in any detail. Even if you already have created a couple of MVC projects, you might find the content in this book useful as a refresher. You might have worked in previous versions of Visual Studio and MVC and want a fast no-fluff way to get up to speed with MVC 5.

Other titles by the author
The author has written other books and produced video courses that you might find helpful.

MVC 5 - How to build a Membership Website
This is a comprehensive video course showing how to build the membership site that you will be building going through this book. The course has in excess of **24 hours!** of video.

In this video course you will learn how to build a membership website from scratch. You will create the database using Entity Framework code-first, scaffold an Administrator UI and build a front-end UI using HTML5, CSS3, Bootstrap, JavaScript, C# and MVC 5. Prerequisites for this course are: a good knowledge of the C# language and basic knowledge of MVC 5, HTML5, CSS3, Bootstrap and JavaScript.

You can watch the video course on Udemy following this link: www.udemy.com/building-a-mvc-5-membership-website

C# for Beginners: The tactical guidebook
This book is for **YOU** if you are new to C# or want to brush up on your skills and like a **CHALLENGE**. This is not your run-of-the-mill encyclopedic programming book; it is highly modularized, tactical and practical – meaning that you learn by reading theory, and then implement targeted exercises building many applications.

You can buy **C# for Beginners: The tactical guidebook** at Amazon following this link: https://www.amazon.com/dp/B017OAFR8I

Source code and bonus materials
The source code accompanying this book is shared under the MIT License and can be downloaded after registering for free with this site www.csharpschool.com or by emailing the author. At this link, you can also download a free e-book describing MVC 5, CSS 3, HTML 5, Bootstrap, JavaScript JQuery, Ajax for beginners.

Disclaimer – Who is this book for?

It's important to mention that this book is not meant to be a *get-to-know-it-all* book; it's more on the practical and tactical side where you will learn as you progress through the examples and build a real application in the process. Because I personally dislike having to read hundreds upon hundreds of pages of irrelevant fluff (filler material) not necessary for the tasks at hand, and also view it as a disservice to the readers, I will assume that we are of the same mind on this, and will therefore only include important information pertinent for the tasks at hand; thus making the book both shorter and more condensed, and also saving you time and effort in the process. Don't get me wrong, I will describe the important things in great detail, leaving out only the things that are not directly relevant to your first experience with MVC 5. The goal is for you to have created a working MVC application upon finishing this book. You can always look into details at a later time when you have a few projects under your belt. *If you prefer encyclopedic books describing everything in minute detail with short examples, and value a book by how many pages it has rather than its content, then this book is NOT for you.*

The examples in this book are presented using Visual Studio 2015, but they will work with 2013 Professional Update 4 as well. The free express version should do fine when you follow along and implement them yourself.

Rights

All rights reserved. The content is presented as is and the publisher and author assume no responsibility for errors or omissions. Nor is any liability assumed for damages resulting from the use of the information in the book or the accompanying source code.

It is strictly prohibited to reproduce or transmit the whole book, or any part of the book, in any form or by any means without the prior written permission of the author.

You can reach the author at: info@csharpschool.com.

ISBN-13: 978-1535167864, ISBN-10: 1535167866

Copyright © 2015 by Jonas Fagerberg, All rights reserved.

About the author

Jonas started a company back in 1994 focusing on education in Microsoft Office and the Microsoft operating systems. While still studying at the university in 1995, he wrote his first book about Widows 95, as well as a number of course materials.

In the year 2000, after working as a Microsoft Office developer consultant for a couple of years, he wrote his second book about Visual Basic 6.0.

Between 2000 and 2004, he worked as a Microsoft instructor with two of the largest educational companies in Sweden. First teaching Visual Basic 6.0, when Visual Basic.NET and C# were released, he started teaching those languages, as well as the .NET Framework. He was also involved in teaching classes at all levels for beginner to advanced developers.

From the year 2005, Jonas shifted his career towards consulting once again, working hands-on with the languages and framework he taught.

Jonas wrote his third book *C# programming* aimed at beginner to intermediate developers in 2013, and in 2015, his fourth book C# for beginners - The Tactical Guide was published.

Jonas has also produced a 24h+ video course titled MVC 5 – How to build a Membership Website (www.udemy.com/building-a-mvc-5-membership-website), showing in great detail how to build a membership website.

2. Entity Framework

Introduction
In this chapter you will learn the basics of Entity Framework and how to create a code-first database; meaning that no design surface will be used – only plain C# classes. The database will be used throughout the remainder of this book to fetch and update data. You will implement two scenarios. The first is a rudimentary admin portal for adding, deleting and updating memberships, courses and content. The second scenario is successively building a user interface where users can log in and view the content they subscribe to. The content will be in the form of videos, articles and downloadable content.

The database will constitute the backend storage for the content you share through your products.

The database you will handle four areas which are connected to one another: users, subscriptions, products and content.

Technologies used in this chapter
- **Entity Framework Code-First** - You will model the database using entity classes which then are used to create the tables when building the database.
- **C#** - Is used to create the entity classes.
- **Attributes** - Will decorate classes and properties to enable specific functionality such as storing HTML in a column, client side validation, and restricting the content size.

The use case
The customer wants you to build a database for their upcoming membership site. They request that you create it using *Entity Framework Code-First* technology since there is no existing database to model it on. They have however provided a database diagram for you which is available later in this chapter. Below is a brief description of the tables.

All id fields are of integer type, except the **UserId** field which must be stored as a string with a max length of 128 characters, since that is a limitation imposed by the Entity Framework user id in the **AspNetUser** table. A more in-depth description of each table is available in their respective section in this chapter.

A brief description of the tables

- **Section** - Stores a list of available section titles which can be used by multiple content pieces (items). The section title *Module 1* could for instance be used by *Video 1* and *Video 2*. One scenario could be that the product you are creating has videos, articles and downloadable material belonging to the same section, which means that the same chapter title must be reusable. Other scenarios could be that you have a series of videos or articles on the same subject.
- **ItemType** - Stores a list of the different item types an item can have, for instance *Video*, *Article* and *Download*.
- **Part** - Can be viewed as a sub-categorization of a section. A section can contain many parts or sub-headers.
- **Item** - Is a content piece which can be part of one or many products.
- **Product** - Is a list of available products. A product can have many content pieces (items) tied to it through the **ProductItem** connection table, and can belong to many subscriptions through the **ProductSubscription** connection table.
- **Subscription** – A list of available subscriptions a user can subscribe to. A subscription can have many products tied to it through the **ProductSubscription** connection table.
- **UserSubscription** – A list of subscriptions a specific user has access to. This is the "entry point" for a user, granting access to certain content based on which subscriptions are listed here. The primary key for the table is a composite key of a subscription id (from the **Subscription** table) and a user id (from the **AspNetUser** table).
- **ProductItem** - A connection table between the **Product** and **Item** tables storing information about what content belongs to what product.
- **ProductSubscription** - A connection table between the **Subscription** and **Product** tables storing information about what products are part of what subscription.

- **ProductLinkText** - Contains label texts that can be displayed with the product thumbnail.

Creating the membership solution

In this section you will focus on creating the solution for the membership site. Because the name *Membership* is already used in the .NET Framework, you can use the plural version *Memberships* instead when naming the MVC Web Application project. Add a folder called **Entities** to the MVC project after you have created the solution. You will later add the entity (table) classes to this folder and use them to generate the database.

1. Click on the **New Project** link on Visual Studio's start page. The Dialog boxes in Visual Studio 2013 and Visual Studio 2015 are very similar; the difference is that you have more project templates in Visual Studio 2015.
2. Select **ASP.NET Web Application** in the list, name the project *Memberships* in the **Name** field and make sure the **Create directory for solution** checkbox is selected. If you are using Team Foundation Server (TFS) or GIT for source control, then check the **Add to source control** checkbox. Click the **OK** button.

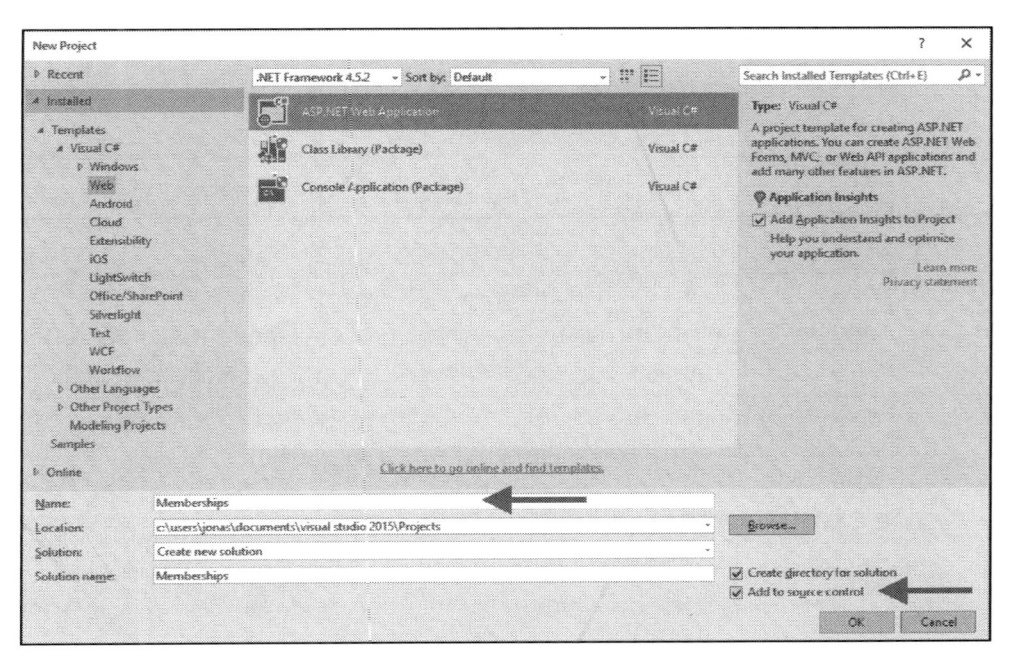

3. Select the **MVC** template in the dialog's list, and make sure that **Individual User Accounts** is selected, then click **OK**. If you have or want to create an Azure account to host the application in the cloud, then check the **Host in the cloud** checkbox and follow the steps outlined in the guide. Hosting this web application in the cloud is not necessary, you can run and debug the web application locally. You can add the application to Azure at a later time.

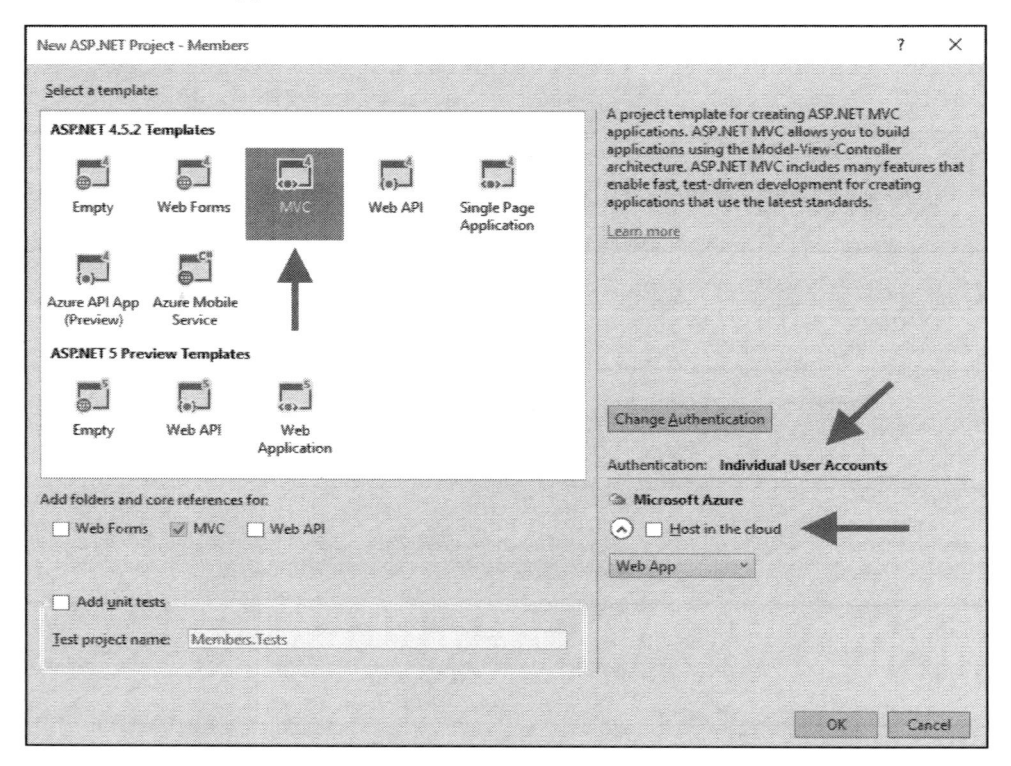

4. Add a folder called **Entities** to the project where you add the entity classes. This helps keep the project organized. Right-click on the project name in the Solution Explorer and select **New-Folder** and name it **Entities**.

Enable Migrations

To keep track of the changes made to the database, a migrations folder will be created in the project when the database is first created. There will also be a __**MigrationHistory** table in the database keeping track of the changes in case you need to revert back to an older version.

You can let .NET Framework create a database with the default **AspNet** tables for you the first time you launch the application.

To be able to make changes to the database and seed it with data, you need to enable migrations to create the **Migrations** folder and files. To enable migrations, you open the *Package Manager Console* window and execute the **enable-migrations** command.

When the **enable-migrations** command has finished executing, you can enable two properties in the *Configuration.cs* migrations file to make it easier to work with database updates and migrations. By enabling these two settings you are telling Entity Framework that you allow it to perform automatic migrations, and that you allow loss of data while doing a database update. If you don't enable automatic migrations, you have to manually create a new migration before attempting any database updates. These settings are normally disabled for production databases, but can be of great help when designing a new database.

```
Public Configuration()
{
    AutomaticMigrationsEnabled = true;
    AutomaticMigrationDataLossAllowed = true;
}
```

Enable database migrations

1. Open the *Package Manager Console* by typing in *Package Manager* into the quick launch search bar at the top right corner of Visual Studio and select it. Or select **View-Other Windows-Package Manager Console** in the menu.
2. Type in the command **enable-migrations** and press **Enter** on the keyboard.
3. When the *Configuration.cs* migrations file is displayed, you can set the following two properties in the constructor to be able to work more smoothly with updates to the database. *Note that it's not recommended to have these enabled when working in a production database.*
   ```
   AutomaticMigrationsEnabled = true;
   AutomaticMigrationDataLossAllowed = true;
   ```

```
Package Manager Console
Package source: nuget.org            ▼  ⚙  Default project: Memberships
Each package is licensed to you by its owner. Microsoft is not responsible fo
licenses. Follow the package source (feed) URL to determine any dependencies.

Package Manager Console Host Version 2.8.50926.663

Type 'get-help NuGet' to see all available NuGet commands.

PM> enable-migrations
Checking if the context targets an existing database...
Code First Migrations enabled for project Memberships.
PM>
```

What's in the database?

Many tables are involved when storing information about memberships. I have however tried to keep the number of tables down in this book to give you a foundation on which you can build when you create your own membership site.

Content tables

The individual items (content pieces), information about available videos, articles and downloadable files, are stored in a table called **Item,** which in turn reference the **ItemType** table which stores information about available item types such as video, article and download. The **Section** table stores information about available sections that the items can belong to. The **Part** table stores information about available parts items can belong to. The Idea is that an item (a piece of content) can belong to a section which has a number of parts; think of a book where each section has a main heading (chapter) and sub headings (parts) or videos can be divided into parts.

Creating the database

Now that you have seen an overview of what tables the database will contain, it is time to actually create the database; without it you won't be able to complete upcoming exercises in this book. Let's start with the peripheral tables and work our way to the core tables.

When you want to add a table to the database using code-first, it has to be represented by an entity class describing its columns and settings by using properties and attributes. If, for instance, you want to add a **Name** column to a table, you define it as a **string** property and assign attributes to it. Attributes can for instance limit the number of characters allowed, or define it as a required value in the table.

Let's start by exploring how to add a table and how to create and update the database by adding the **Section** table.

Changing the database name

You can change the database name before you create it by opening the *Web.Config* file and altering the **DefaultConnection** property; change the *database name* and *Initial Catalog* values to the name you want the database to have. By default, the name is set to *aspnet-YourProjectName-UniqueNumber.mdf*. For example *aspnet-Memberships-20150125111*.

The first occurrence of the name in the **DefaultConnection** property is the database file name, and the second is the name used internally by SQL Server.

Default connection string:

```
<connectionStrings>
    <add name="DefaultConnection" connectionString="Data Source=(LocalDb)\v11.0;AttachDbFilename=|DataDirectory|\aspnet-Memberships-20150411124038.mdf;Initial Catalog=aspnet-Memberships-20150411124038;Integrated Security=True"
providerName="System.Data.SqlClient" />
</connectionStrings>
```

Modified connection string:

```
<connectionStrings>
    <add name="DefaultConnection" connectionString="Data Source=(LocalDb)\v11.0;AttachDbFilename=|DataDirectory|\MembershipsDb.mdf;Initial Catalog=MembershipsDb;Integrated Security=True"
providerName="System.Data.SqlClient" />
</connectionStrings>
```

Enabling Data Annotations

Enabling data annotations in the project will make it possible to add certain database-related attributes to properties and entity classes, specifying the name of the table as well as column behaviors in the database table. Annotations can also be used when verifying form input on the client.

ASP.NET MVC 5 - How to build a Membership Website

To enable data annotations, you have to add a reference to the *System.Components.DataAnnotations* assembly if it's not already added, as well as **using** statements in the desired parts of the added assembly in the entity classes.

1. Open the **References** folder in the Solution Explorer and make sure that the *DataAnnotations* assembly is referenced in the list of references; if it's not, then continue with the rest of the bullets in this list to add it.
2. Right-click on the **References** folder in the Solution Explorer.
3. Select **Add Reference** in the context menu.
4. Search for *DataAnnotations*, select the assembly in the list and click **OK**.

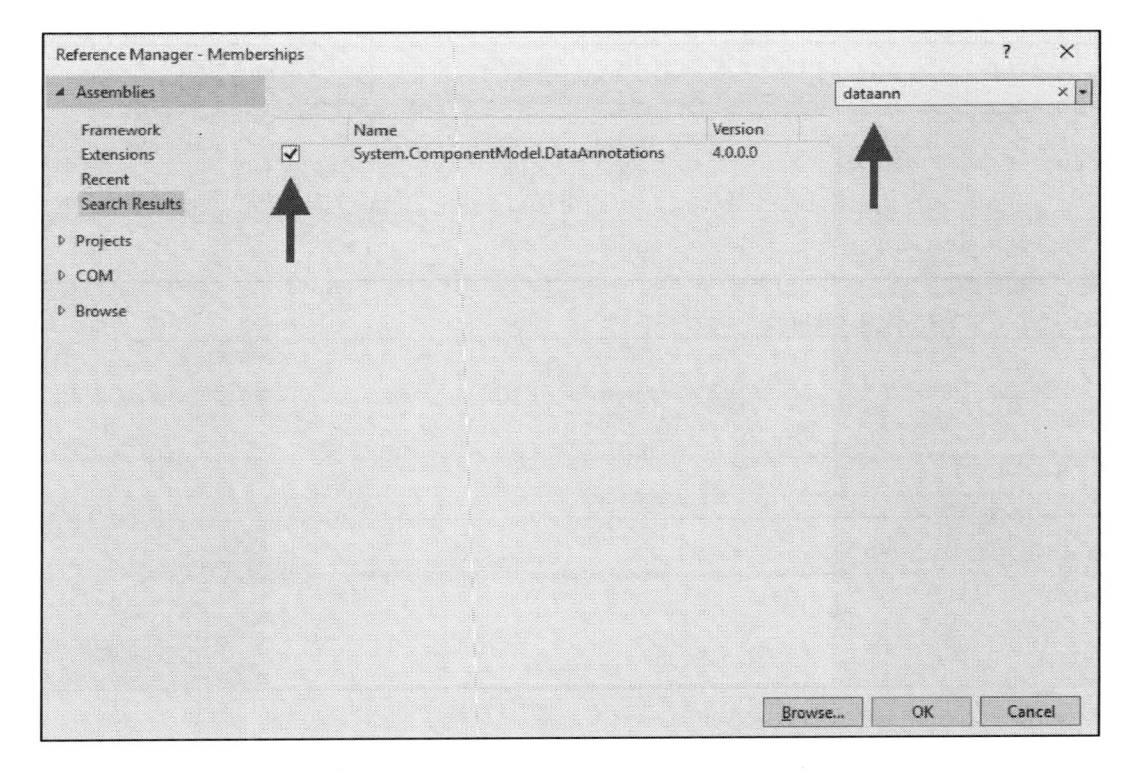

Data Annotation Attributes

Attribute	Description
DatabaseGenerated	The database will automatically generate the value for this field in the table. This attribute is used to create an identity field in the table.

15

Attribute	Description
MaxLength	Sets the maximum number of characters allowed to be entered into a table column. Can also be used to verify user input on the client side (in the browser).
Required	Requires a value to be inserted in the column when adding a new row to the table.
AllowHtml	This attribute must be added to a property if you want the column to store HTML content. _Never_ let users alter and store HTML in the database; in certain scenarios you might want administrators to be able to store HTML.
NotMapped	This attribute will keep Entity Framework from creating a column for the property in the database. This can come in handy if for instance you want to add properties for calculated values.

The Section class

The **Section** table is defined by a class with the same name that you will add to the **Entities** folder. This folder will eventually contain classes representing all the tables in the database. The **Section** table is very simple and contains only two columns *Id* of type **int** and a *Title* of type **string**.

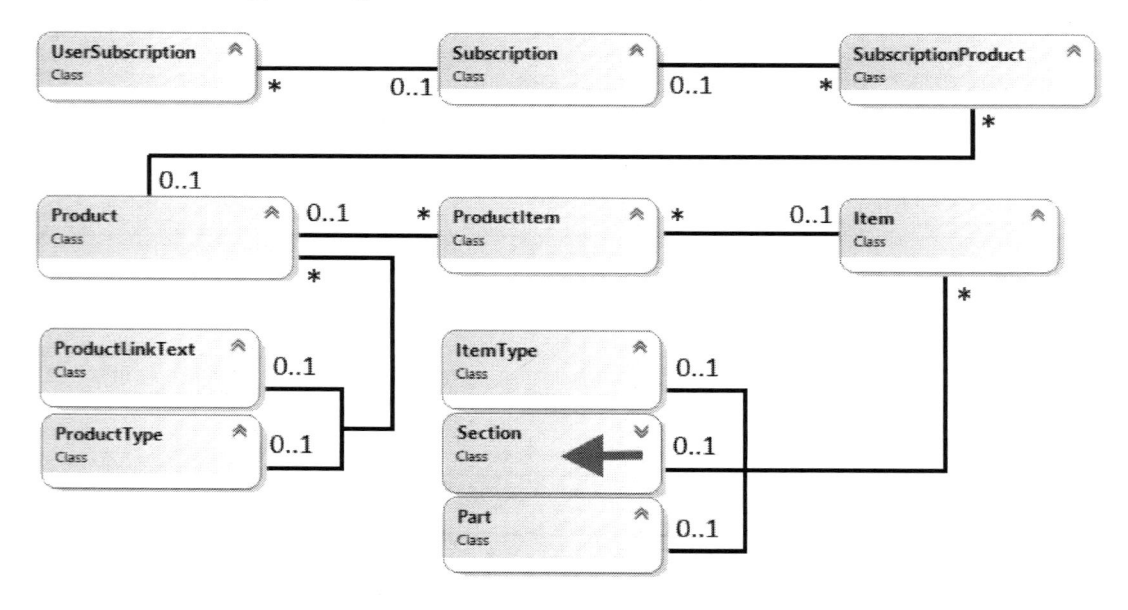

Note that the class name is given in singular but the auto-generated table name in the database will be in plural. This is a matter of choice and preference. You can change this by adding the **Table** attribute to the class.

Adding the table
To be able to add data annotation attributes to the properties, you must add a reference to the **DataAnnotations** assembly and then add the following two using statements to the class.

```
using System.ComponentModel.DataAnnotations;
using System.ComponentModel.DataAnnotations.Schema;
```

Section
Class

Properties
- Id
- Title

1. Right-click on the project name in the Solution Explorer and select **Add-New Folder** in the context menu. Name the folder **Entities**.
2. Right-click on the **Entities** folder and select **Add-Class** in the context menu.
3. Enter *Section* in the **Name** textbox and click **Add**.
4. Add the following two namespaces to the class to be able to use data annotations. You can add them manually or right-click on the attribute name and select **resolve-using xyz** in the context menu.
   ```
   using System.ComponentModel.DataAnnotations;
   using System.ComponentModel.DataAnnotations.Schema;
   ```
5. Add the **Table** attribute to the class to specify the name you want the table to have. If you leave this attribute out, the table name will be pluralized in the database.
   ```
   [Table("Section")]
   public class Section
   ```
6. Add the **Id** property and decorate it with the **DatabaseGenerated** attribute.

```
[DatabaseGenerated(DatabaseGeneratedOption.Identity)]
public int Id { get; set; }
```

7. Add the **Title** property and restrict it to allow a maximum of 255 characters and that it is a required field.
   ```
   [MaxLength(255)]
   [Required]
   public string Title { get; set; }
   ```

The complete **Section** class:
```
[Table("Section")]
public class Section
{
    [DatabaseGenerated(DatabaseGeneratedOption.Identity)]
    public int Id { get; set; }

    [MaxLength(255)]
    [Required]
    public string Title { get; set; }
}
```

The dbContext
When creating and interacting with the database in the exercises, you will use the default **dbContext** class called **ApplicationDbContext**. In a real world scenario you might opt to rename the **ApplicationDbContext** or have multiple contexts responsible for different parts of the database such as **Identity** and **Membership**. Because the focus of this book is geared toward MVC and not the Entity Framework, it will only describe how to use the default context.

The **ApplicationDbContext** class is located in the *IdentityModels.cs* file in the **Models** folder.

For a table to be created in the database, you have to add a **DbSet** entry for it as a property in the **ApplicationDbContext** class. The **DbSet** will, among other things, make it possible to query tables for data with LINQ and Lambda.

Adding a DbSet for the Section class
For the **Section** class to be used as a model for the **Section** table, you have to add a **DbSet** property for it in the **ApplicationDbContext** class.

public DbSet<Section> Sections { get; set; }

1. Open the *IdentityModel.cs* file in the **Models** folder.
2. Locate the **ApplicationDbContext** class.
3. Add the following **DbSet** property to the class.
   public DbSet<Section> Sections { get; set; }

Create and inspect the database

Now that everything is set up for creating the database and the **Section** table, you can execute the **update-database** command in the *Package Manager Console*. This command will look at the uncommitted migrations and run them against the database. In this case, it entails creating the database and then adding the **Section** table and the **AspNet** tables.

1. Open the *Package Manager Console*.
2. Enter the **update-database** command and press **Enter** on the keyboard.

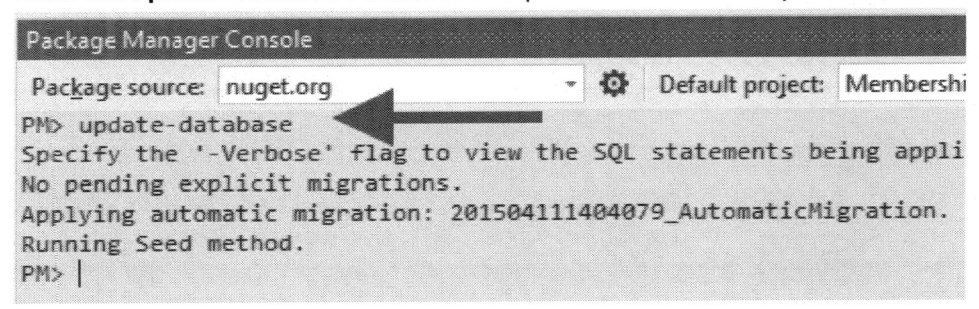

```
Package Manager Console
Package source: nuget.org          ▼ ⚙  Default project: Membershi
PM> update-database
Specify the '-Verbose' flag to view the SQL statements being appli
No pending explicit migrations.
Applying automatic migration: 201504111404079_AutomaticMigration.
Running Seed method.
PM>
```

3. When the execution has finished, click on the **Show All Files** button in the Solution Explorer and expand the **App_Data** folder to make the database visible.

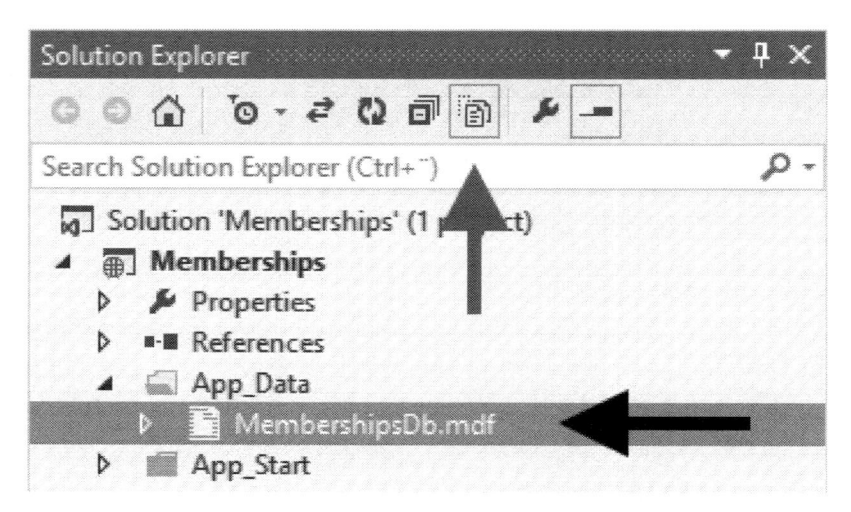

4. Double-click on the database name in the Solution Explorer to open it in the Server Explorer window. As you can see, the **Section** table has been created along with the **AspNet** tables.

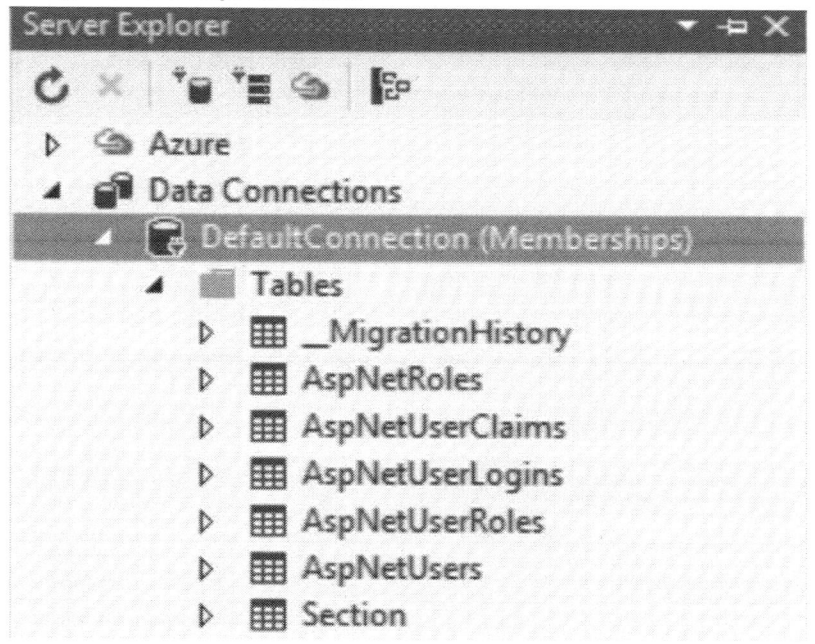

5. To open the **Section** table, right-click on it and select **Show table data**. Then when it is open, you can add and modify its data inside Visual Studio.

Id	Title	Item_Id
NULL	NULL	NULL

The Part class

The **Part** table is defined by a class with the same name and contains only two columns *Id* of type **int** and *Title* of type **string**. The properties have the same attributes as the properties in the **Section** class.

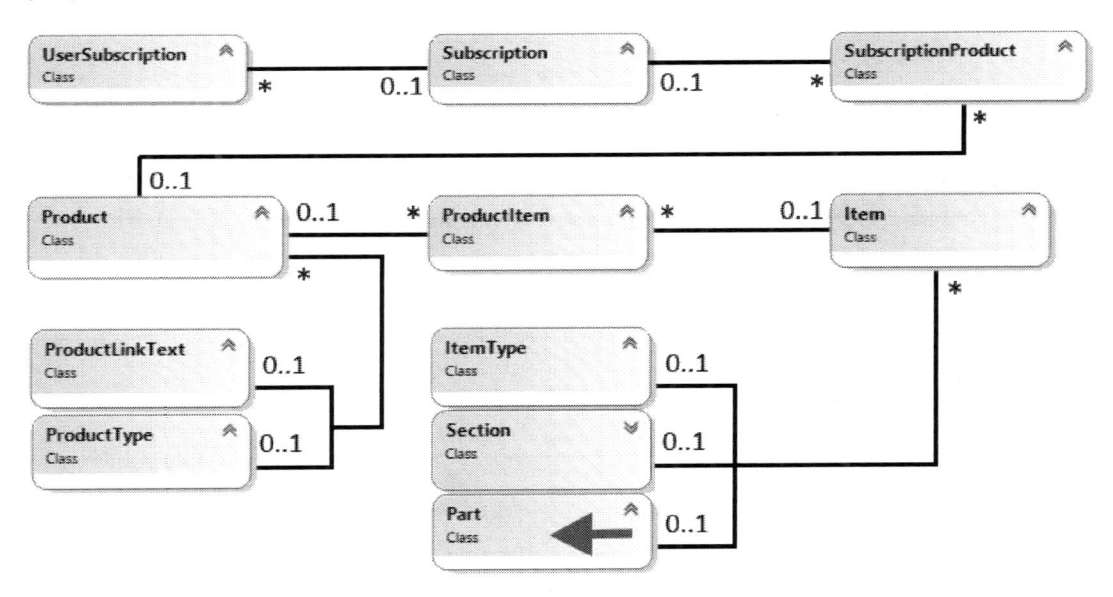

Adding the table

To be able to add data annotation attributes to the properties, you must already have added a reference to the **DataAnnotations** assembly and add the following two using statements to the class.

```
using System.ComponentModel.DataAnnotations;
using System.ComponentModel.DataAnnotations.Schema;
```

```
Part                    ▲
Class

⊟ Properties
  🔧 Id
  🔧 Title
```

1. Add the **Part** class to the **Entities** folder.
2. Add the **Table** attribute to the class to specify the same table name as the class name.
3. Add the **Id** property and decorate it with the **DatabaseGenereated** attribute.
4. Add the **Title** property and decorate it with the **Required** and **MaxLength(255)** attributes.
5. Add a **DbSet** for the **Part** class and name it **Parts** in the *IdentityModels.cs* file.
6. Open the *Package Manager Console* and execute the **update-database** command.
7. Open the **Tables** folder in the database and make sure that the table has been added.

The complete **Part** class:

```
[Table("Part")]
public class Part
{
    [DatabaseGenerated(DatabaseGeneratedOption.Identity)]
    public int Id { get; set; }

    [MaxLength(255)]
    [Required]
    public string Title { get; set; }
}
```

The ItemType class

The **ItemType** table is defined by a class with the same name and contains only two columns *Id* of type **int** and *Title* of type **string**. The properties have the same attribute decorations as the ones in the **Part** class.

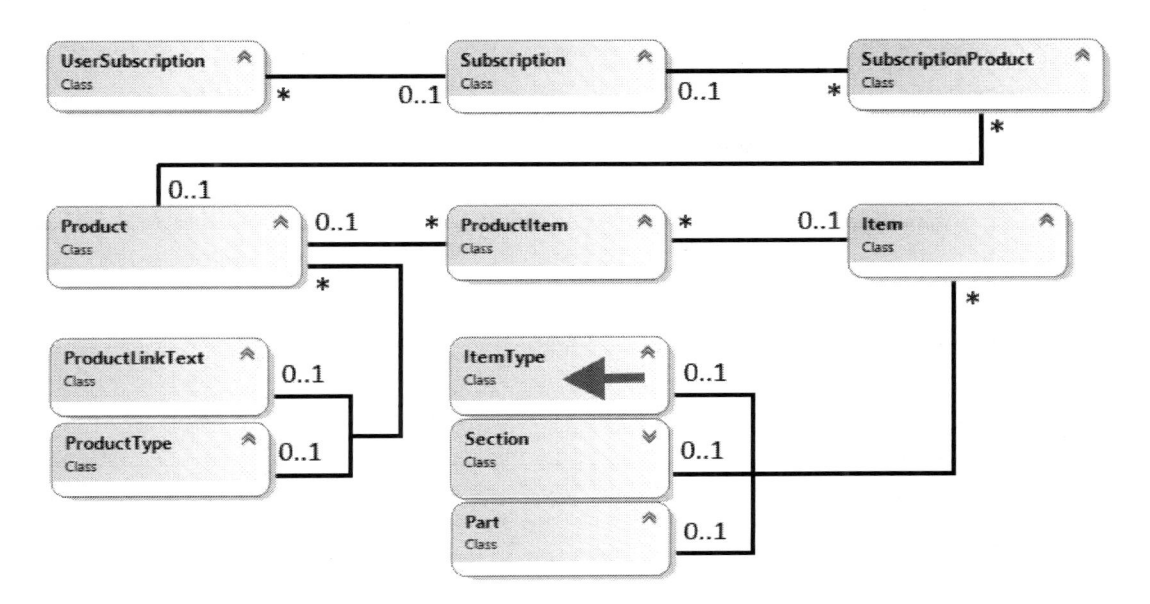

Adding the table

To be able to add data annotation attributes to the properties, you must already have added a reference to the **DataAnnotations** assembly and add the following three using statements to the class.

```
using System.ComponentModel;
using System.ComponentModel.DataAnnotations;
using System.ComponentModel.DataAnnotations.Schema;
```

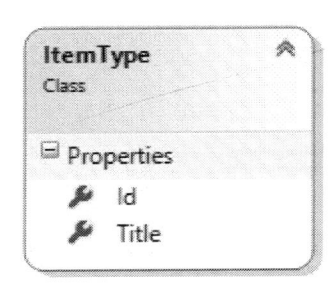

1. Add the **ItemType** class to the **Entities** folder.
2. Add the **Table** attribute to the class to specify the same name for the table as the class name.
3. Add the **Id** property and decorate it with the **DatabaseGenereated** attribute.

4. Add the **Title** property and decorate it with the **Required** and **MaxLength(255)** attributes.
5. Add a **DbSet** for the **ItemType** class and name it **ItemTypes** in the *IdentityModels.cs* file.
6. Open the *Package Manager Console* and execute the **update-database** command.
7. Open the **Tables** folder in the database and make sure that the table has been added.

The complete **ItemType** class:

```
[Table("ItemType")]
public class ItemType
{
    [DatabaseGenerated(DatabaseGeneratedOption.Identity)]
    public int Id { get; set; }

    [MaxLength(255)]
    [Required]
    public string Title { get; set; }
}
```

The Item class

The **Item** table is defined by a class with the same name. This is one of the most significant tables in the database because it stores data about each piece of content that can be added to a product. It has many properties, and among them are connection properties referencing the three previously added tables: **Section**, **Part** and **ItemType**.

One row in this table represents one piece of content that you want to share, it therefore has to store a URL to the physical file through a property called **Url** (which for instance can be a path to a YouTube video or a PDF document). The URL should not be longer than 1024 characters, since that is the max length for a URL. The **ItemType** will also determine how to handle the different types of content stored in the table.

Articles will be stored as HTML markup through a **string** property called **HTML**. An error will occur if you try to store HTML in a table without adding the **[AllowHtml]** attribute to the property representing the database field.

*Note that you **never** should allow your users to store raw HTML in your database. In this system, you will restrict the access only to users belonging to the admin role, and separate out the views in a separate area of the project. To have access to the view where the HTML is sent to the database, the user has to be registered with the system and be in the admin role; which only you manually can add users to (there is no view to add a user to the admin role for security reasons).*

The property called **HTMLShort** should be marked with the **[NotMapped]** attribute to prevent it from being stored in the database. This property will return the 50 first characters of the **HTML** property. If there are no characters or less than 50 characters, then the unmodified content of the **HTML** property should be returned.

The class must also have an **Id** property decorated with the **DatabaseGenerated** attribute to have the database automatically generate the value for the field: a required **Title** restricted to 255 characters and a **Description** restricted to 2048 characters.

You also want to link the **Section**, **Part** and **ItemType** tables to this table storing the primary key value for the tables when they are assigned to a specific item row; which will happen when the row is added or modified by a member of the admin role. To make it easier for Entity Framework to add references between the tables, you can add id columns for each table as well as a collection representing the table values. Don't worry, the collections will not be filled with data automatically. You can use a **public virtual ICollection<T>** for each of the three tables, for instance:

```
public virtual ICollection<Section> Sections { get; set; }
```

Note that you can use the plural form on the property name if you want it to appear that way on the **dbContext** object when coding, inspecting it in Visual Studio during debugging and in IntelliSense lists.

By creating the reference properties as **public virtual ICollection<T>** *lazy loading* is enabled, as well as more efficient change tracking. *Lazy loading* means that no data is loaded into the collection until you request it; this can make the data you need load much faster.

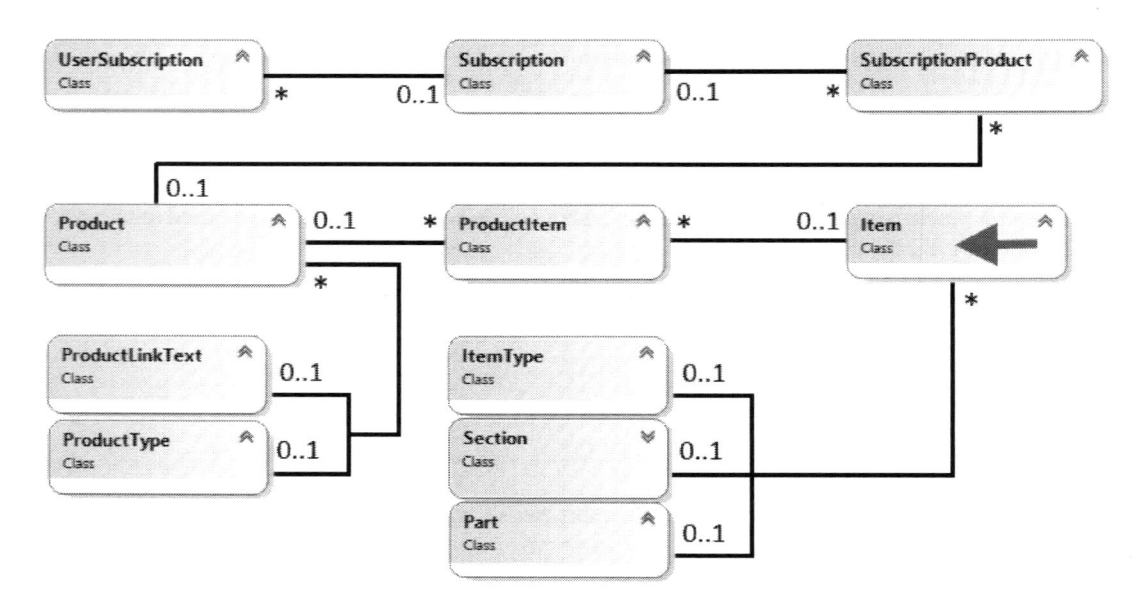

Adding the table

To be able to add data annotation attributes to the properties, you must already have added a reference to the **DataAnnotations** assembly and add the following two using statements to the class.

```
using System.ComponentModel.DataAnnotations;
using System.ComponentModel.DataAnnotations.Schema;
```

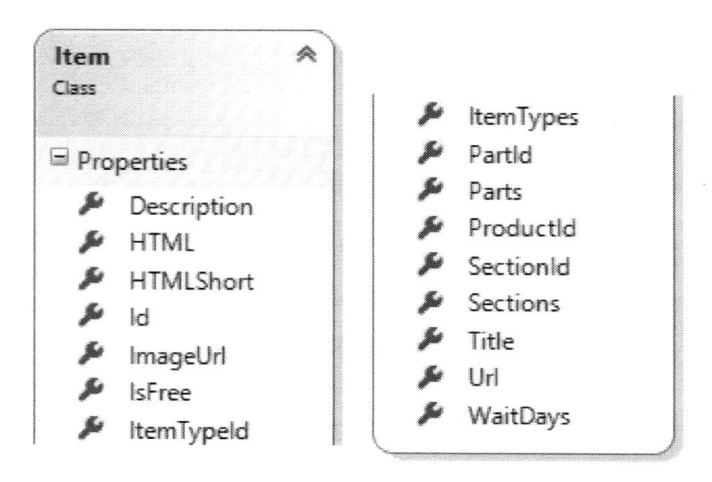

Item
Class

Properties
- Description
- HTML
- HTMLShort
- Id
- ImageUrl
- IsFree
- ItemTypeId
- ItemTypes
- PartId
- Parts
- ProductId
- SectionId
- Sections
- Title
- Url
- WaitDays

1. Add the **Item** class to the **Entities** folder.
2. Add the **Table** attribute to the class to specify the same name for the table as the class name.
3. Add the **Id** property and decorate it with the **DatabaseGenereated** attribute.
4. Add the **Title** property and decorate it with the **Required** and **MaxLength(255)** attributes.
5. Add the **Description** property and decorate it with the **MaxLength(2048)** attribute.
6. Add the **Url** property and decorate it with the **MaxLength(1024)** attribute.
7. Add the **ImageUrl** property and decorate it with the **MaxLength(1024)** attribute.
8. Add the **HTML** property and decorate it with the **AllowHtml** attribute.
9. Add the **HTMLShort** property and decorate it with the **NotMapped** attribute.
10. Add three **int** properties representing the primary key value of the referenced tables **ItemTypeId**, **PartId** and **SectionId**.
11. Add the **Sections** property as a **public virtual ICollection<Section>**.
    ```
    public virtual ICollection<Section> Sections { get; set; }
    ```
12. Add the **Parts** property as a **public virtual ICollection<Part>**.
    ```
    public virtual ICollection<Part> Parts { get; set; }
    ```
13. Add the **ItemTypes** property as a **public virtual ICollection<ItemType>**.
    ```
    public virtual ICollection<ItemType> ContentTypes { get; set; }
    ```
14. Add the **DisplayName** attribute to the properties with composite names to add a space between the words making up the property names in order to make them more readable.
15. Add a **DbSet** for the **Item** class and name it **Items** in the *IdentityModels.cs* file.
16. Open the *Package Manager Console* and execute the **update-database** command.
17. Open the **Tables** folder in the database and make sure that the table has been added.

The complete **Item** class:

```
[Table("Item")]
public class Item
{
   [DatabaseGenerated(DatabaseGeneratedOption.Identity)]
   public int Id { get; set; }
   [MaxLength(255)]
   [Required]
   public string Title { get; set; }
   [MaxLength(2048)]
   public string Description { get; set; }
   [MaxLength(1024)]
   public string Url { get; set; }
   [MaxLength(1024)]
   [DisplayName("Image Url")]
   public string ImageUrl { get; set; }
   [AllowHtml]
   public string HTML { get; set; }
   [DefaultValue(0)]
   [DisplayName("Wait Days")]
   public int WaitDays { get; set; }
   public string HTMLShort { get { return HTML == null ||
       HTML.Length < 50 ? HTML : HTML.Substring(0, 50); } }
   public int ItemTypeId { get; set; }
   public int SectionId { get; set; }
   public int PartId { get; set; }
   DisplayName("Is Free")]
   public bool IsFree { get; set; }
   DisplayName("Item Types")]
   public ICollection<ItemType> ItemTypes { get; set; }
   public ICollection<Section> Sections { get; set; }
   public ICollection<Part> Parts { get; set; }
}
```

The Product class

The **Product** table is defined by a class with the same name. This is one of the most significant tables in the database because it stores information about specific products. Each row in the table represents one product which can be referenced by many subscriptions. A product can be comprised of several content pieces (items) represented by rows in the **Item** table connected through the **ProductItem** table which you will add later.

This table references two other tables with a many-to-many relationship; which means that connection tables have to be involved. You will create these tables later, but for now let's concentrate on the **Product** table. You have already created one of the tables that will be referenced through one of the intermediary tables: the **Item** table.

The **Product** table has the following properties: an **Id** of type **int** decorated with the **DatabaseGenerated** attribute, a required **Title** of type **string** limited to 255 characters and a **Description** of type **string** limited to 2048 characters.

It also has some reference ids to other tables, all of type **int**: **ProductTypeId** and **Product-LinkTextId**.

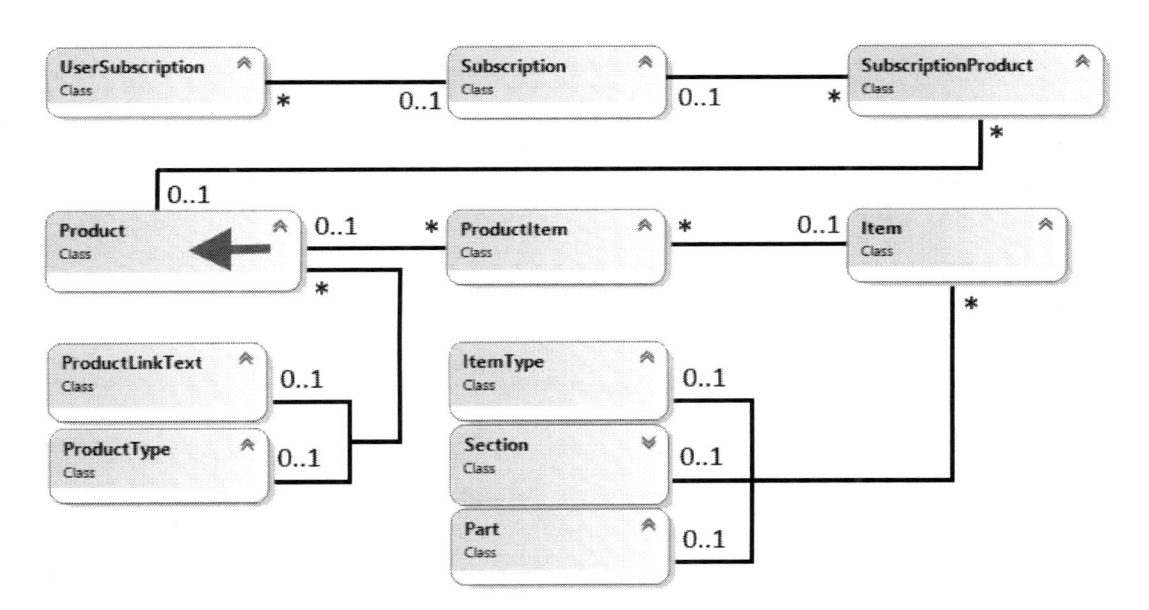

Adding the table
To be able to add data annotation attributes to the properties, you must already have added a reference to the **DataAnnotations** assembly and add the following three using statements to the class.

```
using System.ComponentModel;
using System.ComponentModel.DataAnnotations;
using System.ComponentModel.DataAnnotations.Schema;
```

Product
Class

Properties
- Description
- Id
- ImageUrl
- ProductLinkTextId
- ProductTypeId
- Title

1. Add the **Product** class to the **Entities** folder.
2. Add the **Table** attribute to the class to specify the same name for the table as the class name.
3. Add the **Id** property and decorate it with the **DatabaseGenereated** attribute.
4. Add the **Title** property and decorate it with the **Required** and **MaxLength(255)** attributes.
5. Add the **Description** property and decorate it with the **MaxLength(2048)** attribute.
6. Add two **int** properties representing the primary key values of the referenced tables **ProductTypeId** and **ProductLinkTextId**.
7. Add the **ImageUrl** property and decorate it with the **MaxLength(1024)** attribute.
8. Add a **DbSet** for the **Product** class in the **IdentityModels.cs** file and name it **Products**.
9. Open the *Package Manager Console* and execute the **update-database** command.
10. Open the **Tables** folder in the database and make sure that the **Product** table has been added.

The complete **Product** class would look like this:

```
[Table("Product")]
public class Product
{
```

```
    [DatabaseGenerated(DatabaseGeneratedOption.Identity)]
    public int Id { get; set; }
    [MaxLength(255)]
    [Required]
    public string Title { get; set; }
    [MaxLength(1024)]
    [DisplayName("Image Url")]
    public string ImageUrl { get; set; }
    [MaxLength(2048)]
    public string Description { get; set; }
    public int ProductLinkTextId { get; set; }
    public int ProductTypeId { get; set; }
}
```

The ProductType class

The **ProductType** table is defined by a class with the same name and will hold the possible product types a product can have. A product type could for instance be a course, a book, articles or something else.

The entity class defining the table contains two properties: one called **Id** of type **int** and one called **Title** of type **string** limited to a maximum of 25 characters . The **Id** should be generated automatically by the database when new product types are added.

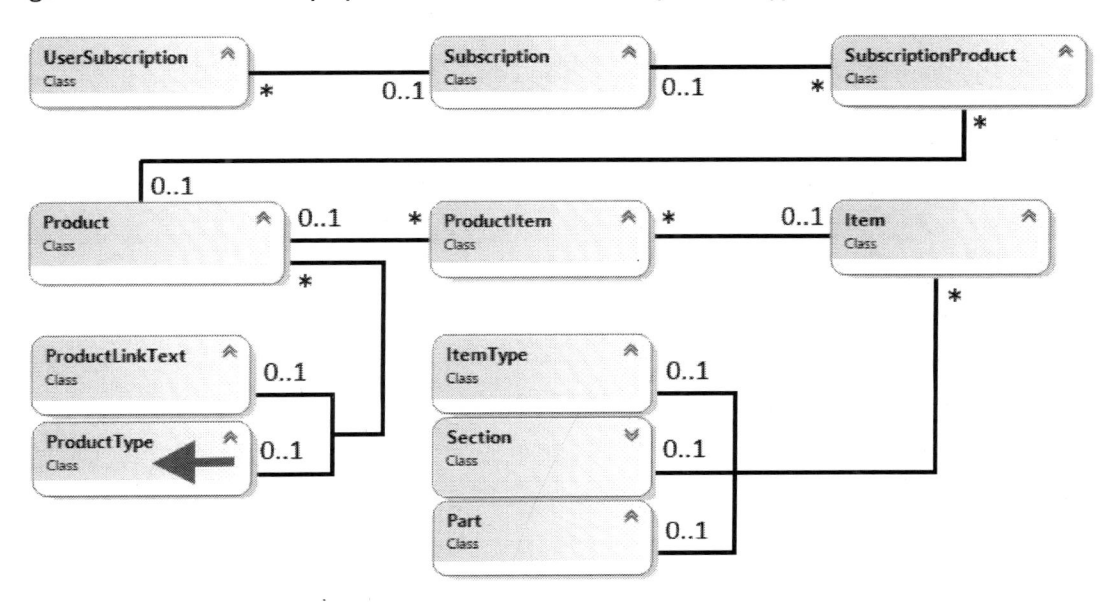

Adding the table

To be able to add data annotation attributes to the properties, you must already have added a reference to the **DataAnnotations** assembly and add the following two using statements to the class.

```
using System.ComponentModel.DataAnnotations;
using System.ComponentModel.DataAnnotations.Schema;
```

```
ProductType
Class

Properties
  Id
  Title
```

1. Add the **ProductType** class to the **Entities** folder.
2. Add the **Table** attribute to the class and name the class **ProductType**.
3. Add the **Id** property and decorate it with the **DatabaseGenereated** attribute.
4. Add the **Title** property and decorate it with the **Required** and **MaxLength(25)** attributes.
5. Open the *Package Manager Console* and execute the **update-database** command.
6. Open the **Tables** folder in the database and make sure that the **ProductType** table has been added.

The complete **ProductType** class:

```
[Table("ProductType")]
public class ProductType
{
    [DatabaseGenerated(DatabaseGeneratedOption.Identity)]
    public int Id { get; set; }
    [MaxLength(25)]
    [Required]
    public string Title { get; set; }
}
```

The ProductLinkText class

The **ProductLinkText** table is defined by a class with the same name, and it holds link descriptions which are displayed on product thumbnails. The description can be part of a clickable link that navigates to the product content view when clicked.

The entity class defining the table contains two properties called **Id** of type **int** and **Title** of type **string** limited to a maximum of 255 characters. The **Id** should be generated automatically by the database when new product links are added.

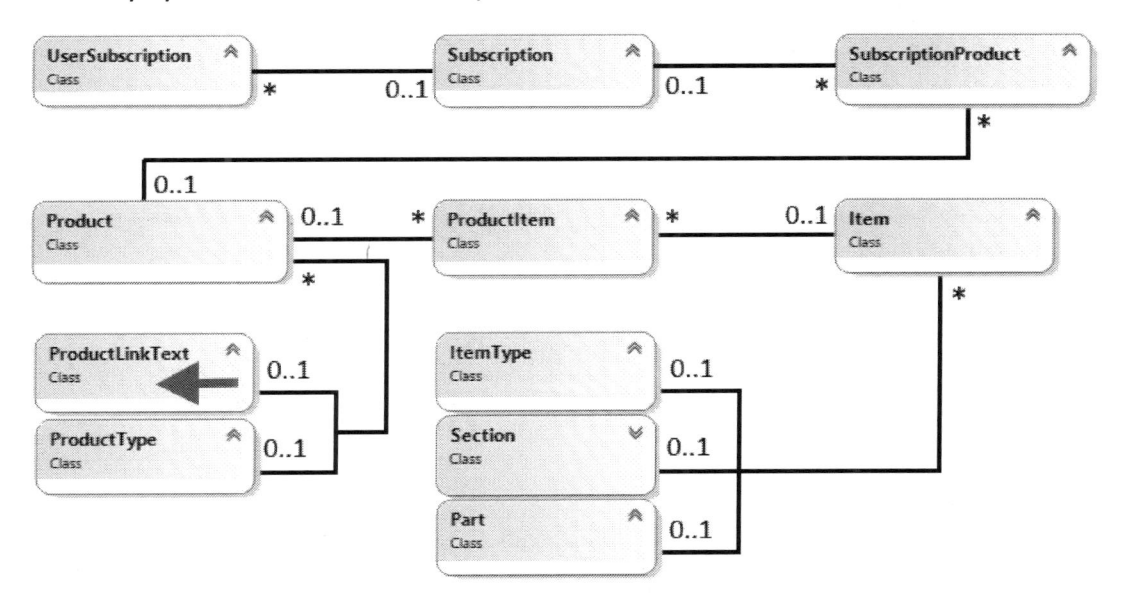

Adding the table

To be able to add data annotation attributes to the properties, you must already have added a reference to the **DataAnnotations** assembly and add the following two using statements to the class.

```
using System.ComponentModel.DataAnnotations;
using System.ComponentModel.DataAnnotations.Schema;
```

ProductLinkText Class
Properties:
- Id
- Title

1. Add the **ProductLinkText** class to the **Entities** folder.
2. Add the **Table** attribute to the class to specify the same name for the table as the class name.
3. Add the **Id** property and decorate it with the **DatabaseGenerated** attribute.
4. Add the **Title** property and decorate it with the **Required** and **MaxLength(25)** attributes.
5. Open the *Package Manager Console* and execute the **update-database** command.
6. Open the **Tables** folder in the database and make sure that the **ProductLinkText** table has been added.

The complete **ProductLinkText** class:

```
[Table("ProductLinkText")]
public class ProductLinkText
{
    [DatabaseGenerated(DatabaseGeneratedOption.Identity)]
    public int Id { get; set; }
    [MaxLength(25)]
    [Required]
    public string Title { get; set; }
}
```

The Subscription class

The **Subscription** table is defined by a class with the same name. This is one of the most significant tables in the database because it stores information about specific subscriptions. Each row in the table represenst one subscription which can be referenced by many users in the **UserSubscription** table. A subscription can be comprised of several products represented by rows in the **Product** table and connected through the **SubscriptionProduct** table which you will add later.

This table references another table with a many-to-many relationship; which means that a connection table has to be involved. You will create this table later, but for now let's concentrate on the **Subscription** table.

The **Subscription** table has the following properties: an **Id** of type **int** decorated with the **DatabaseGenerated** attribute, a required **Title** of type **string** limited to 255 characters, a **Description** of type **string** limited to 2048 characters and a **RegistrationCode** of type **string** limited to 20 characters. This code will be entered into a form by the user to gain access to the subscription content.

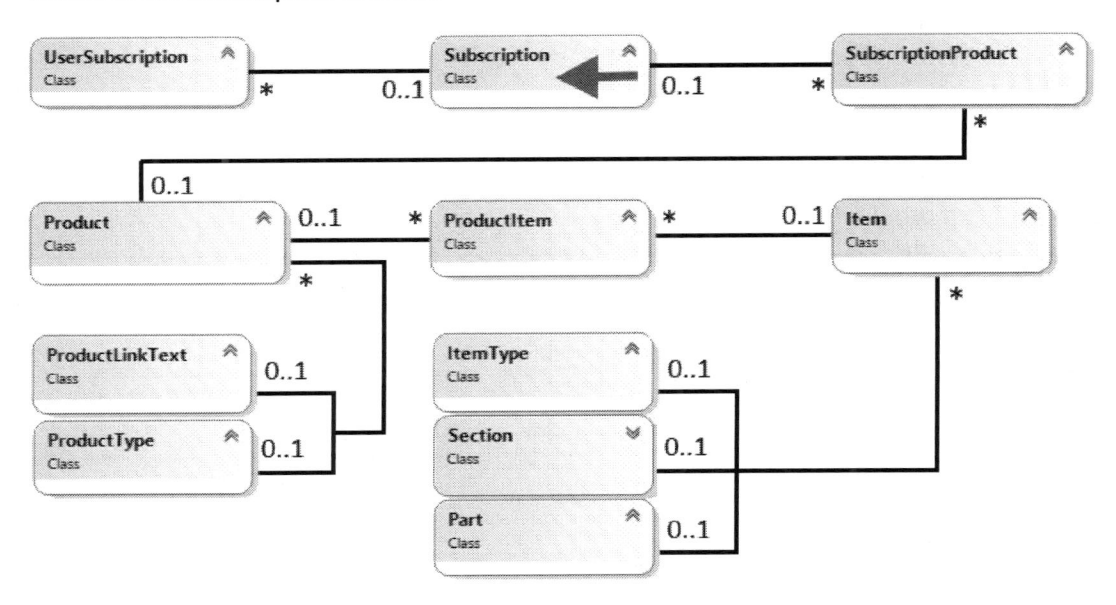

Adding the table

To be able to add data annotation attributes to the properties, you must already have added a reference to the **DataAnnotations** assembly and add the following three using statements to the class.

```
using System.ComponentModel;
using System.ComponentModel.DataAnnotations;
using System.ComponentModel.DataAnnotations.Schema;
```

Subscription
Class

Properties
- Description
- Id
- RegistrationCode
- Title

1. Add the **Subscription** class to the **Entities** folder.
2. Add the **Table** attribute to the class to specify the same name for the table as the class name.
3. Add an **Id** property of type **int** and decorate it with the **DatabaseGenereated** attribute.
4. Add a **Title** property of type **string** and decorate it with the **Required** and **MaxLength(255)** attributes.
5. Add a **Description** property of type **string** and decorate it with the **MaxLength(2048)** attribute.
6. Add a **RegistrationCode** property of type **string** and decorate it with the **MaxLength(20)** attribute.
7. Add a **DbSet** for the **Subscription** class and name it **Subscription** in the *IdentityModels.cs* file.
8. Open the *Package Manager Console* and execute the **update-database** command.

9. Open the **Tables** folder in the database and make sure that the **Subscription** table has been added.

The complete **Subscription** class:

```
[Table("Subscription")]
public class Subscription
{
    [DatabaseGenerated(DatabaseGeneratedOption.Identity)]
    public int Id { get; set; }
    [MaxLength(255)]
    [Required]
    public string Title { get; set; }
    [MaxLength(2048)]
    public string Description { get; set; }
    [MaxLength(20)]
    [DisplayName("Registration Code")]
    public string RegistrationCode { get; set; }
}
```

The ProductItem class

The **ProductItem** table is defined by a class with the same name. This table is a connection table between the rows in the **Item** table and the rows in the **Product** table. Each row in the table connects a piece of content (item) with a product. By adding the **ProductItem** table, one piece of content (item) can be added to multiple products without duplicating its data.

Adding the **ProductItem** class also makes it easier to gain access to the table data for a product and its corresponding items from the code.

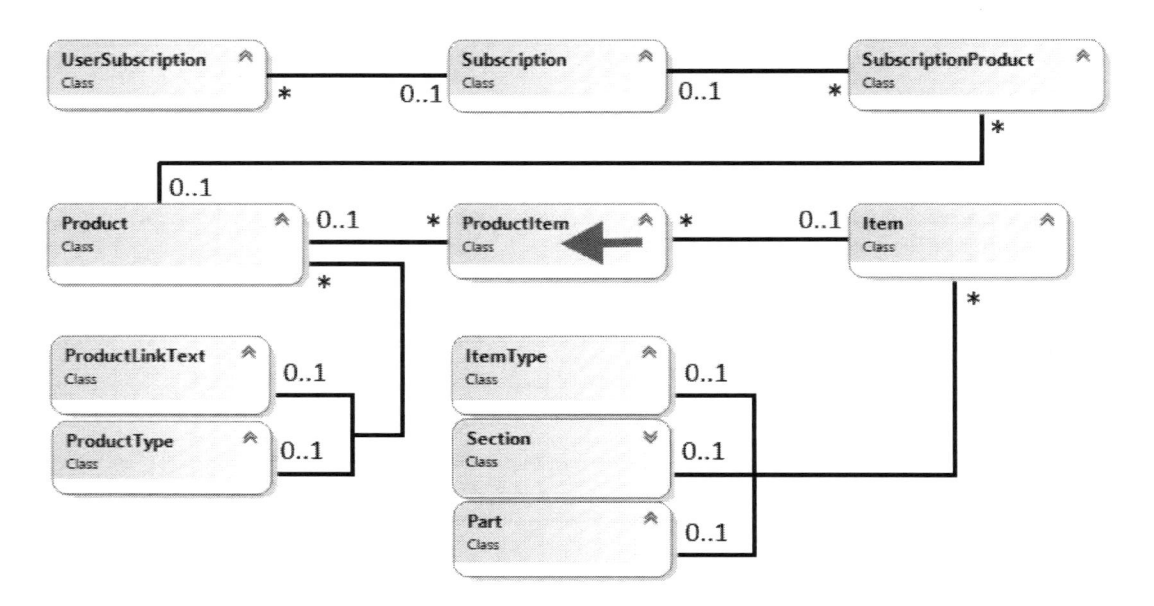

This is a small class consisting of two properties which are persisted in the **ProductItem** table and two properties which are used to store temporary ids during application execution. The trick here is to use the primary keys from the tables that you want to connect as a composite key – the **ProductId** and **ItemId**. To achieve this, you add two attributes to each of the properties, specifying that they should be considered part of the primary key of the **ProductItem** table; where the **Key** attribute specifies that the properties should be part of a composit key and the **Column** attribute specifies in which order they will make up the composite key. The two properties should also be marked as **Required** values. Below is an example of how the attributes can be added.

The two **int** properties, **OldProductId** and **OldItemId,** should not be mapped to the table. Adding these properties saves you the hassle of creating a separate view model. Some puritans say that you only should include properties that will map to columns in the table. In my opinion, it comes down to preference. I personally would create view models if there are many properties that are calculated or don't map to the table. I would also think twice before adding methods to an entity class. Try to keep the entity classes as clean as possible.

```
[Required]
[Key, Column(Order = 1)]
public int ProductId { get; set; }
[Required]
[Key, Column(Order = 2)]
public int ContentId { get; set; }
```

Adding the table

To be able to add data annotation attributes to the properties, you must already have added a reference to the **DataAnnotations** assembly and add the following two using statements to the class.

```
using System.ComponentModel.DataAnnotations;
using System.ComponentModel.DataAnnotations.Schema;
```

ProductItem
Class

Properties
- ItemId
- OldItemId
- OldProductId
- ProductId

1. Add the **ProductItem** class to the **Entities** folder.
2. Add the **Table** attribute to the class to specify the same name for the table as the class name.
3. Add the **ProductId** property and decorate it with the **Required, Key** and **Column** attributes.
4. Add the **ItemId** property and decorate it with the **Required, Key** and **Column** attributes.
5. Add the **OldProductId** and the **OldItemId** properties and decorate them with the **NotMapped** attribute, denoting that they should not be columns in the table.
   ```
   [NotMapped]
   public int OldProductId { get; set; }
   [NotMapped]
   public int OldItemId { get; set; }
   ```

6. Add a **DbSet** for the **ProductItem** class and name it **ProductItems** in the *IdentityModels.cs* file.
7. Open the *Package Manager Console* and execute the **update-database** command.
8. Open the **Tables** folder in the database and make sure that the **ProductItem** table has been added.

The complete **ProductItem** class:

```
[Table("ProductItem")]
public class ProductItem
{
    [Required]
    [Key, Column(Order = 1)]
    public int ProductId { get; set; }
    [Required]
    [Key, Column(Order = 2)]
    public int ItemId { get; set; }

    [NotMapped]
    public int OldProductId { get; set; }
    [NotMapped]
    public int OldItemId { get; set; }
}
```

The SubscriptionProduct class

The **SubscriptionProduct** table is defined by a class with the same name. This table is a connection table between the rows in the **Subscription** table and the rows in the **Product** table. Each row in the table connects a product with a subscription. By adding the **SubscriptionProduct** table, one product can be added to multiple subscriptions without duplicating its data.

Adding the **SubscriptionProduct** class makes it easier to gain access to the involved tables from the code.

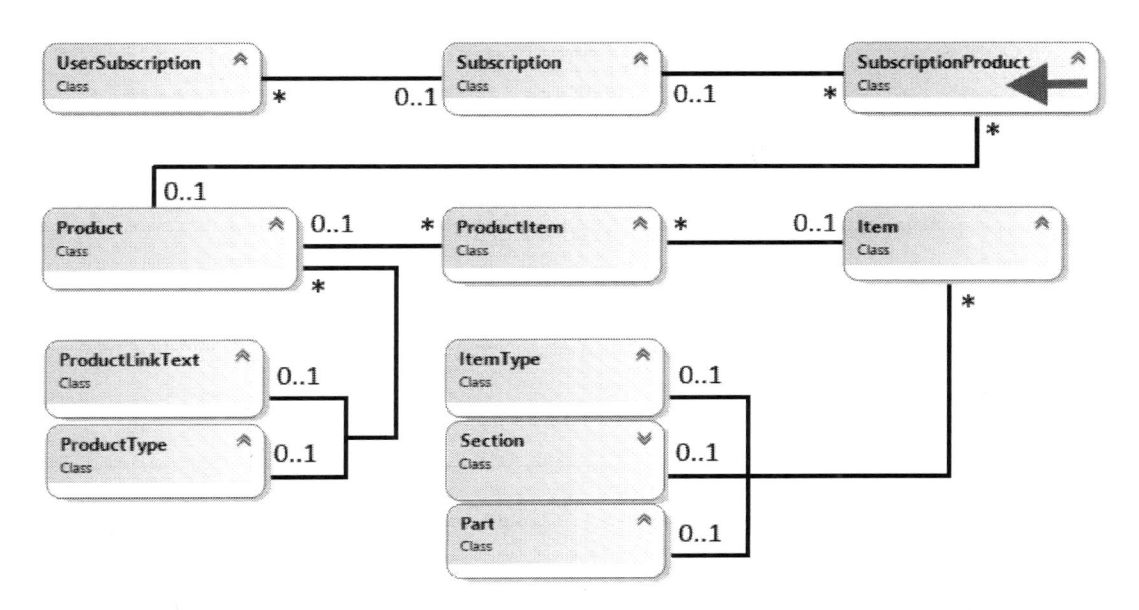

```
UserSubscription          Subscription                  SubscriptionProduct
Class          *    0..1  Class          0..1      *    Class
                                                                    *
         0..1
Product        0..1   *   ProductItem    *     0..1   Item
Class                     Class                       Class
               *                                                *

ProductLinkText           ItemType
Class          0..1       Class           0..1

ProductType               Section
Class          0..1       Class           0..1

                          Part
                          Class           0..1
```

This is a small class consisting of two properties which are persisted in the **Subscription-Product** table and two properties which are used to store temporary ids during application execution. The trick here is to use the two table primary keys that you want to connect as a composite key, the **SubscriptionId** and **ProductId**. To achieve this you add two attributes to each of them, specifying that they should be considered part of the primary key of the **SubscriptionProduct** table, where the **Key** attribute specifies that the properties should be part of a composite key and the **Column** attribute specifies in which order they will make up the composite key. The two properties should also be marked as required values. See the previous section for an example of how the attributes can be added.

The two **int** properties **OldSubscriptionId** and **OldProductId** should not be mapped to the table. Adding these properties saves you the hassle of creating a separate view model. Some puritans say that you only should include properties that will map to columns in the table, in my opinion it comes down to taste. I personally would create view models if there are many properties that are calculated or do not map to the table. I would also think twice of adding methods to an entity class. Try to keep the entity classes as clean as possible.

Adding the table

To be able to add data annotation attributes to the properties, you must already have added a reference to the **DataAnnotations** assembly and add the following two using statements to the class.

```
using System.ComponentModel.DataAnnotations;
using System.ComponentModel.DataAnnotations.Schema;
```

SubscriptionProduct
Class

Properties
- OldProductId
- OldSubscriptionId
- ProductId
- SubscriptionId

1. Add the **SubscriptionProduct** class to the **Entities** folder.
2. Add the **Table** attribute to the class to specify the same name for the table as the class name.
3. Add the **SubscriptionId** property and decorate it with the **Required, Key** and **Column** attributes.
4. Add the **ProductId** property and decorate it with the **Required, Key** and **Column** attributes.
5. Add the **OldSubscriptionId** and the **OldProductId** properties and decorate them with the **NotMapped** attribute. See how the attributes can be added in the code below.
6. Add a **DbSet** for the **SubscriptionProduct** class and name it **SubscriptionProduct** in the *IdentityModels.cs* file.
7. Open the *Package Manager Console* and execute the **update-database** command.
8. Open the **Tables** folder in the database and make sure that the **SubscriptionProduct** table has been added.

The complete **SubscriptionProduct** class:

```
[Table("SubscriptionProduct")]
public class SubscriptionProduct
{
   [Required]
   [Key, Column(Order = 1)]
   public int ProductId { get; set; }
   [Required]
   [Key, Column(Order = 2)]
   public int SubscriptionId { get; set; }

   [NotMapped]
   public int OldProductId { get; set; }
   [NotMapped]
   public int OldSubscriptionId { get; set; }
}
```

The UserSubscription class

The **UserSubscription** table is defined by a class with the same name. This table handles the connection between users stored in the .NET Framework generated table called **AspNetUser** where users are stored, and the **Subscription** table which stores all available subscriptions.

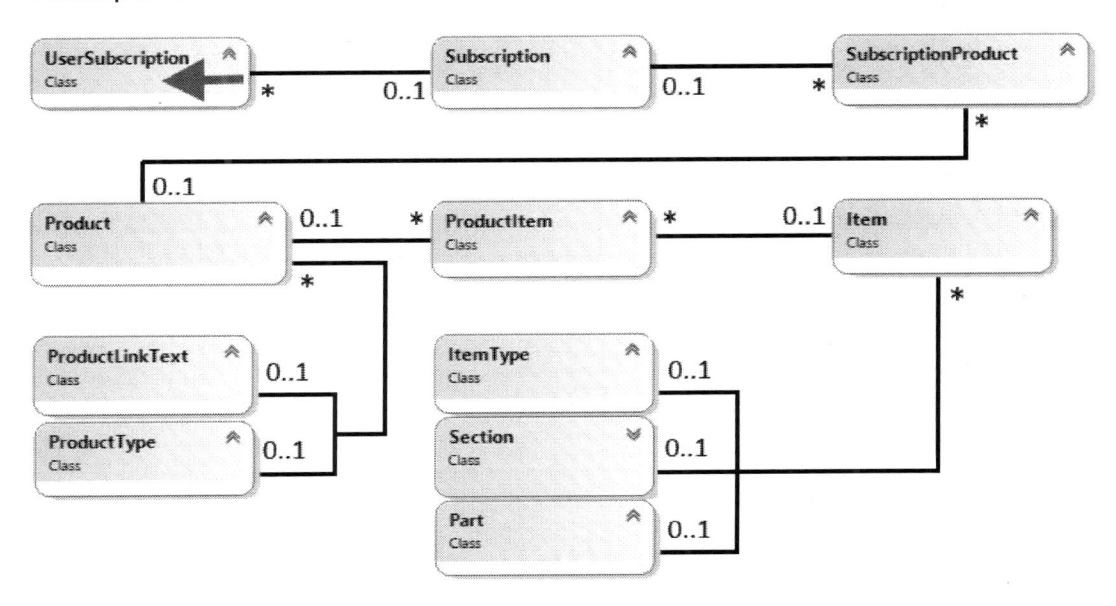

There is a one-to-many relationship between the **AspNetUser** table and the **UserSubscription** table to keep them separated from one another and not mix .NET Framework-created data with your data. Instead, the user id can be used multiple times in the **UserSubscription** table as part of a composite key containing the **UserId** and **SubscriptionId** columns.

There is a one-to-many relationship between the **UserSubscription** table and the **Subscription** table making it possible for a user to have many subscriptions but only one entry for a specific subscription.

There should also be two **null**-able **DateTime** properties called **StartDate** and **EndDate** keeping track of whether the user has access to the registered subscriptions based on when the subscription was registered and when it runs out.

Adding the table
To be able to add data annotation attributes to the properties, you must already have added a reference to the **DataAnnotations** assembly and add the following four using statements to the class.

```
Using System;
using System.ComponentModel;
using System.ComponentModel.DataAnnotations;
using System.ComponentModel.DataAnnotations.Schema;
```

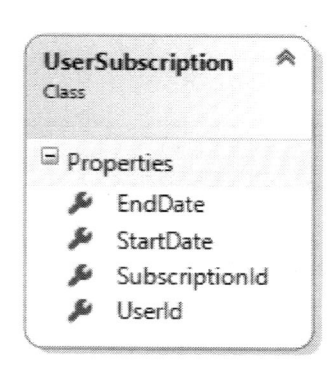

UserSubscription
Class

Properties
- EndDate
- StartDate
- SubscriptionId
- UserId

1. Add the **UserSubscription** class to the **Entities** folder.
2. Add the **Table** attribute to the class to specify the same name for the table as the class name.

3. Add the **SubscriptionId** property of type **int** and decorate it with the **Required, Key** and **Column** attributes.
4. Add the **UserId** property of type **string** and decorate it with the **Required, Key** and **Column** attributes. This property must also be restricted to 128 characters because that is the maximum number of characters allowed for the user id in the .NET Framework generated **AspNetUser** table.
5. Add a **null**-able **DateTime** property called **StartDate**.
6. Add a **null**-able **DateTime** property called **EndDate**.
7. Add a **DbSet** for the **UserSubscription** class and name it **UserSubscriptions** in the **IdentityModels.cs** file.
8. Open the *Package Manager Console* and execute the **update-database** command.
9. Open the **Tables** folder in the database and make sure that the **UserSubscription** table has been added.

The complete **UserSubscription** class:

```
[Table("UserSubscription")]
public class UserSubscription
{
    // Composite key: Subscription and AspNetUser tables
    [Key, Column(Order = 1)]
    [Required]
    public int SubscriptionId { get; set; }
    [Key, Column(Order = 2)]
    [MaxLength(128)]
    [Required]
    public string UserId { get; set; }
    public DateTime? StartDate { get; set; }
    public DateTime? EndDate { get; set; }
}
```

Modifying the AspNetUser class

To be able to store additional information about a user such as **FirstName**, **IsActive** and the date when the user **Registered,** you have to alter the **AspNetUser** table. Intuitively, you would search for a class named **AspNetUser** or **User**, but the class has a different name altogether. You would find the **ApplicationUser** class in the *IdentityModels.cs* file. The properties you add to this class will be added to the **AspNetUser** table in the database when you execute the **update-database** command in the *Package Manager Console*.

Modifying the table
1. Open the **ApplicationUser** class located in the *IdentityModels.cs* file in the **Models** folder.
2. Add a **string** property called **FirstName**.
3. Add a **bool** property called **IsActive**.
4. Add a **DateTime** property called **Registered**.
5. Open the *Package Manager Console* and execute the **update-database** command.
6. Open the **Tables** folder in the database and right-click on the **AspNetUser**.
7. Select **Open Table Definition** in the context menu and make sure that the three columns have been added to the table.

The Complete **ApplicationUser** class:

```
public class ApplicationUser : IdentityUser
{
    public string FirstName { get; set; }
    public bool IsActive { get; set; }
    public DateTime Registered { get; set; }

    public async Task<ClaimsIdentity> GenerateUserIdentityAsync(
        UserManager<ApplicationUser> manager)
    {
        var userIdentity = await manager.CreateIdentityAsync(
            this, DefaultAuthenticationTypes.ApplicationCookie);
        return userIdentity;
    }
}
```

The ApplicationDbContext class

The complete code for the **ApplicationDbContext** class in the *IdentityModels.cs* file.

```
public class ApplicationDbContext : IdentityDbContext<ApplicationUser>
{
    public ApplicationDbContext()
        : base("DefaultConnection", throwIfV1Schema: false) { }
```

```
    public static ApplicationDbContext Create()
    {
        return new ApplicationDbContext();
    }

    public DbSet<Section> Sections { get; set; }
    public DbSet<Part> Parts { get; set; }
    public DbSet<ItemType> ItemTypes { get; set; }
    public DbSet<Item> Items { get; set; }
    public DbSet<Product> Products { get; set; }
    public DbSet<ProductType> ProductTypes { get; set; }
    public DbSet<ProductLinkText> ProductLinkTexts { get; set; }
    public DbSet<Subscription> Subscriptions { get; set; }
    public DbSet<ProductItem> ProductItems { get; set; }
    public DbSet<SubscriptionProduct> SubscriptionProducts { get; set; }
    public DbSet<UserSubscription> UserSubscriptions { get; set; }
}
```

What's Next?

In this chapter, you learned about Entity Framework and how to create and update a database. In the next chapter, you will create a user interface for listing, adding, updating and deleting data in the database. The Razor views, models and controllers needed to achieve this will be added to a separate area to avoid mixing them with the views providing the user experience.

You will use scaffolding to create the views from the entity classes you created in this chapter. The views will have to be altered and styled to display the content in a more pleasing manner, creating a better user experience; this is where Bootstrap enters the arena.

Everything is presented in a modularized way, making it super easy to follow along and implement the admin user interface.

3. Create the Admin area & Menu

Introduction
In this chapter, you will add a new area to the project which will separate the Admin functionality from the regular user. It is good practice to separate parts of an application, especially if it is a separate UI, in order to avoid clutter; which otherwise would certainly be a reality when placing all models, views and controllers together in their respective folders.

You will also create a menu to navigate more easily between the different tables' **Index** views.

Technologies used in this chapter
1. **MVC** - To structure the application and scaffold views and controllers and to create partial views for reusable components such as buttons.
2. **C#** - Creating Extension methods, helper methods to keep the controller actions clean and easy to read. Creating the view models needed for all the views. Reflection is used to fetch property values for generic objects.
3. **Razor** - To incorporate C# in the views where necessary.
4. **HTML 5** - To build the views.
5. **Bootstrap** - To style the HTML 5 components.

The use case
The task appointed to you by the company is to create a new admin area in the MVC Web Application containing the database you added in the previous chapter. This area should have its own MVC structure but not be a separate project; the area should reside inside the same project as the regular user interface will be created at a later time.

You are also asked to create a "Admin" menu which makes it possible to navigate between the **Index** views you will create for various controllers in upcoming chapters.

The different views

The following views should be present for each table:

- **Index** – An overview of the content presented in table format. If it's the **Section** table you are creating views for, then all section titles should be listed in a table, and there should be three buttons to the **Edit** (blue color), **Detail** (green color) and **Delete** (red color) views for each title. A **Create New** button table leading to the **Create** view should be available above.
- **Create** - For most tables, this view only displays textboxes for user input, but for the **ProductContent** and **SubscriptionProduct** connection tables, a more refined approach is necessary since they only store primary keys from the two tables involved as integer values; but the view should display the product, item and subscription titles in drop downs to provide a better user experience and to avoid erroneous data being entered. The **Create** button should be displayed with the (green) success button style.
- **Delete** - The user can delete the selected record from the table it is stored in. The view should display static data in labels; no input should be possible. The **Delete** button should be easily distinguishable from other buttons in the view by signaling danger (red).
- **Details** - Is essentially the same as the **Delete** view, but instead of a **Delete** button, there should be an **Edit** button.
- **Edit** - This view is essentially the same as the **Create** view with the difference that it has an **Edit** button instead of a **Create** button. The **Edit** button should be displayed with the (green) success button style.

All views except for the **Index** view should have a blue **Back to List** button displaying a list icon and the text *Back to List* on it. This button should take the user back to the **Index** view.

A brief recap of the different tables

- **Section** - Stores a list of available section titles which can be used by multiple content pieces (items); the section title *Chapter 1* could for instance be used by *Video 1* and *Video 2*. One scenario could be that the product you are creating has

videos, articles and downloadable material belonging to the same section which mean that a section title must be reusable.
- **Itemype** - Stores a list of the different item types an **Item** can have such as *Video*, *Article* and *Download*.
- **Part** - Can be viewed as a sub-categorization of the a section. A section can contain many parts or sub-headers.
- **Item** - Is a list of content pieces which can be part of one or many products.
- **Product** - Is a list of available products. A product can have many content pieces tied to it through the **ProductItem** connection table and can belong to many subscriptions through the **SubscriptionProduct** connection table.
- **Subscription** - A list of available subscriptions a user can subscribe to. A subscription can have many products tied to it through the **SubscriptionProduct** connection table.
- **UserSubscription** - A list of the subscriptions a specific user has access to. This is the "entry point" for a user, granting access to certain content based on which subscriptions are listed here. Its primary key is a composite key of a subscription id and a user id (from the **AspNetUser** table).
- **ProductItem** - A connection table between the **Product** and **Item** tables storing information about what content belongs to which product.
- **SubscriptionProduct** - A connection table between the **Subscription** and **Product** tables storing information about what products are part of which subscription.
- **ProductType** - Holds the possible product types a product can have. A product type can for instance be a course, a book, articles or something else.
- **ProductLinkText** - Holds link descriptions which are displayed on a product's thumbnail. The description is part of a clickable link that will navigate to the product content view when clicked.

The Admin area

Adding a new area to an MVC project will add a folder called **Areas** to the project, in which a second set of project folders will be created in a subfolder. In this project, the area subfolder will be called **Admin**, since it will hold the project files for the admin section of the web application.

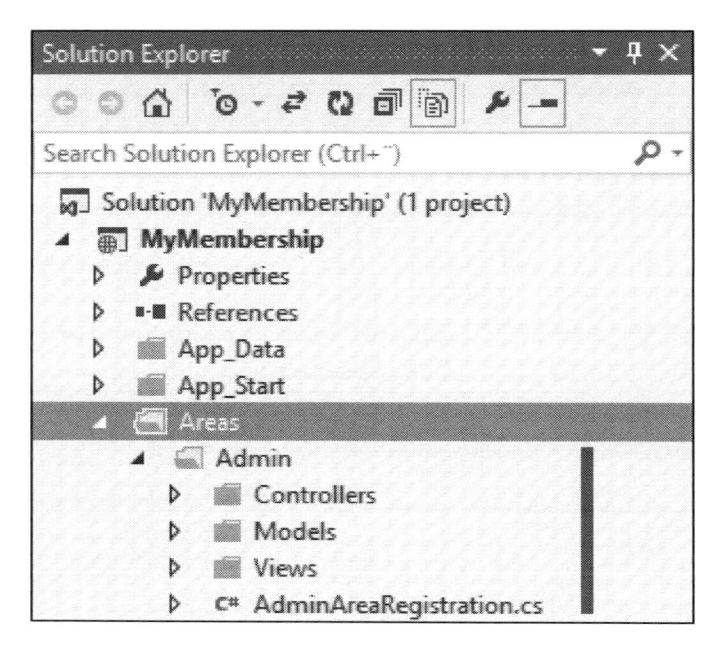

1. Right click on the project name in the Solution Explorer.
2. Select **Add-Area** in the context menu.
3. Enter *Admin* in the **Area name** textbox in the dialog and click the **Add** button.

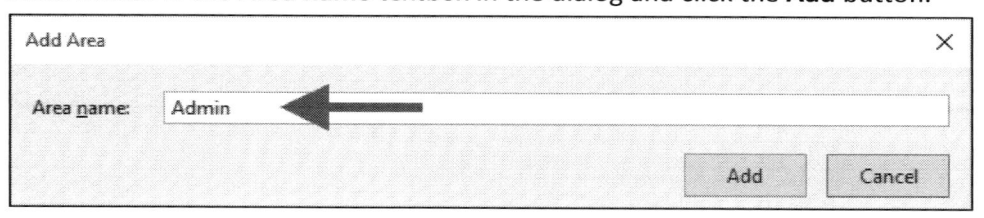

The Admin menu

It might seem counter-intuitive to create the menu before even creating a single view, but you can do it because you know the URLs to the **Index** views for the different tables. A controller's URL consists of the controller name and the view you want to reach, and you know both because the controllers will have the same name as the tables in this admin application. You can even make the URL shorter by leaving out the view name if you are targeting the **Index** view, because there is a default route defined for that scenario in the *RouteConfig.cs* file located in the **App_Start** folder in the Solution Explorer.

So let's create the **Admin** menu before creating the models, views and controllers to make navigation a bit easier as you implement the functionality for the different controllers in upcoming chapters. The links will start to work as you add the necessary controllers and views.

Because the menu will be used in two separate areas in the web application, you will have to add it as a partial view (**_AdminMenuPartial.cshtml**) to the **Views-Shared** folder in the main project (not in the **Admin** area).

The image below show the finished menu.

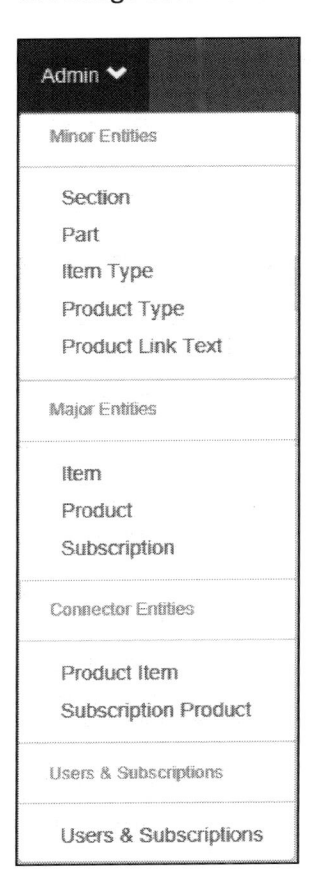

Admin ˅
Minor Entities
Section
Part
Item Type
Product Type
Product Link Text
Major Entities
Item
Product
Subscription
Connector Entities
Product Item
Subscription Product
Users & Subscriptions
Users & Subscriptions

53

Creating the _AdminMenuPartial partial view

You will find the HTML markup you need to begin creating the dropdown menu on the http://getbootstrap.com/components web page under the *Dropdowns* section. It has to be modified slightly though to look good in the menu navigation bar.

The element used to create the **Admin** menu option in the navigation bar should be a list item **<li>** element not a **<div>** element and the **<button>** element should be changed to an anchor tag **<a>** element with a pound sign (#) in its **href** attribute. You can also delete the list items **<li>** elements in the unordered list **<ul>** element since you will create new ones for the menu headers, dividers and menu choices.

The **<li>** element should have an attribute named **data-admin-menu** which will be used from JavaScript to open the menu when hovering over the *Admin* **<a>** anchor element. The attribute will be ignored by the browser but will be available from JavaScript.

The anchor tag **<a>** element will display the **Admin** text as a link which won't navigate away from the current view because it has a **#**-sign in its **href** attribute.

The **<span>** element with the **glypgicon-chevron-down** class inside of the anchor tag will be rendered as a downward pointing triangle denoting that the link will open a menu.

The unordered list **<ul>** element is the area which will drop down when the user hovers over the **Admin** menu as denoted by the **dropdown-menu** class . The **role** attribute is necessary to correctly render the unordered list as a menu.

If you feel that it is easier to just type in the code by hand from the detailed description below then you certainly can do that.

The initial code for the **Admin** menu:

```html
<li class="dropdown" data-admin-menu>
    <a href="#">
        Admin
        <span class="glyphicon glyphicon-chevron-down"></span>
    </a>

    <ul class="dropdown-menu" role="menu">
    </ul>
</li>
```

Add a partial view named **_AdminMenuPartial** to the main project's **Views-Shared** folder not in the **Admin** area and add the code described above to it.

1. Locate the **Views-Shared** folder in the project, **not** in the **Admin** area, and right-click on it.
2. Select **Add-View** in the context menu.
3. Enter **_AdminMenuPartial** in the **View name** textbox.
4. Check the **Create as partial view** checkbox.
5. Leave the rest of the options as they are and click on the **Add** button.
6. Type in the HTML markup above in the view's code window.
7. Save the view by pressing **Ctrl+S** on the keyboard.

Adding the Admin menu to the navigation bars

Let's begin by adding the **Admin** menu to the main project's menu navigation bar and see what it looks like before you add it to the **Admin** menu navigation bar.

Before Admin Menu

Application name   Home   About   Contact

Admin Menu Without Glyphicon

Application name   Home   About   Contact   Admin

With Glyphicon

Application name   Home   About   Contact   Admin ⌄

55

Adding the Admin menu to the main project's navigation bar

Adding it to the main menu bar is very easy because you changed it from being displayed as a **<div>** element to a list item **<li>** element which is used in navigation menus by default. Changing the **<button>** element to an anchor tag **<a>** element makes it appear like text and not as a button in the menu.

All you have to do is to open the **_Layout** partial view and add it to the already existing list of menu items using the **@Html.Partial** method passing in the name of the partial view as a parameter.

1. Locate the **Views-Shared** folder in the project.
2. Open the **_Layout** partial view where the menu navigation resides.
3. Locate the menu item list and add the partial view using the **@Html.Partial** extension method to have it render as part of the navigation bar.
   @Html.Partial("_AdminMenuPartial")
4. Save the **_Layout** view and run the application to view it in the browser.

Adding the Admin menu to the Admin area navigation bar

If you could navigate to a view in the **Admin** area you would find that it has no menu by default. To add the partial view to the Admin navigation bar, you have to locate it in the **_Layout** view in the **Admin** area and find the empty unordered list **<ul>** element to which you add the partial view by searching for *navbar-nav* in the **_Layout** view.

You add the partial Admin menu view using the **@Html.Partial** method.

```
<ul class="nav navbar-nav">
   @Html.Partial("_AdminMenuPartial")
</ul>
```

1. Locate the **Views-Shared** folder in the project **not** in the **Areas** folder.
2. Copy the **_Layout** partial view by right clicking on it and selecting **Copy** in the context menu.
3. Locate the **Areas** folder and expand it.
4. Locate the **Views-Shared** folder in the **Areas** folder and paste in the copied **_Layout** partial view by right-clicking on the **Views-Shared** folder and select **Paste** in the context menu.

5. Open the **_Layout** partial view you pasted in.
6. Locate the navigation bar by searching for *navbar-nav* and add the partial view to the unordered list using the **@Html.Partial** extension method to have it render as part of the navigation bar.
   `@Html.Partial("_AdminMenuPartial")`
7. Remove the three **@Html.ActionLink** extension methods calls.
   ```
   <li>@Html.ActionLink("Home", "Index", "Home")</li>
   <li>@Html.ActionLink("About", "About", "Home")</li>
   <li>@Html.ActionLink("Contact", "Contact", "Home")</li>
   ```
8. Save the **_Layout** view. You cannot view it in the **Admin** navigation bar yet because there are no controllers available in the **Admin** area to navigate to.

Adding menu items to the Admin menu

Now that the Admin menu has been created and added to all the navigation bars it is time to add the menu items that the user can click on to navigate. The menu item links are very easy to figure out; you just take the area name and add on the controller name like **/Admin/Section** for the **SectionController** and its views. The links will take the user to the respective **Index** views.

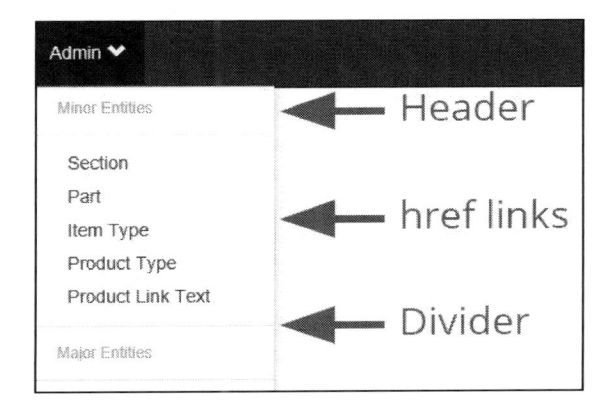

You add **<li>** elements with a nested **<a>** element for all the menu choices you want available in the **Admin** menu. Set the **href** of the **<a>** element to the desired controller path.

`<li><a href="/Admin/Section">  Section</a></li>`

Use the Bootstrap **dropdown-header** class on a **<li>** element to add a menu header.

```
<li class="dropdown-header">Minor Entities</li>
```

Use the Bootstrap **divider** class on a **<li>** element to add a menu divider line.

```
<li class="divider" />
```

1. Open the **_AdminMenuPartial** view in the **Views-Shared** folder.
2. Add a **dropdown-header** with the text *Minor Entities* and a divider to the **<ul>** element.
   ```
   <li class="dropdown-header">Minor Entities</li>
   <li class="divider" />
   ```
3. Add list items for **Section, Part, Item Type, Product Type** and **Product Link Text**. They are all the same except for the description and **href**.
   ```
   <li><a href="/Admin/Section">  Section</a></li>
   ```
4. Add a **dropdown-header** with the text *Major Entities* and a divider to the **<ul>** element.
5. Add list items for **Item, Product** and **Subscription**. They are the same as the **Section <li>** except for the description and **href**.
6. Add a **dropdown-header** with the text *Connector Entities* and a divider to the **<ul>** element.
7. Add list items for **Product Item** and **Subscription Product**. They are the same as the **Section <li>** except for the description and **href**.
8. Add a **dropdown-header** with the text *Users & Subscriptions* and a divider to the **<ul>** element.
9. Add a list item for **Users & Subscriptions** and assign */Account* to its **href**.
10. Save the partial view. There is one more thing you have to do before the menu will drop down, and that is to add a JavaScript for the **hover** method.

The complete code for the **_AdminMenuPartial** view:

```
<li class="dropdown" data-admin-menu>
    <a href="#">
        Admin
        <span class="glyphicon glyphicon-chevron-down"></span>
    </a>

    <ul class="dropdown-menu" role="menu">
```

```html
                <li class="dropdown-header">Minor Entities</li>
                <li class="divider"/>
                <li><a href="/Admin/Section">  Section</a></li>
                <li><a href="/Admin/Part">  Part</a></li>
                <li><a href="/Admin/ItemType">  Item Type</a></li>
                <li><a href="/Admin/ProductType">  Product Type</a></li>
                <li><a href="/Admin/ProductLinkText">
                      Product Link Text</a></li>

                <li class="divider" />
                <li class="dropdown-header">Major Entities</li>
                <li class="divider" />
                <li><a href="/Admin/Item">  Item</a></li>
                <li><a href="/Admin/Product">  Product</a></li>
                <li><a href="/Admin/Subscription">
                      Subscription</a></li>

                <li class="divider" />
                <li class="dropdown-header">Connector Entities</li>
                <li class="divider" />
                <li><a href="/Admin/ProductItem">  Product Item</a></li>
                <li><a href="/Admin/SubscriptionProduct">
                      Subscription Product</a></li>

                <li class="divider" />
                <li class="dropdown-header">Users & Subscriptions</li>
                <li class="divider" />
                <li><a href="/Account">
                      Users & Subscriptions</a></li>
            </ul>
        </li>
```

JavaScript Hover functionality

Now that the **Admin** menu has been finished, it is time to create a JavaScript that wires up the **hover** function to the menu to make it drop down when a user hovers over it.

You can use the JQuery **hover** function to wire up the hover event to the admin menu. To keep the view clean and separate concerns a separate JavaScript file will be used for the **Admin** menu scripts. To keep the registration of this and future JavaScript files for the Admin menu as easy as possible you will create a new minification bundle called **admin** for them in the *BundleConfig.cs* file.

To access the Admin menu list item **<li>** element you will add an attribute called **data-admin-menu** to it which will be referenced from the JavaScript when wiring up the **hover** event and toggling the **open** class, which determines if the menu should be open or closed. Because the **hover** event handles both mouse enter and mouse leave, you only need this one event to handle the toggling.

The **AdminMenu.js** JavaScript file has to be added to the **Scripts** folder in the main project, not in the **Admin** area, to make it reachable from both the **Admin** area and the main project.

Adding the AdminMenu JavaScript file

1. Locate the **Scripts** folder in the main project and expand it, not in the **Admin** area.
2. Right-click on the folder and select **Add-JavaScript File**.
3. Enter **AdminMenu** in the **Item name** textbox and click the **OK** button.
4. Add the *Document Ready* function to make the scripts entered in it load when the DOM elements for the web page have been loaded. The easiest way to do this is to use the **$()** JQuery function.
   ```
   $(function () {
      // Code goes here
   });
   ```
5. Add the **hover** event referencing the **data-admin-menu** attribute from the **Document Ready** function.
   ```
   $('[data-admin-menu]').hover(function () {
      // Code goes here
   });
   ```
6. Add the **toggleClass** method to the **hover** event to hide and show the **Admin** menu. Again you reference the menu by its attribute.
   ```
   $('[data-admin-menu]').toggleClass('open');
   ```
7. Save the JavaScript file.

The complete code in the **AdminMenu** JavaScript file:

```
$(function () {
   $('[data-admin-menu]').hover(function () {
      $('[data-admin-menu]').toggleClass('open');
   });
});
```

Adding the admin bundle for the JavaScript files
1. Locate the **BundleConfig.cs** file in the **App_Start** folder and open it.
2. Copy one of the existing **ScriptBundle** definitions.
3. Change the name of the bundle to **~/bundles/admin**.
4. Change the script file name to **~/Scripts/AdminMenu.js**.
   ```
   bundles.Add(new ScriptBundle("~/bundles/admin").Include(
       "~/Scripts/AdminMenu.js"));
   ```
5. Open both **_Layout** views in the **Views-Shared** folders.
6. Copy one of the **@Scripts.Render** extension methods to the bottom of the **_Layout** views and change the path to **~/bundles/admin**. It has to be placed after the **jquery** and **bootstrap** bundles.
   ```
   @Scripts.Render("~/bundles/admin")
   ```
7. Save the files and run the application.
8. Hover over the **Admin** menu to open it and move away from it to close the menu.

4. Adding UIs for the Minor Entities

Introduction
In this chapter you will use the database you created in a previous chapter and start to build an admin application that ultimately only will be accessible for users in the **Admin** role. You will add the **Admin** role and enforce the security in an upcoming chapter when you implement login functionality.

To make it a soft start, the views in this chapter will be added with scaffolding to show how you can use synchronous calls to the server to fetch, add, update and delete data in the database.

As you add controllers and views to the **Admin** area, the corresponding menu items will start working, making it possible to navigate more easily between the **Index** views.

Technologies used in this chapter
1. **MVC** - To structure the application and scaffold views and controllers and to create partial views for reusable components such as buttons.
2. **C#** - Creating extension methods, helper methods, to keep the controller actions clean and easy to read. Creating the view models needed for all the views. Reflection is used to fetch property values for generic objects.
3. **Razor** - To incorporate C# in the views where necessary.
4. **HTML 5** - To build the views.
5. **Bootstrap** - To style the HTML 5 components.

The use case
Your task is to scaffold the controllers and views for the **Section**, **ItemType**, **Part**, **ProductLinkText** and **ProductType** tables in the database to enable reading and writing data to and from it. The controllers will be called **SectionController, ItemTypeController, PartController, ProductLinkTextController, ProductTypeController;** and for each con-

troller, five views will be created in folders named after the controller's corresponding tables. The views will be created in the **Views-Admin** folder.

- **Index** - The main view with a list of the available table records and buttons to the other views.
- **Create** - A view for adding new table records.
- **Delete** - A view for deleting a selected table record.
- **Edit** - A view to modify the table data.
- **Details** - A view to show one table record.

The customers push really hard for reusability, so that should be honored throughout the solution.

Because the default scaffolded views have a poor layout, you will spruce them up using Bootstrap and create reusable buttons in partial views instead of using the default links.

Scaffold the Section controller and views

When creating the section controller in the **Admin** area, be sure to select the **MVC 5 Controller with views, using Entity Framework** to create actions that can access the database. You also want to select the **Section** class in the **Model class** dropdown, the **ApplicationDbContext** in the **Data context** class dropdown and check the **Use async controller actions** and **Generate views** checkboxes. Note that the controller's name is in plural by default, change it to singular (*SectionController*).

By checking the **Use async controller actions** checkbox, actions decorated with the **async** keyword and a **Task** return type will be added to prepare for asynchronous calls to the database using the **await** keyword. By using **await,** the main thread servicing the controller action will be returned to the system to free it up for other work while the database call is processed.

IMPORTANT: *Although asynchronous calls often lead to better performance, it is not always the case; so you better do bench tests to see if it improves the performance. Asynchronous calls in the wrong scenario can even give slower response times.*

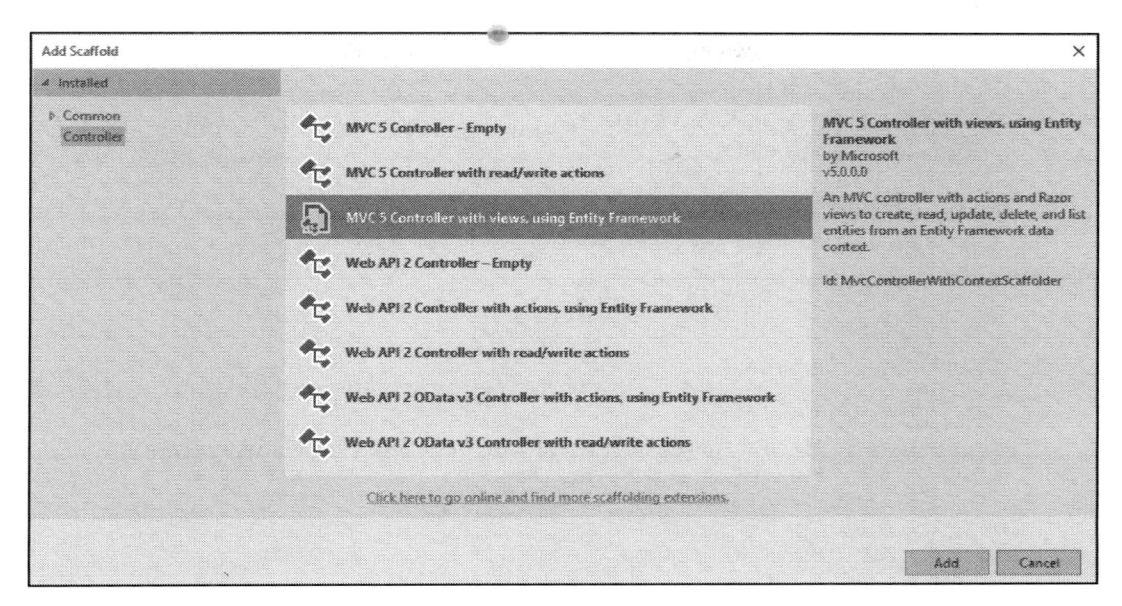

ASP.NET MVC 5 - How to build a Membership Website

Add Scaffold

- MVC 5 Controller – Empty
- MVC 5 Controller with read/write actions
- **MVC 5 Controller with views, using Entity Framework**
- Web API 2 Controller – Empty
- Web API 2 Controller with actions, using Entity Framework
- Web API 2 Controller with read/write actions
- Web API 2 OData v3 Controller with actions, using Entity Framework
- Web API 2 OData v3 Controller with read/write actions

MVC 5 Controller with views, using Entity Framework
by Microsoft
v5.0.0.0

An MVC controller with actions and Razor views to create, read, update, delete, and list entities from an Entity Framework data context.

Id: MvcControllerWithContextScaffolder

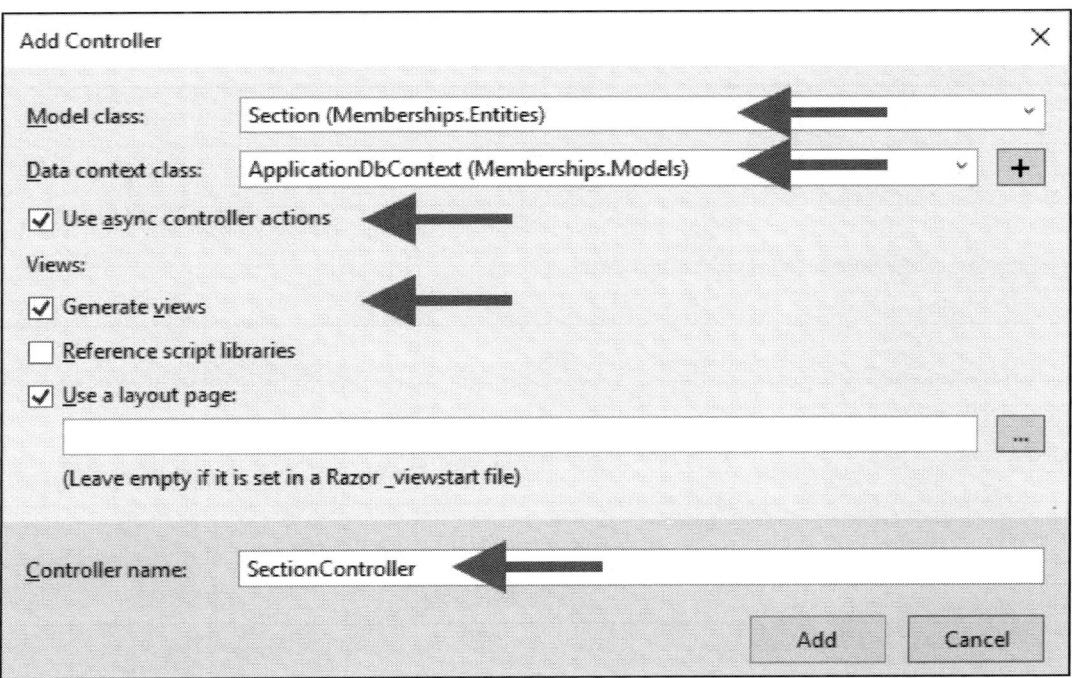

Add Controller

- Model class: Section (Memberships.Entities)
- Data context class: ApplicationDbContext (Memberships.Models)
- ☑ Use async controller actions

Views:
- ☑ Generate views
- ☐ Reference script libraries
- ☑ Use a layout page:

(Leave empty if it is set in a Razor _viewstart file)

Controller name: SectionController

65

ASP.NET MVC 5 - How to build a Membership Website

1. Right-click on the **Controllers** folder in the **Admin** area and select **Add-Controller** in the context menu.
2. Select the **MVC5 Controller with views, using Entity Framework** option in the dialog and click the **Add** button.
3. Select **Section** in the **Model class** dropdown.
4. Select **ApplicationDbContext** in the Data context class dropdown.
5. Check the **Use async controller actions** checkbox to enable asynchronous calls to the database.
6. Check the **Generate views** checkbox to automatically add the views needed for CRUD operations.
7. Change the controller name to *SectionController* and click the **Add** button.

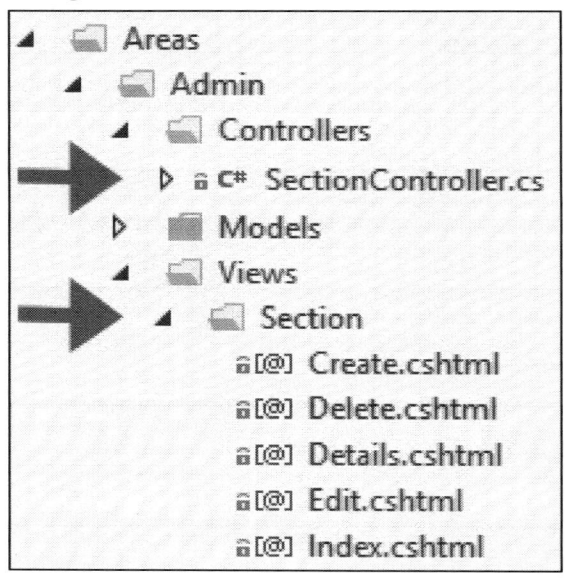

```
▲ 📁 Areas
    ▲ 📁 Admin
        ▲ 📁 Controllers
➡             ▷ C# SectionController.cs
          ▷ 📁 Models
          ▲ 📁 Views
➡             ▲ 📁 Section
                  [@] Create.cshtml
                  [@] Delete.cshtml
                  [@] Details.cshtml
                  [@] Edit.cshtml
                  [@] Index.cshtml
```

8. Run the application and select **Section** in the **Admin** menu to navigate to the page rendered by the **Index** view in the **SectionController**. Note that the URL is */Admin/Section* because the view is located in the **Admin** area.

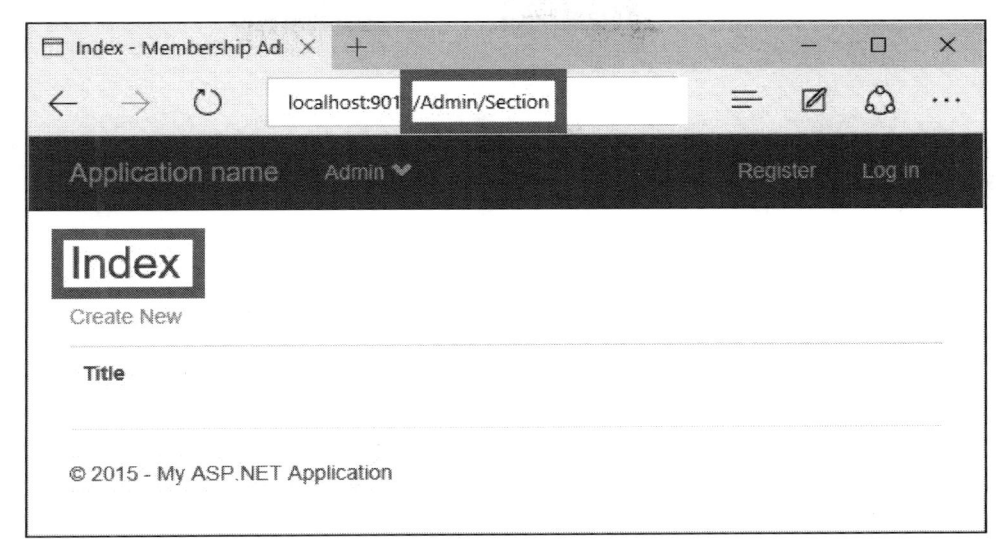

9. Selecting any other **Admin** menu option will generate a 404 error because there are no controllers available to process those requests.

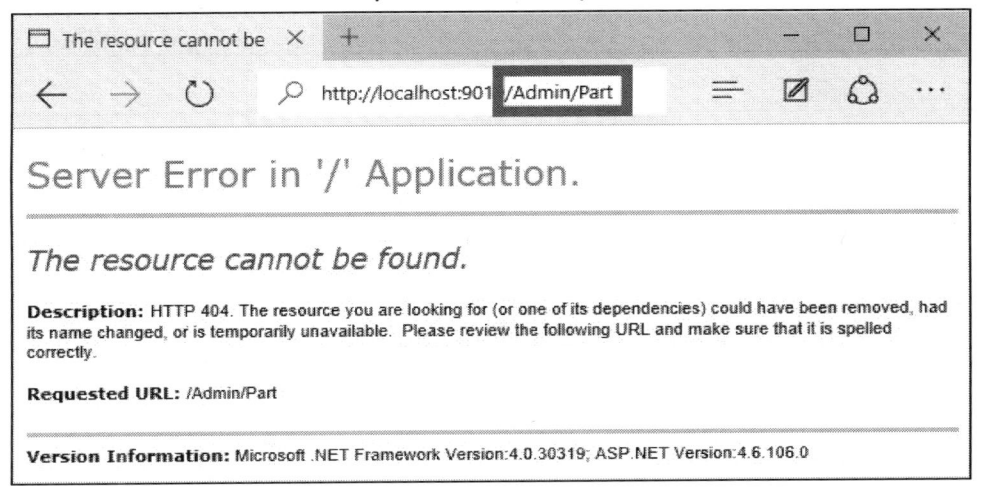

10. Let's add a section entry in the database by clicking on the **Create new** link. If you are still on the error page then click the browser **Back** button first to navigate back to the section **Index** page. Note that the URL changes to */Admin/Section/Create* to target the **Create** action method in the controller and render the view with the same name.

ASP.NET MVC 5 - How to build a Membership Website

11. Enter the text *Chapter 1* into the **Title** textbox and click the **Create** button. When the **Create** action method has finished processing the request, a redirect to the **Index** page is made displaying the newly added section fetched from the **Section** table in the database. Note that three new links are available to the right of the section title – these links are referencing the id of that section entry in the database.

12. Click the **Edit** link to edit the section data. Change the title to *Chapter 2* and click the **Save** button. Again you are redirected to the **Index** page where you can see the updated title.

13. Click the **Details** link to the right of the section title. This will show static data about the section. Click the **Back to List** link to navigate back to the **Index** page.

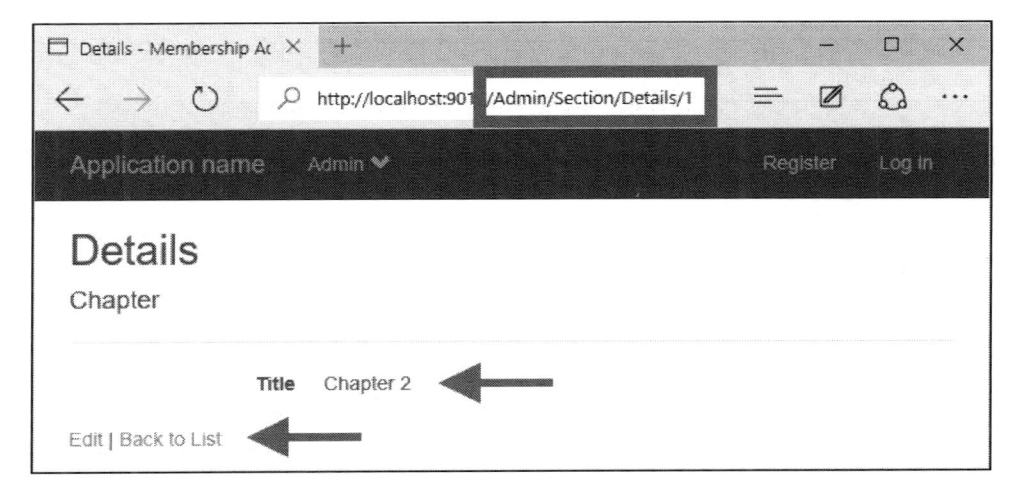

ASP.NET MVC 5 - How to build a Membership Website

14. Click the **Delete** link to the right of the section title. This will take you to a page where you can delete the section. Click the **Delete** button to remove the section and navigate back to the **Index** page.

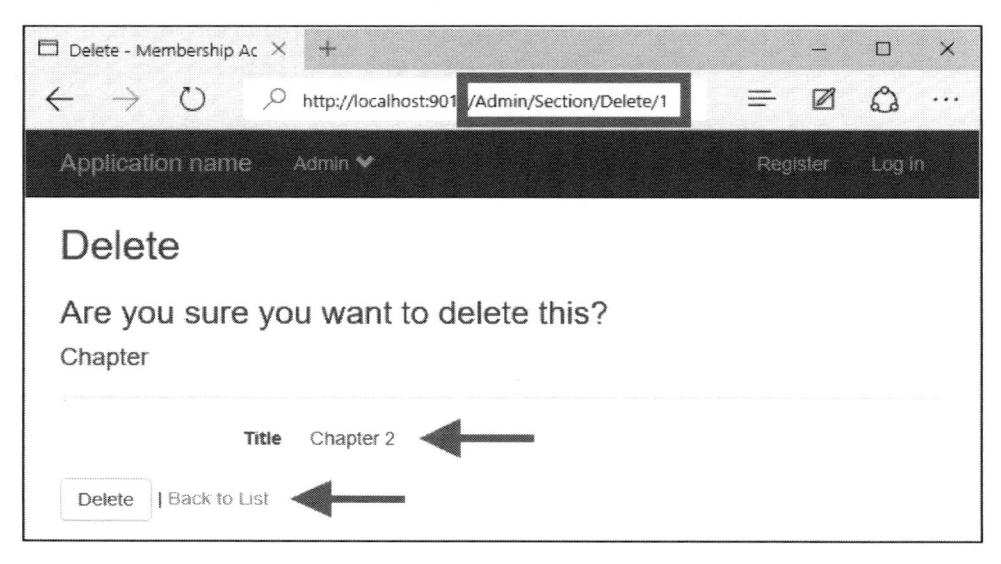

15. Now you are back where you started with an empty list on the **Index** page.

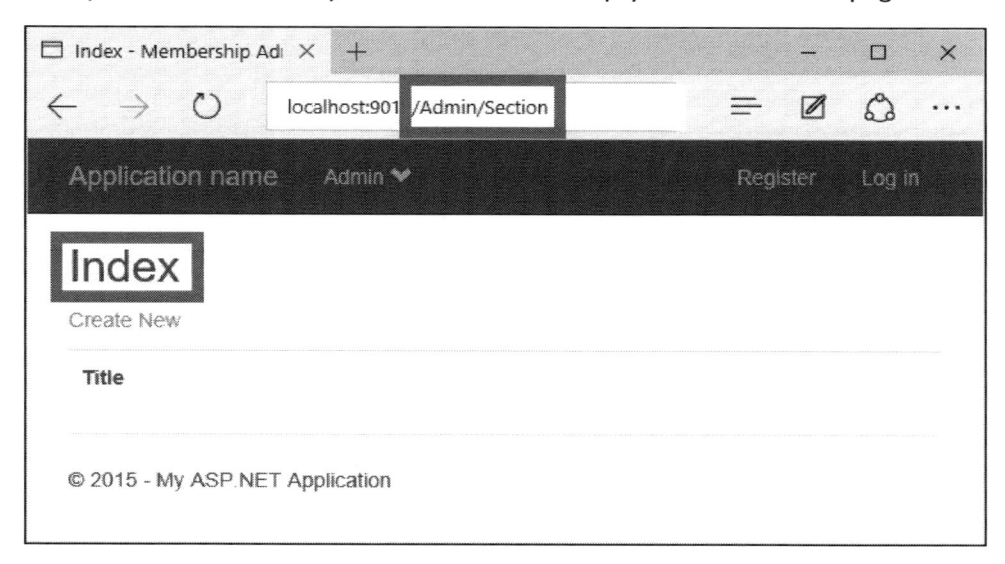

70

The Create View

Let's put some color and buttons in the **Create** view using Bootstrap. Since you will add many views which have a **Back to List** link, it can be beneficial to place that code in a partial view which can replace that link in all the views. While you are at it, you might as well spruce it up a little and change it into a (blue) primary button with a **list** glyph icon.

When you have created the **_BackToListButtonPartial** partial view, you swap out the **@Html.ActionLink** extension method for the **@Html.Partial** passing in the name of the partial view as a parameter.

Also change the **Create** button's background color to the (green) success color by adding the **btn-success** Bootstrap class to it.

This is the end result you will achieve.

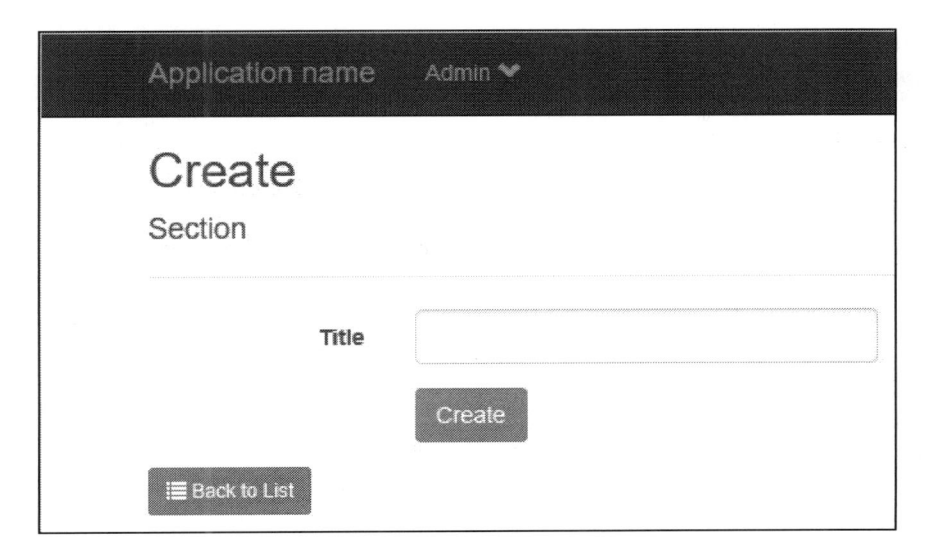

Change the Create button color
1. Open the **Create** view in the **Views-Section** folder in the **Admin** area.
2. Locate the **submit** button and change the class **btn-default** to **btn-success**.
   <input type="submit" value="Create" class="btn btn-success" />

Create the _BackToListButtonPartial view
1. Locate the **Views-Shared** folder in the **Admin** area.

2. Right-click on the folder and select **Add-View**.
3. Enter **_BackToListButtonPartial** in the **View name** textbox.
4. Check the **Create as partial view** checkbox and click the **Add** button.

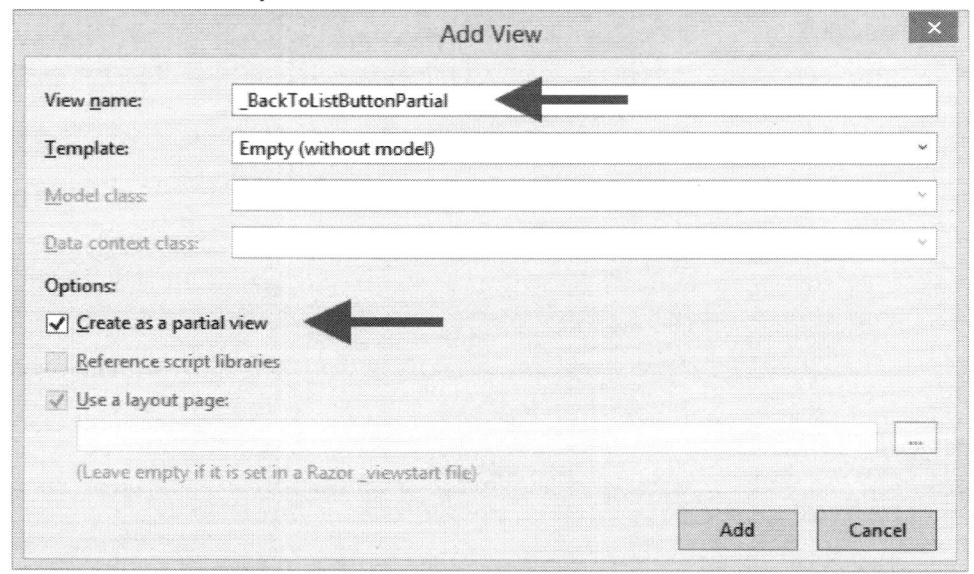

5. Add an anchor tag **<a>** element in the view window which is opened. Set its **type** attribute to **button**. Add the **btn, btn-primary** and **btn-sm** Bootstrap classes to make it into a button with the (blue) primary color and a little smaller than a normal button. Also add the **@Url.Action** extension method to the **href** attribute passing in the name of the **Index** view where the button will navigate when the user clicks it.

```
<a type="button" class="btn btn-primary btn-sm"
href="@Url.Action("Index")"></a>
```

6. Next, add the **list** glyph icon by adding a **<span>** inside the **<a>** element. Note that you have to add both the **glyphicon** and **glyphicon-list** Bootstrap classes for the icon to be displayed on the button. Also note that a glyph icon always is added as a class on an empty **<span>** element.

```
<span class="glyphicon glyphicon-list" aria-hidden="true"></span>
```

7. Then add the description to the right of the icon in a **<span>** element. You have to place it in a **<span>** for it to be displayed correctly when using a glyph icon.

```
<span>Back to List</span>
```

8. Save the **_BackToListButtonPartial** partial view.
9. Locate the **Create** view in the **Views-Section** folder.
10. Find the **@Html.ActionLink** extension method for the *Back to list* link and replace it with an **@Html.Partial** method call passing in the partial view name as a parameter.
    @Html.Partial("_BackToListButtonPartial")
11. Run the application and select **Section** in the **Admin** menu.
12. Click the **Create New** link on the **Index** page. The **Create** page should display the changes.
13. Click the **Back to list** button to see that it works, then add a new section called *Chapter 3*.

Here is the complete code for the **_BackToListButtonPartial** partial view:

```
<a type="button" class="btn btn-primary btn-sm"
href="@Url.Action("Index")">
    <span class="glyphicon glyphicon-list"></span>
    <span>Back to List</span>
</a>
```

The complete code for the **Create** view:

```
@model Memberships.Entities.Section

@{
    ViewBag.Title = "Create";
}

<h2>Create</h2>

@using (Html.BeginForm())
{
    @Html.AntiForgeryToken()

    <div class="form-horizontal">
        <h4>Section</h4>
        <hr />
        @Html.ValidationSummary(true, "", new { @class = "text-danger" })
        <div class="form-group">
            @Html.LabelFor(model => model.Title, htmlAttributes:
                new { @class = "control-label col-md-2" })
```

```
            <div class="col-md-10">
                @Html.EditorFor(model => model.Title, new {
                    htmlAttributes = new { @class = "form-control" } })
                @Html.ValidationMessageFor(model => model.Title, "",
                    new { @class = "text-danger" })
            </div>
        </div>

        <div class="form-group">
            <div class="col-md-offset-2 col-md-10">
                <input type="submit" value="Create" class="btn btn-success" />
            </div>
        </div>
    </div>
}

<div>
    @Html.Partial("_BackToListButtonPartial")
</div>
```

The Edit View

Let's put some color and buttons in the **Edit** view using Bootstrap. As you can see, the **Edit** view is very similar to the **Create** view and has the same **Back to List** link as the **Create** view had before you changed it to a button.

Since you already have created the partial view **_BackToListButtonPartial,** you can simply swap out the **@Html.ActionLink** extension method for a call to the **@Html.Partial** extension method like you did for the **Create** view.

You change the color of the **Save** button in the same way you did for the **submit** button in the **Create** view.

Change the Save button color
1. Open the **Edit** view in the **Views-Section** folder in the **Admin** area.
2. Locate the submit button and change the class **btn-default** to **btn-success**.
   ```
   <input type="submit" value="Save" class="btn btn-success" />
   ```

Change the Back to List link to a button
1. In the **Edit** view, locate the **@Html.ActionLink** extension method and swap it for a **@Html.Partial** extension method call.

```
@Html.Partial("_BackToListButtonPartial")
```

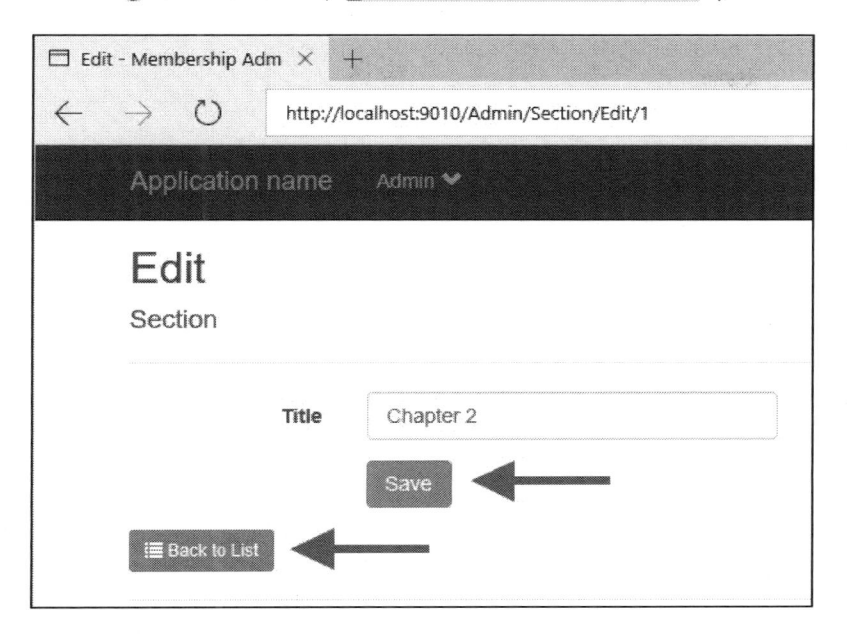

The complete code for the **Edit** view:

```
@model Memberships.Entities.Section

@{
    ViewBag.Title = "Edit";
}

<h2>Edit</h2>

@using (Html.BeginForm())
{
    @Html.AntiForgeryToken()

    <div class="form-horizontal">
        <h4>Section</h4>
        <hr />
        @Html.ValidationSummary(true, "", new { @class = "text-danger" })
        @Html.HiddenFor(model => model.Id)

        <div class="form-group">
            @Html.LabelFor(model => model.Title, htmlAttributes:
```

```
                new { @class = "control-label col-md-2" })
            <div class="col-md-10">
                @Html.EditorFor(model => model.Title, new {
                    htmlAttributes = new { @class = "form-control" } })
                @Html.ValidationMessageFor(model => model.Title, "",
                    new { @class = "text-danger" })
            </div>
        </div>

        <div class="form-group">
            <div class="col-md-offset-2 col-md-10">
                <input type="submit" value="Save" class="btn btn-success" />
            </div>
        </div>
    </div>
}

<div>
    @Html.Partial("_BackToListButtonPartial")
</div>
```

The Details View

Let's put some color and buttons in the **Details** view using Bootstrap. As you can see, the **Details** view only displays static data and has two links: one back to the list and one to the **Edit** view. The latter link requires the current section id as a parameter to be able to correctly navigate to the **Edit** view. A typical **Edit** URL looks like this */Admin/Section/Edit/1* where **1** is a section id in the database's **Section** table.

The section id is passed in to the partial view **_EditButtonPartial** from the **Id** property in the **Model** object in the **Details** view.

```
@Html.Partial("_EditButtonPartial", Model.Id)
```

In the partial view **_EditButtonPartial,** the section id is passed in as a second parameter to the **@Url.Action** method. The **id** property is assigned the view's **Model** value. The property is wrapped in an anonymous object.

```
href="@Url.Action("Edit", new { id = Model })"
```

The **id** property in the anonymous object is then matched with a parameter of the **Edit** action in the **SectionController** class.

ASP.NET MVC 5 - How to build a Membership Website

```
public async Task<ActionResult> Edit(int? id)
```

Two partial views will be used here, the **_BackToListButtonPatial** and a new one called **_EditButtonPartial** which will define the **Edit** button.

This is what the **Details** view will look like after the changes:

Change the Back to List link to a button
1. In the **Details** view, locate the **@Html.ActionLink** extension method and swap it for a **@Html.Partial** extension method call.
   ```
   @Html.Partial("_BackToListButtonPartial")
   ```

Create the _EditButtonPartial view
1. Locate the **Views-Shared** folder in the **Admin** area.
2. Right-click on the folder and select **Add-View**.
3. Enter **_EditButtonPartial** in the **View name** textbox.
4. Check the **Create as partial view** checkbox and click the **Add** button.
5. In the view window, add a **@model** directive of type **int** at the top.
   ```
   @model int
   ```
6. Add an anchor tag **<a>** element in the view window. Set its type attribute to **button**. Add the **btn**, **btn-primary** and **btn-sm** Bootstrap classes to make it into a button with the (blue) primary color and a little smaller than a normal button.

77

Also add the **@Url.Action** extension method to the **href** attribute passing in the name of the **Edit** view where the button will navigate, and the current section id through the **@model** directive.

```
<a type="button" class="btn btn-primary btn-sm"
href="@Url.Action("Edit", new { id = Model })"></a>
```

7. Next, add the **pencil** glyph icon by adding a **<span>** inside the **<a>** element. Note that you have to add both the **glyphicon** and **glyphicon-pencil** Bootstrap classes for the icon to be displayed on the button. Also note that a glyph icon is always added as two classes on an empty **<span>** element.

```
<span class="glyphicon glyphicon-pencil" aria-hidden="true"></span>
```

8. Then add the text to be displayed to the right of the icon in a **<span>** element. You have to place it in a **<span>** for it to be displayed correctly when using a glyph icon.

```
<span>Edit</span>
```

9. Save the **_EditButtonPartial** partial view.
10. Locate the **Details** view in the **Views-Section** folder.
11. Add a second **@Html.Partial** method call passing in **_EditButtonPartial** as its parameter.

```
@Html.Partial("_EditButtonPartial")
```

12. Run the application and select **Section** in the **Admin** menu.
13. Click the **Details** link on the **Index** page next to the section you want to view.
14. Check that the view's layout has changed.

Here is the complete code for the **_EditButtonPartial** partial view:

```
@model int

<a type="button" class="btn btn-primary btn-sm"
href="@Url.Action("Edit", new { id = Model })">
    <span class="glyphicon glyphicon-pencil" aria-hidden="true"></span>
    <span>Edit</span>
</a>
```

In the **Details** view swap the following two rows:

```
@Html.ActionLink("Edit", "Edit", new { id = Model.Id }) |
@Html.ActionLink("Back to List", "Index")
```

with

```
@Html.Partial("_EditButtonPartial", Model.Id)
@Html.Partial("_BackToListButtonPartial")
```

The complete code for the **Details** view:

```
@model Memberships.Entities.Section

@{
    ViewBag.Title = "Details";
}

<h2>Details</h2>

<div>
    <h4>Section</h4>
    <hr />
    <dl class="dl-horizontal">
        <dt>@Html.DisplayNameFor(model => model.Title)</dt>
        <dd>@Html.DisplayFor(model => model.Title)</dd>
    </dl>
</div>
<p>
    @Html.Partial("_EditButtonPartial", Model.Id)
    @Html.Partial("_BackToListButtonPartial")
</p>
```

The Delete View

Let's put some color and buttons in the **Delete** view using Bootstrap. Here you will change the color of the **Delete** button to (red) **btn-danger** to signal to the user that they should proceed with caution. The buttons will have different sizes unless you add the **btn-sm** class to the **Delete** button. Then you will swap the **Back to List** link for the partial view **_BackToListButtonPartial**.

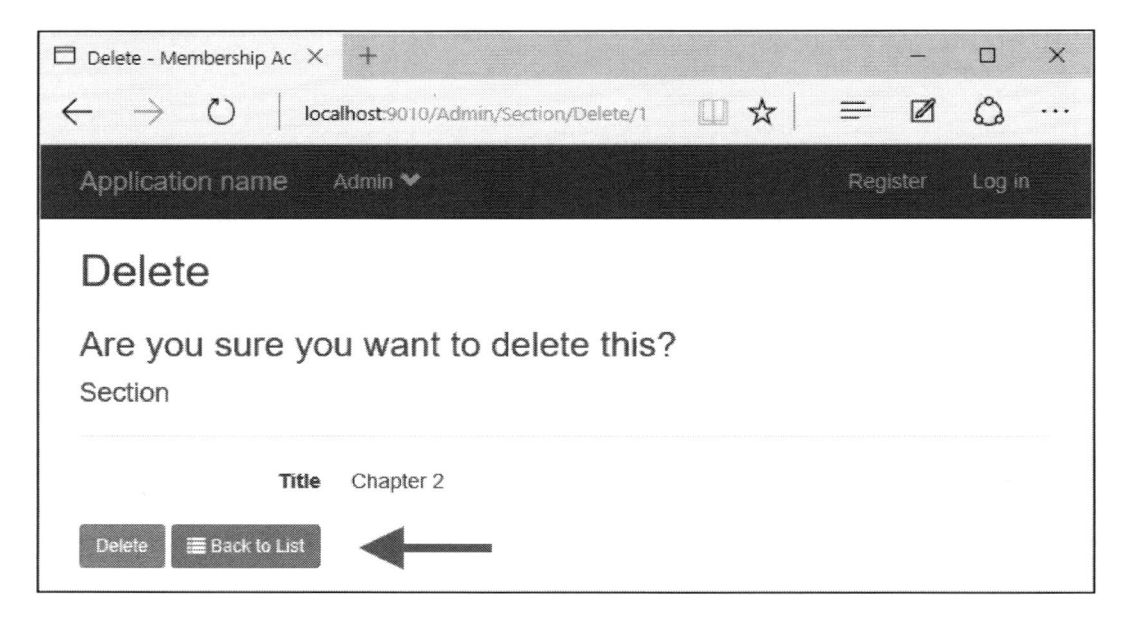

Change the Delete button color
1. Open the **Delete** view in the **Views-Section** folder in the **Admin** area.
2. Locate the **submit** button and change the class **btn-default** to **btn-danger** and add the **btn-sm** class to make this button the same size as the **Back to List** button.
   ```
   <input type="submit" value="Delete" class="btn btn-danger btn-sm" />
   ```

Change the Back to List link to a button
1. In the **Delete** view, locate the **@Html.ActionLink** extension method and swap it for a **@Html.Partial** extension method call.
   ```
   @Html.Partial("_BackToListButtonPartial")
   ```

The complete code for the **Delete** view:

```
@model Memberships.Entities.Section

@{ ViewBag.Title = "Delete"; }

<h2>Delete</h2>
<h3>Are you sure you want to delete this?</h3>
<div>
```

```
<h4>Section</h4>
<hr />
<dl class="dl-horizontal">
    <dt>@Html.DisplayNameFor(model => model.Title)</dt>
    <dd>@Html.DisplayFor(model => model.Title)</dd>
 </dl>

@using (Html.BeginForm()) {
   @Html.AntiForgeryToken()
   <div class="form-actions no-color">
      <input type="submit" value="Delete"
         class="btn btn-danger btn-sm" />
      @Html.Partial("_BackToListButtonPartial")
   </div>
}
</div>
```

The Index View

Let's put some color and buttons in the **Index** view using Bootstrap. It will take a little more effort to get this view looking nice, since you not only have to style links into buttons, but you also have to create a button group for the styled links in the table and style the table itself. Below is an image showing the finished result.

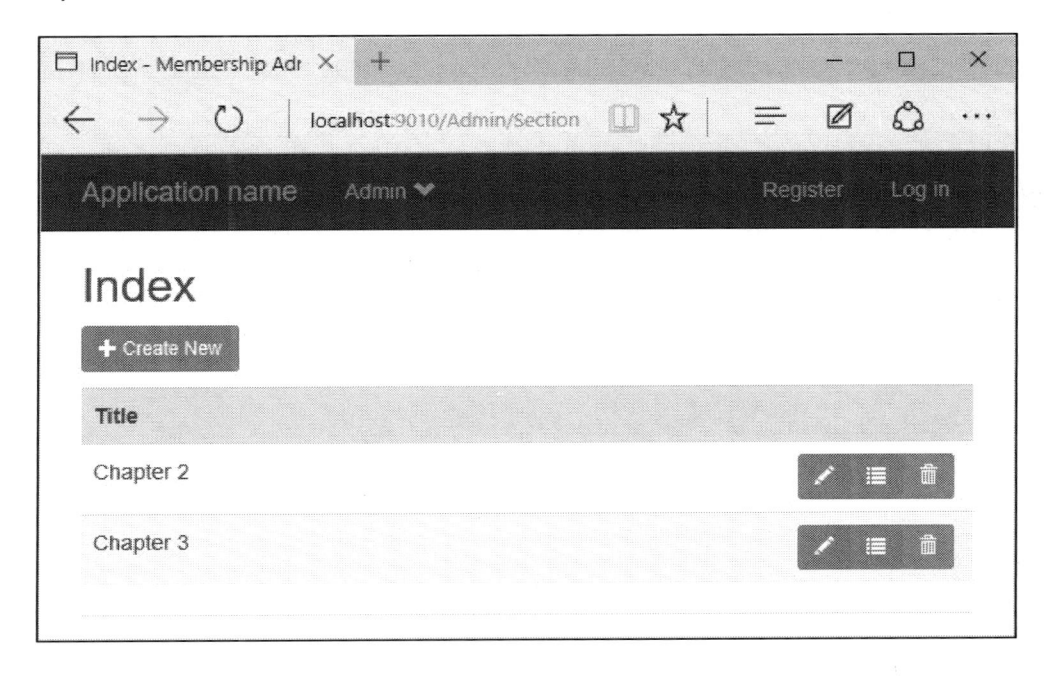

Styling the table

Let's start by styling the table, which oddly enough is the easiest of the tasks you have to complete when styling the **Index** view.

There are only two classes that you have to add in order to get the table to look this dashing.

First, you add the **table-striped** class to the **<table>** element to get the striping effect with every other row in an alternate color.

```
<table class="table table-striped">
```

Then all you have to do is to add the **success** class (green) to the header row to make it stand out in another color.

```
<tr class="success">
```

Styling the Create New link

Next, you will transform the **Create New** link into a button with a plus-sign icon using the **glyphicon** library. Create it as a partial view to enable reuse and get cleaner HTML markup in the **Index** view.

Let's do it faster by copying the **_BackToListButtonPartial** partial view, renaming it **_CreateNewButtonPartial** and then altering its content. You only have to change three values in the view; the first is the action to call when the button is clicked specified by the **@Url.Action** method parameter – it has to be changed from *Index* to *Create*. The second is the glyph icon which has to be changed from **glyphicon-list** to **glyphicon-plus**. The third is the button text which should say *Create New*.

1. Locate the **_BackToListButtonPartial** view in the **Views-Shared** folder in the **Admin** area.
2. Right-click on it and select **Copy** in the context menu.
3. Right-click on the **Shared** folder and select **Paste** in the context menu.
4. Rename the copy **_CreateNewButtonPartial** by right-clicking on it and selecting **Rename** in the context menu.
5. Change **Index** to **Create** in the **@Url.Action** method.

```
<a type="button" class="btn btn-primary btn-sm"
href="@Url.Action("Create")">
```

6. Locate **glyphicon-list** and change it to **glyphicon-plus**.
   ```
   <span class="glyphicon glyphicon-plus" aria-
   hidden="true"></span>
   ```

7. Change the text to *Create New* in the last **<span>** element.
   ```
   <span>Create New</span>
   ```

8. Save the view and open the **Index** view in the **Views-Section** folder.

9. Replace the **@Html.ActionLink** with a call to **@Html.Partial** for the **Create New** link.
   ```
   @Html.Partial("_CreateNewButtonPartial")
   ```

10. Run the application and select **Section** in the **Admin** menu to check that the link has been swapped for a button.

The complete HTML markup for the **_CreateNewButtonPartial** view:

```
<a type="button" class="btn btn-primary btn-sm"
href="@Url.Action("Create")">
    <span class="glyphicon glyphicon-plus" aria-hidden="true"></span>
    <span>Create New</span>
</a>
```

The SmallButtonModel class

Up until now, you have used hard-coded partial views to add buttons, creating one partial view per button. Let's bring it up a notch and create a more dynamic version of a button that can be reused for several upcoming scenarios.

The first thing you need to create is a view model that can be sent to the generic button with values that will be used in the button's partial view. To begin, you will need the following values (you can always add more in the future if you want).

- **Action** - A **string** property holding the name of the controller action you want to call when the button is clicked.
- **ButtonType** - A **string** property defining what type of Bootstrap button will be created, you can use the default button types provided by Bootstrap such as *btn-default*, *btn-primary*, *btn-success*, *btn-warning* and *btn-danger*.

- **Glyph** - A **string** property defining a glyphicon to display in the button. Only use the part after the hyphen in the glyphicon name; you would use *pencil* for *glyphicon-pencil*.
- **Text** - A **string** property for hidden text which can be used for browser optimization.
- **Id** - A **null**-able **int** property storing the id used when only one parameter is received by the action method.
- **ItemId** - A **null**-able **int** property storing the item id used when for instance editing and displaying information about or deleting an item.
- **ProductId** - A **null**-able **int** property storing a product id. In certain scenarios you will have to pass in several ids one of them is the product id.
- **SubscriptionId** - A **null**-able **int** property storing a subscription id. In certain scenarios you will have to pass in several ids one of them is the subscription id.
- **ActionParameters** - A read-only **string** property returning a list of URL parameters for the four id properties: The URL parameter values should be named **id**, **itemId**, **projectId** and **subscriptionId**. (note that the first letter is in lower case). The parameters that can be passed in through the model are **Id**, **ItemId**, **ProductId**, **SubscriptionId**. The **id** parameter is used by default in controller actions where only one id is passed in. Since the model is used from a variety of **Index** views, the property must be able to return URL parameters with the following combinations:
    - Only **Id**, **ItemId**, **ProductId** or **SubscriptionId**
    - **ItemId** and **ProductId**
    - **ItemId**, **ProductId** and **SubscriptionId**
    - **ProductId** and **SubscriptionId**
    - **ItemId** and **SubscriptionId**

Use the information in the list above to add class called **SmallButtonModel** to the **Models** folder in the **Admin** area.

1. Right-click on the **Models** folder in the **Admin** area.
2. Select **Add-Class** in the context menu.
3. Enter **SmallButtonModel** in the **Name** textbox.
4. Add the properties from the list above.

5. The read-only **ActionParameters** property can be a bit tricky so let's create that one together. A read-only property only has a **get**-block.
6. In the **get**-block, add a **StringBuilder** variable called **param** and create an instance of it. Pass in the obligatory URL parmeter **?**-mark to the constructor.
   `var param = new StringBuilder("?");`
7. Check with an if-statement if the **Id** property is not **null** and is greater than 0, then append a formatted string to the **param** variable containing the name and value of the parameter.
   ```
   if (Id != null && Id > 0)
       param.Append(String.Format("{0}={1}&", "id", Id));
   ```
8. Next, do the same for the **ItemId, ProductId** and **SubscriptionId** properties.
9. Return the string representation of the **param** variable by calling the **ToString** and **Substring** methods on it. The **Substring** method is used to remove the last **&**-character or the **?**-mark (if no matching id's were found) from the parameter list.
   `return param.ToString().Substring(0, s.Length - 1);`

The complete **SmallButton** class:

```
public class SmallButtonModel
{
    public string Action { get; set; }
    public string Text { get; set; }
    public string Glyph { get; set; }
    public string ButtonType { get; set; }
    public int? Id { get; set; }
    public int? ItemId { get; set; }
    public int? ProductId { get; set; }
    public int? SubscriptionId { get; set; }
    public string ActionParameters
    {
        get
        {
            var param = new StringBuilder("?");
            if (Id != null && Id > 0)
                param.Append(String.Format("{0}={1}&", "id", Id));

            if (ItemId != null && ItemId > 0)
                param.Append(String.Format("{0}={1}&", "itemId", ItemId));
```

```
            if (ProductId != null && ProductId > 0)
                param.Append(String.Format("{0}={1}&", "productId",
                ProductId));

            if (SubscriptionId != null && SubscriptionId > 0)
                param.Append(String.Format("{0}={1}&", "subscriptionId",
                SubscriptionId));

            return param.ToString().Substring(0, s.Length - 1);
        }
    }
}
```

Creating a generic reusable partial view button
To create the generic button partial view you have to add it to the **Views-Shared** folder with the **SmallButtonModel** as its model. You can use the **_BackToListButtonPatial** view as a starting point when creating the generic button view.

Instead of only using hard coded values in the HTML markup, you will use Razor syntax to add the model properties to select places. Generally, you prefix the **Model** object with an **@**-sign when accessing its properties in HTML markup, the exception to the rule is if the HTML markup already is inside a C# block.

Let's modify the HTML to become more generic using the **Model** properties. The first constant you will replace is the **btn-primary** class defining the button color. Use the **@Model.ButtonType** property. Next, replace the "Index" in the **@Url.Action** method with the **@Model.Action** property and immediately outside the parenthesis, add the **@Model.ActionParameters** property. This combination will render the base URL for the action and append the parameter list to it. Next, replace the hard-coded glyphicon **glyphicon-list** with **glyphicon-@Model.Glyph** property. The last thing to replace is the text *Back to List* with the **@Model.Text** property.

1. Copy the **_BackToListButtonPatial** view in the **Views-Shared** folder and rename the copy **_SmallButtonPartial**.
2. In the **_SmallButtonPartial** view, add the **model** class reference to the **SmallButtonModel** at the very top of the view.
   ```
   @model Memberships.Areas.Admin.Models.SmallButtonModel
   ```

3. Change the **btn-primary** class to the **@Model.ButtonType** property in the **<a>** element's **class** attribute.
4. Replace the "Index" in the **@Url.Action** method with the **@Model.Action** property, and immediately outside the parenthesis, add the **@Model.ActionParameters** property.
   ```
   <a type="button" class="btn @Model.ButtonType btn-sm"
   href="@Url.Action(Model.Action)@Model.ActionParameters">
   ```
5. Replace **glyphicon-list** with **glyphicon-@Model.Glyph** property.
   ```
   <span class="glyphicon glyphicon-@Model.Glyph" aria-
   hidden="true"></span>
   ```
6. Replace is the text *Back to List* with the **@Model.Text** property.
   ```
   <span class="sr-only">@Model.Text</span>
   ```

The complete **_SmallButtonPartial** view:

```
@model Memberships.Areas.Admin.Models.SmallButtonModel

<a type="button" class="btn @Model.ButtonType btn-sm"
    href="@Url.Action(Model.Action)@Model.ActionParameters">
    <span class="glyphicon glyphicon-@Model.Glyph"
        aria-hidden="true"></span>
    <span class="sr-only">@Model.Text</span>
</a>
```

Create the partial view _TableButtonsPartial

This partial view will act as a container for the three buttons displayed on each row in the table on the **Index** view, replacing the default **Edit**, **Details** and **Delete** links.

The three buttons will be added using the generic **_SmallButtonPartial** partial view you just created.

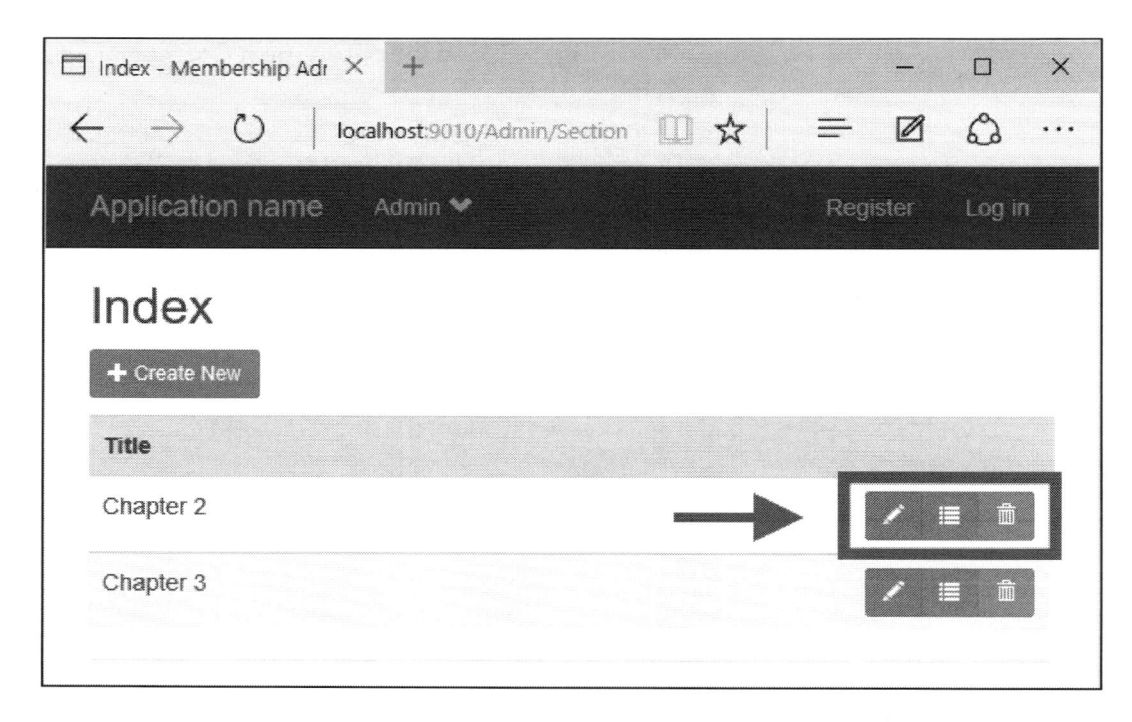

[Screenshot: Index page showing Create New button, a Title column with Chapter 2 and Chapter 3 rows, each with edit/details/delete button group on the right. An arrow points to the button group on the Chapter 2 row.]

Because the buttons are displayed as data in a table row, they have to reside inside a table data **<td>** element to be rendered correctly. The element also needs a width of 120px to be rendered correctly as a button group on the row. Without the width assigned, the buttons will take up too much space in the table since the available width will be divided equally by the two columns, placing the buttons in the middle of the table.

The view has to have the **SmallButtonModel** class as its model as well as a **using** statement to the **Models** folder in the **Admin** area to get access to the **SmallButtonModel** class. The class is used in Razor code to create instances which are sent to the individual buttons added to the button group.

For the buttons to be treated as a group, they have to be placed in a **<div>** element with the class **btn-group** assigned to it, as well as having the **role** attribute set to **group**. Since there can be more than one button group, the **aria-label** attribute has to be assigned a unique value, for instance a Guid.

ASP.NET MVC 5 - How to build a Membership Website

To add a button, you call the **@Html.Partial** method passing in **_SmallButtonPartial** as its first parameter and an instance of the **SmallButtonModel** class as its second parameter.

Use the following values for the **Edit** button: **Action** = "Edit", **ButtonType** = "btn-primary", **Glyph** = "pencil", **Text** = "Edit", **Id** = Model.Id, **ItemId** = Model.ItemId, **ProductId** = Model.ProductId, **SubscriptionId** = Model.SubscriptionId.

Use the following values for the **Details** button: **Action** = "Details", **ButtonType** = "btn-success", **Glyph** = "list", **Text** = "Details", **Id** = Model.Id, **ItemId** = Model.ItemId, **ProductId** = Model.ProductId, **SubscriptionId** = Model.SubscriptionId.

Use the following values for the **Delete** button: **Action** = "Delete", **ButtonType** = "btn-danger", **Glyph** = "trash", **Text** = " Delete", **Id** = Model.Id, **ItemId** = Model.ItemId, **ProductId** = Model.ProductId, **SubscriptionId** = Model.SubscriptionId.

1. Right-click on the **Views-Shared** folder and select **Add-View**.
2. Enter **_TableButtonsPartial** in the **View name** textbox.
3. Make sure that the **Create as a partial view** checkbox is checked.
4. Click on the **Add** button.
5. Add the **@model** directive and the **using** statement.
    ```
    @model Memberships.Areas.Admin.Models.SmallButtonModel
    @using Memberships.Areas.Admin.Models
    ```
6. Add the table data **<td>** element and set its width to 120px.
    ```
    <td style="width:120px;">
        @*Button group goes here*@
    </td>
    ```
7. Add the button group **<div>** element, assign the **btn-group** class and **Role** attribute to it and assign a new Guid to the **aria-label** attribute.
    ```
    <div class="btn-group" role="group" aria-label="@Guid.NewGuid()">
        @*Button code goes here*@
    </div>
    ```
8. Add three **@Html.Partial** method calls to add the buttons (see code below).

The full code for the **TableButtonsPartial** partial view:

```
@model MyMembership.Areas.Admin.Models.SmallButtonModel
@using MyMembership.Areas.Admin.Models

<td style="width:120px;">
    <div class="btn-group" role="group" aria-label="@Guid.NewGuid()">
        @Html.Partial("_SmallButtonPartial",
            new SmallButtonModel { Action = "Edit",
            ButtonType = "btn-primary", Glyph = "pencil", Text = "Edit",
            Id = Model.Id,
            ItemId = Model.ItemId,
            ProductId = Model.ProductId,
            SubscriptionId = Model.SubscriptionId })

        @Html.Partial("_SmallButtonPartial", new SmallButtonModel {
            Action = "Details", ButtonType = "btn-success",
            Glyph = "list", Text = "Details",
            Id = Model.Id,
            ItemId = Model.ItemId,
            ProductId = Model.ProductId,
            SubscriptionId = Model.SubscriptionId })

        @Html.Partial("_SmallButtonPartial", new SmallButtonModel {
            Action = "Delete", ButtonType = "btn-danger", Glyph = "trash",
            Text = "Delete",
            Id = Model.Id,
            ItemId = Model.ItemId,
            ProductId = Model.ProductId,
            SubscriptionId = Model.SubscriptionId })
    </div>
</td>
```

Add the partial view _TableButtonsPartial to the Index view

One last thing remains to complete the **Index** view, and that is to add the **_TableButtonsPartial** partial view to it. To add the buttons you have created, replace the existing links with the partial view.

Replace:
```
<td>
    @Html.ActionLink("Edit", "Edit", new { id=item.Id }) |
    @Html.ActionLink("Details", "Details", new { id=item.Id }) |
    @Html.ActionLink("Delete", "Delete", new { id=item.Id })
</td>
```

With:
```
@Html.Partial("_TableButtonsPartial", new SmallButtonModel { Id = item.Id })
```

1. Open the **Index** view in the **Views-Section** folder.
2. Add a **@using** statement to the **Models** folder in the **Admin** area under the **@model** directive.
   ```
   @using Memberships.Areas.Admin.Models
   ```
3. Find the **foreach** loop and remove the following HTML markup
   ```
   <td>
       @Html.ActionLink("Edit", "Edit", new { id=item.Id })|
       @Html.ActionLink("Details", "Details", new { id=item.Id })|
       @Html.ActionLink("Delete", "Delete", new { id=item.Id })
   </td>
   ```
4. Add the following HTML markup in its place. Note that an instance of the **SmallButtonModel** is passed in as a second parameter to the **@Html.Partial** method.
   ```
   @Html.Partial("_TableButtonsPartial", new SmallButtonModel { ItemId = item.Id })
   ```
5. Save and run the application and check that the buttons are displayed in the table and that they are working.

The complete code for the **Index** view:

```
@model IEnumerable<Memberships.Entities.Section>
@using Memberships.Areas.Admin.Models;

@{ ViewBag.Title = "Index"; }

<h2>Index</h2>
<p>@Html.Partial("_CreateButtonPartial")</p>

<table class="table table-striped table-condensed">
    <tr class="success">
        <th>@Html.DisplayNameFor(model => model.Title)</th>
        <th></th>
    </tr>
```

```
@foreach (var item in Model) {
    <tr>
        <td>@Html.DisplayFor(modelItem => item.Title)</td>
        @Html.Partial("_TableButtonsPartial",
            new SmallButtonModel { Id = item.Id })
    </tr>
}
</table>
```

Scaffold the Part controller and views

The **Part** table is virtually identical to the **Section** table; it's basically just the name that differs, so creating and altering the controller and views should be a breeze by now. If you get stuck you can always go back to the section describing how to set it up for the **Section** table.

The fastest way to implement the controller and views for the **Part** table is probably to create a controller without views, copy the **Section** views and make a couple of small changes to them.

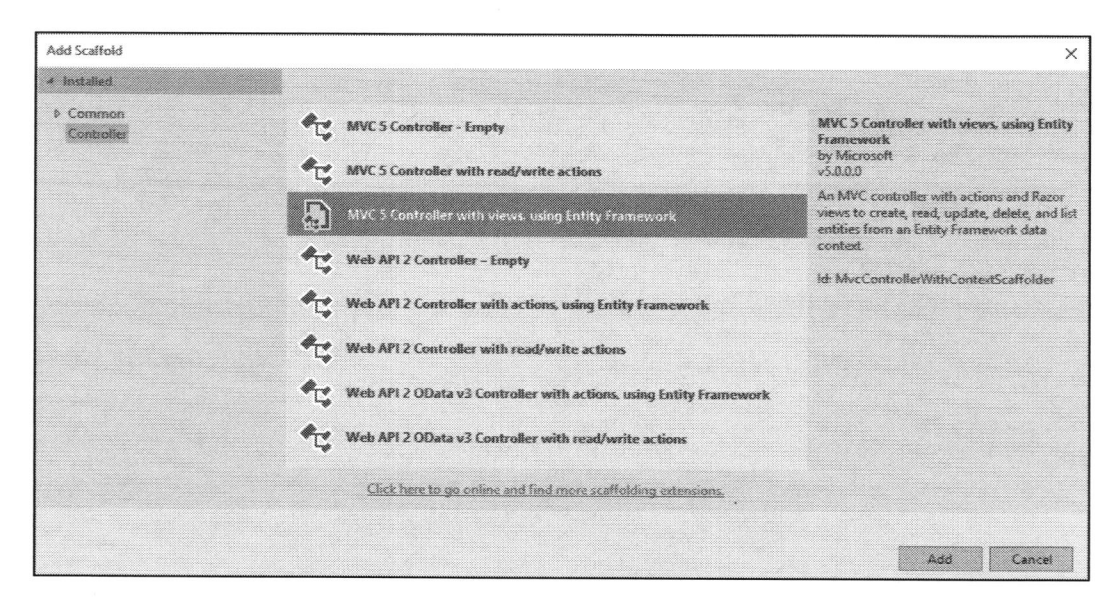

ASP.NET MVC 5 - How to build a Membership Website

Add Controller

- Model class: Part (Memberships.Entities)
- Data context class: ApplicationDbContext (Memberships.Models)
- ☑ Use async controller actions
- Views:
  - ☐ Generate views
  - Reference script libraries
  - ☑ Use a layout page:
    - (Leave empty if it is set in a Razor _viewstart file)
- Controller name: PartController

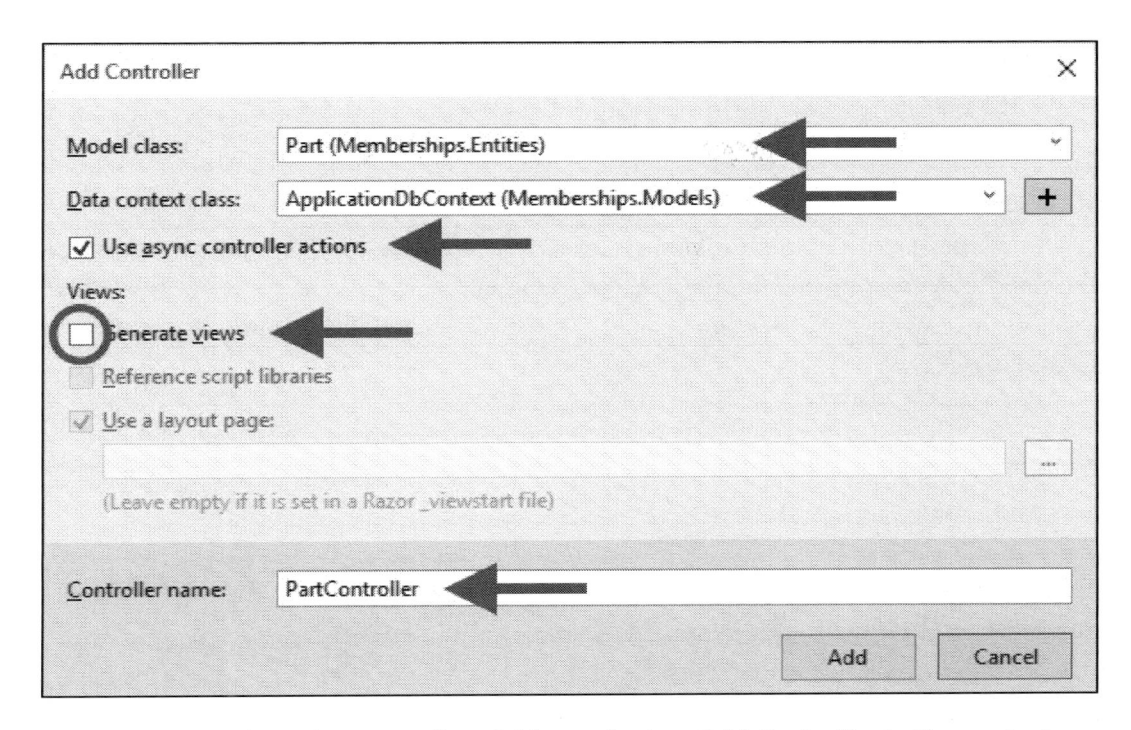

1. Right-click on the **Controllers** folder and select **Add-Controller** in the context menu.
2. Fill in the **Add Controller** dialog according to the image above and make sure that the **Generate views** checkbox is unchecked and the name is *PartController*. Apart from adding the controller, a folder named **Part** will be added to the **Views** folder.
3. Select *all views* in the **Section** folder by selecting the first one and while holding down shift selecting the last one.
4. Right-click on the selection and select **Copy** in the context menu.
5. Right-click on the **Part** folder and select **Paste** in the context menu.
6. Now you have to go through the views in the **Part** folder one by one and change the **@model** directive to point to the **Part** class and the **<h4>** heading in the form to *Part*. The **Index** view does not have the **<h4>** element.
   `@model` IEnumerable<Memberships.Entities.Part>
   and
   <h4>Part</h4>

7. Run the application and select **Part** in the **Admin** menu to check that all the views are working.

Scaffold the ItemType controller and views

The **ItemType** table is virtually identical to the **Section** table; it's basically just the name that differs, so creating and altering the controller and views should be a breeze by now. If you get stuck you can always go back to the section describing how to set it up for the **Section** table.

The fastest way to implement the controller and views for the **ItemType** table is to create a controller without views, copy the **Section** views and make a couple of small changes to them.

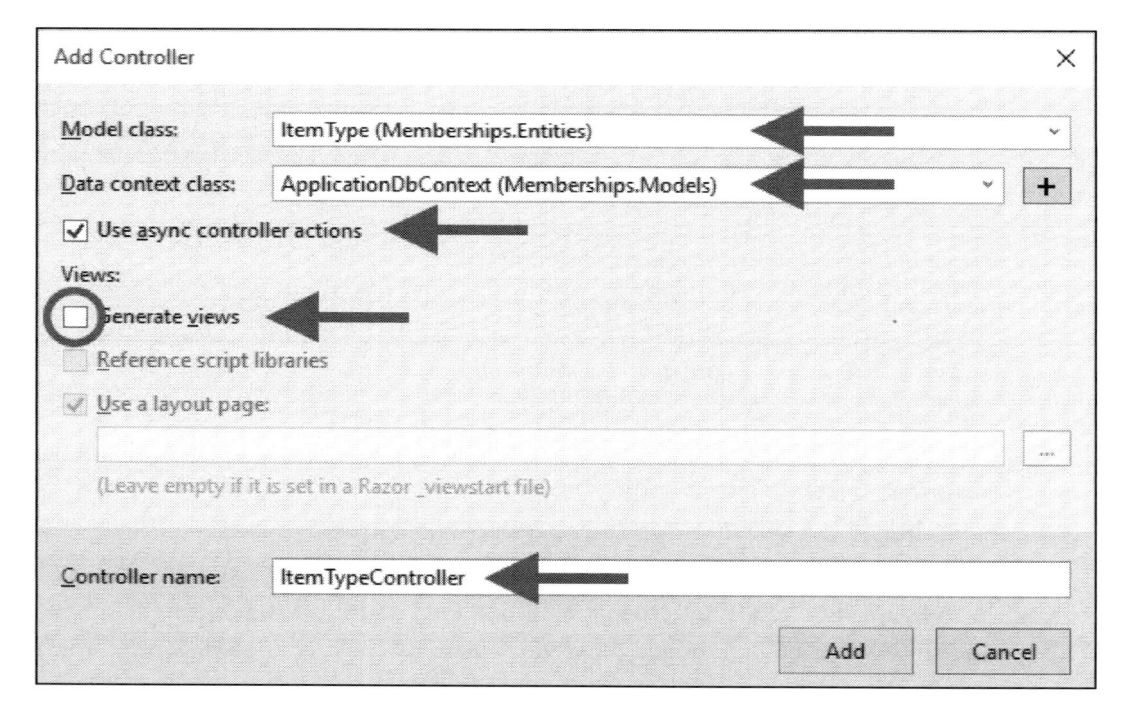

1. Right-click on the **Controllers** folder and select **Add-Controller** in the context menu.

2. Fill in the **Add Controller** dialog as described in the image above and make sure that the **Generate views** checkbox is unchecked and the name is *ItemTypeController*. Apart from adding the controller in the **Controllers** folder, an empty folder named **ItemType** will be added to the **Views** folder.
3. Select *all views* in the **Section** folder by selecting the first one and while holding down shift selecting the last one.
4. Right-click on the selection and select **Copy** in the context menu.
5. Right-click on the **ItemType** folder and select **Paste** in the context menu.
6. Now you have to go through the views in the **ItemType** folder one by one and change the **@model** directive to point to the **ItemType** class and the **<h4>** heading in the form to *Item Type*. The **Index** view doesn't have the **<h4>** element.
   `@model IEnumerable<Memberships.Entities.ItemType>`
   and
   `<h4>Item Type</h4>`
7. Run the application and select **Item Type** in the **Admin** menu and check that all the views are working.

Scaffold the ProductType controller and views

The **ProductType** table is virtually identical to the **Section** table; it's basically just the name that differs, so creating and altering the controller and views should be a breeze by now. If you get stuck, you can always go back to the section describing how to set it up for the **Section** table.

The fastest way to implement the controller and views for the **ProductType** table is to create a controller without views, copy the **Section** views and make a couple of small changes to them.

Add Controller

Model class: ProductType (Memberships.Entities)
Data context class: ApplicationDbContext (Memberships.Models)
☑ Use async controller actions

Views:
☐ Generate views
☐ Reference script libraries
☑ Use a layout page:

(Leave empty if it is set in a Razor _viewstart file)

Controller name: ProductTypeController

[Add] [Cancel]

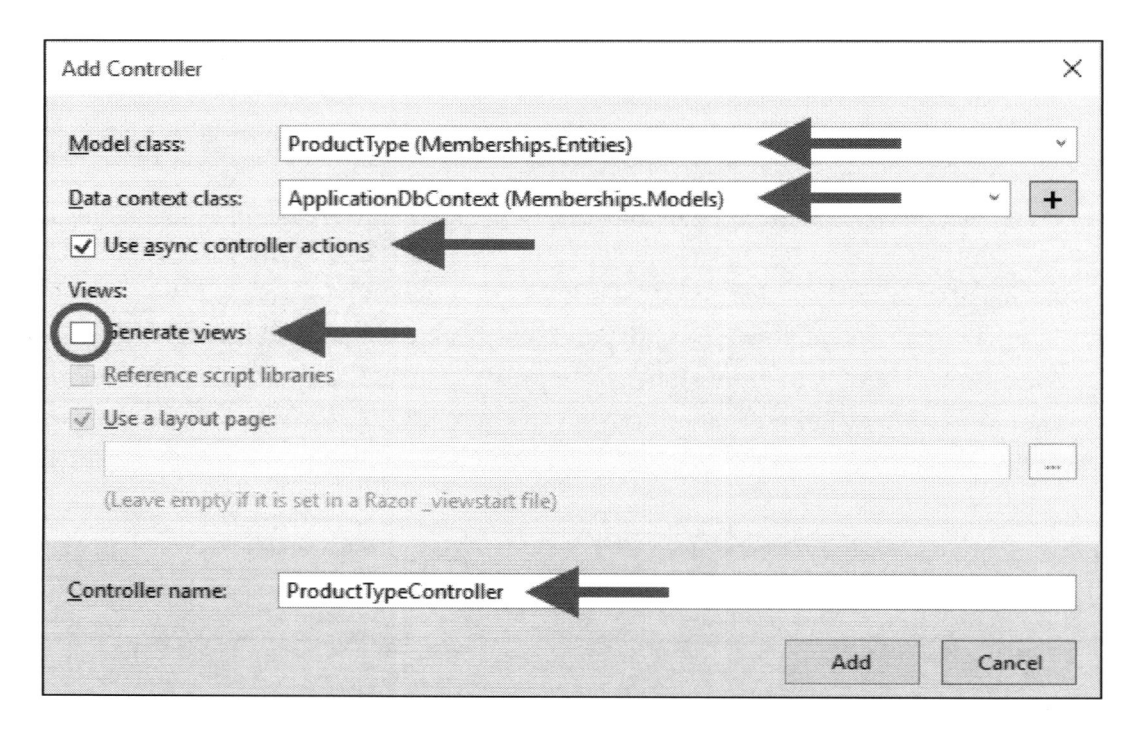

1. Right-click on the **Controllers** folder and select **Add-Controller** in the context menu.
2. Fill in the **Add Controller** dialog as described in the image above and make sure that the **Generate views** checkbox is unchecked and the name is *ProductTypeController*. Apart from the controller in the **Controllers** folder, an empty folder named **ProductType** will be added to the **Views** folder.
3. Select *all views* in the **Section** folder by selecting the first one and while holding down shift selecting the last one.
4. Right-click on the selection and select **Copy** in the context menu.
5. Right-click on the **ProductType** folder and select **Paste** in the context menu.
6. Now you have to go through the views in the **ProductType** folder one by one and change the **@model** directive to point to the **ProductType** class and the **<h4>** heading in the form to *Product Type*. The **Index** view doesn't have the **<h4>** element.
   `@model IEnumerable<Memberships.Entities.ProductType>`
   and
   `<h4>Product Type</h4>`

96

7. Run the application and select **Product Type** in the **Admin** menu and make sure that all the views are working.

Scaffold the ProductLinkText controller and views

The **ProductLinkText** table is virtually identical to the **Section** table; it's basically just the name that differs, so creating and altering the controller and views should be a breeze by now. If you get stuck you can always go back to the section describing how to set it up for the **Section** table.

The fastest way to implement the controller and views for the **ProductLinkText** table is to create a controller without views, copy the **Section** views and make a couple of small changes to them.

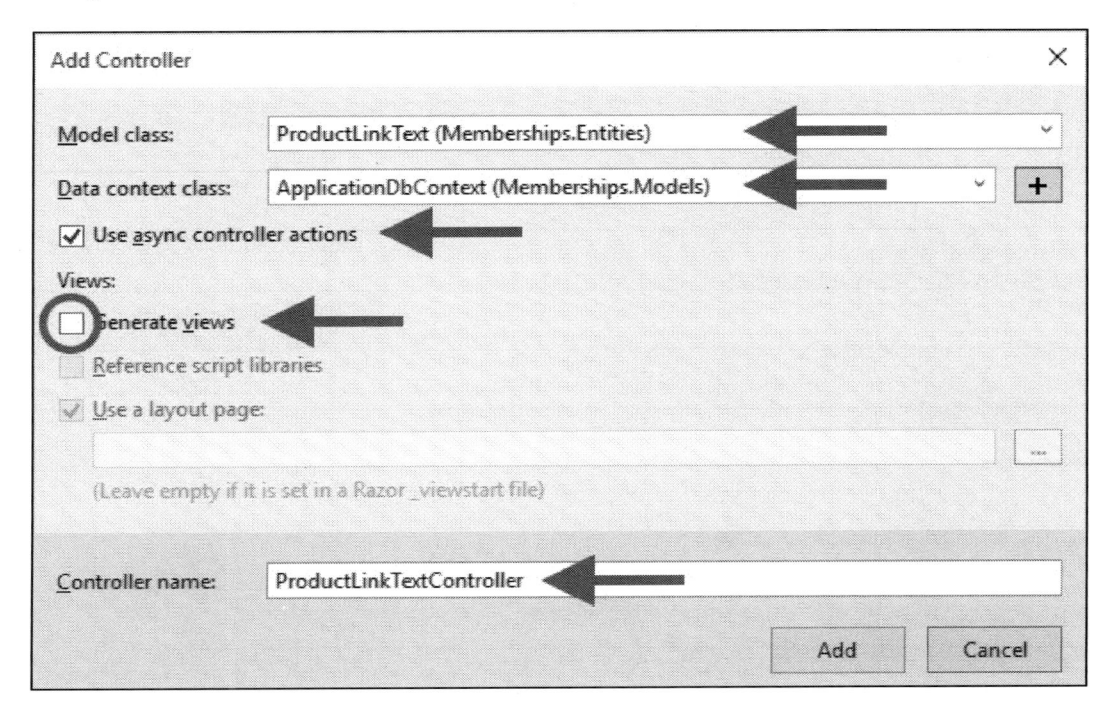

1. Right-click on the **Controllers** folder and select **Add-Controller** in the context menu.

2. Fill in the **Add Controller** dialog as described in the image above and make sure that the **Generate views** checkbox is unchecked and the name is *ProductLinkTextController*. Apart from the controller in the **Controllers** folder, an empty folder named **ProductLinkText** will be added to the **Views** folder.
3. Select *all views* in the **Section** folder by selecting the first one, and while holding down shift, selecting the last one.
4. Right-click on the selection and select **Copy** in the context menu.
5. Right-click on the **ProductLinkText** folder and select **Paste** in the context menu.
6. Now you have to go through the views in the **ProductLinkText** folder one by one and change the **@model** directive to point to the **ProductLinkText** class and the **<h4>** heading in the form to *Product Link Text*. The **Index** view doesn't have the **<h4>** element.
   ```
   @model IEnumerable<Memberships.Entities.ProductLinkText>
   ```
   and
   ```
   <h4>Product Link Text</h4>
   ```
7. Run the application and select **Product Link Text** in the **Admin** menu and check that all the views are working.

5. Adding UIs for the Major Entities

Introduction

As you add controllers and views to the **Admin** area in this chapter, the corresponding **Admin** menu items will begin to work, making it possible to navigate more easily between the **Index** views for the different tables you are using on the back-end to store data.

Technologies used in this chapter

1. **MVC** – To structure the application and scaffold views and controllers and to create partial views for reusable components such as buttons.
2. **C#** - Creating Extension methods, helper methods, to keep the controller actions clean and easy to read. Creating the view models needed for all the views. Reflection is used to fetch property values for generic objects.
3. **Razor** – To incorporate C# in the views where necessary.
4. **HTML 5** – To build the views.
5. **Bootstrap** – To style the HTML 5 components.

The use case

Your task is to scaffold the controllers and views for the **Product**, **Item** and **Subscription** tables in the database to enable reading and writing data to and from them. The controllers will be called **ProductController**, **ItemController** and **SubscriptionController,** and with each controller, five views will be created in a folder with the same name as the controller's corresponding table.

- **Index** - The main view with a list of the available table records and buttons to the other views.
- **Create** - A view for adding new table records.
- **Delete** - A view for deleting a selected table record.
- **Edit** - A view to modify the table data.
- **Details** - A view to show the data stored for one table record.

Scaffold the Item controller and views

The **Item** table contains information about each content piece; items can then be added to a product and subsequently to a subscription. Because the views contain a lot more information than the previously added views, it is best to scaffold them with the **ItemController** controller.

Use scaffolding when creating the **Item** controller and its views in the **Admin** area, then alter the views to use the partial view you have already created and spruce it up with some added Bootstrap design classes.

The controller will be based on the **Item** entity class located in the **Entities** folder in the main project.

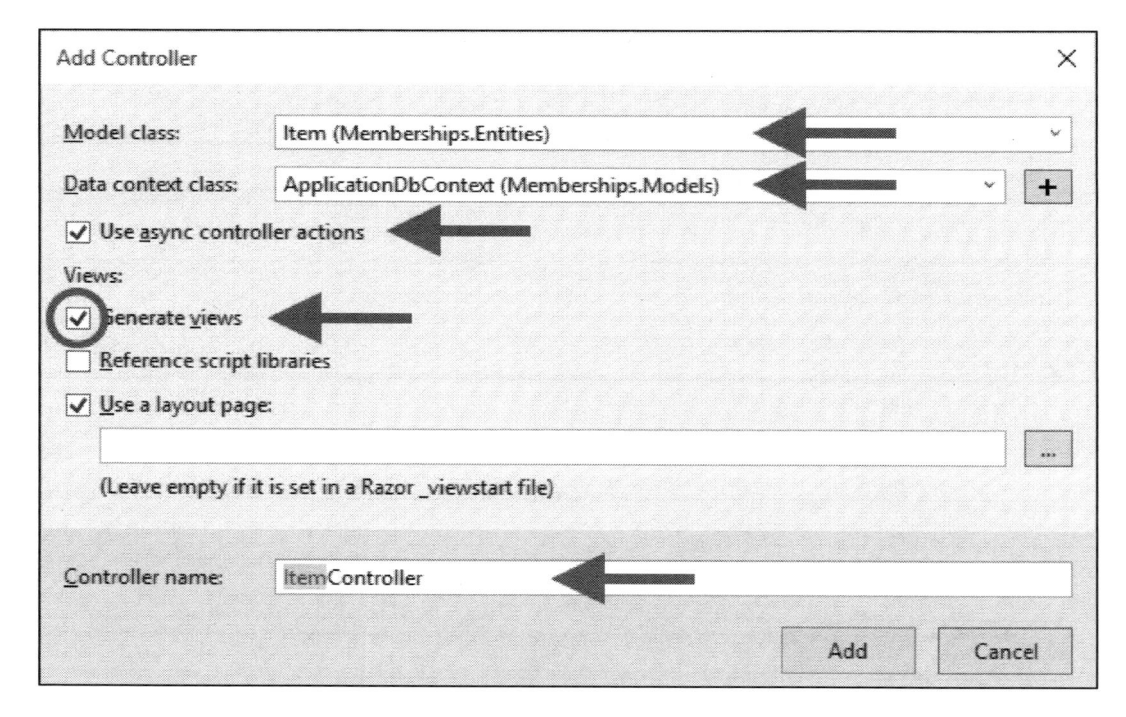

1. Right-click on the **Controllers** folder in the **Admin** area and select **Add-Controller** in the context menu.
2. Select the template for scaffolding a controller with Entity Framework action methods (the same as in the two previous chapters).

3. Fill in the form according to the image above. Remember that the controller name should be in singular and that the **Generate views** checkbox should be checked. This will add a controller called **ItemController** with read and write actions as well as the views associated with the actions.

The Create Action (HttpGet)

Before altering the **Create** view, you have to make some changes to the **Create** action in the **ItemController** class in order to be able to display dropdowns for the **Section**, **Part** and **ItemType** values. If you don't do this, then the values will be handled by textboxes – which isn't a good user experience and invites problems and errors. If possible, it is always best to let the user select from a dropdown rather than typing in a value because then, only the available values can be selected by their title.

There are two actions named **Create,** and the one you want to alter is the one without parameters because it is called when the view is rendered. The other **Create** action, which is called when the user submits the form, doesn't have to be changed.

You have to alter the **Create** action to send an instance of the **Item** class which has been populated from the database.

1. Open the **ItemController** class in the Solution Explorer.
2. Locate the **Create** action without parameters.
   ```
   public ActionResult Create()
   {
       return View();
   }
   ```
3. Create an instance of the **Item** class called **model** and fill its **ItemTypes** collection with data from the **ItemType** table, **Parts** collection with data from the **Part** table and **Sections** collection with data from the **Section** table. Use the **ApplicationDbContext** variable called **db** located at the beginning of the **ItemController** class when accessing the database.
   ```
   var model = new Item()
   {
      ItemTypes = db.ItemTypes.ToList(),
      Parts = db.Parts.ToList(),
      Sections = db.Sections.ToList()
   };
   ```

4. Return the **model** variable as a parameter in the **View** method.
   `return View(model);`

The complete code for the **HttpGet Create** action:

```
public ActionResult Create()
{
   var model = new Item
   {
      ItemTypes = db.ItemTypes.ToList(),
      Parts = db.Parts.ToList(),
      Sections = db.Sections.ToList()
   };

   return View(model);
}
```

The Create View

Now that the **Create** view has a model with lists of products, sections, parts, and item types, you will alter the appearance of the web page, changing the textboxes to drop-down controls. If you look closely you can see that the default labels aren't displayed properly; they have the wrong description. To fix this, you have to add the **DisplayName** attribute to the **ItemTypes** collection in the **Item** model class. You also have to change the Lambda expression in the **LabelFor** method calls for the collections in the Razor view to go to the collection property instead of the id property.

Changes to the **Item** model class and the **Create** view:

```
[DisplayName("Item Types")]
public virtual ICollection<ItemType> ItemTypes { get; set; }
```

```
@Html.LabelFor(model => model.ItemTypes, htmlAttributes: new { @class = "control-label col-md-2" })
```

Displaying dropdown lists is a bit more challenging since you are using models for other tables in your collection as described in the previous section. What makes it challenging is that the **DropDownFor** extension method requires an **Ienumerable<SelectListitem>** which means that you have to convert the lists in your view model to that type of list, and since there are no available convert methods that you can use, you have to create a convert method. Let's create it as a generic extension method which can be used on any collection with a given set of properties, making it possible to reuse it for all **DropDownFor** calls in this and future views. This will require reflection to look at the properties of the passed in collection.

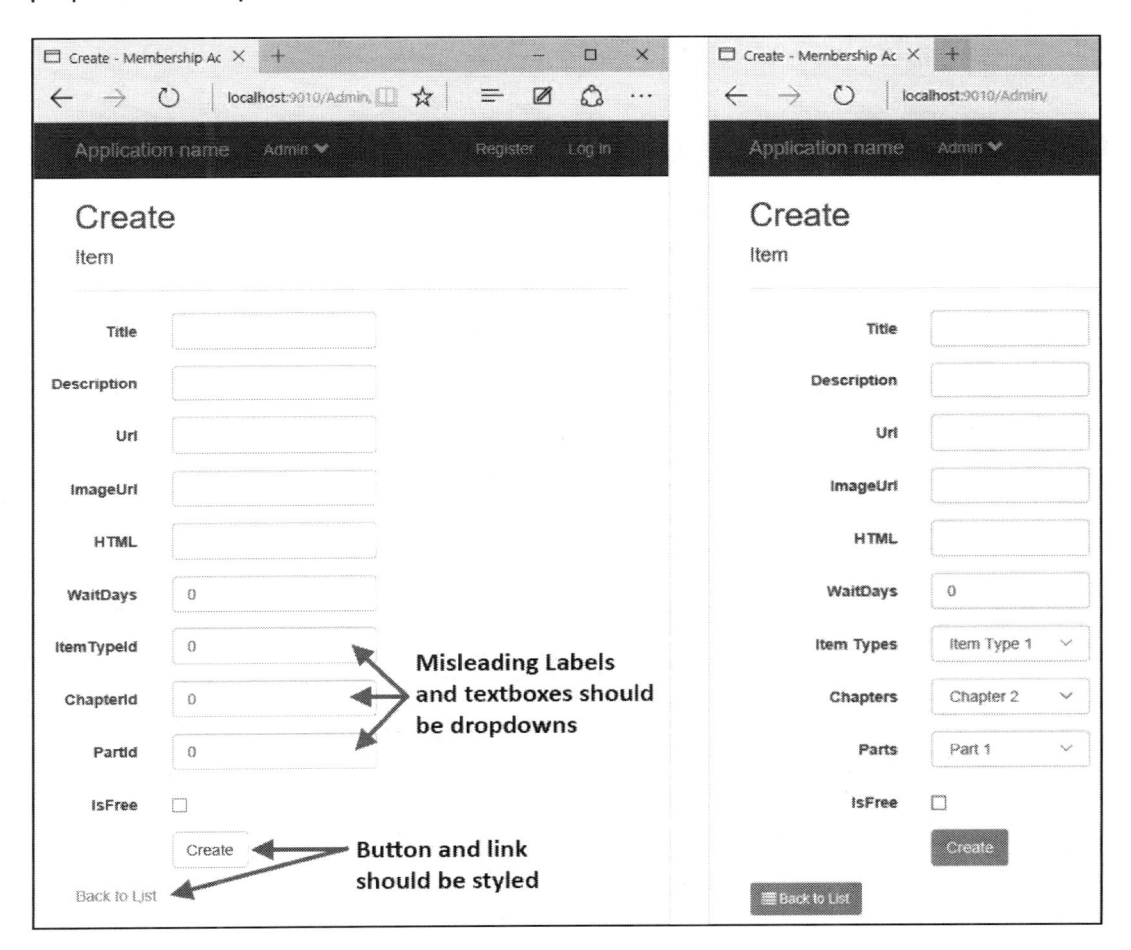

Fixing the dropdown labels
1. Open the **Item** class located in the **Entities** folder.
2. Find the **ItemTypes** collection and add the **DisplayName** attribute to it.
   ```
   [DisplayName("Item Types")]
   public virtual ICollection<ItemType> ItemTypes { get; set; }
   ```
3. Open the **Create** view in the **Views-Item** folder in the **Admin** area.

4. Change the Lambda expression in the **LabelFor** method calls to target the collections.

```
@Html.LabelFor(model => model.ItemTypes, htmlAttributes: new {
    @class = "control-label col-md-2" })
@Html.LabelFor(model => model.Sections, htmlAttributes: new {
    @class = "control-label col-md-2" })
@Html.LabelFor(model => model.Parts, htmlAttributes: new {
    @class = "control-label col-md-2" })
```

Creating the GetPropertyValue extension method

This extension method is called from the **ToSelectListItem** extension method to fetch property values with reflection from individual items in the collection passed into the **ToSelectListItem** extension method.

This method has two parameters: a generic type **T** which represents the item to reflect over (to read its property values) and a **string** which represents the name of the property whose values you want to fetch. The method returns a **string** representing the property value.

Note that the first parameter in an extension method has to be preceded by the **this** keyword which makes it possible to call the method on any object with a data type defined by the **this** parameter.

The generic type **T** makes it possible to use the method on any type. You could restrict this behavior if you wanted. Also note that an extension method must be declared as **public static** and reside in a class which also is declared as **public static**.

```
public static string GetPropertyValue<T>(this T item, string
propertyName)
```

Use reflection in the method to fetch the property value for the property matching the name sent in through the **propertyName** parameter. Use the **GetType** method to find the type definition of the generic object, the **GetProperty** method on the type definition to fetch the property matching the name passed in to it, and lastly the **GetValue** method to fetch the actual value stored in the object.

1. Create a folder called **Extensions** in the project, not in the **Admin** area.

2. Right-click on the folder and select **Add-Class**.
3. Name the class *ReflectionExtensions*.
4. Change the class to **public static**.
   ```
   public static class ReflectionExtensions
   ```
5. Add a **public static** method called **GetPropertyValue** which takes a parameter of type **T** called **item** and is decorated with the **this** keyword and a second parameter of type **string** called **propertyName**.
   ```
   public static string GetPropertyValue<T>(this T item, string propertyName)
   ```
6. Use the **GetType** method to find the type definition of the item object, the **GetProperty** method on the type definition to fetch the property matching the passed in name, and lastly the **GetValue** method to fetch the actual value stored in the object.
   ```
   return item.GetType().GetProperty(propertyName).GetValue(item, null).ToString();
   ```

The complete code for the **GetPropertyValue** extension method looks like this:

```
public static class ReflectionExtensions
{
    public static string GetPropertyValue<T>(this T item,
    string propertyName)
    {
        // Reflecting over the item and pulling out the property value
        return item.GetType().GetProperty(propertyName)
            .GetValue(item, null).ToString();
    }
}
```

Creating the ToSelectListitem extension method

The purpose of calling this method is to convert a collection of type **T** into a collection of type **SelectListItem**.

This method has two parameters: a generic collection of type **ICollection<T>** which contains the items to reflect over to get to their property values, and an **int** which represents the id of the selected item in the list. The method returns a collection of type **IEnumerable<SelectListItem>**.

```
public static IEnumerable<SelectListItem> ToSelectListItem<T>(this
ICollection<T> items, int selectedValue)
```

Loop over the items in the collection parameter to create an **IEnumerable<SelectListItem>** collection and assign values to the **Text**, **Value** and **Selected** properties for each new instance added to it. Assign their values by calling the **GetPropertyValue** extension method you created in the previous section.

```
Text = item.GetPropertyValue("Title")
```

The **Text** property is the text to display for the item in the dropdown, the **Value** property is the item id and the **Selected** property determines if the current item should be the selected dropdown item.

1. Right-click on the **Extension** folder you created in the last section and select **Add-Class**.
2. Name the class *ICollectionExtensions*.
3. Change the class to be **public static**.
   ```
   Public static class IcollectionExtensions
   ```
4. Add a **public static** method called **ToSelectListItem** which takes two parameters: the first is the **ICollection<T>** which has to be decorated with the **this** keyword. The second is of type **int** and is called **selectedValue**. It keeps track of which item in the list should be marked as selected and be displayed when the list is rendered. The purpose of calling this method is to convert a collection of type **T** into a collection of type **SelectListItem**.
   ```
   public static IEnumerable<SelectListItem> ToSelectListItem<T>(this
   ICollection<T> items, int selectedValue)
   {
       // Code goes here
   }
   ```
5. Return an **IEnumerable<SelectListitem>** by iterating over the items in the passed in collection and create instances of the **SelectListItem** class. Call the **GetPropertyValue** extension method when the instance is being created to assign values to the **Text**, **Value** and **Selected** properties. You can use the **Equals** method to determine if the **Id** and **selectedValue** are equal and therefore should be the selected item in the dropdown.

```
        return from item in items
               select new SelectListItem
               {
                  Text = item.GetPropertyValue("Title"),
                  Value = item.GetPropertyValue("Id"),
                  Selected = item.GetPropertyValue("Id")
                     .Equals(selectedValue.ToString())
               };
```

The complete **ICollectionExtensions** class:

```
public static class ICollectionExtensions
{
    public static IEnumerable<SelectListItem> ToSelectListItem<T>(
    this ICollection<T> items, int selectedValue)
    {
        return from item in items
               select new SelectListItem
               {
                  // Cannot get to properties directly
                  // because the item is of type T!
                  // We can use reflection to solve this...
                  // Let's call the GetPropertyValue method
                  // which return a string containing the
                  // property value.
                  Text = item.GetPropertyValue("Title"),
                  Value = item.GetPropertyValue("Id"),
                  Selected = item.GetPropertyValue("Id")
                     .Equals(selectedValue.ToString())
               };
    }
}
```

Fixing the dropdowns

Now it's time to swap the **@Html.EditorFor** method calls for **@Html.DropDownListFor** calls, changing textboxes to dropdowns.

1. Open the **Create** view located in the **Item** folder.
2. Add a using statement to the **Extensions** namespace immediately below the **@model** directive.

   @using Memberships.Extensions

3. Locate the **form-group <div>** containing product information and delete it. When creating a new item, you might not want to link it to a specific product right away.
4. Locate the **@Html.EditorFor** method for the **ItemTypes** and change it to **@Html.DropDownListFor** and add a third parameter in between the existing parameters, calling the **ToSelectListItem** extension method on the **ItemTypes** collection passed in through the model to convert it to a collection suitable for a dropdown.

   ```
   @Html.DropDownListFor(model => model.ItemTypeId,
   Model.ItemTypes.ToSelectListItem(Model.ItemTypeId), new { @class = "form-control" })
   ```

5. Now do the same changes for the **Sections** and the **Parts** collections.

The complete changes for the labels and dropdowns in the **Create** view:

```
<div class="form-group">
    @Html.LabelFor(model => model.ItemTypes,
        htmlAttributes: new { @class = "control-label col-md-2" })
    <div class="col-md-10">
        @Html.DropDownListFor(model => model.ItemTypeId,
            Model.ItemTypes.ToSelectListItem(
                Model.ItemTypeId),new { @class = "form-control" })

        @Html.ValidationMessageFor(model => model.ItemTypeId, "",
            new { @class = "text-danger" })
    </div>
</div>

<div class="form-group">
    @Html.LabelFor(model => model.Sections,
        htmlAttributes: new { @class = "control-label col-md-2" })
    <div class="col-md-10">
        @Html.DropDownListFor(model => model.SectionId,
            Model.Sections.ToSelectListItem(Model.SectionId),
            new { @class = "form-control" })

        @Html.ValidationMessageFor(model => model.SectionId, "",
            new { @class = "text-danger" })
    </div>
</div>
```

```
<div class="form-group">
    @Html.LabelFor(model => model.Parts, htmlAttributes:
        new { @class = "control-label col-md-2" })
    <div class="col-md-10">
        @Html.DropDownListFor(model => model.PartId,
            Model.Parts.ToSelectListItem(Model.PartId),
            new { @class = "form-control" })

        @Html.ValidationMessageFor(model => model.PartId, "",
            new { @class = "text-danger" })
    </div>
</div>
```

The Edit View

The **Edit** view is very similar to the **Create** view. You can copy the code for the **@Html.DropDownListFor** dropdowns from the **Create** view and replace the corresponding **@Html.EditorFor** code in the **Edit** view. You also need to add a using statement to the **Memberships.Extensions** namespace under the **@model** directive in the **Edit** view to get access to the **ToSelectListitem** extension method you created earlier in this chapter.

To style the view a bit, you can change the **btn-default** to **btn-success** for the **submit** button and replace the **@HtmlActionLink** extension method call to a call to the **@Html.Partial** and pass the **_BackToListButtonPartial** name to render that partial view displaying a button instead.

To show data in the dropdown controls for item type, section and part, you have to load their data in the **Edit** controller action method in the **ItemController** class. Since the action is asynchronous, it is possible to load the data from the database tables using the **ToListAsync** extension method on the table in conjunction with the **await** keyword which frees up the current thread for other work. A word of caution: in a production environment, you probably want to run bench tests to see that you get a performance benefit from executing asynchronously.

The image below shows the end result after all the changes to the **Edit** view.

ASP.NET MVC 5 - How to build a Membership Website

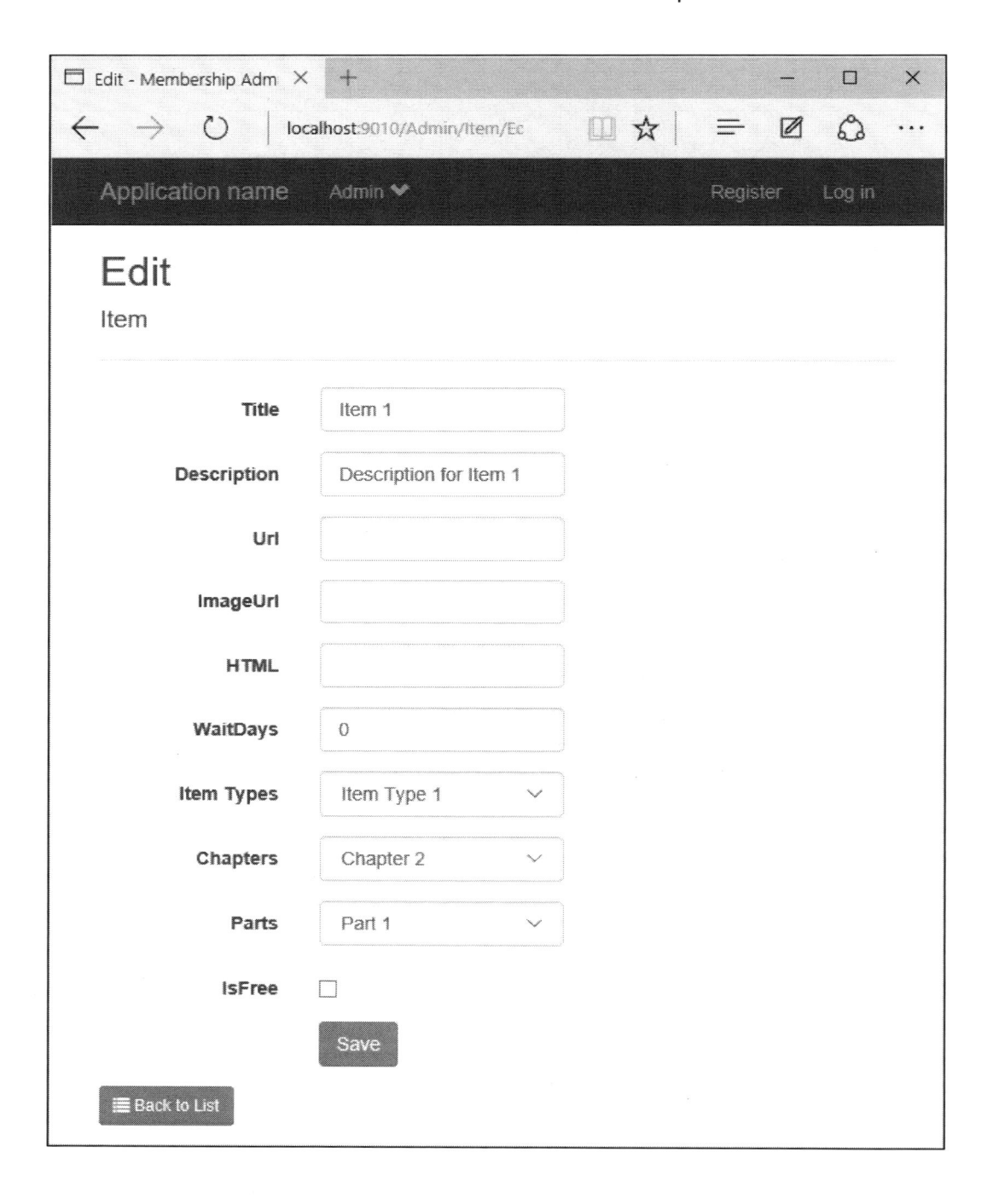

Edit

Item

Title	Item 1
Description	Description for Item 1
Url	
ImageUrl	
HTML	
WaitDays	0
Item Types	Item Type 1
Chapters	Chapter 2
Parts	Part 1
IsFree	☐

Save

≡ Back to List

Modifying the Edit controller action (HttpGet)
1. Open the **ItemController** class and locate the **Edit** action with only one parameter.
2. Add the code to load the data from the **ItemType**, **Section** and **Part** tables immediately above the **return** statement. Store the result in the already existing **content** variable's **ItemTypes**, **Sections** and **Parts** collections.
   ```
   item.ItemTypes = await db.ItemTypes.ToListAsync();
   item.Parts = await db.Parts.ToListAsync();
   item.Sections = await db.Sections.ToListAsync();
   ```

The complete **HttpGet Edit** action:
```
public async Task<ActionResult> Edit(int? id)
{
   if (id == null)
   {
      return new HttpStatusCodeResult(HttpStatusCode.BadRequest);
   }

   Item item = await db.Items.FindAsync(id);
   if (item == null)
   {
      return HttpNotFound();
   }

   item.ItemTypes = await db.ItemTypes.ToListAsync();
   item.Parts = await db.Parts.ToListAsync();
   item.Sections = await db.Sections.ToListAsync();

   return View(item);
}
```

Replacing the textboxes with dropdowns in the view
1. Open the **Create** view and copy the code for the dropdown controls you modified earlier.
2. Open the **Edit** view and replace the existing **@Html.EditorFor** method calls with the **Html.DropDownListFor** code you copied from the **Create** view.

Styling the Edit view
1. Open the **Edit** view and locate the **Save** submit button and replace **btn-default** with **btn-success** (green).
   ```
   <input type="submit" value="Save" class="btn btn-success" />
   ```
2. Locate the **@HtmlActionLink** extension method at the end of the view and replace it with a call to **@Html.Partial** and pass in **_BackToListButtonPartial** to render that partial view.
   ```
   @Html.Partial("_BackToListButtonPartial")
   ```

Changes to the **Edit** view:
```
<div class="form-group">
   @Html.LabelFor(model => model.ItemTypes, htmlAttributes:
      new { @class = "control-label col-md-2" })
   <div class="col-md-10">
      @Html.DropDownListFor(
         model => model.ItemTypeId,
         Model.ItemTypes.ToSelectListItem(Model.ItemTypeId),
         new { @class = "form-control" })
      @Html.ValidationMessageFor(model => model.ItemTypeId, "",
         new { @class = "text-danger" })
   </div>
</div>

<div class="form-group">
   @Html.LabelFor(model => model.Sections, htmlAttributes:
      new { @class = "control-label col-md-2" })
   <div class="col-md-10">
      @Html.DropDownListFor(
         model => model.SectionId,
         Model.Sections.ToSelectListItem(Model.SectionId),
         new { @class = "form-control" })
      @Html.ValidationMessageFor(model => model.SectionId, "",
         new { @class = "text-danger" })
   </div>
</div>

<div class="form-group">
   @Html.LabelFor(model => model.Parts, htmlAttributes:
      new { @class = "control-label col-md-2" })
   <div class="col-md-10">
      @Html.DropDownListFor(
```

```
        model => model.PartId,
        Model.Parts.ToSelectListItem(Model.PartId),
        new { @class = "form-control" })
     @Html.ValidationMessageFor(model => model.PartId, "",
        new { @class = "text-danger" })
   </div>
</div>

<div class="form-group">
   <div class="col-md-offset-2 col-md-10">
      <input type="submit" value="Save" class="btn btn-success" />
   </div>
</div>

<div>
   @Html.Partial("_BackToListButtonPartial")
</div>
```

The Details View

The **Item Details** view is very similar to the **Section Details** view. You can copy the two lines of code you need to change from the **Section Details** view. Locate the **@Html.Partial** for the two buttons and copy the code and then replace the two corresponding **@Html.ActionLink** calls in the **Item Details** view.

The image below shows the **Details** view after the changes.

Details

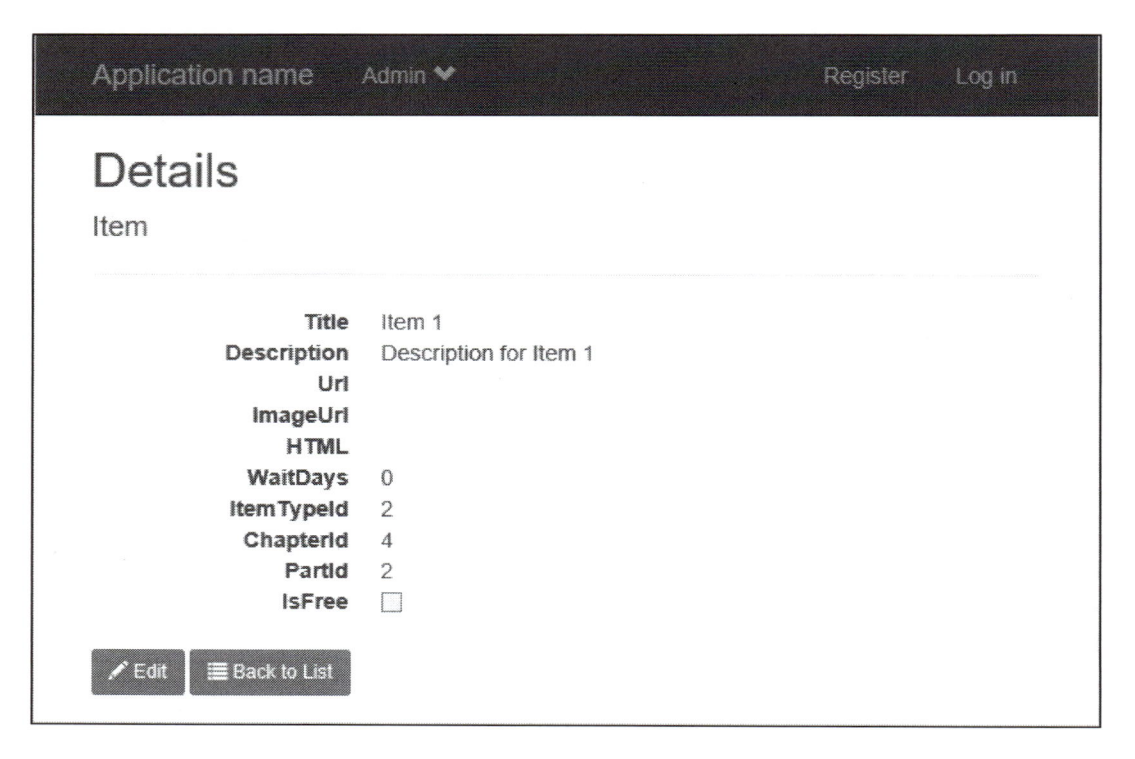

Item

Title	Item 1
Description	Description for Item 1
Url	
ImageUrl	
HTML	
WaitDays	0
ItemTypeId	2
ChapterId	4
PartId	2
IsFree	☐

[Edit] [Back to List]

1. Open the **Details** view in the **Section** folder.
2. Locate the two **@Html.Partial** method calls and copy the code.
   ```
   @Html.Partial("_EditButtonPartial", Model.Id)
   @Html.Partial("_BackToListButtonPartial")
   ```
3. Open the **Details** view in the **Item** folder.
4. Locate the two **@Html.ActionLink** method calls and replace the code below with the code you copied from the other **Details** view.
   ```
   @Html.ActionLink("Edit", "Edit", new { id = Model.Id }) |
   @Html.ActionLink("Back to List", "Index")
   ```

Changes to the **Details** view:

```
<p>
   @Html.Partial("_EditButtonPartial", Model.Id)
   @Html.Partial("_BackToListButtonPartial")
</p>
```

The Delete View

The **Item Delete** view is very similar to the **Section Delete** view. You can copy the two lines of code you need to change from the **Section Delete** view. At the very end of the view, you will find the **Delete** button and the **@Html.Partial** method call you need to copy. Replace the corresponding code in the **Item Delete** view.

The image below shows the **Delete** view after the changes.

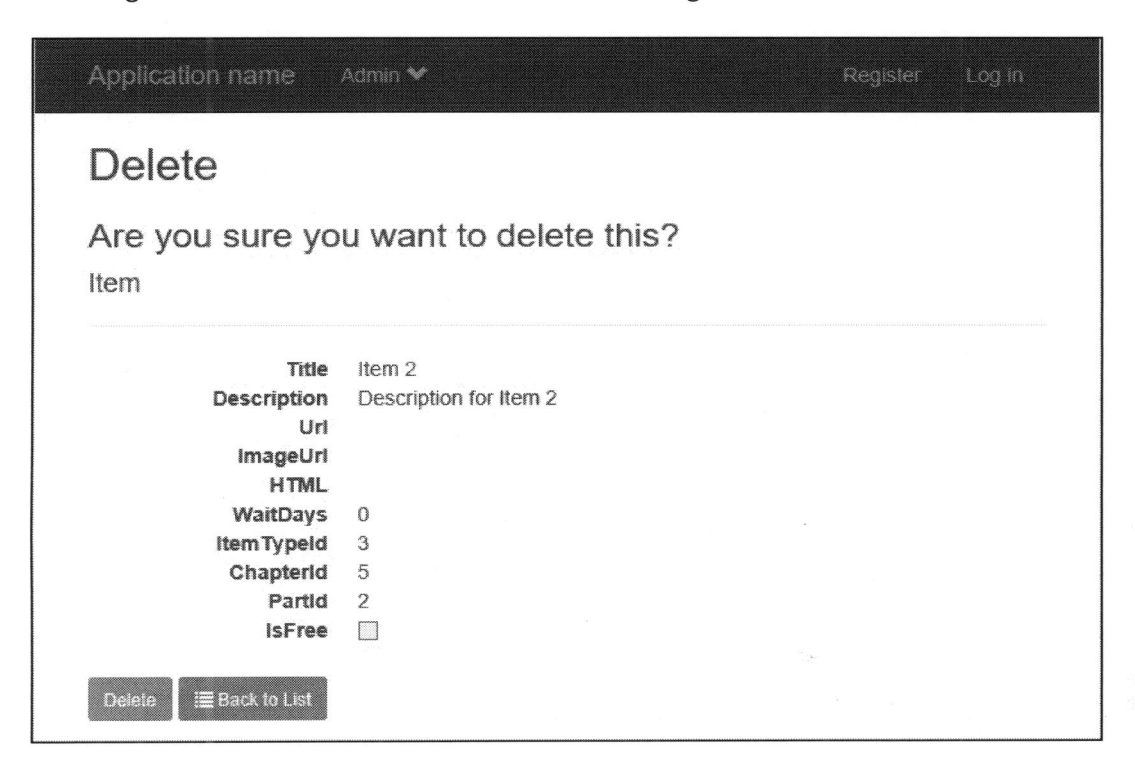

1. Open the **Delete** view in the **Section** folder.
2. Locate the **Delete** button and the **@Html.Partial** method call and copy the code.
   ```
   <input type="submit" value="Delete" class="btn btn-danger btn-sm" />
   @Html.Partial("_BackToListButtonPartial")
   ```
3. Open the **Delete** view in the **Item** folder.
4. Locate the **Delete** button and the **@Html.ActionLink** method call displayed below and replace it with the code you copied.
   ```
   <input type="submit" value="Delete" class="btn btn-default" /> |
   ```

```
@Html.ActionLink("Back to List", "Index")
```

Changes to the **Details** view:

```
<div class="form-actions no-color">
   <input type="submit" value="Delete" class="btn btn-danger btn-sm" />
   @Html.Partial("_BackToListButtonPartial")
</div>
```

The Index View

The **Item Index** view is very similar to the **Section Index** view; it's basically only the number of columns that differs. You can copy a lot of the code from the **Section Index** view and paste it in.

You can copy the **@Html.Partial** code for creating the **_CreateNewButtonPartial** and replace the corresponding **@Html.ActionLink** in the **Item Index** view with the copied code.

You can also copy the **<table>** and first **<tr>** tags from the **Section Index** view which is styled with Bootstrap, and replace the corresponding tags in the **Item Index** view.

Next, you have to copy the **@using** statement at the top of the **Section Index** view to get access to the **SmallButtonModel** class needed to create the three buttons.

Lastly, you can replace the **<td>** element holding the three **@Html.ActionLink** method calls at the bottom of the view with a call to the **@Html.Partial** method call for the **_TableButtonsPartial** view.

Then there is a bit of cleaning up in the table; you do not want to display the URL and id columns. To remove them, simply delete their code from the view.

This is what the **Item Index** view looks like before any changes:

ASP.NET MVC 5 - How to build a Membership Website

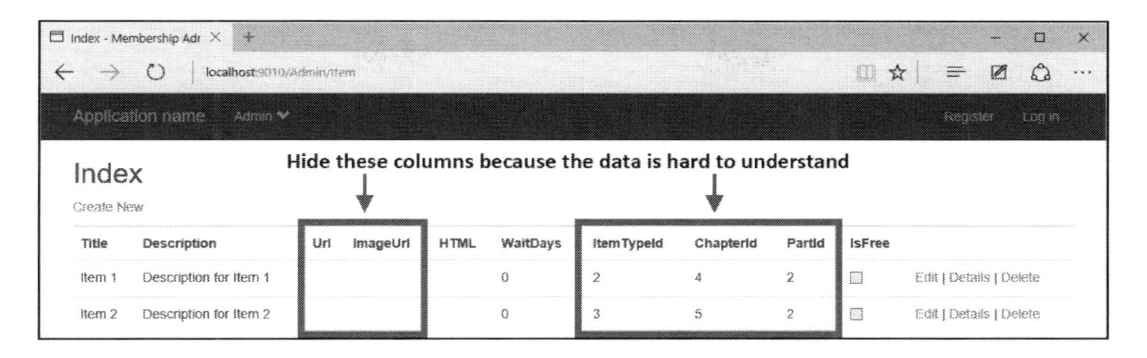

[Screenshot showing Index view with columns: Title, Description, Url, ImageUrl, HTML, WaitDays, ItemTypeId, ChapterId, PartId, IsFree. Annotations point to Url/ImageUrl and ItemTypeId/ChapterId/PartId columns with text: "Hide these columns because the data is hard to understand"]

And this is what it look like after the changes:

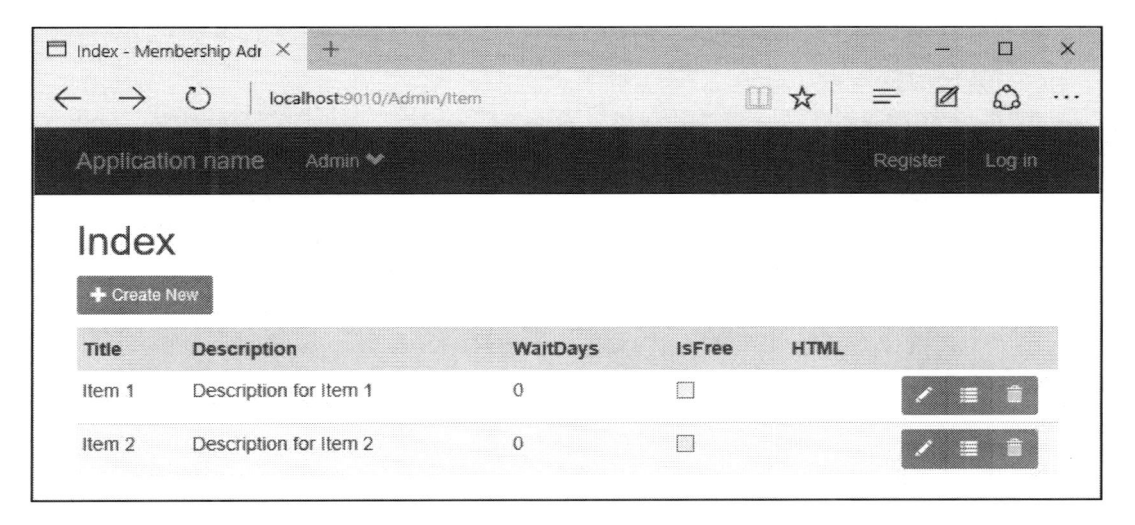

[Screenshot showing simplified Index view with columns: Title, Description, WaitDays, IsFree, HTML and a "+ Create New" button]

Replacing the Create New link with a button

1. Open the **Index** view in the **Section** folder and copy the **@using** statement at the top of the view.
   `@using Memberships.Areas.Admin.Models`

2. Open the **Index** view in the **Item** folder and paste in the code in the corresponding place.

3. Open the **Index** view in the **Section** folder and copy the code for the **Create New** button.
   `@Html.Partial("_CreateNewButtonPartial")`

117

4. Open the **Index** view in the **Item** folder and replace the corresponding **@Html.ActionLink** with the copied code.
   ```
   @Html.ActionLink("Create New", "Create")
   ```

5. Open the **Index** view in the **Section** folder and copy the code for the **<table>** and **<tr>** elements.
   ```
   <table class="table table-striped">
       <tr class="success">
   ```

6. Open the **Index** view in the **Item** folder and replace the corresponding elements with the copied code.
   ```
   <table class="table">
       <tr>
   ```

7. Open the **Index** view in the **Section** folder and copy the code for the partial view for the table buttons.
   ```
   @Html.Partial("_TableButtonsPartial", new SmallButtonModel { Id = item.Id })
   ```

8. Open the **Index** view in the **Item** folder and replace the last **<td>** element and its three **@Html.ActionLink** method calls with the copied code.
   ```
   <td>
       @Html.ActionLink("Edit", "Edit", new { id = item.Id }) |
       @Html.ActionLink("Details", "Details", new { id = item.Id }) |
       @Html.ActionLink("Delete", "Delete", new { id = item.Id })
   </td>
   ```

9. Open the **Index** view in the **Item** folder and delete the following table headings to keep the table clean and more readable.
   ```
   <th>@Html.DisplayNameFor(model => model.Url)</th>
   <th>@Html.DisplayNameFor(model => model.ImageUrl)</th>
   <th>@Html.DisplayNameFor(model => model.ItemTypeId)</th>
   <th>@Html.DisplayNameFor(model => model.SectionId)</th>
   <th>@Html.DisplayNameFor(model => model.PartId)</th>
   ```

10. Delete the following table data columns.
    ```
    <td>@Html.DisplayFor(modelItem => item.ImageUrl)</td>
    <td>@Html.DisplayFor(modelItem => item.Url)</td>
    <td>@Html.DisplayFor(modelItem => item.ItemTypeId)</td>
    <td>@Html.DisplayFor(modelItem => item.SectionId)</td>
    <td>@Html.DisplayFor(modelItem => item.PartId)</td>
    ```

The complete code for the **Index** view:

```
@model IEnumerable<Memberships.Entities.Item>
@using Memberships.Areas.Admin.Models

@{
    ViewBag.Title = "Index";
}

<h2>Index</h2>

<p>
    @Html.Partial("_CreateNewButtonPartial")
</p>
<table class="table table-striped table-condensed">
    <tr class="success">
        <th>@Html.DisplayNameFor(model => model.Title)</th>
        <th>@Html.DisplayNameFor(model => model.Description)</th>
        <th>@Html.DisplayNameFor(model => model.WaitDays)</th>
        <th>@Html.DisplayNameFor(model => model.IsFree)</th>
        <th>@Html.DisplayNameFor(model => model.HTML)</th>
        <th></th>
    </tr>

    @foreach (var item in Model) {
        <tr>
            <td>@Html.DisplayFor(modelItem => item.Title)</td>
            <td>@Html.DisplayFor(modelItem => item.Description)</td>
            <td>@Html.DisplayFor(modelItem => item.WaitDays)</td>
            <td>@Html.DisplayFor(modelItem => item.IsFree)</td>
            <td>@Html.DisplayFor(modelItem => item.HTML)</td>
            @Html.Partial("_TableButtonsPartial", new SmallButtonModel {
                Id = item.Id })
        </tr>
    }
</table>
```

Scaffold the Product controller and views

A product is a "container" for content items stored in the **item** table. A single piece of content can belong to many products, and a product can have many content pieces – in other words, a *many-to-many* relationship that warrants a connection table between the **Product** and **item** table called **ProductItem** which you will implement views for.

The **Product** table also has a *many-to-many* relationship with the **Subscription** table warranting a connection table between the two called **SubscriptionProduct** which you will implement views for in the next chapter. Each product can be part of several subscriptions and a subscription can have many products.

In this section, you will focus on implementing a UI for the **Product** table.

The views for this table are very similar to the views in the **Item** folder, so you can use them as a starting point to save time. Below is an image of the **Index** view for the **Product** table.

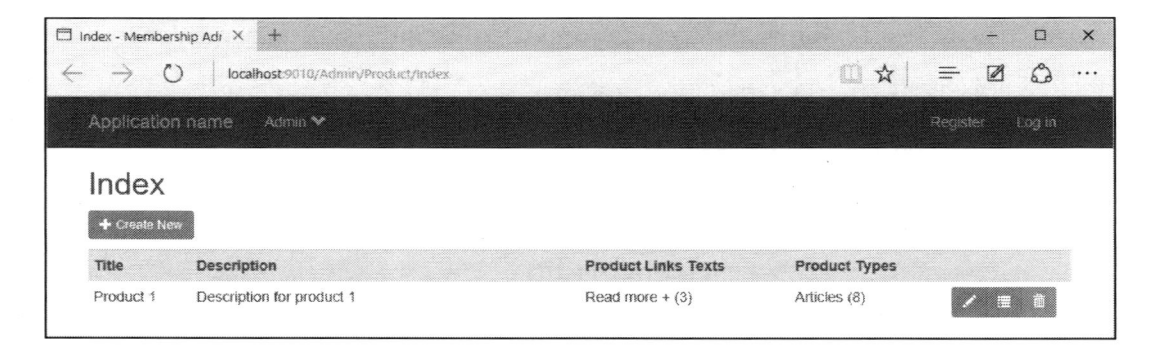

Adding necessary data

Because the **Create** and **Edit** views contain dropdown lists with values that can be selected when adding and changing a product, you will have to add some real data to be able to select it in the views.

Navigate to the **Create** view for **Product Types** and add the following data as separate product types: "Course", "Book", "Articles" and "Misc.".

Navigate to the **Create** view for **Product Link Texts** and add the following data: "Read more +".

Adding the ProductModel

Because a product is dependent on information from other tables, you will have to create a view model called **ProductModel** for the **Product** table and its related tables in the **Models** folder in the **Admin** area.

This model will contain properties for the columns in the **Product** table as well as **ICollection** properties for the data in the **ProductLinkText** and **ProductType** tables called **ProductLinkTexts** and **ProductTypes**, and also **int** properties called **ProductLinkTextId** and **ProductTypeId** for their primary key columns.

Right-click on the **Models** folder in the **Admin** area and select **Add-Class** and name it **ProductModel** to add the view model.

1. Right-click on the **Model** folder in the **Admin** area and select **Add-Class** in the context menu.
2. Name the class **ProductModel** and click the **Add** button.
3. Add an **int** property called **Id**.
4. Add two **string** properties called **Title** and **ImageUrl** which can hold a maximum of 255 characters each.
5. Add a **string** property called **Description** which can hold a maximum of 2048 characters.
6. Add two **int** properties for foreign key values called **ProductLinkTextId** and **ProductTypeId**.
7. Add two **ICollection** properties called **ProductLinkTexts** and **ProductTypes** for the values in the tables referenced by the foreign key id properties.
8. Add display member attributes to **ProductLinkTexts**, **ProductTypes** and **ImageUrl** to change the text to "Product Link Texts", "Product Types" and "Image Url".
   ```
   [DisplayName("Product Link Texts")]
   public ICollection<ProductLinkText> ProductLinkTexts { get; set; }
   ```
9. Add a string property called **ProductType** with the **set**-block removed which returns the title from the **ProductTypes** collection based on the **ProductTypeId**. Return an empty string if the **ProductTypes** collection is **null** or if it has no values.
   ```
   public string ProductType {
      get {
         return ProductTypes == null ||
            ProductTypes.Count.Equals(0) ?
               string.Empty : ProductTypes.First(pt =>
               pt.Id.Equals(ProductTypeId)).Title;
      }
   ```

                }
10. Repeat step 9 for the **ProductLinkTexts** property.
11. Save the **ProductModel** class.

The complete code for the **ProductModel** class:

```
public class ProductModel
{
    public int Id { get; set; }
    [MaxLength(255)]
    [Required]
    public string Title { get; set; }
    [MaxLength(1024)]
    [DisplayName("Image Url")]
    public string ImageUrl { get; set; }
    [MaxLength(2048)]
    public string Description { get; set; }
    public int ProductLinkTextId { get; set; }
    public int ProductTypeId { get; set; }
    [DisplayName("Product Link Texts")]
    public ICollection<ProductLinkText> ProductLinkTexts { get; set; }
    [DisplayName("Product Types")]
    public ICollection<ProductType> ProductTypes { get; set; }

    public string ProductType
    {
        get
        {
            return ProductTypes == null || ProductTypes.Count.Equals(0) ?
                string.Empty :
                ProductTypes.First(pt =>
                    pt.Id.Equals(ProductTypeId)).Title;
        }
    }

    public string ProductLinkText
    {
        get
        {
            return ProductLinkTexts == null ||
            ProductLinkTexts.Count.Equals(0) ?
                string.Empty :
                ProductLinkTexts.First(pt =>
```

```
            pt.Id.Equals(ProductLinkTextId)).Title;
        }
    }
}
```

Adding the ProductController and views

The fastest way to implement the controller and views for the **Product** table is to create a controller without views, copy the **Item** views to the **Views-Product** folder and make a couple of small changes to them.

There are only two things you need to change in the views – the **@model** directive from **Item** to **Product** and the **<h4>** heading from *Item* to *Product*.

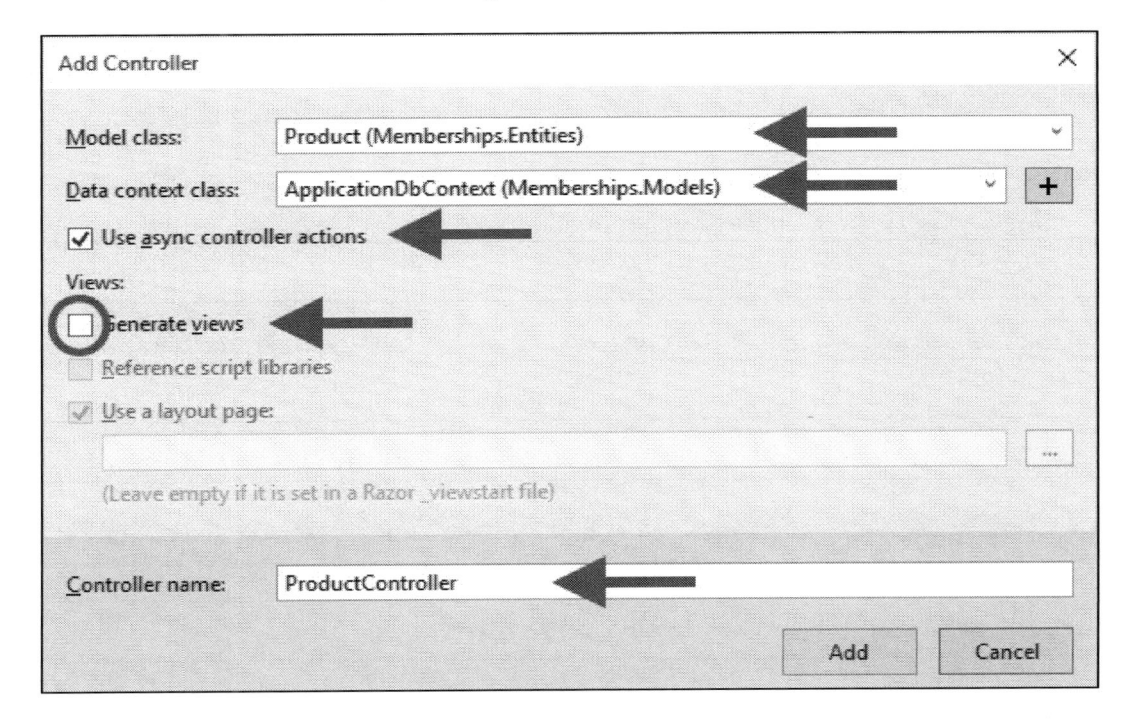

Add Controller

- Model class: Product (Memberships.Entities)
- Data context class: ApplicationDbContext (Memberships.Models)
- ☑ Use async controller actions
- Views:
  - ☐ Generate views
  - ☐ Reference script libraries
  - ☑ Use a layout page:

    (Leave empty if it is set in a Razor _viewstart file)
- Controller name: ProductController

[Add] [Cancel]

1. Right-click on the **Controllers** folder and select **Add-Controller** in the context menu.
2. Fill in the **Add Controller** dialog according to the image above and make sure that the **Generate views** checkbox is unchecked and the name is

ProductController. Apart from the controller, a folder named **Product** will be added to the **Views** folder.

3. Select *all views* in the **Item** folder by selecting the first one, and while holding down shift, selecting the last one.
4. Right-click on the selection and select **Copy** in the context menu.
5. Right-click on the **Product** folder and select **Paste** in the context menu.
6. Now you have to go through the views in the **Product** folder one by one and change the **@model** directive to point to the **Product** class and change the **<h4>** heading in the form to *Product*. The **Index** view doesn't have the **<h4>** element.
   `@model IEnumerable<Memberships.Areas.Admin.Models.ProductModel>`
   and
   `<h4>Product</h4>`
7. Remove the HTML elements for the **Url**, **HTML** and **WaitDays** labels, textboxes and validation. Also remove the **IsFree** checkbox and label.

Altering the Index view

In order to display all the necessary information in the **Index** view, you have to modify the view itself, as well as the **ProductModel** class, and create a new asynchronous extension method called **Convert** which converts an **IEnumerable<Product>** into an **Ienumerable<ProductModel>**. The **Convert** method is used in the **ProductController's Index** action.

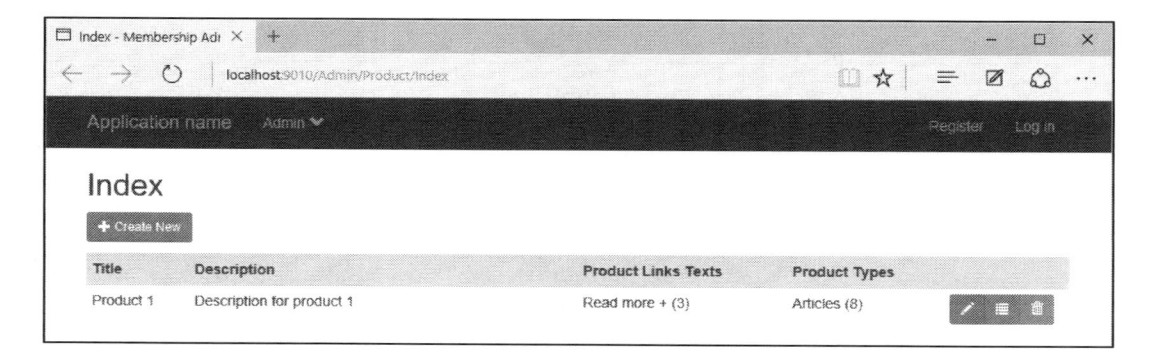

Creating the asynchronous Convert extension method

To be able to display the product link text and product type as text in the **Index** view, the two properties you just created must be filled with data when the **ProductModel** is created in the **ProductController's** Index action.

To keep the code clean in the controller, you will create an asynchronous extension method called **Convert** which will take an **IEnumerable<Product>** and convert it to an **IEnumerable<ProductModel>** while at the same time filling the **ProductTypes** and **ProductLinkTexts** collections with data.

The method is declared as **async** to make it possible to fetch data asynchronously from the **ProductType** and **ProductLinkText** tables in the database and to enable an asynchronous call to the method from the **ProductController's Index** action. Asynchronous calls can speed up the execution of the overall application since the main thread is temporarily given back to the application while long running tasks are being performed, such as fetching data from a table. It can prevent the application from becoming unresponsive during long running tasks.

1. Create a class called **ConversionExtensions** in the **Extensions** folder in the **Admin** area.
2. Add a **using** statement to the **System.Data.Entity** namespace to gain access to the asynchronous list methods.
   using System.Data.Entity;
3. Add an **async** method called **Convert** which takes two parameters and returns **Task<IEnumerable<ProductModel>>**. The two parameters are the product list to act on and an instance of the **ApplicationDbContext** enabling database access.
   public static async Task<IEnumerable<ProductModel>> Convert(
   this IEnumerable<Product> products, ApplicationDbContext db)
   {
   }
4. Return an empty list of **ProductModel** if there are no products in the list of products passed into the method in the **products** parameter to avoid returning **null**.
5. Use the **await** keyword and the **ToListAsync** method to fetch data from the two tables involved and store the result in two variables called **texts** and **types**.

```
var texts = await db.ProductLinkTexts.ToListAsync();
```

6. Use a LINQ query to convert the products in the **products** collection to **ProductModel** instances, assigning the **texts** and **types** variables to the corresponding collection in the **ProductModel** instances.
7. Return the resulting collection of **ProductModel** instances from the method.

The complete code for the **Convert** method:

```
using System.Data.Entity;

public static class ConversionExtensions
{
    public static async Task<IEnumerable<ProductModel>> Convert(
    this IEnumerable<Product> products, ApplicationDbContext db)
    {
        if (products.Count().Equals(0))
            return new List<ProductModel>();

        var texts = await db.ProductLinkTexts.ToListAsync();
        var types = await db.ProductTypes.ToListAsync();

        return from p in products
            select new ProductModel
            {
                Id = p.Id,
                Title = p.Title,
                Description = p.Description,
                ImageUrl = p.ImageUrl,
                ProductLinkTextId = p.ProductLinkTextId,
                ProductTypeId = p.ProductTypeId,
                ProductLinkTexts = texts,
                ProductTypes = types
            };
    }
}
```

Altering the ProductController's Index action

Because another model will be used with the **Index** view than originally was added, you have to make two small changes to the **Index** action in the **ProductController**.

First you have to fetch the products in the **Product** table asynchronously using the **await** keyword, then you will pass that result to the **Convert** method along with an **Applica-**

tionDbContext instance making it possible to access the database from the method. The result from the asynchronous call to the **Convert** method will then be used as the model for the view.

1. Open the **ProductController** class located in the **Controllers** folder in the **Admin** area.
2. Locate the **Index** action method.
3. Fetch the products asynchronously from the **Products** table and store the result in a variable called **products**.
   `var products = await db.Products.ToListAsync();`
4. Pass the result in the **products** variable to the **Convert** method and store the result in a variable called **model**.
   `var model = await products.Convert(db);`
5. Pass the result in the **model** variable to the view.
   `return View(model);`

The complete code for the **Index** action:

```
public async Task<ActionResult> Index()
{
    var products = await db.Products.ToListAsync();
    var model = await products.Convert(db);
    return View(model);
}
```

Altering the Index view

Because the model has been changed from **Product** to **ProductModel** for the **Index** view in the **ProductController's Index** action, you will have to change the view model in the **Index** view as well.

`@model Ienumerable<Memberships.Areas.Admin.Models.ProductModel>`

You will also have to change the missing **WaitDays**, **IsFree** and **HTML** properties in the HTML table to the **ProductLinkText** and **ProductType** properties in the model. Then you will add the corresponding id's in parenthesis to the right of the property texts (see previous image).

1. Open the **Index** view in the **Product** folder in the **Admin** area.

2. Change the **@model** directive to use the **ProductModel** class.
   ```
   @model Ienumerable<Memberships.Areas.Admin.Models.ProductModel>
   ```
3. Change the properties used for label descriptions in the table headers for the missing data.
   ```
   <th>
       @Html.DisplayNameFor(model => model.ProductLinkTexts)
   </th>
   ```
4. Change the missing properties in the loop to the **ProductLinkText** and **ProductType** properties and add the id in parenthesis to the right of the text.
   ```
   <td>
       @Html.DisplayFor(modelItem => item.ProductLinkTexts)
       (@{@Html.DisplayFor(modelItem => item.ProductLinkTextId)})
   </td>
   ```
5. Run the application and select **Product** in the **Admin** menu to check that the view is rendered correctly.

The complete HTML markup for the **Index** view:

```
@model Ienumerable<Memberships.Areas.Admin.Models.ProductModel>
@using Memberships.Areas.Admin.Models

@{
    ViewBag.Title = "Index";
}

<h2>Index</h2>

<p>
    @Html.Partial("_CreateNewButtonPartial")
</p>
<table class="table table-striped table-condensed">
    <tr class="success">
        <th>@Html.DisplayNameFor(model => model.Title)</th>
        <th>@Html.DisplayNameFor(model => model.Description)</th>
        <th>@Html.DisplayNameFor(model => model.ProductLinkTexts)</th>
        <th>@Html.DisplayNameFor(model => model.ProductTypes)</th>
        <th></th>
    </tr>

    @foreach (var item in Model) {
        <tr>
            <td>@Html.DisplayFor(modelItem => item.Title)</td>
            <td>@Html.DisplayFor(modelItem => item.Description)</td>
```

```
            <td>@Html.DisplayFor(modelItem => item.ProductLinkText)
                (@{@Html.DisplayFor(modelItem => item.ProductLinkTextId)})
            </td>
            <td>@Html.DisplayFor(modelItem => item.ProductType)
                (@{@Html.DisplayFor(modelItem => item.ProductTypeId)})
            </td>
             @Html.Partial("_TableButtonsPartial", new SmallButtonModel {
                Id = item.Id })
        </tr>
    }
</table>
```

Altering the Create view

You have to change the **@model** directive to **ProductModel** in the **Create** view as well as the dropdown properties, so that they reflect the correct properties in the **ProductModel**.

You also have to create a **ProductModel** instance in the **Create** action and fill the **ProductLinkTexts** and **ProductTypes** collections with data from the **ProductLinkText** and **ProductType** tables in the database. Then you have to return that model with the view.

Create

Product

Title	
Description	
Image Url	
Product Links Texts	Read more +
Product Types	Course

[Create]

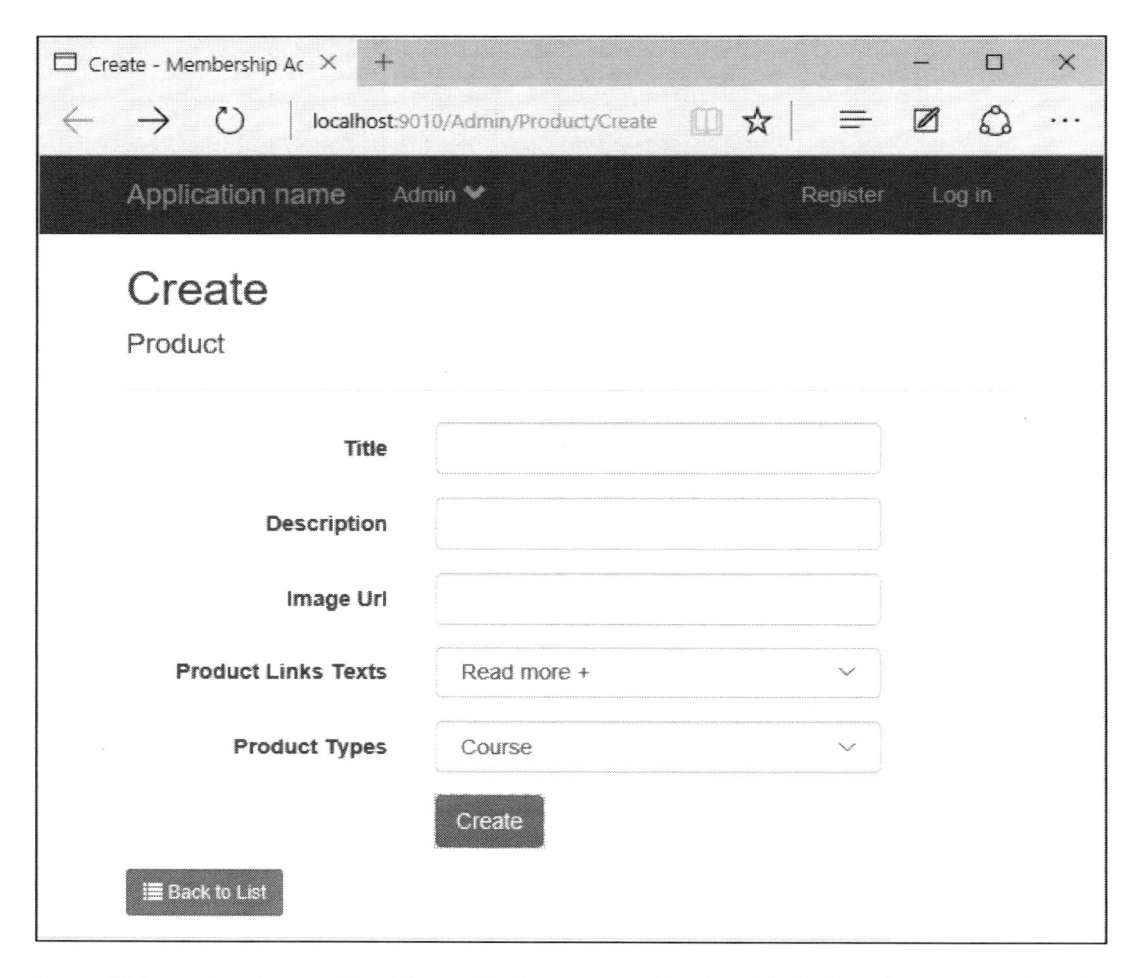

[Back to List]

You will have to change the **@model** directive to **ProductModel** in the **Create** view in order to display items in the dropdowns.

Remove the form groups for the **Url**, **HTML**, **IsFree** and **WaitDays** properties since they don't exist in the view model.

Change the dropdowns for the **ItemTypes**, **Sections** and **Parts** collections to display items from the **ProductLinkTexts** and **ProductTypes** collections.

1. Open the **Create** view located in the **Product** folder in the **Admin** area.
2. Change the **@model** directive to **ProductModel**.

130

@model Memberships.Areas.Admin.Models.ProductModel

3. Remove the **form-groups** for the **Url**, **HTML**, **IsFree** and **WaitDays** properties.
4. Change the dropdowns for the **ItemTypes**, **Sections** and **Parts** collections to display items from the **ProductLinkTexts** and **ProductTypes** collections.

```
@Html.DropDownListFor(model => model.ProductLinkTextId,
    Model.ProductLinkTexts.ToSelectListItem(
    Model.ProductLinkTextId), new { @class = "form-control" })

@Html.ValidationMessageFor(model => model.ProductLinkTextId, "",
    new { @class = "text-danger" })
```

The changes to the **Create** view:

```
@model Memberships.Areas.Admin.Models.ProductModel

...

<div class="form-group">
    @Html.LabelFor(model => model.ProductLinkTexts, htmlAttributes:
        new { @class = "control-label col-md-2" })
    <div class="col-md-10">
        @Html.DropDownListFor(model => model.ProductLinkTextId,
        Model.ProductLinkTexts.ToSelectListItem(Model.ProductLinkTextId),
            new { @class = "form-control" })

        @Html.ValidationMessageFor(model => model.ProductLinkTextId, "",
            new { @class = "text-danger" })
    </div>
</div>

<div class="form-group">
    @Html.LabelFor(model => model.ProductTypes, htmlAttributes:
        new { @class = "control-label col-md-2" })
    <div class="col-md-10">
        @Html.DropDownListFor(model => model.ProductTypeId,
            Model.ProductTypes.ToSelectListItem(Model.ProductTypeId),
            new { @class = "form-control" })
        @Html.ValidationMessageFor(model => model.ProductTypeId, "",
            new { @class = "text-danger" })
    </div>
</div>
```

Altering the Create action in the ProductController class

In order for the **Create** view to display data correctly the **Create** action in the **ProductController** must return an instance of the **ProductModel** class where the **ProductLinkTexts** and **ProductTypes** collections have been populated from the database. These collections will be used when displaying data in the view's dropdowns.

1. Open the parameter-less **Create** action located in the **ProductController** class in the **Controllers** folder in the **Admin** area.
2. Add a variable called **model** which is assigned an instance of the **ProductModel** class.
3. Fetch all the items asynchronously from the **ProductLinkText** and **ProductType** database tables and assign the results to the **ProductLinkTexts** and **ProductTypes** collections.
   ProductLinkTexts = await db.ProductLinkTexts.ToListAsync()
4. Return the **model** variable with the view.
5. Run the application and select **Product** in the **Admin** menu.
6. Click the **Create New** button and add a product. It should appear in the **Index** view afterwards.

The changes to the **Create** action in the **ProductController** class:

```
public async Task<ActionResult> Create()
{
    var model = new ProductModel
    {
        ProductLinkTexts = await db.ProductLinkTexts.ToListAsync(),
        ProductTypes = await db.ProductTypes.ToListAsync(),
    };

    return View(model);
}
```

Altering the Details view

In order to display all the necessary information in the **Details** view, you have to modify the view itself, as well as add an overloaded version of the asynchronous **Convert** extension method which returns a filled instance of the **ProductModel** class given an instance of the **Product** class. The **Convert** method is used in the **ProductController's Details** action.

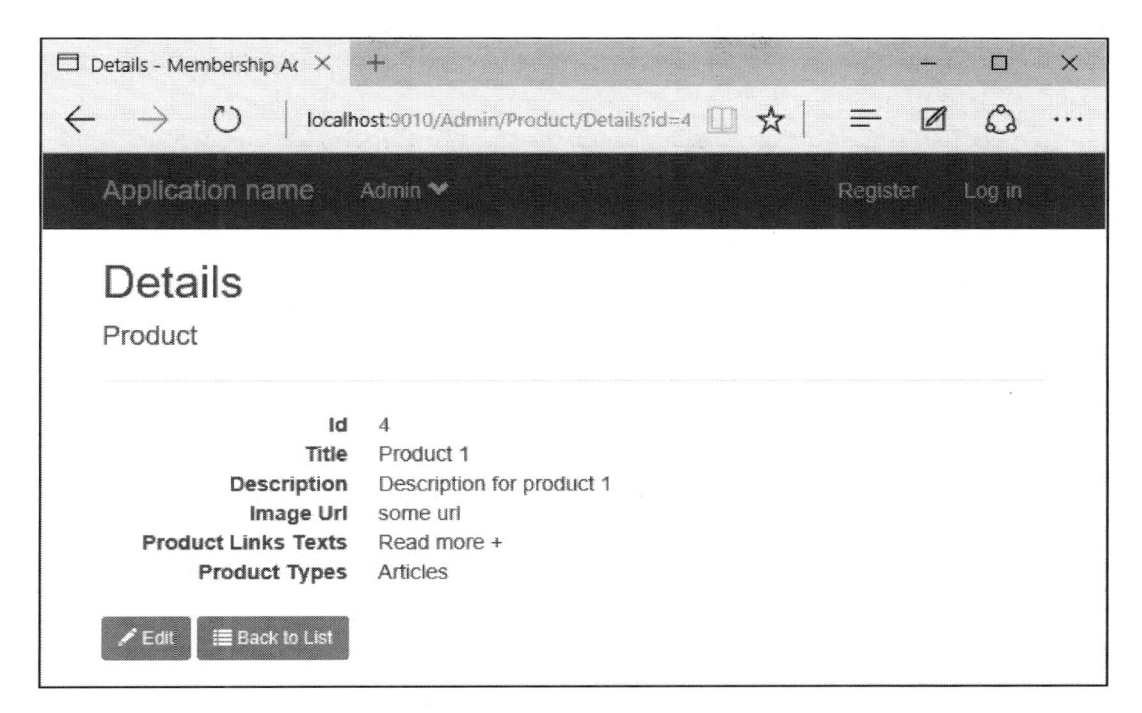

Altering the view

Because the model has been changed from **Product** to **ProductModel** for the **Details** view in the **ProductController's Details** action, you will have to change the view model in the **Details** view as well.

You will also have to add a new list item in the HTML data list for the **Id** property and change the missing **HTML, WaitDays,** and **ProductId** properties in the HTML data list to the **ProductLinkTexts/ProductLinkText** and **ProductTypes/ProductType** properties in the model. Then you will have to remove the HTML data list items for the **Url, ItemTypeId, SectionId, PartId** and **IsFree** properties.

1. Open the **Details** view in the **Product** folder in the **Admin** area.
2. Change the **@model** directive to use the **ProductModel** class.
   `@model Memberships.Areas.Admin.Models.ProductModel`

133

3. Change the missing **HTML**, **WaitDays**, and **ProductId** properties in the HTML data list to the **ProductLinkTexts/ProductLinkText** and **ProductTypes/ProductType** properties in the model.

   ```
   <dt>@Html.DisplayNameFor(model => model.ProductLinkTexts)</dt>
   <dd>@Html.DisplayFor(model => model.ProductLinkText)</dd>
   ```

4. Remove the HTML data list items for the **Url**, **ItemTypeId**, **SectionId**, **PartId** and **IsFree** properties.

The complete **Details** view:

```
@model Memberships.Areas.Admin.Models.ProductModel

@{
    ViewBag.Title = "Details";
}

<h2>Details</h2>

<div>
    <h4>Product</h4>
    <hr />
    <dl class="dl-horizontal">
        <dt>@Html.DisplayNameFor(model => model.Title)</dt>
        <dd>@Html.DisplayFor(model => model.Title)</dd>
        <dt>@Html.DisplayNameFor(model => model.Description)</dt>
        <dd>@Html.DisplayFor(model => model.Description)</dd>
        <dt>@Html.DisplayNameFor(model => model.ImageUrl)</dt>
        <dd>@Html.DisplayFor(model => model.ImageUrl)</dd>
        <dt>@Html.DisplayNameFor(model => model.ProductTypes)</dt>
        <dd>@Html.DisplayFor(model => model.ProductType)</dd>
        <dt>@Html.DisplayNameFor(model => model.ProductLinkTexts)</dt>
        <dd>@Html.DisplayFor(model => model.ProductLinkText)</dd>
    </dl>
</div>
<p>
    @Html.Partial("_EditButtonPartial", Model.Id)
    @Html.Partial("_BackToListButtonPartial")
</p>
```

Adding the asynchronous Convert extension method

Because the model has been changed from **Product** to **ProductModel** for the **Details** view in the **ProductController's Details** action, you will have to add an overloaded version of the **Convert** method which takes a single product and converts it to an instance of the **ProductModel** class.

You can copy the already existing **Convert** method in the **static ConversionExtension** class and alter it.

Remove the **IEnumerable** for the return data type and the **Product** parameter to make it act on a single product and return a single instance of the **ProductModel** class.

Change the two variable names **texts** and **types** to **text** and **type**. Then change the **ToListAsync** method call to **FirstOrDefaultAsync** to return a single item instead of a list. Fetch the item in the **ProductLinkText** table that matches the product's **ProductLinkTextId** property and store it in the **text** variable. Fetch the item in the **ProductType** table that matches the product's **ProductTypeId** property and store it in the **type** variable.

Switch out the **return** statement for a variable named **model** and assign a new empty for the **ProductType** and **ProductLinkText** properties using **List<ProductType>** and **List<ProducLinkText>**.

Add the two variables **text** and **type** to their corresponding list in the **ProductModel** instance.

Return the **model** variable.

1. Open the **ConversionExtensions** class located in the **Extensions** folder in the **Admin** area.
2. Copy the **Convert** method and paste it into the same class.
3. Change the return data type to **Task<ProductModel>**.
4. Change the name of the **products** parameter to **product** and its data type to **Product**.
    ```
    public static async Task<ProductModel> Convert(
    this Product product, ApplicationDbContext db)
    {
    }
    ```
5. Change the names of the variables **texts** and **types** to **text** and **type**.

6. Change the **ToListAsync** method calls to **FirstOrDefaultAsync** to return a single item instead of a list for each of the tables. Use the id properties when fetching the data.
   ```
   var text = await db.ProductLinkTexts.FirstOrDefaultAsync(p =>
       p.Id.Equals(product.ProductLinkTextId));
   ```
7. Switch out the **return** statement for a variable named **model** and assign a new empty lists to the **ProductLinkText** and **ProductType** properties.
   ```
   var model = new ProductModel
   {
       ...
       ProductLinkTexts = new List<ProductLinkText>(),
       ProductTypes = new List<ProductType>()
   };
   ```
8. Add two variables (**text** and **type**) to their corresponding list in the **ProductModel** instance.
   ```
   model.ProductLinkTexts.Add(text);
   ```
9. Return the **model** variable from the method.

The complete code for the **Convert** extension method:

```
public static async Task<ProductModel> Convert(
this Product product, ApplicationDbContext db)
{
    var text = await db.ProductLinkTexts.FirstOrDefaultAsync(p =>
        p.Id.Equals(product.ProductLinkTextId));
    var type = await db.ProductTypes.FirstOrDefaultAsync(p =>
        p.Id.Equals(product.ProductTypeId));

    var model = new ProductModel
    {
        Id = product.Id,
        Title = product.Title,
        Description = product.Description,
        ImageUrl = product.ImageUrl,
        ProductLinkTextId = product.ProductLinkTextId,
        ProductTypeId = product.ProductTypeId,
        ProductLinkTexts = new List<ProductLinkText>(),
        ProductTypes = new List<ProductType>()
    };
```

```
      model.ProductLinkTexts.Add(text);
      model.ProductTypes.Add(type);

      return model;
}
```

Changing the Details action in the ProductController

Because the model has been changed from **Product** to **ProductModel** for the **Details** view in the **ProductController's Details** action, you will have convert the fetched product to a **ProductModel** instance using the asynchronous **Convert** method you just added to the **ConvertExtensions** class.

Use the **await** keyword when calling the **Convert** method on the fetched product immediately above the **return** statement in the **Details** action and store the result in a variable called **model**.

Return the **model** variable with the view.

1. Open the **ProductController** class located in the **Controllers** folder in the **Admin** area.
2. Locate the **Details** action method.
3. Add the **model** variable above the **return** statement and store the result from an asynchronous call to the **Convert** method on the **product** variable. Then return the **model** with the view.
   ```
   var model = await product.Convert(db);
   return View(model);
   ```
4. Run the application and click the **Product** item in the **Admin** menu.
5. Click on the **Details** button (the green middle button) for a product to make sure that the details are displayed.

The complete **Details** action:
```
public async Task<ActionResult> Details(int? id)
{
   if (id == null)
   {
      return new HttpStatusCodeResult(HttpStatusCode.BadRequest);
   }
   Product product = await db.Products.FindAsync(id);
```

```
    if (product == null)
    {
        return HttpNotFound();
    }
    var model = await product.Convert(db);
    return View(model);
}
```

Altering the Delete view

In order to display all the necessary information in the **Delete** view, you have to modify the view itself, in addition to using the overloaded version of the asynchronous **Convert** extension method which returns a filled instance of the **ProductModel** class given an instance of the **Product** class. The **Convert** method is used in the **ProductController's Delete** action.

Change the **@model** directive in the **Delete** view to the **ProductModel** class.

```
@model Memberships.Areas.Admin.Models.ProductModel
```

Change the properties in the HTML data list to the properties in the **ProductModel**. You can copy the **<dl>** element and its sub-elements from the **Details** view.

Change the **Delete** action in the **ProductController**. Copy the **model** variable and the call to the **View** method at the end of the **Details** action and replace the call to the **View** method in the **Delete** action with the copied code.

Delete

Are you sure you want to delete this?

Item

Id	4
Title	Product 1
Description	Description for product 1
Image Url	some url
Product Links Texts	Read more +
Product Types	Articles

[Delete] [Back to List]

Altering the Delete view

You have to change the **@model** directive to **ProductModel** and replace the existing HTML data list with the one from the **Details** view.

1. Open the **Details** view located in the **Product** folder in the **Admin** area.
2. Copy the **@model** directive located at the top of the view.
   `@model Memberships.Areas.Admin.Models.ProductModel`
3. Open the **Delete** view located in the **Product** folder in the **Admin** area.
4. Replace the current **@model** directive with the one you just copied.
5. Switch to the **Details** view and copy the HTML data list and its content.
   ```
   <dl class="dl-horizontal">
       ... Content ...
   </dl>
   ```
6. Switch to the **Delete** view again and replace the current HTML data list with the one you copied.

The complete **Delete** view:

```
@model Memberships.Areas.Admin.Models.ProductModel

@{
    ViewBag.Title = "Delete";
}
```

```
<h2>Delete</h2>

<h3>Are you sure you want to delete this?</h3>
<div>
   <h4>Product</h4>
   <hr />
   <dl class="dl-horizontal">
      <dt>@Html.DisplayNameFor(model => model.Title)</dt>
      <dd>@Html.DisplayFor(model => model.Title)</dd>
      <dt>@Html.DisplayNameFor(model => model.Description)</dt>
      <dd>@Html.DisplayFor(model => model.Description)</dd>
      <dt>@Html.DisplayNameFor(model => model.ImageUrl)</dt>
      <dd>@Html.DisplayFor(model => model.ImageUrl)</dd>
      <dt>@Html.DisplayNameFor(model => model.ProductTypes)</dt>
      <dd>@Html.DisplayFor(model => model.ProductType)</dd>
      <dt>@Html.DisplayNameFor(model => model.ProductLinkTexts)</dt>
      <dd>@Html.DisplayFor(model => model.ProductLinkText)</dd>
   </dl>

   @using (Html.BeginForm()) {
      @Html.AntiForgeryToken()

      <div class="form-actions no-color">
         <input type="submit" value="Delete" class="btn btn-danger btn-sm" />
         @Html.Partial("_BackToListButtonPartial")
      </div>
   }
</div>
```

Altering the Delete action in the ProductController

You have to change the **Delete** action in the **ProductController** class to fetch an instance of the **ProductModel** class and fill it with product data by calling one of the overloaded **Convert** methods. Then you have to return the new model with the view.

The easiest way to achieve this is to copy the two last statements of the **Details** action in the **ProductController** class and replace the call to the **View** method in the **Delete** action with the copied code.

1. Open the **ProductController** class located in the **Controllers** folder in the **Admin** area.
2. Locate the **Details** action method.

3. Copy the last two code lines in the action.
   ```
   var model = await product.Convert(db);
   return View(model);
   ```
4. Locate the **Delete** action method and replace the call to the **View** method with the copied code.
5. Run the application and click the **Product** item in the **Admin** menu.
6. Click on the **Delete** button (the right most red button) on a product row in the **Index** view and make sure that the data in the **Delete** view is displayed properly.

The complete **Delete** action:

```
public async Task<ActionResult> Delete(int? id)
{
   if (id == null)
   {
      return new HttpStatusCodeResult(HttpStatusCode.BadRequest);
   }
   Product product = await db.Products.FindAsync(id);
   if (product == null)
   {
      return HttpNotFound();
   }
   var model = await product.Convert(db);
   return View(model);
}
```

Altering the Edit view

You have to change the **@model** directive to the **ProductModel** class and the form to display the correct properties. You can do this by copying the **@model** directive and the **<div>** containing the form controls from the **Create** view and replacing the corresponding code in the **Edit** view.

Then you have to alter the **Edit** action in the **ProductController** class. You can use the already exisisting **Convert** extension method to change a product to a **ProductModel,** but you have to wrap the product in a list because the **Convert** method takes a list of products.

Lastly, you pass the first product model in the result from the call to the **Convert** method to the **View** method as its model.

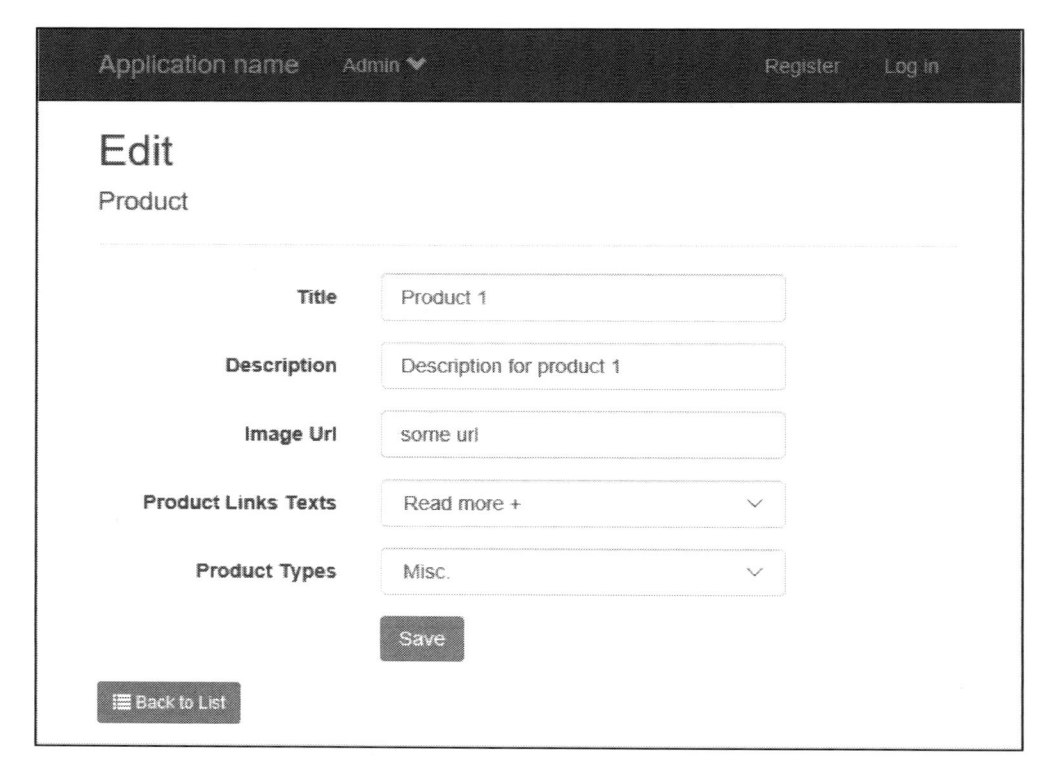

Altering the Edit view
You have to change the **@model** directive to **ProductModel** and replace the existing **<div>** containing the form controls with the one you copy from the **Create** view.

1. Open the **Create** view located in the **Product** folder in the **Admin** area.
2. Copy the **@model** directive located at the top of the view.
   `@model Memberships.Areas.Admin.Models.ProductModel`
3. Open the **Edit** view located in the **Product** folder in the **Admin** area.
4. Replace the current **@model** directive with the one you just copied.
5. Switch to the **Create** view and copy the **<div>** containing the form controls.
   ```
   <div class="form-horizontal">
       ... Form Controls ...
   </div>
   ```
6. Switch to the **Edit** view again and replace the **<div>** containing the form controls with the one you copied.

7. Change the text displayed on the button from **Create** to **Save** in the **<input>** element.
   ```
   <input type="submit" value="Save" class="btn btn-success" />
   ```

Altering the Edit action in the ProductController

You have to change the **Edit** action in the **ProductController** class to fetch an instance of the **ProductModel** class and fill it with product and collection data by calling one of the overloaded **Convert** methods. Then you have to return the new model with the view.

The easiest way to achieve this is to wrap the product in a **List<Product>** and call the **Convert** method on that list. Then you pass the first item in the result from the **Convert** method to the **View** method in the **Edit** action.

1. Open the **ProductController** class located in the **Controllers** folder in the **Admin** area.
2. Locate the **Edit** action method.
3. Add a variable called **prod** which is a new empty **List<Product>** immediately above the **return** statement.
   ```
   var prod = new List<Product>();
   ```
4. Add the product that was fetched earlier in the **Edit** action to the list.
5. Add a variable called **productModel** which stores the result from the call to the **Convert** method on the **prod** variable.
   ```
   var productModel = await prod.Convert(db);
   ```
6. Replace the current **return** statement with one that returns the first **ProductModel** instance from the **productModel** list variable. It will only contain one item but since the **Convert** method return a list you have to fetch the first item from it.
   ```
   return View(productModel.First());
   ```
7. Run the application and click the **Product** item in the **Admin** menu.
8. Click on the **Edit** button (the left most blue button) on a product row in the **Index** view and check that the data in the **Edit** view is displayed properly and that you can alter and save data for the product.

The complete **Edit** action:

```
public async Task<ActionResult> Edit(int? id)
{
   if (id == null)
   {
      return new HttpStatusCodeResult(HttpStatusCode.BadRequest);
   }
   Product product = await db.Products.FindAsync(id);
   if (product == null)
   {
      return HttpNotFound();
   }

   var prod = new List<Product>();
   prod.Add(product);
   var ProductModel = await prod.Convert(db);
   return View(ProductModel.First());
}
```

Scaffold the Subscription controller and views

This is one of the most important tables since it holds information about available subscriptions. A subscription is a collection of products that can be assigned to users when they subscribe or sign up with the web site. You could give the users access to free teaser subscriptions without them having to sign up and other subscriptions they get automatically when they register with the web site. You could then have paid subscriptions that they can buy from you to gain access to the content.

The first thing you need to do is to scaffold out the **Subscription** controller and its views, then you have to do some minor modifications to the views.

Scaffold the controller and views

The image below shows the settings needed to scaffold the **Subscription** controller and its views.

Add Controller dialog

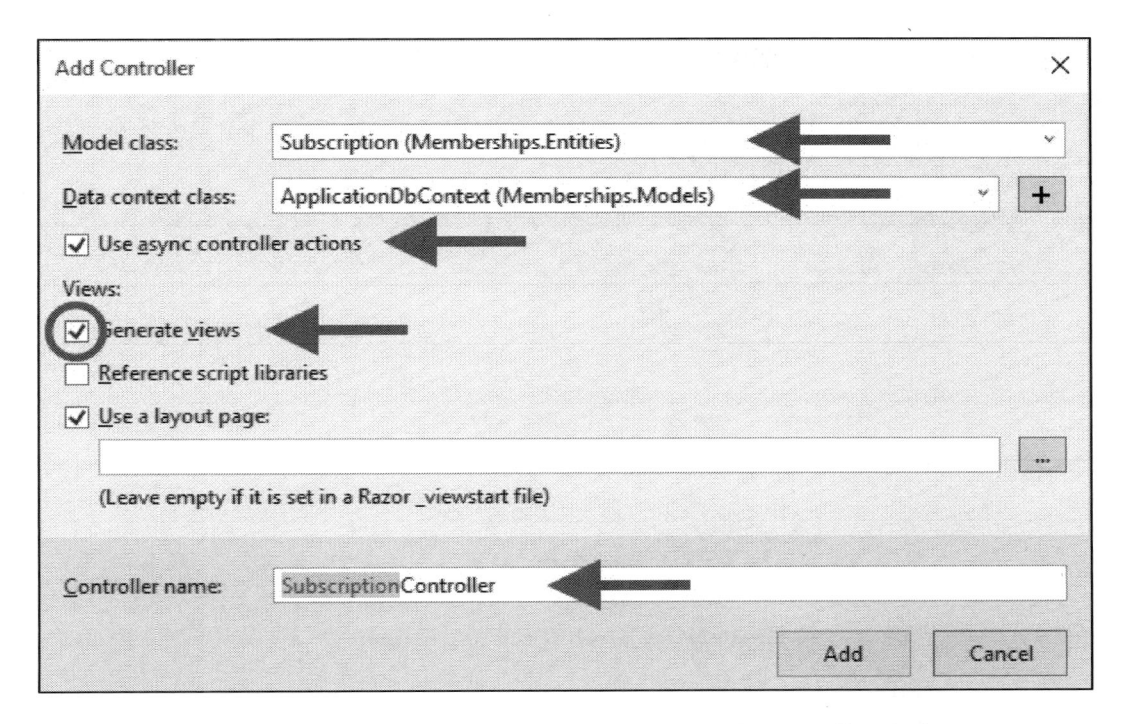

- **Model class:** Subscription (Memberships.Entities)
- **Data context class:** ApplicationDbContext (Memberships.Models)
- ☑ Use async controller actions
- **Views:**
  - ☑ Generate views
  - ☐ Reference script libraries
  - ☑ Use a layout page:
    - (Leave empty if it is set in a Razor _viewstart file)
- **Controller name:** SubscriptionController

1. Right-click on the **Controllers** folder and select **Add-Controller** in the context menu.
2. Select **MVC 5 Controller with views, using Entity Framework** and click the **Add** button.
3. Fill in the dialog according to the image above and click the **Add** button.

The Index View

The **Index** view is almost done out of the box. You only have to replace the *Create New* link with the partial view **_CreateNewButtonPartial**, replace the table row links with the buttons in the partial view **_TableButtonsPartial**, style the table and its header using the **table-striped** and **success** Bootstrap classes and remove the **ProductId** column.

ASP.NET MVC 5 - How to build a Membership Website

This is what the **Index** view looks like out of the box:

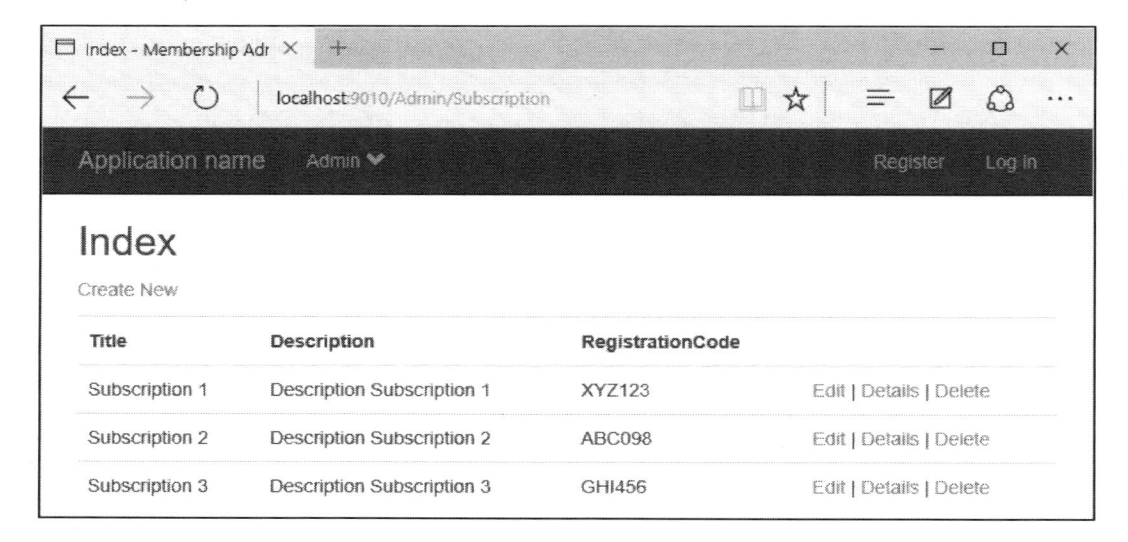

This is what the **Index** view look like after it has been modified:

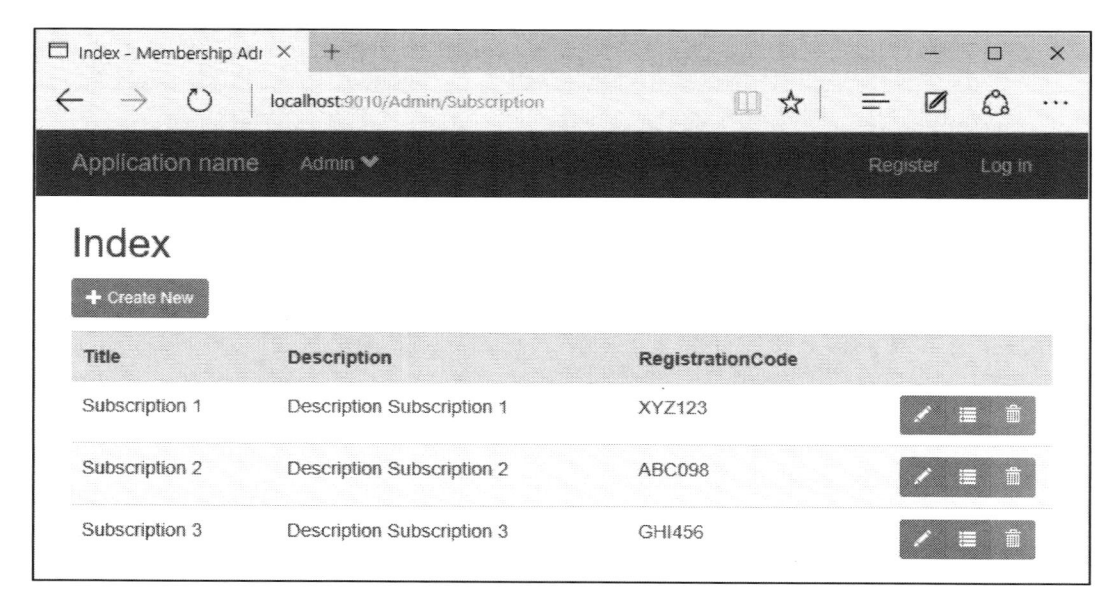

1. Open the **Index** view in the **Section** folder and copy the **@Html.Partial** method call to the partial view **_CreteButtonPartial**.
   @Html.Partial("_CreateNewButtonPartial")

2. Open the **Index** view in the **Subscriptions** folder and replace the **submit** button and the **@Html.ActionLink** method call with the copied code.
3. Add a **using** statement to the **Admin-Models** folder immediately below the **@model** directrive at the top of the view.
   ```
   @using Memberships.Areas.Admin.Models
   ```
4. Locate the **<th>** element and **<td>** elements displaying the **ProductId** property and delete them.
   ```
   <th>@Html.DisplayNameFor(model => model.ProductId)</th>
   <td>@Html.DisplayFor(modelItem => item.ProductId)</td>
   ```
5. Locate the **<table>** element and add the class **table-striped** to its class attribute.
   ```
   <table class="table table-striped">
   ```
6. Locate the **<tr>** element under the **<table>** element and add the class **success** to a new class attribute.
   ```
   <tr class="success">
   ```
7. Find the last **<td>** which contains the **@Html.ActionLink** calls and replace the entire **<td>** element with the partial view **_TableButtonsPartial**.
   ```
   @Html.Partial("_TableButtonsPartial", new SmallButtonModel { Id = item.Id })
   ```

The complete code for the **Index** view:

```
@model IEnumerable<Memberships.Entities.Subscription>
@using Memberships.Areas.Admin.Models;

@{
    ViewBag.Title = "Index";
}

<h2>Index</h2>

<p>
    @Html.Partial("_CreateButtonPartial")
</p>
<table class="table table-condensed table-striped">
    <tr class="success">
        <th>@Html.DisplayNameFor(model => model.Title)</th>
        <th>@Html.DisplayNameFor(model => model.Description)</th>
        <th>@Html.DisplayNameFor(model => model.RegistrationCode)</th>
        <th></th>
```

```
      </tr>

@foreach (var item in Model) {
   <tr>
      <td>@Html.DisplayFor(modelItem => item.Title)</td>
      <td>@Html.DisplayFor(modelItem => item.Description)</td>
      <td>@Html.DisplayFor(modelItem => item.RegistrationCode)</td>
      @Html.Partial("_TableButtonsPartial",
         new SmallButtonModel { Id = item.Id })
   </tr>
}
</table>
```

The Create View

The **Create** view is almost done out of the box. You only have to style the **Create** button using the **btn-success** Bootstrap class and replace the *Back to List* link with the partial view **_BackToListButtonPartial**.

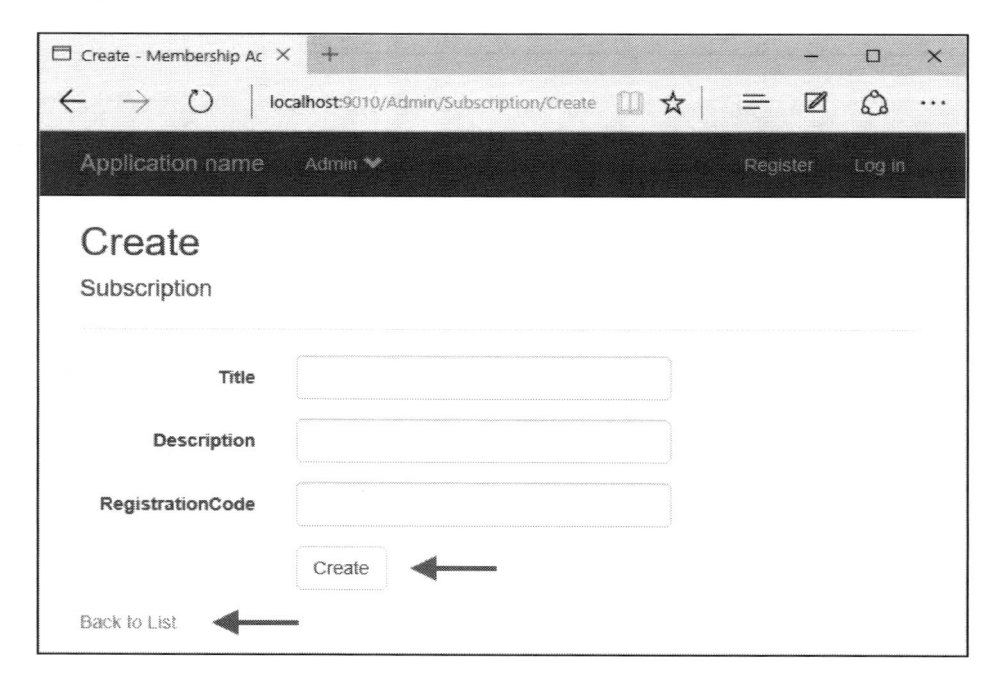

Here's what the **Create** view looks like when modified:

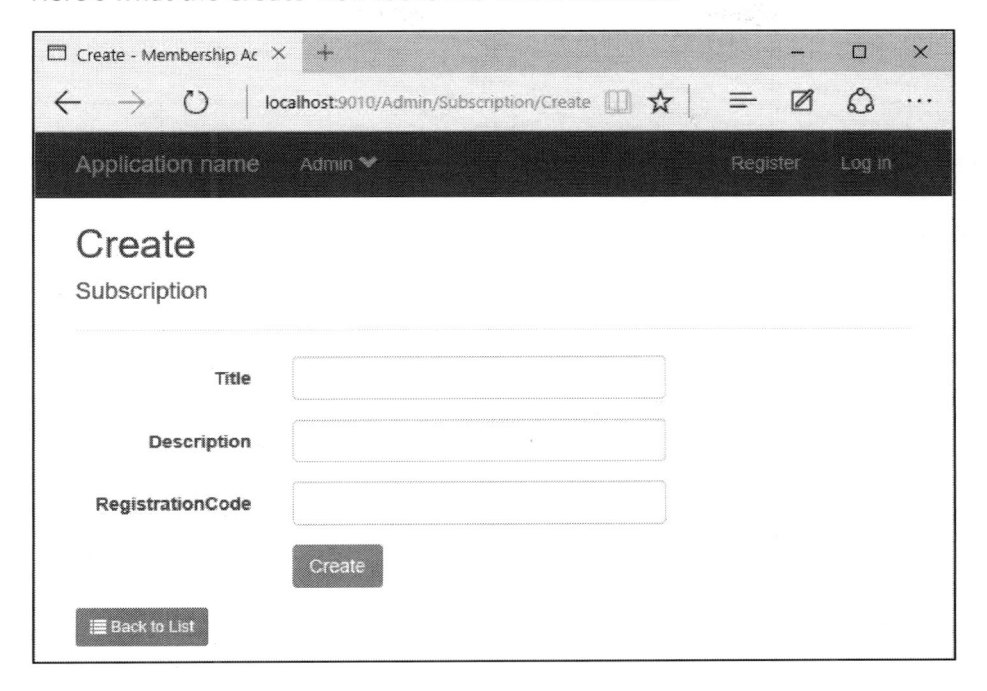

1. Open the **Create** view in the **Subscription** folder.
2. Locate the **Create** button and add the **btn-success** Bootstrap class to its **class** attribute.
   ```
   <input type="submit" value="Create" class="btn btn-success" />
   ```
3. Open the **Create** view in the **Section** folder and copy the **@Html.Partial** for the partial view **_BackToListButtonPartial**.
4. Open the **Create** view in the **Subscription** folder and replace the *Back to List* **@Html.ActionLink** with the copied code.

Changes to the **Create** view:

```
<div class="form-group">
   <div class="col-md-offset-2 col-md-10">
     <input type="submit" value="Create" class="btn btn-success" />
   </div>
</div>
```

```
<div>
   @Html.Partial("_BackToListButtonPartial")
</div>
```

The Edit View

The **Edit** view is almost done out of the box. You only have to style the **Save** button using the **btn-success** Bootstrap class and replace the *Back to List* link with the partial view **_BackToListButtonPartial**.

This is what the **Edit** view looks like out of the box:

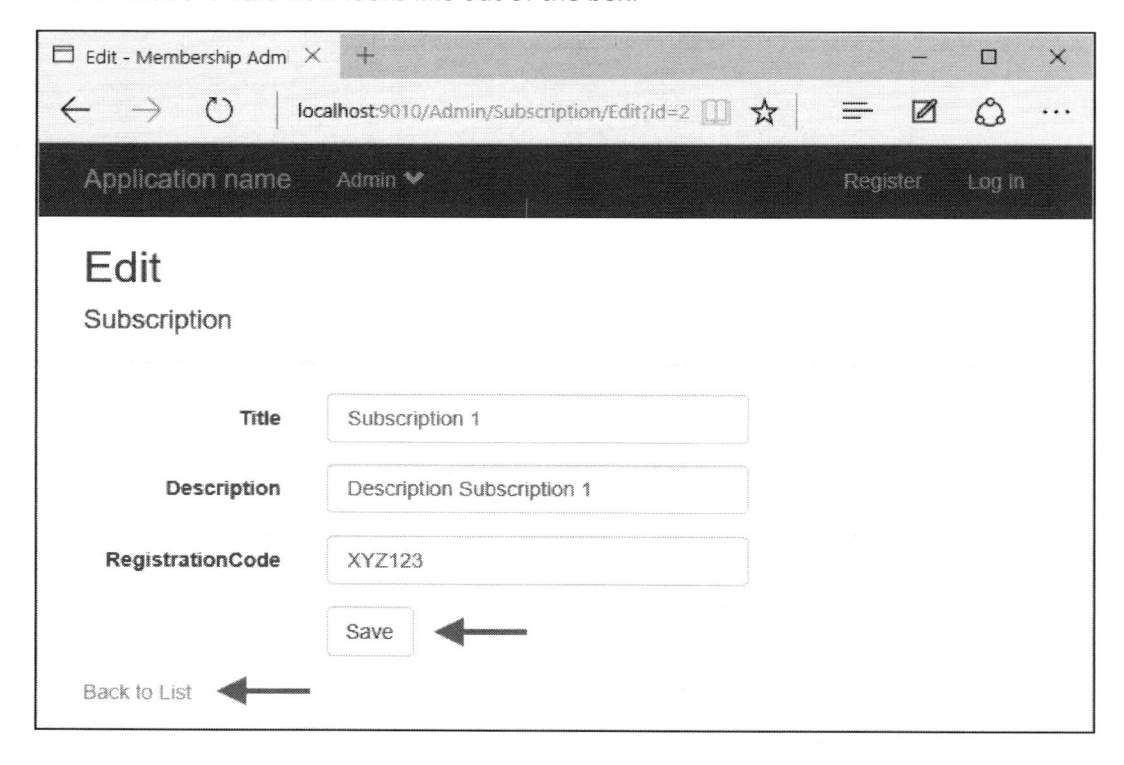

Here is what the **Edit** view looks like when modified:

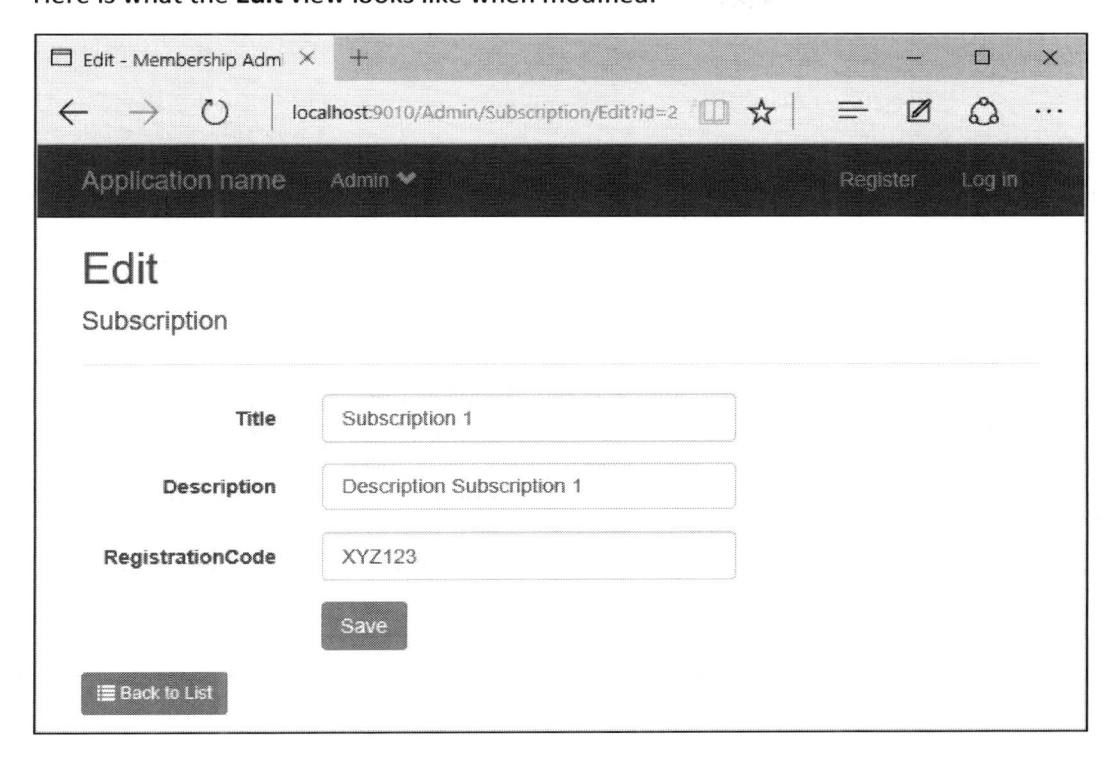

1. Open the **Edit** view in the **Subscription** folder.
2. Locate the **Save** button and add the **btn-success** Bootstrap class to its **class** attribute.
   `<input type="submit" value="Save" class="btn btn-success" />`
3. Open the **Edit** view in the **Section** folder and copy the **@Html.Partial** for the partial view **_BackToListButtonPartial**.
4. Open the **Edit** view in the **Subscription** folder and replace the *Back to List* **@Html.ActionLink** with the copied code.

Changes to the **Edit** view:

```
<div class="form-group">
   <div class="col-md-offset-2 col-md-10">
      <input type="submit" value="Create" class="btn btn-success" />
   </div>
</div>
```

```
<div>
    @Html.Partial("_BackToListButtonPartial")
</div>
```

The Details View

The **Details** view is almost done out of the box. You only have to replace the *Back to List* link with the partial view **_BackToListButtonPartial** and the **Edit** link with the partial view **_EditButtonPartial**.

This is what the **Details** view looks like out of the box:

This is what the **Details** view looks like after it has been modified:

ASP.NET MVC 5 - How to build a Membership Website

1. Open the **Details** view in the **Section** folder and copy the two **@Html.Partial** method calls at the bottom of the view.
2. Open the **Details** view in the **Subscriptions** folder and replace the two **@Html.ActionLink** method calls with the copied code.

Changes to the **Details** view:

```
<p>
    @Html.Partial("_EditButtonPartial", Model.Id)
    @Html.Partial("_BackToListButtonPartial")
</p>
```

The Delete View

The **Delete** view is almost done out of the box. You only have to replace the *Back to List* link with the partial view **_BackToListButtonPartial** and style the **Delete** button with the two Bootstrap classes **btn-danger** (red) and **btn-sm** (small button).

This is what the **Delete** view looks like out of the box:

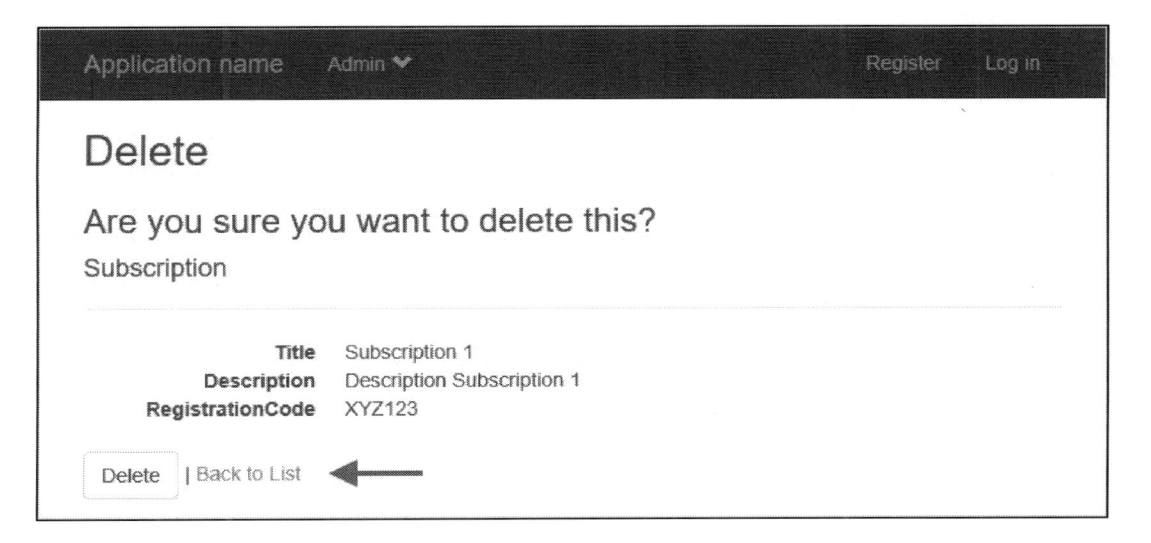

This is what the **Delete** view looks like after it has been modified:

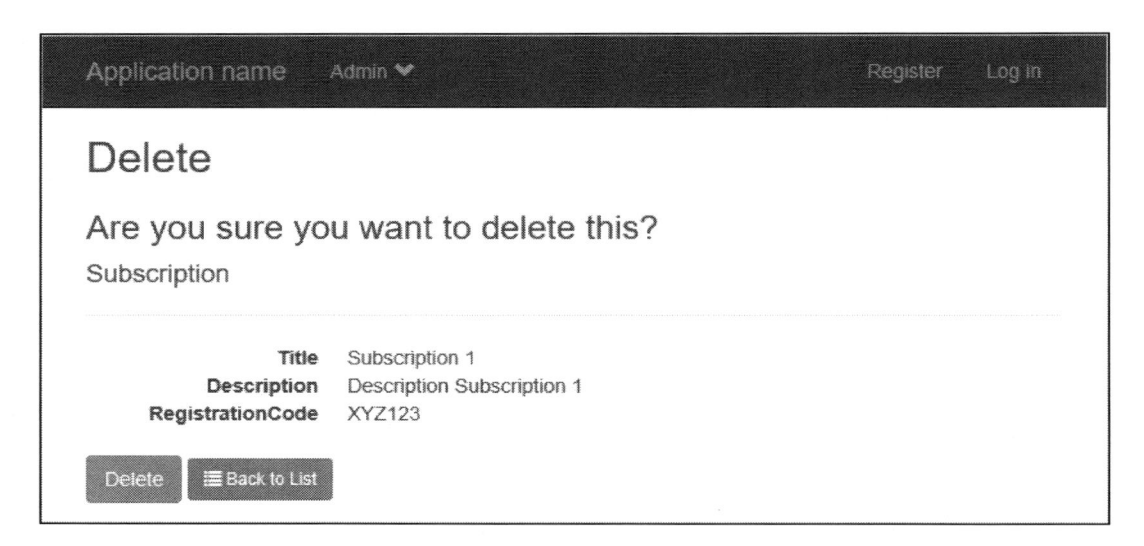

Delete

Are you sure you want to delete this?

Subscription

Title	Subscription 1
Description	Description Subscription 1
RegistrationCode	XYZ123

Delete   Back to List

1. Open the **Delete** view in the **Section** folder and copy the submit button and the **@Html.Partial** method call at the bottom of the view.
   ```
   <input type="submit" value="Delete" class="btn btn-danger btn-sm"/>
   @Html.Partial("_BackToListButtonPartial")
   ```
2. Open the **Delete** view in the **Subscriptions** folder and replace the **submit** button and the **@Html.ActionLink** method call with the copied code.

Changes to the **Delete** view:

```
<div class="form-actions no-color">
   <input type="submit" value="Delete" class="btn btn-danger btn-sm" />
   @Html.Partial("_BackToListButtonPartial")
</div>
```

6. Adding UIs for the Connecting Entities

Introduction
In this chapter you will continue to implement controllers and views for the database you have created. As you add controllers and views to the **Admin** area, the corresponding menu items will work, making it possible to navigate between the **Index** views.

Technologies used in this chapter
1. **MVC** - To structure the application and scaffold views and controllers and to create partial views for reusable components such as buttons.
2. **C#** - Creating Extension methods, helper methods, to keep the controller actions clean and easy to read. Creating the view models needed for all the views. Reflection is used to fetch property values for generic objects.
3. **Razor** - To incorporate C# in the views where necessary.
4. **HTML 5** - To build the views.
5. **Bootstrap** - To style the HTML 5 components.

The use case
Your task is to scaffold the controllers and views for the **ProductItem** and **Subscription-Product** tables in the database to enable reading and writing data to and from them, and in so doing, connecting a product with an item or a subscription. The controllers will be called **ProductItemController** and **SubscriptionProductController** and with each controller five views will be created in a folder with the same name as the controller's corresponding table.

- **Index** - The main view with a list of the available table records and buttons to the other views.
- **Create** - A view for adding new table records.
- **Delete** - A view for deleting a selected table record.

- **Edit** - A view to modify the data in table record.
- **Details** - A view to show the data stored about one table record in the corresponding table.

Scaffold the ProductItem controller and views

The connection table ties a piece of content in the **Item** table to one or more products in the **Product** table. Even though it only contains two values, it is one of the more complex tables to create a controller and views for, the reason being that the values are stored as integer values in the table; but you want to display the descriptive titles in dropdowns instead of as integers in textboxes, creating a better user experience and minimizing the risk for errors.

The image below displays the settings in the *Add Controller* dialog for the **PrductItem-Controller**.

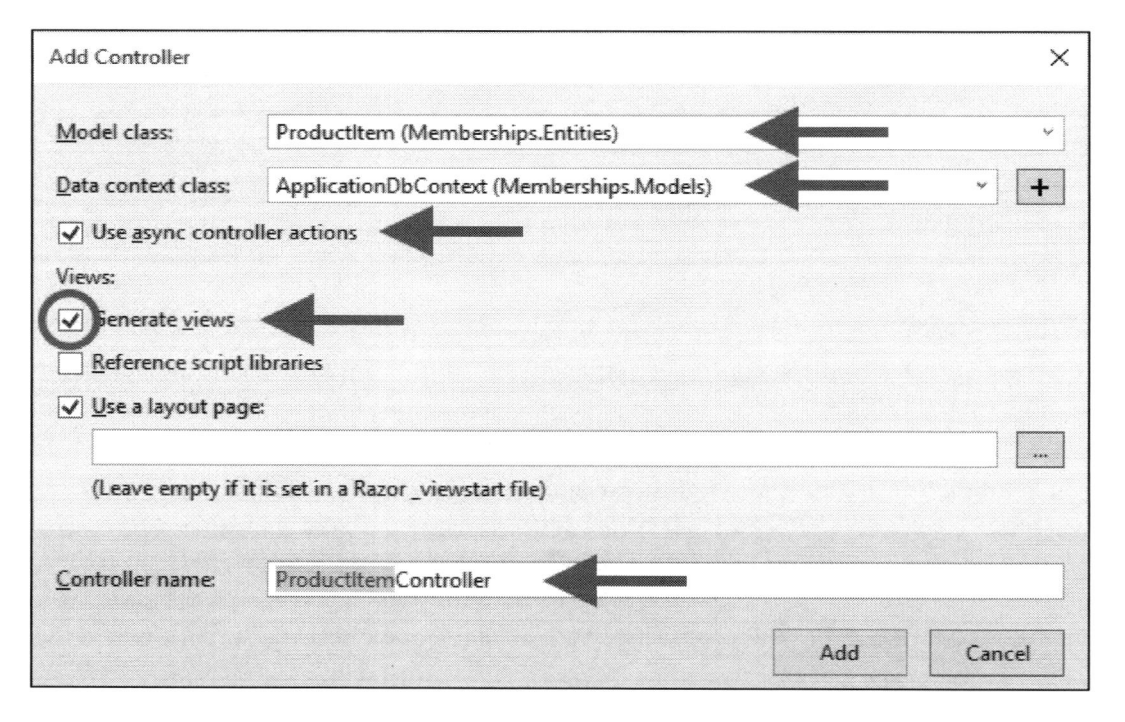

The first thing you need to do is to scaffold out the **ProductItemController** and its views.

1. Right-click on the **Controllers** folder in the **Admin** area.
2. Select **Add-Controller** in the context menu.
3. Select the **ProductItem** entity model in the **Model class** dropdown.
4. Make sure that the **Generate views** checkbox is checked.
5. Change the name to its singular form and click the **Add** button.

Adding the ProductItemModel

To be able to display the title from the **Product** and **Item** tables in the **Create** view, you need to create a view model which has collections for the products and items, as well as the product id and item id which will represent the selected dropdown values. Thinking ahead, you can also add two **string** properties for the product and item titles which will be used when displaying information about a product-item connection in other views.

1. Right-click on the **Models** folder in the **Admin** area.
2. Select **Add-Class** in the context menu.
3. Name the class **ProductItemModel**.
   ```
   Public class ProductItemModel
   {
   }
   ```
4. Add two **int** properties called **ProductId** and **ItemtId**.
   ```
   Public int ProductId { get; set; }
   public int ItemId { get; set; }
   ```
5. Add two **string** properties called **ProductTitle** and **ItemTitle**.
   ```
   Public string ProductTitle { get; set; }
   public string ItemTitle { get; set; }
   ```
6. Add a property of type **Icollection<Product>** called **Products** which will hold the available products in the **Products** table.
   ```
   Public Icollection<Product> Products { get; set; }
   ```
7. Add a property of type **Icollection<Item>** called **Items** which will hold the available content pieces in the **Item** table.
   ```
   Public Icollection<Item> Items { get; set; }
   ```
8. Add the **DisplayName** attribute where applicable to change the lable text in the view.

The complete code for the **ProductItemModel**:

```
public class ProductItemModel
{
   [DisplayName("Product Id")]
   public int ProductId { get; set; }
   [DisplayName("Item Id")]
   public int ItemId { get; set; }
   [DisplayName("Product Title")]
   public string ProductTitle { get; set; }
   [DisplayName("Item Title")]
   public string ItemTitle { get; set; }
   public Icollection<Product> Products { get; set; }
   public Icollection<Item> Items { get; set; }
}
```

The Create View

The first view you will alter is the **Create** view which adds a new connection between a product in the **Product** table and an item in the **Item** table, adding a piece of content to a product. As you can see in the image below, the data is displayed in textboxes by default. You need to change this to dropdowns to provide a better user experience and minimize the risk of errors.

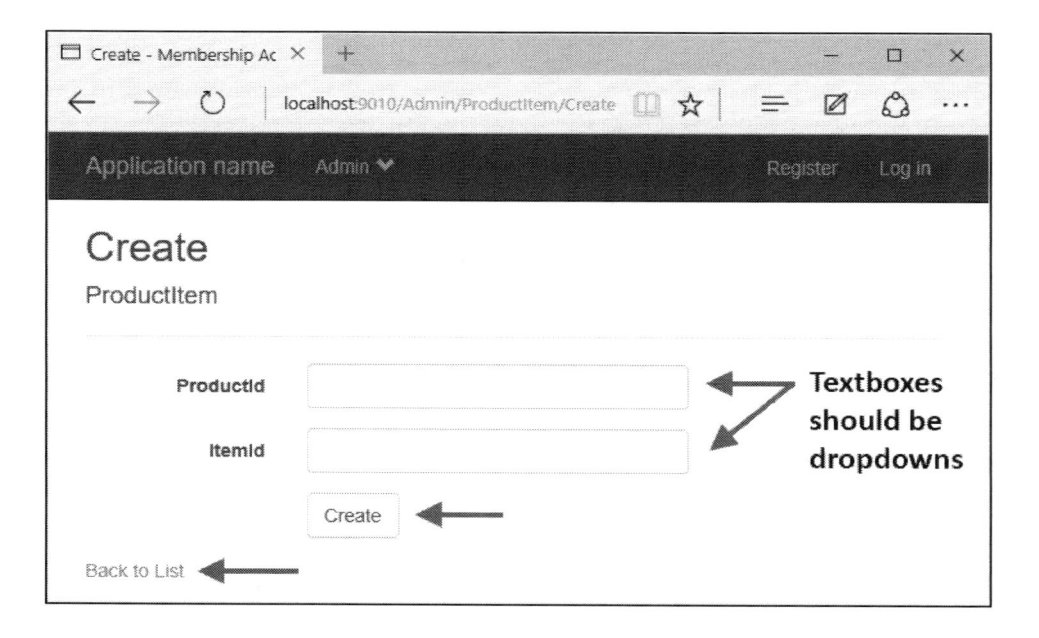

The image below shows the finished view.

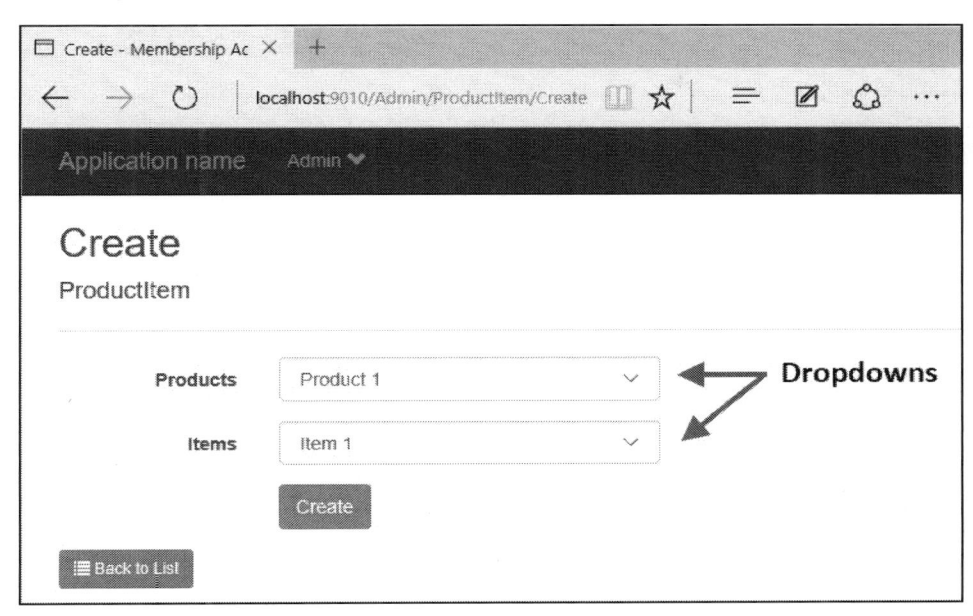

The first thing you need to do is to change the **@model** directive to use the **ProductItem-Model** class and add a **using** statement to the **Memberships.Areas.Admin.Extensions** namespace below the **@model** directive to gain access to the **ToSelectListItem** extension method you created earlier, which is needed to convert an **ICollection<T>** to an **IEnumerable<SelectListItem>** to display items in a dropdown.

```
@model Memberships.Areas.Admin.Models.ProductItemModel
@using Memberships.Areas.Admin.Extensions
```

Next, you need to change the textboxes to dropdowns using the **@Html.DropDownFor** extension method. Looking back, you have already done this for textboxes in the **Create** view for the **Product** table, so you copy one of the **form-group <div>** elements and replace the existing two **form-group <div>** elements in the **Create** view for the **ProdutItem**. Then you simply change the id and collection in the **@Html.DropDownFor** extension methods.

159

Next, you need to change the **@Html.LabelFor** method calls to reference the **Products** and **Items** collections instead of **ProductId** and **ItemId**; this will change the label text for the controls.

```
@Html.LabelFor(model => model.Products ...
```

Because you have changed the textboxes to dropdowns, they need values in the model collections that you used when adding the **@Html.DropDownFor** method calls. To fill the collections, you need to call the database from the parameter-less **Create** action in the **ProductItem** controller. Create an instance of the **ProductItemModel** class in the **Create** action and fill its two collections with values from the **Product** and **Item** tables. Return the model with the view.

The last thing you need to do is to style the button and link. Give the button green color by replacing the **btn-default** Bootstrap class with **btn-success**. Replace the *Back to List* link with the partial view **_BakToLinkButtonPartial**.

Change @model and add @using
1. Open the **Create** view in the **ProductItem** folder.
2. Change the **@model** directive to **ProductItemModel**.
   ```
   @model Memberships.Areas.Admin.Models.ProductItemModel
   ```
3. Add a **@using** statement to the **Memberships.Areas.Admin.Extensions** namespace below the **@model** directive.
   ```
   @using Memberships.Areas.Admin.Extensions
   ```

Changing the label descriptions and the textboxes
1. Delete the two **form-group <div>** elements and their content.
2. Open the **Create** view in the **Product** folder and copy two **form-group <div>** elements and their content.
3. Open the **Create** view in the **ProductItem** folder and paste in the code where you previously deleted the **form-group <div>** elements.
4. Locate the first **@Html.LabelFor** method call and change the Lambda expression to go to **Products** instead of the current id. This will change the label to display the text *Products*.
   ```
   @Html.LabelFor(model => model.Products ...
   ```

5. Locate the second **@Html.LabelFor** method call and change the Lambda expression to go to **Item** instead of the current id. This will change the label to display the text *Items*.
   @Html.LabelFor(model => model.Items ...

6. Locate the first **@Html.DropDownFor** and change the id to **ProductId** and the collection to **Products**.
   ```
   @Html.DropDownListFor(model => model.ProductId,
       Model.Products.ToSelectListItem(Model.ProductId),
          new { @class = "form-control" })
   ```

7. Locate the second **@Html.DropDownFor** and change the id to **ItemId** and the collection to **Items**.
   ```
   @Html.DropDownListFor(model => model.ItemId,
       Model.Items.ToSelectListItem(Model.ItemId),
          new { @class = "form-control" })
   ```

The complete code for the **Create** view:

```
@model Memberships.Areas.Admin.Models.ProductItemModel
@using Memberships.Extensions

@{
    ViewBag.Title = "Create";
}

<h2>Create</h2>

@using (Html.BeginForm())
{
    @Html.AntiForgeryToken()

    <div class="form-horizontal">
        <h4>ProductItem</h4>
        <hr />
        @Html.ValidationSummary(true, "", new { @class = "text-danger" })

        <div class="form-group">
            @Html.LabelFor(model => model.Products, htmlAttributes:
                new { @class = "control-label col-md-2" })
            <div class="col-md-10">
                @Html.DropDownListFor(
                    model => model.ProductId,
```

```
            Model.Products.ToSelectListItem(Model.ProductId),
              new { @class = "form-control" })
          @Html.ValidationMessageFor(model => model.ProductId, "",
              new { @class = "text-danger" })
        </div>
      </div>

      <div class="form-group">
        @Html.LabelFor(model => model.Items, htmlAttributes:
            new { @class = "control-label col-md-2" })
        <div class="col-md-10">
          @Html.DropDownListFor(
              model => model.ItemId,
              Model.Items.ToSelectListItem(Model.ItemId),
              new { @class = "form-control" })
          @Html.ValidationMessageFor(model => model.ItemId, "",
              new { @class = "text-danger" })
        </div>
      </div>

      <div class="form-group">
        <div class="col-md-offset-2 col-md-10">
          <input type="submit" value="Create" class="btn btn-success" />
        </div>
      </div>
    </div>
}

<div>
  @Html.Partial("_BackToListButtonPartial")
</div>
```

Changing the Create controller action (HttpGet)

Because you have changed the textboxes to dropdowns, they need values in the model collections that you used when adding the **@Html.DropDownFor** method calls. To fill the collections, you need to call the database from the parameter-less **Create** get action in the **ProductItem** controller and fill the two collections with values.

1. Open the **ProductItemController** class in the **Controllers** folder in the **Admin** area.
2. Locate the parameter-less **Create** action method.

3. Change it to an asynchronous method adding the **async** keyword and return the data as a **Task**.
   Public async Task<ActionResult> Create()

4. Add a variable called **model** to which you assign an instance of the **ProductItemModel** class. Fill the collections in the **ProductItemModel** instance asynchronously with data from the **Product** and **Item** tables.
   ```
   Var model = new ProductItemModel
   {
       Items = await db.Items.ToListAsync()
       Products = await db.Product.ToListAsync()
   };
   ```

5. Return the model variable in the **View** method call.
   Return View(model);

The complete code for the **HttpGet Create** action:

```
public async Task<ActionResult> Create()
{
   var model = new ProductItemModel
   {
      Items = await db.Items.ToListAsync(),
      Products = await db.Products.ToListAsync()
   };
   return View(model);
}
```

Styling the Create button and the Back to List link

The last task for the **Create** view is to give the **Create** button a green color by replacing the **btn-default** Bootstrap class with the **btn-success** class and to replace the *Back to List* link with the partial view **_BackToLinkButtonPartial**.

1. Open the **Create** view located in the **ProductItem** folder.
2. Find the **submit** button and replace **btn-default** with **btn-success**.
   <input type="submit" value="Create" class="btn btn-success" />
3. Locate the **@Html.ActionLink** and replace it with an **@Html.Partial** method call passing in **_BackToLinkButtonPartial** as its parameter.
   @Html.Partial("_BackToListButtonPartial")

The Index view

To be able to display the table listing with all **ProductItem** records, you need to change the **@model** directive to use the **ProductItemModel** class and add a **@using** statement to the **Memberships.Areas.Admin.Models** namespace.

Replace the *Create New* **@Html.ActionLink** with the partial view **_CreateNewButtonPartial**.

Use Bootstrap classes on the table to make it striped with the **table-striped** class, and the table header displayed in the success color (green) with the **success** class.

Use the **@Html.DisplayNameFor** extension method to display the property name for the model's **ProductTitle** and **ItemTitle** properties in the table header.

Use the **@Html.DisplayFor** extension method to display the values for the model's **ProductTitle** and **ItemTitle** properties on each row in the table.

Use the partial view **_TableButtonsPartial** you created earlier to display the three buttons for each row in the table. Pass in the **ProductId** and **ItemId** to the partial view for the corresponding record on each table row through an instance of the **SmallButtonModel** class.

Replace the *Edit*, *Details* and *Delete* **@Html.ActionLinks** with the partial view.

Add a new overloaded version of the **Convert** method which will convert a list of **ProductItem** instaces from an **IQueryable<ProductItem>**, sent in to the method through a parameter, to a **Task<List<ProductItemModel>>** which is returned from the method. The method also needs an **ApplicationDbContext** parameter to be able to fetch data from the database. Use the **IQueryable** collection to be able to use the **ToListAsync** method on the database table sent in to the method from the **ProductItemController**.

This is what the finished **Index** view will look like:

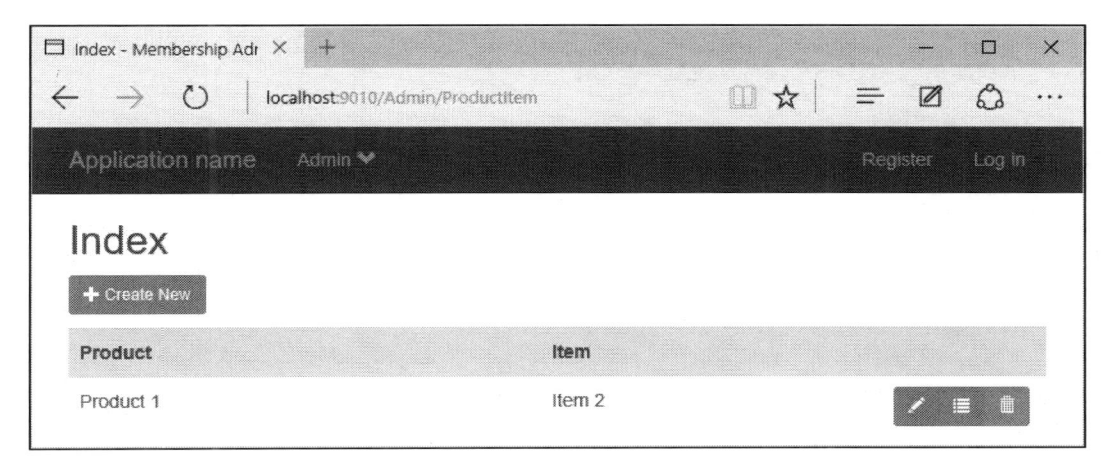

Modify the table
1. Open the **Index** view in the **Views-ProductItem** folder.
2. Change the **@model** directive to use an **IEnumerable<ProductItemModel>** and add a **@using** statement to the **Memberships.Areas.Admin.Models** namespace.
   ```
   @model
   IEnumerable<Memberships.Areas.Admin.Models.ProductItemModel>
   @using Memberships.Areas.Admin.Models
   ```
3. Style the table adding the **table-striped** Bootstrap class to the **<table>** element and the **success** class to the table header row **<tr>** element.
   ```
   <table class="table table-striped">
       <tr class="success">
   ```
4. Change the table headers to display the display name of the **ProductTitle** and **ItemTitle** properties and add an empty table header for the button column.
   ```
   <th>@Html.DisplayNameFor(model => model.ProductTitle)</th>
   <th>@Html.DisplayNameFor(model => model.ItemTitle)</th>
   <th></th>
   ```
5. Add the data in the loop using **@Html.DisplayFor** method calls for the **ProductTitle** and **ItemTitle** properties.
   ```
   <td>@Html.DisplayFor(modelItem => item.ProductTitle)</td>
   <td>@Html.DisplayFor(modelItem => item.ItemTitle)</td>
   ```
6. Open the **ProductItemModel** class and add the **DisplayName** attribute displaying "Product" and "Item" for the **ProductTitle** and **ItemTitle** properties.

```
[DisplayName("Product")]
public string ProductTitle { get; set; }
[DisplayName("Item")]
public string ItemTitle { get; set; }
```

Changing the links to buttons

1. Open the **Index** view and replace the **<td>** element containing the three **@Html.ActaionLink** method calls with a call to the **@Html.Partial** method passing in the name of the partial view **_TableButtonsPartial** and an instance of the **SmallButtonModel** class where its **ItemId** and **ProductId** properties are assigned values from the current loop item.
   ```
   @Html.Partial("_TableButtonsPartial", new SmallButtonModel {
       ItemId = item.ItemId, ProductId = item.ProductId })
   ```

2. Locate the **@Html.ActaionLink** for the *Create New* link and replace it with a call to the **@Html.Partial** method passing in the name of the **_CreateNewButtonPartial** partial view.
   ```
   @Html.Partial("_CreateNewButtonPartial")
   ```

The complete code for the **Index** view:

```
@model IEnumerable<Memberships.Areas.Admin.Models.ProductItemModel>
@using Memberships.Areas.Admin.Models

@{
    ViewBag.Title = "Index";
}

<h2>Index</h2>

<p>
    @Html.Partial("_CreateNewButtonPartial")
</p>
<table class="table table-striped">
    <tr class="success">
        <th>@Html.DisplayNameFor(model => model.ProductTitle)</th>
        <th>@Html.DisplayNameFor(model => model.ItemTitle)</th>
        <th></th>
    </tr>

    @foreach (var item in Model) {
        <tr>
```

```
            <td>@Html.DisplayFor(modelItem => item.ProductTitle)</td>
            <td>@Html.DisplayFor(modelItem => item.ItemTitle)</td>
            @Html.Partial("_TableButtonsPartial", new SmallButtonModel {
                ItemId = item.ItemId, ProductId = item.ProductId })
        </tr>
    }
</table>
```

Modify the Index action and create a Convert method

1. Open the **ConversionExtension** class located in the **Extensions** folder in the **Admin** area.
2. Add a new overloaded version of the **Convert** method which takes an **IQueryable<ProductItem>** called **productItems** and an instance of the **ApplicationDbContext** called **db** and return a **Task<List<ProductItemModel>>**.
   ```
   public static async Task<List<ProductItemModel>> Convert(this
   IQueryable<ProductItem> productItems, ApplicationDbContext db) { }
   ```
3. Return an empty list of **ProductItemModel** if there are no items in the **productItems** parameter.
4. Add a LINQ query based on the **ProductItem** table sent in through the **productItems** parameter and create instances of the **ProductItemModel** class. Use the **Item** and **Product** tables in the LINQ query to assign values to the **ItemTitle** and **ProductTitle** properties. Use the **ItemId** and **ProductId** values from the **ProductItem** table when fetching the titles. Also, assign values to the **ItemId** and **ProductId** properties from the current item in the LINQ query. Use the **ToListAsync** mehod to fetch the result asynchronously.
   ```
   var model = await (
       from pi in productItems
       select new ProductItemModel
       {
           ItemId = pi.ItemId,
           ProductId = pi.ProductId,
           ItemTitle = db.Items.FirstOrDefault(
               i => i.Id.Equals(pi.ItemId)).Title,
           ProductTitle = db.Products.FirstOrDefault(
               p => p.Id.Equals(pi.ProductId)).Title
       }).ToListAsync();
   ```
5. Return the **model** variable from the method.
   ```
   return model;
   ```

6. Open the **ProductItemController** class and locate the **Index** action method and change the **return** statement to call the **Convert** extension method on the **ProductItems** collection.
   ```
   return View(await db.ProductsItems.Convert(db));
   ```

The complete **Convert** method:

```
public static async Task<List<ProductItemModel>> Convert(
this IQueryable<ProductItem> productItems, ApplicationDbContext db)
{
   if (productItems.Count().Equals(0))
      return new List<ProductItemModel>();

   var model = await (
      from pi in productItems
      select new ProductItemModel
      {
         ItemId = pi.ItemId,
         ProductId = pi.ProductId,
         ItemTitle = db.Items.FirstOrDefault(
            i => i.Id.Equals(pi.ItemId)).Title,
         ProductTitle = db.Products.FirstOrDefault(
            p => p.Id.Equals(pi.ProductId)).Title
      }).ToListAsync();

   return model;
}
```

The complete **Index** action:

```
public async Task<ActionResult> Index()
{
   return View(await db.ProductItems.Convert(db));
}
```

The Edit View

The **Edit** view is very similar to the **Create** view you just created. The default **Edit** view doesn't allow any changes since it only contains two hidden fields for the **ProductId** and **ItemId**. You therefore have to alter the view to make it possible to select a product and an item, like in the **Create** view, to update the **ProductItem** table based on the selections the user make.

The image below shows the altered **Edit** view.

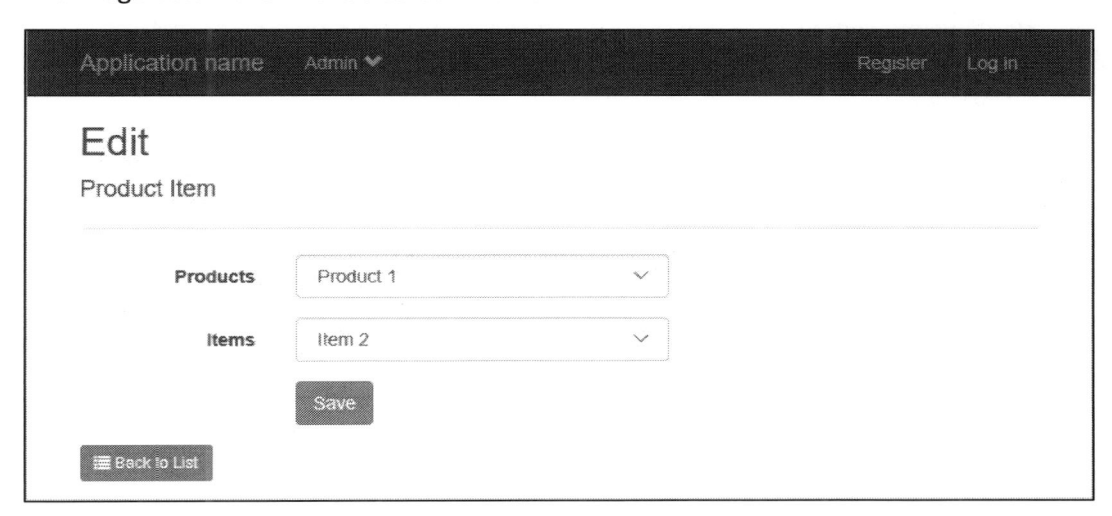

The Edit View - Display data (HttpGet)

You can start by copying the **@model** directive and the **@using** statement in the **Create** view located in the **ProductItem** folder and paste it into the **Edit** view located in the same folder. Then, copy the two **form-grooup <div>** elements from the **Create** view and paste it into the **Edit** view below the last **HiddenFor** method call.

Modify the two **HiddenFor** method calls storing the **ProductId** and **ItemId** in hidden form fields to instead store the property values as hidden form fields called **OldProductId** and **OldItemId** using **@Html.Hidden** method calls. You will need these values to do a look up in the database from the **ProductItem** controller's **HttpPost Edit** action method.

```
@Html.Hidden("OldProductId", Model.ProductId)
```

For the view to work properly, you need to modify its **Edit** controller action. The first thing you need to do is to add second **int?** (null-able **int**) parameter called **productId**. after the already existing **id** parameter.

Because you are changing the parameter list, you also have to change the first if-statement handling the *bad request* **return** to check if the **productId** parameter is **null**. If either of them are **null** then the if-block should be executed.

The existing **FindAsync** method call no longer works and needs to be replaced with a new look up in the **ProductItem** table. Create a new asynchronous method called **GetProductItem** at the end of the **ProfductItemContoller** class; use a LINQ query to find the record in the table matching the two ids you send in to the **Edit** action as parameters. You do this to check that the record actually exists before displaying the data in the view.

If the record exists in the **ProductItem** table, then call a new overloaded version of the **Convert** method which creates a new model using the **ProductItemModel** class and assigns the values to the id properties with data from the passed in **ProductItem** item. Also, assign items from the **Item** table to the **Items** property and the products from the **Product** table to the **Products** property. Use the **await** keyword with the **ToListAsync** method to call the database asynchronously.

When the **model** is complete, return it with the **View** method in the **Edit** view.

Modifying the Edit view
1. Open the **Create** view located in the in the **ProductItem** folder and copy the **@model** directive and the **@using** statement.
2. Open the **Edit** view located in the in the **ProductItem** folder and replace the existing **@model** directive with the copied code.
3. Hide the **ProductId** and **ItemId** as hidden form fields called **OldProductId** and **OldItemId** using **@Html.Hidden** method calls inside the **Html.BeginForm** code block. You can modify the exisiting **HiddenFor** method calls or delete them and write new **Hidden** method calls.
   ```
   @Html.Hidden("OldProductId", Model.ProductId)
   @Html.Hidden("OldItemId", Model.ItemId)
   ```
4. Open the **Create** view again and copy the two **form-group <div>** elements and their content.
5. Open the **Edit** view and paste in the copied code below the last **Hidden** method call.
6. Replace the **btn-default** Bootstrap class with **btn-success** for the **submit** button.
   ```
   <input type="submit" value="Save" class="btn btn-success" />
   ```
7. Replace the **ActionLink** method call with the partial view **_BackToListButtonPartial**.

```
        @Html.Partial("_BackToListButtonPartial")
```

The complete code for the **Edit** view:

```
@model Memberships.Areas.Admin.Models.ProductItemModel
@using Memberships.Extensions

@{
    ViewBag.Title = "Edit";
}

<h2>Edit</h2>

@using (Html.BeginForm())
{
    @Html.AntiForgeryToken()

    <div class="form-horizontal">
        <h4>ProductItem</h4>
        <hr />
        @Html.ValidationSummary(true, "", new { @class = "text-danger" })
        @Html.Hidden("OldProductId", Model.ProductId)
        @Html.Hidden("OldItemId", Model.ItemId)

        <div class="form-group">
            @Html.LabelFor(model => model.Products, htmlAttributes:
                new { @class = "control-label col-md-2" })
            <div class="col-md-10">
                @Html.DropDownListFor(
                    model => model.ProductId,
                    Model.Products.ToSelectListItem(Model.ProductId),
                    new { @class = "form-control" })
                @Html.ValidationMessageFor(model => model.ProductId, "",
                    new { @class = "text-danger" })
            </div>
        </div>

        <div class="form-group">
            @Html.LabelFor(model => model.Items, htmlAttributes:
                new { @class = "control-label col-md-2" })
            <div class="col-md-10">
                @Html.DropDownListFor(
                    model => model.ItemId,
                    Model.Items.ToSelectListItem(Model.ItemId),
```

```
                new { @class = "form-control" })
            @Html.ValidationMessageFor(model => model.ItemId, "",
                new { @class = "text-danger" })
        </div>
    </div>

    <div class="form-group">
        <div class="col-md-offset-2 col-md-10">
            <input type="submit" value="Save" class="btn btn-success" />
        </div>
    </div>
  </div>
}

<div>
    @Html.Partial("_BackToListButtonPartial")
</div>
```

Modifying the Edit controller action (HttpGet)

This action is called when the **Edit** view is displayed.

1. Open the **ProductItem** controller located in the **Controllers** folder.
2. Locate the **Edit** action and add a new parameter of type **int?** (null-able **int**) called **productId**. You need both ids to find the correct record in the **ProductItem** table.
   `public async Task<ActionResult> Edit(int? id, int? productId)`
3. Because you added the **productId** parameter, you have to check if it is **null** in the first if-statement (*bad request*). Neither paramter can be **null** when changing the **ProductItem**.
   `if (id == null || productId == null)`
4. Create a new asynchronous method called **GetProductItem** at the end of the **ProductItemController** class. The method should have two **int?** parameters called **itemId** and **productId** and return a **Task<ProductItem>**.
   `private async Task<ProductItem> GetProductItem(int? itemId, int? productId) { }`
5. Add a **try/catch**-block to the method where the **catch**-block return **null**. Add all the remaining code you write for this method in the **try**-block.
6. Parse the the two parameters with the **int.TryParse** method and store the **out** parameter value in variables called **itmId** and **prdId** of type **int**.

```
int itmId = 0, prdId = 0;
int.TryParse(itemId.ToString(), out itmId);
```

7. Create a variable called **productItem** which holds the result from a LINQ query that fetches the **ProductItem** matching the parameter values.
   ```
   var productItem = await db.ProductsItems.FirstOrDefaultAsync(pi =>
       pi.ProductId.Equals(prdId) && pi.ItemId.Equals(itmId));
   ```

8. Return the **productItem** variable from the method.

9. Replace the existing **FindAsync** method call with a call to the **GetProductItem** method passing in the two ids from the **Edit** action. You do this to check that the **ProductItem** actually exists before displaying the data in the view.
   ```
   ProductItem productItem = await GetProductItem(id, productId);
   ```

10. If the record exists in the **ProductItem** table, then create a model by calling a new overloaded version of the **Convert** method acting on a **ProductItem** instance which will be created in the **ConversionExtensions** class. The method should have two parameters, the first called **productItem** of type **ProductItem** which holds the instance that the method is acting on and an instance of the **ApplicationDbContext** class called **db**. The method should be asynchronous and return a **Task<ProductItemModel>**.
    ```
    public static async Task<ProductItemModel> Convert(this
    ProductItem productItem, ApplicationDbContext db) { }
    ```

11. Create a model using the **ProductItemModel** class in the current method. Assign the ids from the **productItem** parameter to their corresponding properties in the **model** instance and fill the two collections in the **model** by calling the **ToListAsync** method on the **Item** and **Product** tables. Use the **await** keyword with the **ToListAsync** method to call the database asynchronously.
    ```
    var model = new ProductItemModel
    {
        ItemId = productItem.ItemId,
        ProductId = productItem.ProductId,
        Items = await db.Items.ToListAsync(),
        Products = await db.Products.ToListAsync()
    };
    ```

12. When the **Convert** method call has finished, then return it with the **View** method.
    ```
    return View(model);
    ```

The complete altered **HttpGet Edit** action:

```
public async Task<ActionResult> Edit(int? itemId, int? productId)
{
   if (itemId == null || productId == null)
   {
      return new HttpStatusCodeResult(HttpStatusCode.BadRequest);
   }
   ProductItem productItem = await GetProductItem(itemId, productId);
   if (productItem == null)
   {
      return HttpNotFound();
   }
   return View(await productItem.Convert(db));
}
```

The complete code for the **GetProductItem** method:

```
private async Task<ProductItem> GetProductItem(int? itemId,
int? productId)
{
   try
   {
      int itmId = 0, prdId = 0;
      int.TryParse(itemId.ToString(), out itmId);
      int.TryParse(productId.ToString(), out prdId);

      var productItem = await db.ProductsItems.FirstOrDefaultAsync(pi =>
      pi.ProductId.Equals(prdId) && pi.ItemId.Equals(itmId));

      return productItem;
   }
   catch { return null; }
}
```

The complete code for the **Convert** method:

```
public static async Task<ProductItemModel> Convert(this ProductItem
productItem, ApplicationDbContext db)
{
   var model = new ProductItemModel
   {
      ItemId = productItem.ItemId,
      ProductId = productItem.ProductId,
```

```
        Items = await db.Items.ToListAsync(),
        Products = await db.Products.ToListAsync()
    };

    return model;
}
```

The Edit View - Update data (HttpPost)
To be able to save changes when the user clicks the **Edit** button, you have to make some changes to the **Edit** action decorated with the **[HttpPost]** attribute in the **ProductItem-Controller** class.

First, you need to add two **OldProductId** and **OldItemId** to the **Bind** statement in the parameter list. The **Bind** statement will now match the form field names stated in the view represented by the properties in the model passed in to the **Edit** action. This makes it impossible to maliciously add property values to the post. The added names represent the two form fields you added to the **Edit** view as hidden fields using **@Html. Hidden**.

Add an **async** extension method called **CanChange** in the **ConversionExtensions** class which takes two parameters; where the first is an instance of the **ProductItem** class called **productItem** and the second is an instance of the **ApplicationDbContext** class called **db**. The method should return **Task<bool>** which represents the result from checking if a record with the **OldItemId** and **OldProductId** exists in the **ProductItem** table, and that a record with the **ItemId** and **ProductId** doesn't exist in the **ProductItem** table.

Add an **async** extension method called **Change** in the **ConversionExtensions** class which takes two parameters where the first is an instance of the **ProductItem** class called **productItem** and the second is an instance of the **ApplicationDbContext** class called **db**. The method should be **void** and thus return **Task**. The purpose of the method is to remove the existing record and add a new record with the new values.

The first thing the method should do is to try to fetch the records from the **ProductItem** table using the **OldItemId**, **OldProductId**, **ItemId** and **ProductId** which are properties in the passed in **ProductItem** instance.

If a record exists with the **OldItemId** and **OldProductId** values, and no record exists with the **ItemId** and **ProductId** values, then create a new instance of the **ProductItem** class and assign the values from the **ItemId** and **ProductId** properties in the passed in **ProductItem** instance.

Add a reference to the **System.Transactions** asembly to get access to the **TransactionScope** class which makes it possible to use transactions with the database updates the **Change** method make.

Using an instance of the **TransactionScope** class with a **using**-block ensures that both the removal and adding of the two records complete successfully. If any of the database calls fails, both updates will roll back to their original state. Use the **TransactionScopeAsyncFlowOption.Enabled** setting for the **TransactionScope** instance to ensure that the transaction flows across threads.

```
using (var transaction = new TransactionScope(
    TransactionScopeAsyncFlowOption.Enabled))
```

Add a **try/catch**-block inside the **using**-block where the **catch**-block calls the **Dispose** method on the **transaction** variable ending the transaction.

Remove the old **ProductItem** record and add the new **ProductItem** record to the **ProductItem** database table and call the **db.SaveChangesAsync** method asynchronously to add the changes to the database. Then, commit the transaction to persist the changes to the database or roll them back if either the **Remove** or **Add** method fails, by calling the **Complete** method on the **transaction** variable.

Call the **CanChange** method on the **productItem** variable at the beginning of the **ModelState.Valid** if-block to make sure that the record can be changed. Store the result in a variable called **canChange**.

If the value in the **canChange** variable is **true**, then call the **Change** method on the **productItem** variable to persist the changes to the database.

Remove the following two lines of code:

```
db.Entry(productItem).State = EntityState.Modified;
await db.SaveChangesAsync();
```

Adding the CanChange method

The purpose of this method is to check that there is a **ProductItem** in the **ProductItem** database table with the **productId** and **ItemId** combination from the **OldProductId** and **OldItemId** values; this would be the **ProductItem** that is being changed (or removed rather). Then it checks that no **ProductItem** exists with the **productId** and **ItemId** combination from the **ProductId** and **ItemId** values; the new values selected in the view's dropdown controls. If the "old" **ProductItem** exists and the "new" **ProductItem** doesn't exist, then the method will return **true,** signalling that the **ProductItem** can be updated.

1. Open the **ConversionExtensions** class located in the **Extensions** folder.
2. Create an **async** extension method called **CanChange** which takes one instance of the **ProductItem** class called **productItem** (this is the instance the method acts on) and one instance of **ApplicationDbContext** called **db**. The method should return return **Task<bool>**.
   ```
   public static async Task<bool> CanChange(this ProductItem
   productItem, ApplicationDbContext db)
   {
   }
   ```
3. Use the **CountAsync** method on the **ProductItem** table to count the number of times the combination of **OldProductId** and **OldItemId** exist in the table and store the result in a variable called **oldPI**.
   ```
   var oldPI = await db.ProductsItems.CountAsync(pi =>
       pi.ProductId.Equals(productItem.OldProductId) &&
       pi.ItemId.Equals(productItem.OldItemId));
   ```
4. Use the **CountAsync** method on the **ProductItem** table to count the number of times the combination of **ProductId** and **ItemId** exist in the table and store the result in a variable called **newPI**.
5. Return **true** if the **oldPi** equals 1 and the **newPI** variable equals 0 which mean that the original **ProductItem** exist but the new don't.
   ```
   return oldPI.Equals(1) && newPI.Equals(0);
   ```

The complete code for the **CanChange** method:

```
public static async Task<bool> CanChange(this ProductItem productItem,
ApplicationDbContext db)
{
    var oldPI = await db.ProductsItems.CountAsync(pi =>
```

```
            pi.ProductId.Equals(productItem.OldProductId) &&
            pi.ItemId.Equals(productItem.OldItemId));

    var newPI = await db.ProductsItems.CountAsync(pi =>
            pi.ProductId.Equals(productItem.ProductId) &&
            pi.ItemId.Equals(productItem.ItemId));

    return oldPI.Equals(1) && newPI.Equals(0);
}
```

Adding the Change method
1. Open the **ConversionExtensions** class located in the **Extensions** folder.
2. Create an **async** extension method called **Change** which takes one instance of the **ProductItem** class called **productItem** (this is the instance the method acts on) and one instance of **ApplicationDbContext** called **db**, the method shouldn't return any value which is represented by returning **Task**.
   ```
   public static async Task Change(this ProductItem productItem,
   ApplicationDbContext db)
   {
   }
   ```
3. Use the **FirstOrDefaultAsync** method to fetch the original (old) **ProductItem** from the **ProductItem** table and store it in a variable called **oldProducItem**.
   ```
   var oldProductItem = await db.ProductsItems.FirstOrDefaultAsync(
       pi => pi.ProductId.Equals(productItem.OldProductId) &&
           pi.ItemId.Equals(productItem.OldItemId));
   ```
4. Use the **FirstOrDefaultAsync** method to try to fetch a **ProductItem** from the **ProductItem** table with the values from the **ProductId** and **ItemId** properties and store the result in a variable called **newProducItem**.
5. Add an if-block checking that the **oldProductItem** variable is not **null** and that the **newProductItem** is **null**. This means that the new values can be stored because no record exists with the new values in the database.
6. Create a new **ProductItem** instance in the **newProductId** variable inside the if-block and assign the **ItemId** and **ProductId** from the **productItem** parameter to the **ItemId** and **ProductId** properties of the **newProductItem** instance.
7. To be able to use transactions with the **TransactionScope** class, you will have to add a reference to the **System.Transactions** assembly in the **References** folder.

8. Add a **using**-block with a **TransactionScope** instance variable called **transaction** using the **TransactionScopeAsyncFlowOption** set to **Enabled** to allow the transaction to flow between threads.
   ```
   Using (var transaction = new TransactionScope(
   TransactionScopeAsyncFlowOption.Enabled)){ }
   ```
9. Add a **try/catch**-block inside the **using**-block where the **catch**-block calls the **Dispose** method on the **transaction** variable to end the transaction if something has gone wrong.
10. Call the **Remove** method on the **ProductItems** collection in the **try**-block to remove the original record from the **ProductItem** table.
    ```
    Db.ProductsItems.Remove(oldProductItem);
    ```
11. Call the **Add** method on the **ProductItems** collection in the **try**-block to add the new record to the **ProductItem** table.
    ```
    Db.ProductsItems.Add(newProductItem);
    ```
12. Call the **SaveChangesAsync** method on the **db** instance in the **try**-block to save the changes to the database.
    ```
    Await db.SaveChangesAsync();
    ```
13. Because a transaction is handling the two database changes, it has to be completed for the data to be persisted in the table. Add a call to the **Complete** method on the **transaction** variable in the **try**-block to persist the changes.
    ```
    transaction.Complete();
    ```

The complete code for the **Change** method:

```
public static async Task Change(this ProductItem productItem,
ApplicationDbContext db)
{
    var oldProductItem = await db.ProductsItems.FirstOrDefaultAsync(pi =>
        pi.ProductId.Equals(productItem.OldProductId) &&
        pi.ItemId.Equals(productItem.OldItemId));

    var newProductItem = await db.ProductsItems.FirstOrDefaultAsync(pi =>
        pi.ProductId.Equals(productItem.ProductId) &&
        pi.ItemId.Equals(productItem.ItemId));
```

```
if (oldProductItem != null && newProductItem == null)
    {
        newProductItem = new ProductItem
        {
            ItemId = productItem.ItemId,
            ProductId = productItem.ProductId
        };

        // TransactionScope requires a reference to System.Transactions
        using (var transaction = new TransactionScope(
        TransactionScopeAsyncFlowOption.Enabled))
        {
            try
            {
                // Remove the exisiting ProductItem
                db.ProductsItems.Remove(oldProductItem);

                // Add the new (changed) ProductItem
                db.ProductsItems.Add(newProductItem);

                await db.SaveChangesAsync();

                transaction.Complete();
            }
            catch
            {
                transaction.Dispose();
            }
        }
    }
}
```

Modifying the Edit controller action (HttpPost)
1. Open the **ProductItem** controller located in the **Controllers** folder.
2. Locate the **Edit** action decorated with the **[HttpPost]** attribute and add the two hidden form fields called **OldProductId** and **OldItemId** you added to the **Edit** view as hidden fields using **@Html.Hidden**.
   ```
   public async Task<ActionResult> Edit([Bind(Include =
   "ProductId,ItemId,OldProductId,OldItemId")] ProductItem
   productItem)
   ```

3. Call the **CanChange** method from within the **ModelState.Valid** if-block and store the result in a variable called **canChange**.
   `var canChange = await productItem.CanChange(db);`
4. Add an if-block checking if the **canChange** variable value is **true**.
5. Call the **Change** method on the **productItem** parameter asynchronously inside the if-block.
6. Remove the following two lines of code:
   `db.Entry(productItem).State = EntityState.Modified;`
   `await db.SaveChangesAsync();`
7. Run the application and edit an existing **ProductItem**. Add one if none exist and then edit it.

The complete code for the **Edit** action (**HttpPost**) looks like this:

```
[HttpPost]
[ValidateAntiForgeryToken]
public async Task<ActionResult> Edit([Bind(Include =
"ProductId,ItemId,OldProductId,OldItemId")] ProductItem productItem)
{
    if (ModelState.IsValid)
    {
        // Check if the ProductItem can be changed
        var canChange = await productItem.CanChange(db);

        if (canChange)
        {
            // Change the ProductItem
            await productItem.Change(db);
        }

        return RedirectToAction("Index");
    }
    return View(productItem);
}
```

The Details View

To be able to display the details for a **ProductItem** record with user friendly data such as the item and product titles, the **Details** view and **Details** action in the **ProductItem-Controller** have to be drastically changed.

The image below shows the finished **Details** view.

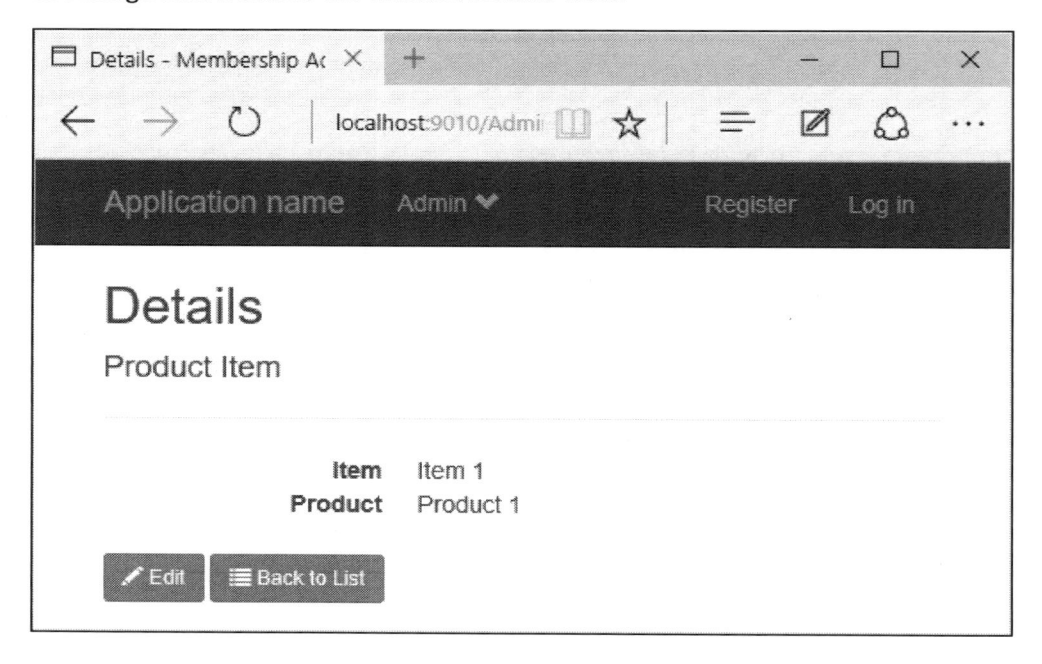

The Details controller action

First you have to add a new **int?** parameter called **productId** to the **Details** action method. Then you have to add a **null** check for that parameter in the first (BadRequest) if-statement; if either of the **id** or **productId** are **null** then the if-block should be executed.

Next, you need to change how the **ProductItem** is fetched from the database which can be done by calling the **GetProductItem** method you created earlier.

The **ProductItem** instance can then be converted to a **ProductListModel** using an altered version of the **Convert** method you created earlier. Store the instance in a variable called **model**.

When the **model** is complete, return it with the **View** method.

1. Open the **ProductItemController** located in the **Controllers** folder in the **Admin** area.

2. Change the name of the **id** parameter to **itemId** for all occurences in this action method.
3. Add a new **int?** parameter called **productId** to the **Details** action method.
   ```
   public async Task<ActionResult> Details(int? itemId, int? productId) { ... }
   ```
4. Change the first (BadRequest) if-statement to check if the **productId** is **null**.
   ```
   if (itemId == null || productId == null)
   ```
5. Change how the **ProductItem** instance is fetched from the database by calling the asynchronous **GetProductItem** method you created earlier.
   ```
   ProductItem productItem = await GetProductItem(itemId, productId);
   ```
6. Create a new model of the **ProductItemModel** class by calling a modified version of the asynchronous **Convert** extension method. In the next section, you will alter this method; so don't be alarmed when an error occurs at this point, it will be fixed automatically when the **Convert** method has been altered.
   ```
   var model = await productItem.Convert(db, false);
   ```
7. Return the model with the **View**.
   ```
   return View(model);
   ```

The altered **Details** action method:

```
public async Task<ActionResult> Details(int? itemId, int? productId)
{
   if (itemId == null || productId == null)
   {
      return new HttpStatusCodeResult(HttpStatusCode.BadRequest);
   }
   ProductItem productItem = await GetProductItem(itemId, productId);
   if (productItem == null)
   {
      return HttpNotFound();
   }

   return View(await productItem.Convert(db, false));
}
```

Altering the Convert method

1. Open the **ConversionExtensions** class located in the **Extensions** folder.

2. Locate the **Convert** method which takes a single instance of the **ProductItem** class and return **Task<ProductItemModel>**.
3. Add a **bool** parameter called **addListData** with a default value of **true**. This parameter will determine if the model being created should contain the items and products from the **Item** and **Product** tables.

   ```
   public static async Task<ProductItemModel> Convert(this
   ProductItem productItem, ApplicationDbContext db, bool addListData
   = true)
   ```
4. Add item and product titles for the **ItemTitle** and **ProductTitle** properties in the model by fetching the matching item and product from the **Item** and **Product** tables and use their **Title** values. You can use the **await** keyword with the **FirstOrDefaultAsync** method to fetch the titles asynchronously.

   ```
   ItemTitle = (await db.Items.FirstOrDefaultAsync(i =>
   i.Id.Equals(productItem.ItemId))).Title,
   ```

The altered **Convert** method:

```
public static async Task<ProductItemModel> Convert(this ProductItem
productItem, ApplicationDbContext db, bool addListData = true)
{
    var model = new ProductItemModel
    {
        ItemId = productItem.ItemId,
        ProductId = productItem.ProductId,
        Items = addListData ? await db.Items.ToListAsync() : null,
        Products = addListData ? await db.Products.ToListAsync() : null,
        ItemTitle = (await db.Items.FirstOrDefaultAsync(i =>
            i.Id.Equals(productItem.ItemId))).Title,
        ProductTitle = (await db.Products.FirstOrDefaultAsync(p =>
            p.Id.Equals(productItem.ProductId))).Title
    };

    return model;
}
```

Creating the _EditButtonDetailsPartial partial view

Because the **Edit** action method in the **ProductItemController** requires two parameters to display the product item, you have to create a new **Edit** button that has the item id and product id in its URL.

To make this partial view more dynamic, you will create a new model called **EditButton-Model** which will have three id properties called **ItemId**, **ProductId** and **SubscriptionId**. It will also have a property called **Link** which returns a concatenated string with the id properties that have a value greater than 0. This string will then be used as part of a URL for the **Edit** button.

The easiest way to create the partial view is to copy the existing **_EditButtonPartial** partial view lodated in the **Shared** views folder and then change the model from **int?** to **EditButtonModel** and use the **Link** property in conjunction with the **@Url.Action** method.

1. Copy the **_EditButtonPartial** partial view located in the **Shared** views folder and paste the copy into the **Shared** views folder. Rename the copy **_EditButtonDetailsPartial**.
2. Change the **@model** directive to use the **EditButtonModel** class. Don't be alarmed that the model shows an error, the error will disappear when the model class has been created.
   `@model Memberships.Areas.Admin.Models.EditButtonModel`
3. Replace the **@Url.Action** method call with the one described below. Note that the **Link** property is outside the parenthesis.
   `href="@Url.Action("Edit")@Model.Link"`

The modified **_EditButtonDetailsPartial** view:

```
@model Memberships.Areas.Admin.Models.EditButtonModel

<a type="button" class="btn btn-primary btn-sm"
    href="@Url.Action("Edit")@Model.Link">
    <span class="glyphicon glyphicon-pencil" aria-hidden="true"></span>
    <span>Edit</span>
</a>
```

Creating the EditButonModel class

The purpose of this class is to store values in any of its three id properties (**ItemId**, **ProductId** and **SubscriptionId**) and a URL parameter list will be generated in the fourth **Link** property. This parameter list is then concatenated to the base URL with a controller and action.

1. Create a new class called **EditButtonModel** in the **Models** folder in the **Admin** area.
2. Add three **int** properties called **ItemId**, **ProductId** and **SubscriptionId**.
3. Add a **string** property which only has a **get**-block. Build a URL parameter list in the get-block using only the properties whare the value is greater than 0. You can use a **StringBuilder** instance to assemble the parameter list. A URL parameterlist begins with a question mark (?) and each parameter is separated by an anpersand (&).
    ```
    var s = new StringBuilder("?");
    if (ItemId > 0) s.Append(String.Format("{0}={1}&", "itemId", ItemId));
    ```
4. Return the resulting string from the property. Note that the last character is removed since it is an ampersand that shouldn't be part of the paraemter list.
    ```
    return s.ToString().Substring(0, s.Length - 1);
    ```

The complete **EditButtonModel** class:

```
public class EditButtonModel
{
    public int ItemId { get; set; }
    public int ProductId { get; set; }
    public int SubscriptionId { get; set; }
    public string Link
    {
        get
        {
            var s = new StringBuilder("?");
            if (ItemId > 0) s.Append(String.Format("{0}={1}&",
                "itemId", ItemId));
            if (ProductId > 0) s.Append(String.Format("{0}={1}&",
                "productId", ProductId));
            if (SubscriptionId > 0) s.Append(String.Format("{0}={1}&",
                "subscriptionId", SubscriptionId));

            return s.ToString().Substring(0, s.Length - 1);
        }
    }
}
```

Modifying the Details view

To be able to display the details for a **ProductItem** record with user friendly data such as the Item and product titles, the **Details** view has to be changed.

The first change you have to make in the **Details** view is to change the **@model** directive to use the **ProductItemModel** class.

Next, add a space between the words in the **<h4>** heading (*Product Item*) then list the data for the **ItemTitle** and **ProductTitle** properties in the model using **<dt>** and **<dd>** elements. You can copy a pair of **<dt>** and **<dd>** elements from the **Details** view in the **Product** folder and alter them to display the values in the **ItemTitle** and **ProductTitle** properties of the model.

Replace the incomplete **Edit** link with the partial view **_EditButtonDetailsPartial** which you will create in an upcoming section.

Replace the *Back to List* link with the with the partial view **_BackToListButtonPartial**.

1. Change the **@model** directive to use the **ProductItemModel** class.
   ```
   @model Memberships.Areas.Admin.Models.ProductItemModel
   ```
2. Change the **<h4>** heading to:
   ```
   <h4>Product Item</h4>
   ```
3. Add name-value pairs to the **<dl>** element using **<dt>** and **<dd>** elements. Add key-value pairs for the **ItemTitle** and **ProductTitle** properties in the model.
   ```
   <dl class="dl-horizontal">
       <dt>@Html.DisplayNameFor(model => model.ItemTitle)</dt>
       <dd>@Html.DisplayFor(model => model.ItemTitle)</dd>

       <dt>@Html.DisplayNameFor(model => model.ProductTitle)</dt>
       <dd>@Html.DisplayFor(model => model.ProductTitle)</dd>
   </dl>
   ```
4. Replace the incomplete **Edit** link with the partial view **_EditButtonDetailsPartial**. Send in an instance of the **EditButtonModel** class with the appropriate properties assigned from values in the **Model** properties.
   ```
   @Html.Partial("_EditButtonDetailsPartial", new EditButtonModel {
   ItemId = Model.ItemId, ProductId = Model.ProductId }))
   ```

5. Replace the *Back to List* link with the with the partial view **_BackToListButtonPartial**.

   `@Html.Partial("_BackToListButtonPartial")`

6. Run the application and cllick the **Details** button to view the product item's details.

7. Click the **Edit** button in the **Details** view to make sure that the **Edit** view is displayed for the current product item.

The modified **Details** view:

```
@model Memberships.Areas.Admin.Models.ProductItemModel

@{
    ViewBag.Title = "Details";
}

<h2>Details</h2>

<div>
    <h4>Product Item</h4>
    <hr />
    <dl class="dl-horizontal">
        <dt>@Html.DisplayNameFor(model => model.ItemTitle)</dt>
        <dd>@Html.DisplayFor(model => model.ItemTitle)</dd>
        <dt>@Html.DisplayNameFor(model => model.ProductTitle)</dt>
        <dd>@Html.DisplayFor(model => model.ProductTitle)</dd>
    </dl>
</div>
<p>
    @Html.Partial("_EditButtonDetailsPartial", new EditButtonModel {
        ItemId = Model.ItemId, ProductId = Model.ProductId }))
    @Html.Partial("_BackToListButtonPartial")
</p>
```

The Delete view

The **Delete** view is very similar to the **Details** view in that it displays the same information about the current product and item.

The first thing you need to do is to change the **@model** directive to use the **ProductItemModel** class.

Copy the **<h4>**, **<hr/>** , **<dl>**, **<dt>** and **<dd>** elements in the **Details** view and replace the **<h4>**, **<hr/>** and **<dl>** elements in the **Delete** view with the copied code.

Change the **submit** button by adding the two **btn-danger** (red) and **btn-sm** (small button) Bootstrap classes.

Replace the *Back to List* **@Html.ActionLink** with a call to the **@Html.Partial** extension method passing in the **_BackToListButtonPartial** view.

Open the **ProductItem** controller and copy the **Details** action and replace the **Delete** action with the copied code and change the method name to **Delete**.

Alter the **DeleteConfirmed** action method to take another **int** parameter called **productId**.

Replace the current way of fetching the **ProcuctItem** instance with a call to the asynchronous **GetProductItem** method you created earlier.

This is what the **Delete** view look like after it has been modified:

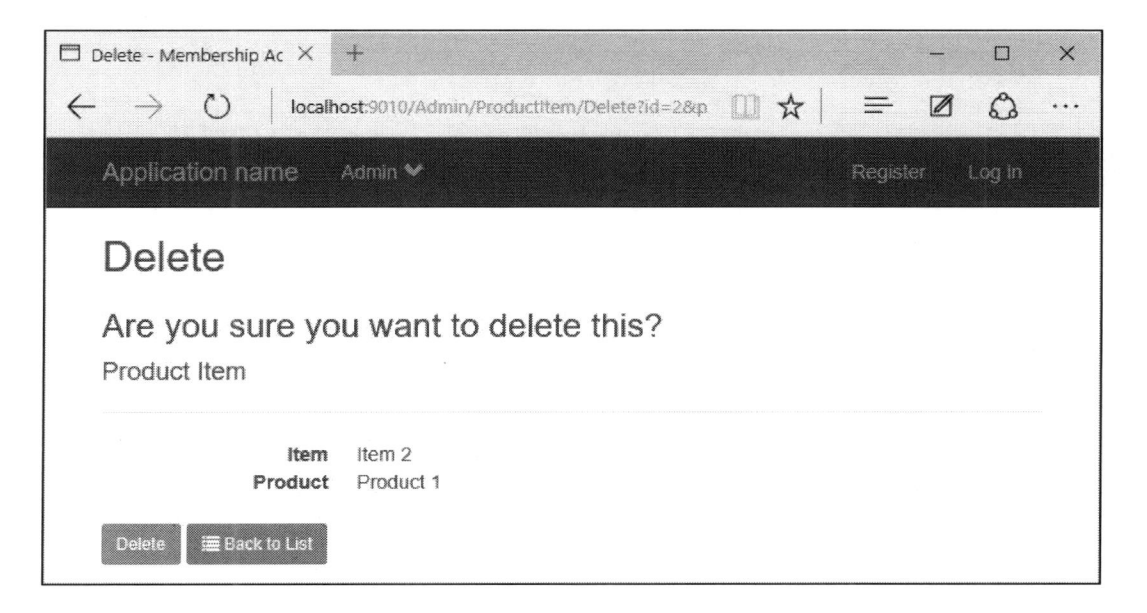

Modifying the view

1. Open the **Details** view in the **ProcuctItem** folder and copy the **@model** directive at the top of the view.
   `@model` `Memberships.Areas.Admin.Models.ProductItemModel`

2. Open the **Delete** view in the **ProcuctItem** folder and replace the existing **@model** directive with the copied code.

3. Open the **Details** view and copy the **<h4>**, **<hr/>** and **<dl>** elements and their content.
   ```
   <h4>Product Item</h4>
   <hr />
   <dl class="dl-horizontal">
       <dt>@Html.DisplayNameFor(model => model.ItemTitle)</dt>
       <dd>@Html.DisplayFor(model => model.ItemTitle)</dd>

       <dt>@Html.DisplayNameFor(model => model.ProductTitle)</dt>
       <dd>@Html.DisplayFor(model => model.ProductTitle)</dd>
   </dd>
   ```

4. Open the **Delete** view and replace the same elements.

5. Add the **btn-danger** (red) and **btn-sm** (small button) Bootstrap classes to the **submit** button.
   ```
   <input type="submit" value="Delete" class="btn btn-danger btn-sm" />
   ```

6. Open the **Details** view and copy the **@Html.Partial** extension method for the **_BackToListButtonPartial** view.
   `@Html.Partial("_BackToListButtonPartial")`

7. Replace the *Back to List* **@Html.ActionLink** with the copied code.

The complete code for the **Delete** view:

```
@model Memberships.Areas.Admin.Models.ProductItemModel

@{
    ViewBag.Title = "Delete";
}

<h2>Delete</h2>

<h3>Are you sure you want to delete this?</h3>
```

```
<div>
    <h4>Product Item</h4>
    <hr />
    <dl class="dl-horizontal">
        <dt>@Html.DisplayNameFor(model => model.ItemTitle)</dt>
        <dd>@Html.DisplayFor(model => model.ItemTitle)</dd>
        <dt>@Html.DisplayNameFor(model => model.ProductTitle)</dt>
        <dd>@Html.DisplayFor(model => model.ProductTitle)</dd>
    </dl>

    @using (Html.BeginForm()) {
        @Html.AntiForgeryToken()
        <div class="form-actions no-color">
            <input type="submit" value="Delete"
                class="btn btn-sm btn-danger" />
            @Html.Partial("_BackToListButtonPartial")
        </div>
    }
</div>
```

Modifying the Delete controller action (HttpGet)

1. Open the **ProcuctItemController** class in the **Controllers** folder.
2. Copy the **Details** action method.
3. Find the **Delete** action method and replace it with the copied code.
4. Change the name of the action method to **Delete**.

Here is the complete **Delete** action code:

```
public async Task<ActionResult> Delete(int? itemId, int? productId)
{
    if (itemId == null || productId == null)
    {
        return new HttpStatusCodeResult(HttpStatusCode.BadRequest);
    }

    ProductItem productItem = await GetProductItem(itemId, productId);
    if (productItem == null) {
        return HttpNotFound();
    }

    var model = await productItem.Convert(db, false);
    return View(model);
}
```

Modifying the DeleteConfirmed controller action (HttpPost)
1. Open the **ProcuctItemController** class in the **Controllers** folder.
2. Locate the **DeleteConfirmed** action method.
3. Change the name of the **id** parameter to **itemId** and all occurrences in the action method.
4. Add another **int** parameter called **productId**.
   `public async Task<ActionResult> DeleteConfirmed(int itemId, int productId)`
5. Replace the call to the **FindAsync** method with a call to the **GetProductItem** method passing in the two parameters to it.
   `ProductItem productItem = await GetProductItem(itemId, productId);`

Here is the complete **DeleteConfirmed** action code:

```
[HttpPost, ActionName("Delete")]
[ValidateAntiForgeryToken]
public async Task<ActionResult> DeleteConfirmed(int itemId, int productId)
{
    ProductItem productItem = await GetProductItem(itemId, productId);
    db.ProductsItems.Remove(productItem);
    await db.SaveChangesAsync();
    return RedirectToAction("Index");
}
```

Adding UI for the SubscriptionProduct Table

The **SubscriptionProduct** table is the connection between the **Subscription** and **Product** tables. One subscription can have multiple products and a product can belong to more than one subscription.

Since the views are working with data from the **SubscriptionProduct** table, you will have to create a model class called **SubscriptionProductModel** which is almost identical to the **ProductItemModel** class. You can copy the **ProductItemModel** class and replace all the ocurrances of the word *Item* with the word *Subscription*.

The fastest way to implement the controller and views for this table is to create a controller without views and then copy the views from the **ProductDetails** folder and modify them to work with the **SubscriptionProductController**.

Even though the **SubscriptionProduct** table only contains two values, it is one of the more complex tables to create a controller and views for; the reason being that the values are stored as integer values in the table. But you want to display the descriptive titles in dropdowns instead of as integers in textboxes, creating a better user experience and minimizing the risk for errors.

When you added the views and controller for the **ProductItem** table, you created four extension methods called **CanChange**, **Change** and **Convert** (which is overloaded). The same methods acting on the **SubscriptionProduct** table must be created; you can copy the exisitng methods and have them fetch data from the Subscription and **Product** tables. You also have to change the **ItemId**, **ItemTitle** and **Items** property names to **SubscriptionId**, **SubscriptionTitle** and **Subscriptions**.

The last thing you need to do is to copy and modify the **Index**, **Edit**, **Create**, **Delete** and **Details** action methods from the **ProductItemController** and replace the already existing actions in the **SubscriptionProductController**. Then modify the action methods to work with the **SubscriptionProductModel**.

Generating the SubscriptionProduct Controller and its views

To create a controller without views, you have to uncheck the **Generate views** checkbox in the *Add Controller* dialog. Then copy the views from the **Views-ProductDetails** folder and paste them into the **Views-SubscriptionProduct** folder and modify them to work with the **SubscriptionProduct** controller.

The image below shows the settings needed to create the **SubscriptionProduct** controller.

1. Right-click on the **Controllers** folder in the **Admin** area.
2. Select **Add-Controller** in the context menu.
3. Select the **SubscriptionProduct** entity model in the **Model class** dropdown.
4. Make sure that the **Genereate views** checkbox is *unchecked*.
5. Change the name to its singular form and click the **Add** button.

6. Open the **Views-ProductItem** folder, select all the views and copy them.
7. Right-click on the **Views-SubscriptionProduct** folder and select **Paste** in the context menu.

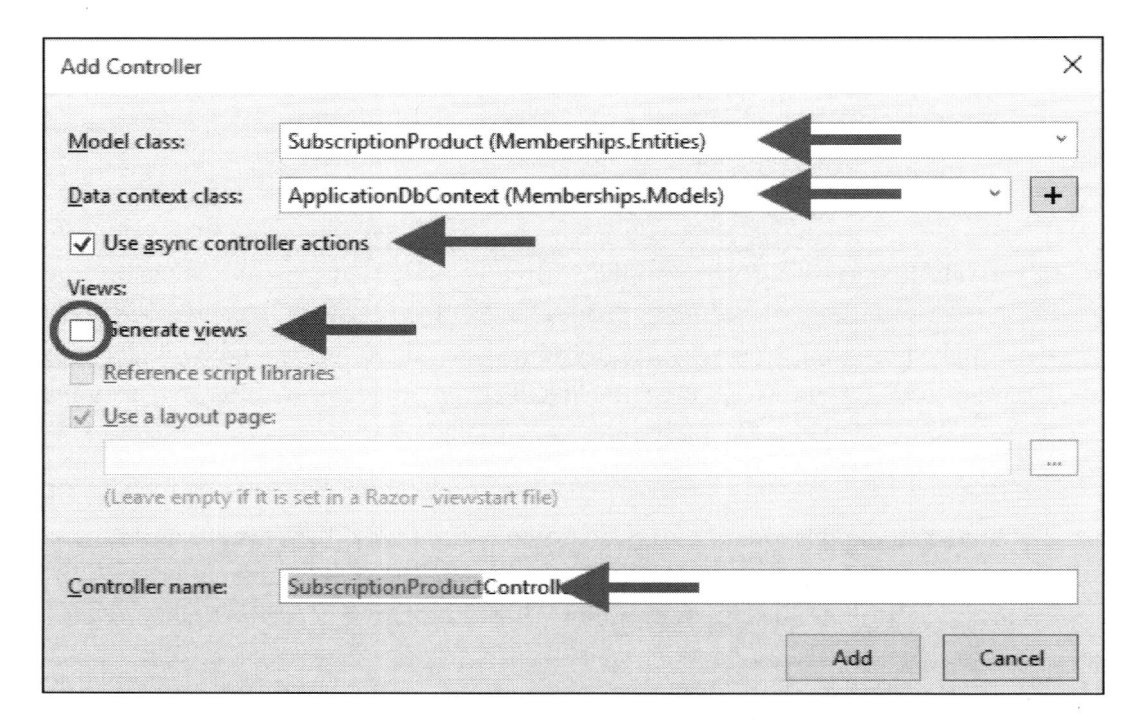

Create the SubscriptionProductModel class

This is the model class used to send data to the views, it is very similar to the **ProductItemModel** class. The fastest way to create the **SubscriptionProductModel** is to copy the **ProductItemModel** and alter its content. The properties you need to change are those containing *Item* in the name, replace the word *Item* with *Subscription*.

1. Open the **Models** folder in the **Admin** area.
2. Right-click on the **ProductItemModel** class and select **Copy** in the context menu.
3. Right-click on the **Models** folder and select **Paste** in the context menu.
4. Right-click on the copied class and select **Rename** in the context menu.
5. Name it **SubscriptionProductModel**.
6. Open the **SubscriptionProductModel** class.
7. Change the class name to **SubscriptionProductModel**.

8. Replace all occurences of the word *Item* in the class with the word *Subscription*.
9. Add the **DisplayName** attribute to properties where applicable to change the label text displayed in the view for the controls.

The complete code for the **SubscriptionProductModel** class:

```
public class SubscriptionProductModel
{
    [DisplayName("Product Id")]
    public int ProductId { get; set; }
    [DisplayName("Subscription Id")]
    public int SubscriptionId { get; set; }
    [DisplayName("Product Title")]
    public string ProductTitle { get; set; }
    [DisplayName("Subscription Title")]
    public string SubscriptionTitle { get; set; }
    public ICollection<Product> Products { get; set; }
    public ICollection<Subscription> Subscriptions { get; set; }
}
```

Copy and alter the Convert method which return a list

This asynchronous method returns a list of records from the **SubscriptionProduct** table matching the values passed in through its **productId** and **subscriptionId** parameters.

1. Open the **ConversionExtensions** class and copy the **Convert** method that return **Task<List<ProductItemModel>>** and paste it in at the end of the class. Change the return type to **Task<List<SubscriptionProductModel>>** and its first parameter to **IQueryable<SubscriptionProduct> subscriptionProduct**.

    ```
    public static async Task<List<SubscriptionProductModel>> Convert(
    this IQueryable<SubscriptionProduct> subscriptionProduct,
    ApplicationDbContext db)
    ```

2. Return an empty list of **SubscriptionProduct** to avoid returning **null** if the **subscriptionProduct** parameter is empty.
3. Change the LINQ query to use the **subscriptionProduct** parameter and have it select new instances of the **SubscriptionProductModel** class. Replace **ItemId** with **SubscriptionId**, **Items** with **Subscriptions** and **ItemTitle** with **SubscriptionTitle**.

    ```
    var model = await (
        from pi in subscriptionProduct
    ```

```
            select new SubscriptionProductModel
            {
                ...
            }).ToListAsync();
```

The complete code for the **Convert** method:

```
public static async Task<List<SubscriptionProductModel>> Convert(
this IQueryable<SubscriptionProduct> subscriptionProduct,
ApplicationDbContext db)
{
    if (subscriptionProducts.Count().Equals(0))
        return new List<SubscriptionProductModel>();

    var model = await (
        from pi in subscriptionProduct
        select new SubscriptionProductModel
        {
            SubscriptionId = pi.SubscriptionId,
            ProductId = pi.ProductId,
            SubscriptionTitle = db.Subscriptions.FirstOrDefault(
                i => i.Id.Equals(pi.SubscriptionId)).Title,
            ProductTitle = db.Products.FirstOrDefault(
                p => p.Id.Equals(pi.ProductId)).Title
        }).ToListAsync();

    return model;
}
```

Copy and alter the Convert method which return a single item

This asynchronous method returns a single record from the **SubscriptionProduct** table matching the values passed in through its **productId** and **subscriptionId** parameters.

1. Open the **ConversionExtensions** class and copy the **Convert** method that return **Task< ProductItemModel>** and paste it in at the end of the class. Change the return type to **Task<SubscriptionProductModel>** and its first parameter to **SubscriptionProduct subscriptionProduct**.

    ```
    public static async Task<SubscriptionProductModel> Convert(
    this SubscriptionProduct subscriptionProduct,
    ApplicationDbContext db, bool addListData = true)
    ```

2. Change the **model** variable to create a new instance of the **SubscriptionProductModel** class. Replace **ItemId** with **SubscriptionId**, **Items** with **Subscriptions** and **ItemTitle** with **SubscriptionTitle**.

```
var model = new SubscriptionProductModel
{
    ...
}).ToListAsync();
```

The complete code for the **Convert** method:

```
public static async Task<SubscriptionProductModel> Convert(
this SubscriptionProduct subscriptionProduct,
ApplicationDbContext db, bool addListData = true)
{
    var model = new SubscriptionProductModel
    {
        SubscriptionId = subscriptionProduct.SubscriptionId,
        ProductId = subscriptionProduct.ProductId,

        Subscriptions = addListData ?
            await db.Subscriptions.ToListAsync() : null,

        Products = addListData ? await db.Products.ToListAsync() : null,

        SubscriptionTitle = (await db.Subscriptions.FirstOrDefaultAsync(
            i => i.Id.Equals(subscriptionProduct.SubscriptionId))).Title,

        ProductTitle = (await db.Products.FirstOrDefaultAsync(p =>
            p.Id.Equals(subscriptionProduct.ProductId))).Title
    };

    return model;
}
```

Copy and alter the CanChange method

This asynchronous method returns **true** if there is a record with the **OldProductId** and **OldSubscriptionId** values in the **SubscriptionProduct** table and no record exists matching the values in the **ProductId** and **SubscriptionId** properties.

1. Open the **ConversionExtensions** class and copy the **CanChange** method and paste it in at the end of the class. Change its first parameter to **SubscriptionProduct subscriptionProduct**.
   ```
   public static async Task<bool> CanChange(this SubscriptionProduct subscriptionProduct, ApplicationDbContext db)
   ```
2. Add a LINQ query which counts the records matching the **OldProductId** and **OldSubscriptionId** values in a variable called **oldPI**.
   ```
   var oldPI = await db.SubscriptionProducts.CountAsync(pi =>
       pi.ProductId.Equals(subscriptionProduct.OldProductId) &&
       pi.SubscriptionId.Equals(subscriptionProduct.OldSubscriptionId));
   ```
3. Add a LINQ query which counts the records matching the **ProductId** and **SubscriptionId** values in a variable called **newPI**.
4. If the **oldPI** equals 1, a record with the original values exists; and if the **newPI** equals 0, no record for the new values from the dropdowns exists. Return **true** if **oldPI** equals 1 and **newPI** equals 0.
   ```
   return oldPI.Equals(1) && newPI.Equals(0);
   ```

The complete code for the **CanChange** method:

```
public static async Task<bool> CanChange(
this SubscriptionProduct subscriptionProduct, ApplicationDbContext db)
{
    var oldPI = await db.SubscriptionProducts.CountAsync(pi =>
        pi.ProductId.Equals(subscriptionProduct.OldProductId) &&
        pi.SubscriptionId.Equals(
            subscriptionProduct.OldSubscriptionId));

    var newPI = await db.SubscriptionProducts.CountAsync(pi =>
        pi.ProductId.Equals(subscriptionProduct.ProductId) &&
        pi.SubscriptionId.Equals(
            subscriptionProduct.SubscriptionId));

    return oldPI.Equals(1) && newPI.Equals(0);
}
```

Copy and alter the Change method

This asynchronous method returns a **Task (void)**. The method uses a transaction to ensure that both the old record is removed and the new record is added, or all the changes are rolled back.

1. Open the **ConversionExtensions** class and copy the **Change** method and paste it in at the end of the class. Change its first parameter to **SubscriptionProduct subscriptionProduct**.
   ```
   public static async Task Change(this SubscriptionProduct
   subscriptionProduct, ApplicationDbContext db)
   ```
2. Add a LINQ query that fetches the record matching the **OldProductId** and **OldSubscriptionId** values and store it in a variable called **oldSubscriptionProduct**.
   ```
   var oldSubscriptionProduct = await
      db.SubscriptionProducts.FirstOrDefaultAsync(pi =>
      pi.ProductId.Equals(subscriptionProduct.OldProductId) &&
      pi.SubscriptionId.Equals(subscriptionProduct.OldSubscriptionId
   ));
   ```
3. Add a LINQ query that fetches the record matching the **ProductId** and **SubscriptionId** values and store it in a variable called **newSubscriptionProduct**.
4. Add an if-block checking that the **oldSubscriptionProduct** is not **null** (the record exist) and the **newSubscriptionProduct** is **null** (don't exist).
   ```
   if (oldSubscriptionProduct != null && newSubscriptionProduct ==
   null){ }
   ```
5. The rest of the code will be placed inside the if-block. Create a new instance of the **SubscriptionProduct** class and store it in the **newSubscriptionProduct** variable. Assign the **SubscriptionId** and **ProductId** from the **subscriptionProduct** parameter to the instance's **SubscriptionIs** and **ProductId** properties.
   ```
   newSubscriptionProduct = new SubscriptionProduct
   {
       SubscriptionId = subscriptionProduct.SubscriptionId,
       ProductId = subscriptionProduct.ProductId
   };
   ```
6. Add a reference to the **System.Transactions** assembly in the **References** folder.
7. Add a **using**-block with a **TransactionScope** instance. Use **TransactionScopeAsyncFlowOption.Enabled** to let the transaction flow through threds.
   ```
   using (var transaction = new TransactionScope(
   TransactionScopeAsyncFlowOption.Enabled))
   {
   }
   ```

8. Add a **try/catch**-block inside the **using**-block where the **catch**-block calls the **Dispose** method on the **transaction** variable to end the transaction if anything goes wrong.
9. Remove the existing **SubscriptionProduct** record from the **SubscriptionProduct** table and add the new **SubscriptionProduct** record to the table.

```
// Remove the exisiting ProductItem
db.SubscriptionProducts.Remove(oldSubscriptionProduct);

// Add the new (changed) ProductItem
db.SubscriptionProducts.Add(newSubscriptionProduct);
```

10. Save the changes by calling the **SaveToChangesAsync** method with the **await** keyword.
11. Persist the changes by completing the transaction calling the **Complete** method on the **transaction** variable. If you skip this step, no data will be saved to the database since the transaction ends without committing the changes.

The complete code for the **Change** method:

```
public static async Task Change(this SubscriptionProduct
subscriptionProduct, ApplicationDbContext db)
{
    var oldSubscriptionProduct = await
        db.SubscriptionProducts.FirstOrDefaultAsync(pi =>
        pi.ProductId.Equals(subscriptionProduct.OldProductId) &&
        pi.SubscriptionId.Equals(subscriptionProduct.OldSubscriptionId));

    var newSubscriptionProduct = await
        db.SubscriptionProducts.FirstOrDefaultAsync(pi =>
        pi.ProductId.Equals(subscriptionProduct.ProductId) &&
        pi.SubscriptionId.Equals(subscriptionProduct.SubscriptionId));

    if (oldSubscriptionProduct != null && newSubscriptionProduct == null)
    {
        newSubscriptionProduct = new SubscriptionProduct
        {
            SubscriptionId = subscriptionProduct.SubscriptionId,
            ProductId = subscriptionProduct.ProductId
        };

        // TransactionScope requires a reference to System.Transactions
        using (var transaction = new TransactionScope(
```

```
            TransactionScopeAsyncFlowOption.Enabled))
            {
                try
                {
                    // Remove the exisiting SubscriptionProduct
                    db.SubscriptionProducts.Remove(oldSubscriptionProduct);

                    // Add the new (changed) SubscriptionProduct
                    db.SubscriptionProducts.Add(newSubscriptionProduct);

                    await db.SaveChangesAsync();

                    transaction.Complete();
                }
                catch
                {
                    transaction.Dispose();
                }
            }
        }
    }
}
```

The Index view

Because you copied the **Index** view from the **ProductItem** folder, a few changes have to be made to it. You have to change the **@model** directive to use the **SubscriptionProductModel** class and replace all **ItemId** properties with **SubscriptionId** and replace all **ItemTitle** properties with **SubscriptionTitle**

One of the new asynchronous **Convert** methods will have to be called from the **Index** action method in the **SubscriptionProductController** to fetch the necessary data from the database.

This is what the finished **Index** view will look like:

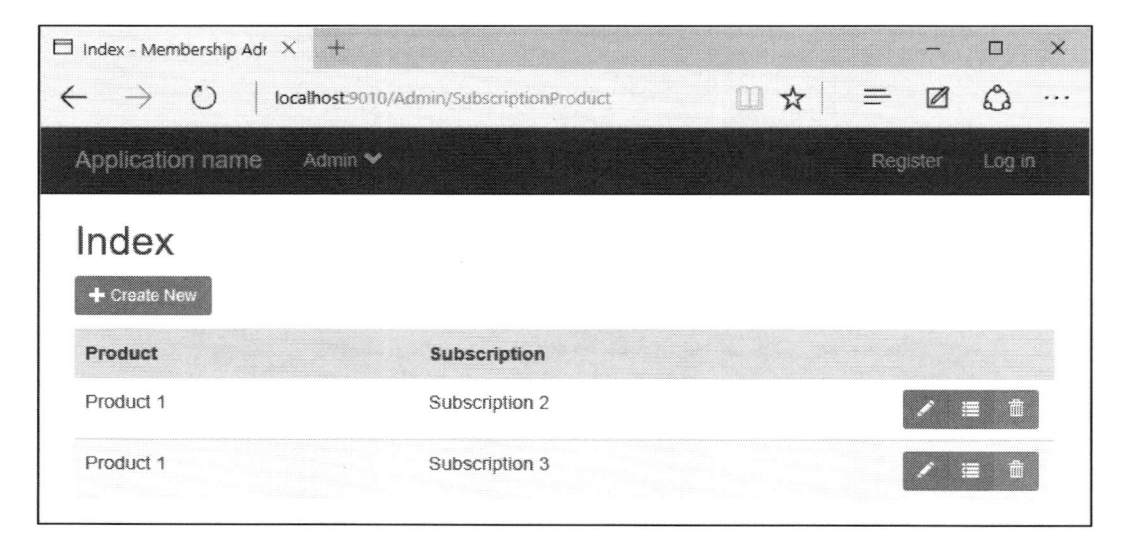

Modify the Index view
1. Open the **Index** view located in the **SubscriptionProduct** folder.
2. Change the **@model** directive to use the **SubscriptionProductModel** class.
   `@model Memberships.Areas.Admin.Models.SubscriptionProductModel`
3. Replace all **ItemId** properties with **SubscriptionId**.
4. Replace all **ItemTitle** properties with **SubscriptionTitle**.

Modify the Index controller action
1. Open the **SubscriptionProductController** class in the **Controllers** folder.
2. Locate the **Index** action method.
3. Replace the **ToListAsync** method call with a call to the **Convert** method in the **ConversionExtensions** class.
   `return View(await db.SubscriptionProducts.Convert(db));`

The complete code for **Index** view:

```
@model 
IEnumerable<Memberships.Areas.Admin.Models.SubscriptionProductModel>
@using Memberships.Areas.Admin.Models;

@{
```

```
        ViewBag.Title = "Index";
}

<h2>Index</h2>

<p>
    @Html.Partial("_CreateButtonPartial")
</p>

<table class="table table-striped table-condensed">
    <tr class="success">
        <th>
            @Html.DisplayNameFor(model => model.ProductTitle)
        </th>
        <th>
            @Html.DisplayNameFor(model => model.SubscriptionTitle)
        </th>
        <th></th>
    </tr>

    @foreach (var item in Model)
    {
        <tr>
            <td>
                @Html.DisplayFor(modelItem => item.ProductTitle)
            </td>
            <td>
                @Html.DisplayFor(modelItem => item.SubscriptionTitle)
            </td>

            @Html.Partial("_TableButtonsPartial", new SmallButtonModel {
                SubscriptionId = item.SubscriptionId, ProductId =
                item.ProductId })
        </tr>
    }
</table>
```

The Create view

In this view, you need to change the **@model** directive to point to the **Subscription-ProductModel** class and change all occurrences of **Items** to **Subscriptions** and **ItemId** with **SubscriptionId**.

ASP.NET MVC 5 - How to build a Membership Website

The finished view will look like the image below.

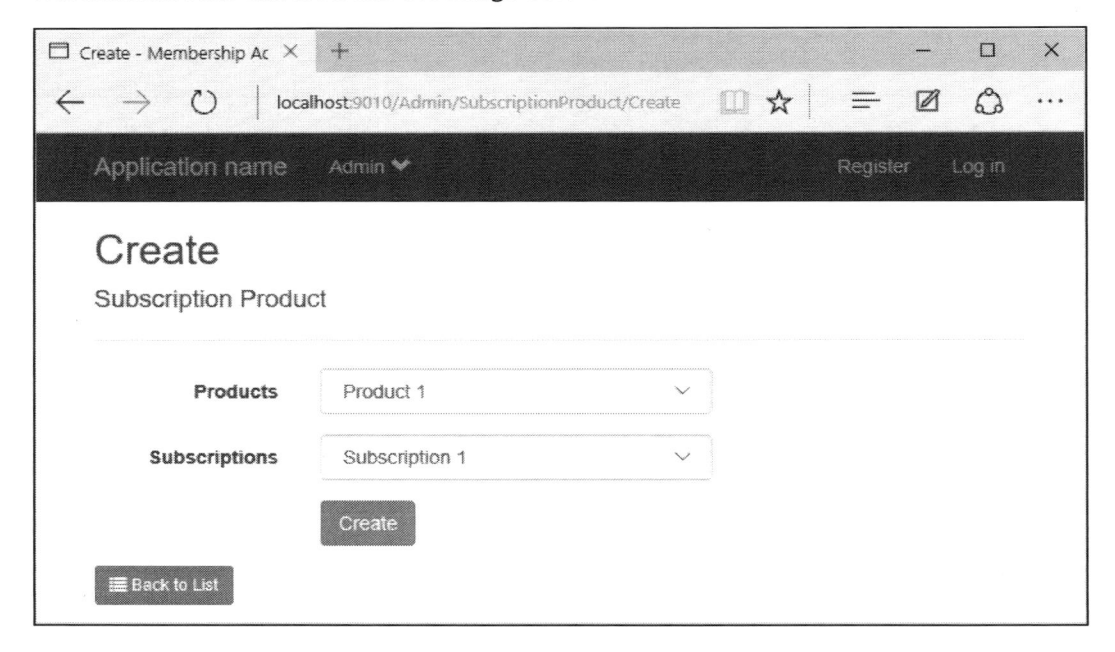

1. Change the **@model** directive.

   ```
   @model Memberships.Areas.Admin.Models.SubscriptionProductModel
   ```
2. Change all occurrences containing *Item* to *Subscription*.

   ```
   <div class="form-group">
      @Html.LabelFor(model => model.Subscriptions, htmlAttributes:
         new { @class = "control-label col-md-2" })
      <div class="col-md-10">
         @Html.DropDownListFor(model => model.SubscriptionId,
            Model.Subscriptions.ToSelectListItem(Model.SubscriptionId),
            new { @class = "form-control" })
         @Html.ValidationMessageFor(model => model.SubscriptionId,
            "", new { @class = "text-danger" })
      </div>
   </div>
   ```

The complete code for **Create** view:

```
@model Memberships.Areas.Admin.Models.SubscriptionProductModel
@using Memberships.Extensions

@{
    ViewBag.Title = "Create";
}

<h2>Create</h2>

@using (Html.BeginForm())
{
    @Html.AntiForgeryToken()

    <div class="form-horizontal">
        <h4>Subscription Product</h4>
        <hr />
        @Html.ValidationSummary(true, "", new { @class = "text-danger" })

        <div class="form-group">
            @Html.LabelFor(model => model.Products, htmlAttributes:
                new { @class = "control-label col-md-2" })
            <div class="col-md-10">
                @Html.DropDownListFor(
                    model => model.ProductId,
                    Model.Products.ToSelectListItem(Model.ProductId),
                    new { @class = "form-control" })
                @Html.ValidationMessageFor(model => model.ProductId, "",
                    new { @class = "text-danger" })
            </div>
        </div>
        <div class="form-group">
            @Html.LabelFor(model => model.Subscriptions, htmlAttributes:
                new { @class = "control-label col-md-2" })
            <div class="col-md-10">
                @Html.DropDownListFor(
                    model => model.SubscriptionId,
                    Model.Subscriptions.ToSelectListItem(
                        Model.SubscriptionId),
                    new { @class = "form-control" })
                @Html.ValidationMessageFor(model => model.SubscriptionId,
                    "", new { @class = "text-danger" })
            </div>
```

```
        </div>

        <div class="form-group">
            <div class="col-md-offset-2 col-md-10">
                <input type="submit" value="Create"
                    class="btn btn-success" />
            </div>
        </div>
    </div>
}

<div>
    @Html.Partial("_BackToListButtonPartial")
</div>
```

Modify the Create controller action (HttpGet)

Because you have changed the **@model** directive to use another model class, you need to alter the **Create** action in the **SubscriptionProduct** controller class.

A new model has to be created using the **SubscriptionProductModel** class, and its two collections have to be filled from the **Subscription** and **Product** database tables.

1. Open the **SubscriptionProduct** controller class and locate the parameter-less **Create** action.
2. Create an instance of the **SubscriptionProductModel** class and store it in a variable called **model**.
3. Fill the model's **Subscription** collection asynchronously with data from the **Subscription** table.
4. Fill the model's **Product** collection asynchronously with data from the **Product** table.
   ```
   var model = new SubscriptionProductModel
   {
       Subscriptions = await db.Subscriptions.ToListAsync(),
       Products = await db.Products.ToListAsync()
   };
   ```
5. Return the **model** variable with the view.
   ```
   return View(model);
   ```

The complete code for **HttpGet Create** action:

```
public async Task<ActionResult> Create()
{
    var model = new SubscriptionProductModel
    {
        Subscriptions = await db.Subscriptions.ToListAsync(),
        Products = await db.Products.ToListAsync()
    };
    return View(model);
}
```

The Edit view

The **Edit** view can be used to change a subscription-product connection; you can change the product associated with a subscription or vice-versa. You will need to change the **Edit** controller action as well as the copied **Edit** view.

The **@model** directive has to be changed to use the **SubscriptionProductModel** class for view model data. The hidden value for **ItemId** has to be changed to **SubscriptionId**. All the places in the **form-group <div>** element where *Item* is referenced has to be changed to *Subscription*.

The finished view will look like the image below.

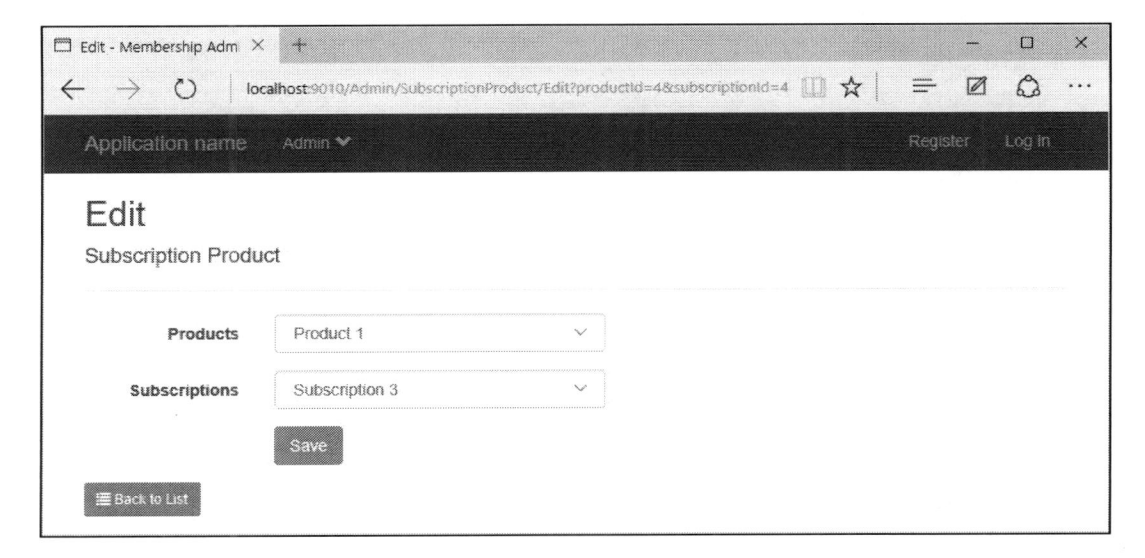

1. Change the **@model** directive.
   @model Memberships.Areas.Admin.Models.SubscriptionProductModel
2. Change the hidden value called **OldItemId** to **OldSubscriptionId** and replace the property with **Model.SubscriptionId**.
   @Html.Hidden("OldSubscriptionId", Model.SubscriptionId)
3. Change all occurrences containing *Item* to **Subscription**.
   ```
   <div class="form-group">
      @Html.LabelFor(model => model.Subscription,
         htmlAttributes: new { @class = "control-label col-md-2" })
      <div class="col-md-10">
         @Html.DropDownListFor(model => model.SubscriptionId,
            Model.Subscription.ToSelectListItem(
            Model.SubscriptionId), new { @class = "form-control" })
         @Html.ValidationMessageFor(model => model.SubscriptionId,
            "", new { @class = "text-danger" })
      </div>
   </div>
   ```

The complete code for **Edit** view:

```
@model Memberships.Areas.Admin.Models.SubscriptionProductModel
@using Memberships.Extensions

@{
    ViewBag.Title = "Edit";
}

<h2>Edit</h2>

@using (Html.BeginForm())
{
    @Html.AntiForgeryToken()

    <div class="form-horizontal">
        <h4>Subscription Product</h4>
        <hr />
        @Html.ValidationSummary(true, "", new { @class = "text-danger" })
        @Html.Hidden("OldProductId", Model.ProductId)
        @Html.Hidden("OldSubscriptionId", Model.SubscriptionId)

        <div class="form-group">
            @Html.LabelFor(model => model.Products, htmlAttributes:
                new { @class = "control-label col-md-2" })
```

```
            <div class="col-md-10">
                @Html.DropDownListFor(
                    model => model.ProductId,
                    Model.Products.ToSelectListItem(Model.ProductId),
                    new { @class = "form-control" })
                @Html.ValidationMessageFor(model => model.ProductId, "",
                    new { @class = "text-danger" })
            </div>
        </div>
        <div class="form-group">
            @Html.LabelFor(model => model.Subscriptions, htmlAttributes:
                new { @class = "control-label col-md-2" })
            <div class="col-md-10">
                @Html.DropDownListFor(
                    model => model.SubscriptionId,
                        Model.Subscriptions.ToSelectListItem(
                            Model.SubscriptionId),
                    new { @class = "form-control" })
                @Html.ValidationMessageFor(model => model.SubscriptionId,
                    "", new { @class = "text-danger" })
            </div>
        </div>

        <div class="form-group">
            <div class="col-md-offset-2 col-md-10">
                <input type="submit" value="Save"
                    class="btn btn-success" />
            </div>
        </div>
    </div>
}

<div>
    @Html.Partial("_BackToListButtonPartial")
</div>
```

Modify the Edit controller action (HttpGet)

Because you have changed the **@model** directive to another class, you need to alter the **Edit** action in the **SubscriptionProduct** controller class.

You have to change the action method to take two **int** parameters called **subscriptionId** and **productId**. If either of the parameters are **null,** then return *Bad Request*.

Replace the call to the **FindAsync** method with a call to a new method called **GetSubscriptionProduct** with two **int? parameters** named **subscriptionId** and **productId**. Pass in the **subscriptionId** and **productId** action parameters to it.

If a matching **SubscriptionProduct** record was found, then call the **Convert** method which returns a single instance of the **SubscriptionProduct** class. Pass the result to the view.

1. Open the **SubscriptionProductController** class and locate the **Edit** action which takes one parameter.
2. Change the name of the **id** parameter to **subscriptionId** for all occurrences in the action method.
3. Add another **int?** parameter called **productId**.
   ```
   public async Task<ActionResult> Edit(int? subscriptionId, int? productId)
   ```
4. Change the first if-statement to check that none of the parameters are **null**.
   ```
   if (subscriptionId == null || productId == null)
   ```
5. Replace the call to the **FindAsync** method with a call to a method called **GetSubscriptionProduct** and pass in the **SubscriptionId** and **productId** as parameters to it. Use the **await** keyword to call the method asynchronously. Don't be alarmed that the call reports an error it will be fixed when the method is created in the next section.
   ```
   SubscriptionProduct subscriptionProduct = await
       GetSubscriptionProduct(subscriptionId, productId);
   ```
6. Create an new variable called **model** by calling the **Convert** method on the **subscriptionProduct** instance you just fetched.
   ```
   var model = await subscriptionProduct.Convert(db);
   ```
7. Return the **model** variable with the view.
   ```
   return View(model);
   ```

The complete code for the **HttpGet Edit** action:

```
public async Task<ActionResult> Edit(int? subscriptionId, int? productId)
{
    if (subscriptionId == null || productId == null)
    {
        return new HttpStatusCodeResult(HttpStatusCode.BadRequest);
    }

    SubscriptionProduct subscriptionProduct = await
        GetSubscriptionProduct(subscriptionId, productId);

    if (subscriptionProduct == null)
    {
        return HttpNotFound();
    }

    var model = await subscriptionProduct.Convert(db);
    return View(model);
}
```

The GetSubscriptionProduct method

You can copy and modify the **GetProductItem** method when implementing the **GetSubscriptionProduct** method. Change the method and parameter/property names and replace the **ProductItems** collection with **SubscriptionProducts**.

1. Open the **ProductItemController** class and copy the **GetProductItem** method.
2. Open the **SubscriptionProductController** class and go to the end of the class and paste in the copied method.
3. Change the method name to **GetSubscriptionProduct**, the return type to **Task<SubscriptionProduct>** and the first parameter name to **subscriptionId**.
   ```
   private async Task<SubscriptionProduct> GetSubscriptionProduct(
       int? subscriptionId, int? productId)
   ```
4. Change all ocurrences of the **itmId** variable name to **subscrId**.
5. Change all ocurrences of the **itemId** parameter to **subscriptionId**.
6. Change the collection from **ProductItems** to **SubscriptionProducts**.
7. The method should return **null** if an exception occurs.

The complete code for the **GetSubscriptionProduct** method:

```
private async Task<SubscriptionProduct> GetSubscriptionProduct(
int? subscriptionId, int? productId)
{
   try
   {
      int subscrId = 0, prdId = 0;
      int.TryParse(subscriptionId.ToString(), out subscrId);
      int.TryParse(productId.ToString(), out prdId);

      var subscriptionProduct = await
         db.SubscriptionProducts.FirstOrDefaultAsync(pi =>
            pi.ProductId.Equals(prdId) &&
            pi.SubscriptionId.Equals(subscrId));

      return subscriptionProduct;
   }
   catch { return null; }
}
```

Modify the Edit controller action (HttpPost)

To be able to save changes when the user clicks the **Edit** button, you have to make some changes to the **Edit** action decorated with the **[HttpPost]** attribute in the **Subscription-ProductController** class.

First, you need to add two parameters called **OldProductId** and **OldSubscriptionId** to the **Bind** statement. The **Bind** statement will match the form field with the properties in the model passed in to the **Edit** action. This makes it impossible to maliciously add property values to the post. The added parameters represent the two form fields you added to the **Edit** view as hidden fields with **@Html.Hidden**.

Delete all code in the **ModelState.Valid** if-block and copy the code from the **ModelState.Valid** if-block in the **Edit** action of the **ProductItemController** class. Change the **product-Item** parameter name in the copied code to **susbscriptionProduct**.

1. Open the **ProductItemController** located in the **Controllers** folder and copy the content in the **ModelState.Valid** if-block in the **Edit** action decorated with the **[HttpPost]** attribute.

2. Open the **SubscriptionProduct** controller located in the **Controllers** folder and replace the code in the **ModelState.Valid** if-block with the copied code.
3. Add parameter names (**OldProductId** and **OldSubscriptionId**) representing the two form fields you added to the **Edit** view as hidden fields using **@Html.Hidden**.
   ```
   public async Task<ActionResult> Edit([Bind(Include =
   "SubscriptionId,ProductId,OldSubscriptionId,OldProductId")]
   SubscriptionProduct subscriptionProduct)
   ```
4. Replace all occurrences of **productItem** with **subscriptionProduct**.
5. Run the application and change the values of an existing **SubscriptionProduct** record. Create a new **SubscriptionProduct** record if none exists and change its values.

The complete code for the **HttpPost Edit** action:

```
public async Task<ActionResult> Edit([Bind(Include =
"SubscriptionId,ProductId,OldSubscriptionId,OldProductId")]
SubscriptionProduct subscriptionProduct)
{
    if (ModelState.IsValid)
    {
        // Check if the SubscriptionProduct can be changed
        var canChange = await subscriptionProduct.CanChange(db);

        if (canChange)
        {
            // Change the SubscriptionProduct
            await subscriptionProduct.Change(db);
        }

        return RedirectToAction("Index");

    }

    return View(subscriptionProduct);
}
```

The Details View

You could actually argue that this view is redundant since you could display the same information in the **Index** view, but it is included here to show how data that is not directly stored in the **SubscriptionProduct** table can be displayed.

The **Details** view is very similar to the **Details** view in the **ProductItem** folder; the only changes you have to make is to use a different model class (**SubscriptionProduct**) and **SunscriptionId** and **SubscriptionTitle** properties instead of **ItemId** and **ItemTitle**.

The **Details** action is basically the same as the **Edit** action in same controller, so you can copy the **Edit** action and replace the **Details** action with the copy. The only things you have to alter are the parameter name **subscriptionId** to **id** and add **false** as a second parameter value in the **Convert** method call. The value **false** will ensure that the title values are fetched instead of a list of all subscriptions and products.

The image below shows the finished **Details** view.

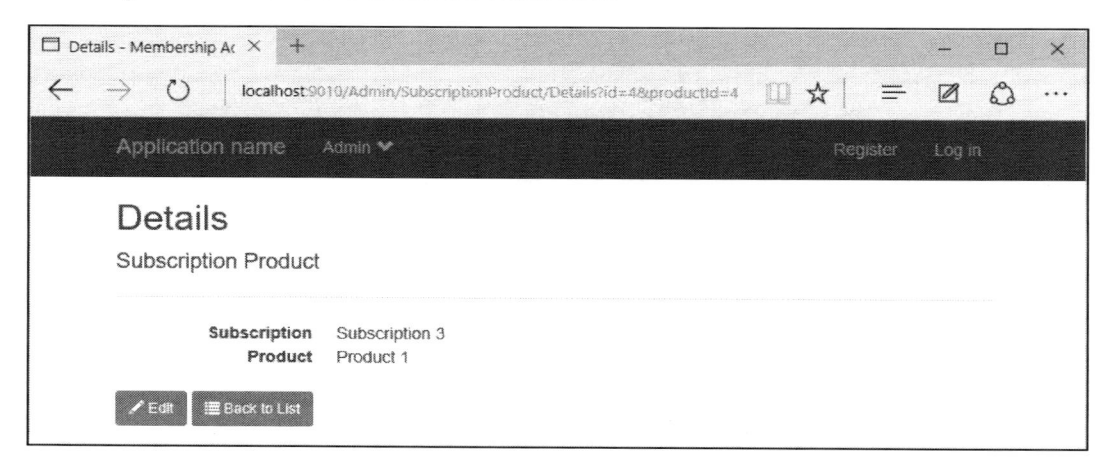

Modify the Details view
1. Open the **Details** view located in the **SubscriptionProduct** folder.
2. Change the **@model** directive to use the **SubscriptionProductModel**.
   `@model Memberships.Areas.Admin.Models.SubscriptionProductModel`
3. Change the **<h4>** heading to say *Subscription-Product*.
   `<h4>Subscription-Product</h4>`
4. Replace all **ItemId** properties with **SubscriptionId**.
5. Replace all **ItemTitle** properties with **SubscriptionTitle**.

The complete code for the **Details** view:

```
@model Memberships.Areas.Admin.Models.SubscriptionProductModel
@using Memberships.Areas.Admin.Models

@{
    ViewBag.Title = "Details";
}

<h2>Details</h2>

<div>
    <h4>Subscription Product</h4>
    <hr />
    <dl class="dl-horizontal">
        <dt>@Html.DisplayNameFor(m => m.SubscriptionTitle)</dt>
        <dd>@Html.DisplayFor(m => m.SubscriptionTitle)</dd>
        <dt>@Html.DisplayNameFor(m => m.ProductTitle)</dt>
        <dd>@Html.DisplayFor(m => m.ProductTitle)</dd>
    </dl>
</div>
<p>
    @Html.Partial("_EditButtonDetailPartial", new EditButtonModel {
        SubscriptionId = Model.SubscriptionId, ProductId =
        Model.ProductId })

    @Html.Partial("_BackToListButtonPartial")
</p>
```

Modify the Details controller action

1. Open the **SubscriptionProductController** class located in the **Controllers** folder.
2. Locate the **Edit** action method which has two parameters and copy it.
3. Locate the **Details** action method and replace it with the copied **Edit** action.
4. Rename the pasted in action **Details**.
5. Run the application and navigate to the **Details** view, then click on the **Edit** button, to display the **Edit** view.

The complete code for the **Details** action:

```
public async Task<ActionResult> Details(
int? subscriptionId, int? productId)
{
    if (subscriptionId == null || productId == null)
    {
        return new HttpStatusCodeResult(HttpStatusCode.BadRequest);
    }

    SubscriptionProduct subscriptionProduct =
        await GetSubscriptionProduct(subscriptionId, productId);

    if (subscriptionProduct == null)
    {
        return HttpNotFound();
    }

    return View(await subscriptionProduct.Convert(db));
}
```

The Delete View

Since you copied the **Delete** view from the **ProductItem** folder, you have to make a few modifications to it. You have to change the **@model** directive to use the **Subscription-ProductModel** class, change the **<h4>** heading to say *Subscription-Product*, replace all **ItemId** properties with **SubscriptionId** and Replace all **ItemTitle** properties with **Subscription-Title**.

Apart from the name, the **Delete** controller action is identical to the **Details** action in the **SubscriptionProductController**.

The **FindAsync** method call in the **DeleteConfirmed** controller action has to be changed to a call to the **GetSubscriptionProduct** method and because the method takes two **int** parameters (**subscriptionId** and **productId**) you have to pass those into the action.

The **Back To List** button won't work because the **Index** view hasn't been fixed yet and the **Delete** button will throw an exception for the same reason but the record will be deleted from the database table anyway.

ASP.NET MVC 5 - How to build a Membership Website

This is what the finished **Delete** view will look like:

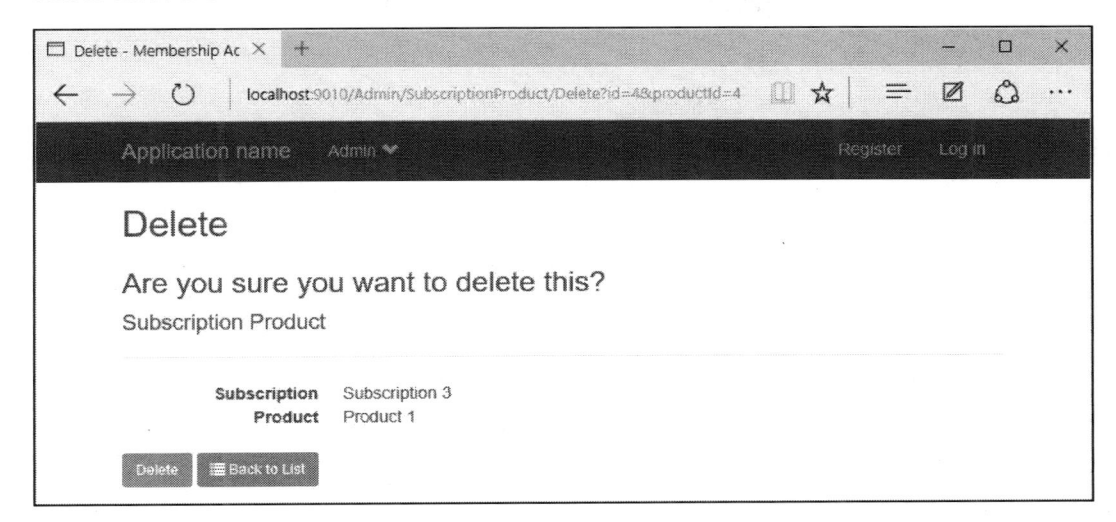

Modify the Delete view
1. Open the **Delete** view located in the **SubscriptionProduct** folder.
2. Change the **@model** directive to use the **SubscriptionProductModel** class.
   `@model Memberships.Areas.Admin.Models.SubscriptionProductModel`
3. Change the **<h4>** heading to say *Subscription-Product*.
   `<h4>Subscription-Product</h4>`
4. Replace all **ItemId** properties with **SubscriptionId**.
5. Replace all **ItemTitle** properties with **SubscriptionTitle**.

The complete code for the **Dlete** action:

```
@model Memberships.Areas.Admin.Models.SubscriptionProductModel
@using Memberships.Areas.Admin.Models

@{
    ViewBag.Title = "Delete";
}

<h2>Delete</h2>

<h3>Are you sure you want to delete this?</h3>
<div>
    <h4>Subscription Product</h4>
```

217

```
    <hr />
    <dl class="dl-horizontal">
        <dt>@Html.DisplayNameFor(m => m.SubscriptionTitle)</dt>
        <dd>@Html.DisplayFor(m => m.SubscriptionTitle)</dd>
        <dt>@Html.DisplayNameFor(m => m.ProductTitle)</dt>
        <dd>@Html.DisplayFor(m => m.ProductTitle)</dd>
    </dl>

    @using (Html.BeginForm()) {
        @Html.AntiForgeryToken()

        <div class="form-actions no-color">
            <input type="submit" value="Delete"
                class="btn btn-danger btn-sm" />
            @Html.Partial("_EditButtonDetailPartial",
                new EditButtonModel { SubscriptionId =
                Model.SubscriptionId, ProductId = Model.ProductId })

            @Html.Partial("_BackToListButtonPartial")
        </div>
    }
</div>
```

Modify the HttpGet Delete controller action

1. Open the **SubscriptionProductController** class in the **Controllers** folder.
2. Locate the **Details** action and copy it.
3. Replace the existing **Delete** action with the **Details** action you copied.
4. Rename the pasted in method **Delete**.

The complete code for the **HttpGet Delete** action:

```
public async Task<ActionResult> Delete(
int? subscriptionId, int? productId)
{
    if (subscriptionId == null || productId == null)
    {
        return new HttpStatusCodeResult(HttpStatusCode.BadRequest);
    }

    SubscriptionProduct subscriptionProduct =
        await GetSubscriptionProduct(subscriptionId, productId);

    if (subscriptionProduct == null)
```

```
    {
        return HttpNotFound();
    }

    return View(await subscriptionProduct.Convert(db));
}
```

Modify the DeleteConfirmed controller action
1. Open the **SubscriptionProductController** class in the **Subscriptions** folder.
2. Locate the **DeleteConfirmed** action.
3. Rename the **id** parameter **subscriptionId** as well as all occurrences in the action method.
4. Add another **int** parameter called **productId**.
5. Replace the **FindAsync** method call with a call to the **GetSubscriptionProduct** method.
6. Run the application and delete an existing subscription-product entry.

The complete code for the **HttpPost DeleteConfirmed** action:

```
[HttpPost, ActionName("Delete")]
[ValidateAntiForgeryToken]
public async Task<ActionResult> DeleteConfirmed(
int subscriptionId, int productId)
{
    SubscriptionProduct subscriptionProduct =
        await GetSubscriptionProduct(subscriptionId, productId);

    db.SubscriptionProducts.Remove(subscriptionProduct);
    await db.SaveChangesAsync();

    return RedirectToAction("Index");
}
```

7. Adding transactions to the DeleteConfirmed actions

Introduction
In this chapter you will modify the **DeleteConfirmed** actions for the **Product**-, **Item**- and **Subscription** controllers. It is essential to not only delete the item from its table when it is removed, you also need to remove the items in the connecting **ProductItem** and **SubscriptionProduct** tables to avoid leaving records without id's for exising records from both tables invloved.

If, for instance, you remove a product, you also have to remove any records with that product id in the the **SubscriptionProdut** and **ProductItem** connecting tables; otherwise you will end up with subscriptions and items without a product in the **Index** listings.

You will also implement a safety check when removing minor entities to make sure that only records that are unused can be deleted from the table.

Technologies used in this chapter
1. **C#** - Creating controller actions and view models to handle users and subscriptions.
2. **Entity framework** - To remove records from the involved tables.

Adding a transaction to the Item's DeleteConfirmed action
Let's start by adding a transaction to the **ItemController**'s **DeleteConfirmed** action. Apart from removing the item itself from the **Item** table we also have to remove any entry in the **ProductItem** table with that item id; and to be certain that both the item and the entries in the **ProductItem** table are removed as an atomic action where all or notihng is removed then a transaction has to surround the database calls.

1. Open the **ItemController** class.
2. Locate the **DeleteConfirmed** acation.

3. Add a **using**-block with a **TransactionScope** instance around the **Remove** and **SaveChanges** method calls.
   ```
   using (var transaction = new TransactionScope(
   TransactionScopeAsyncFlowOption.Enabled))
   {
       db.Items.Remove(item);
       await db.SaveChangesAsync();
   }
   ```
4. Fetch all records in the **ProductItem** table matching the item id passed into the **DeleteConfirmed** action above the **Remove** method call. Then remove those records from the **ProductItem** table.
   ```
   var prodItems = db.ProductItems.Where(
       pi => pi.ItemId.Equals(id));
   db.ProductItems.RemoveRange(prodItems);
   ```
5. Add a call to the **Complete** method on the transaction object variable (from the transaction scope) below the **SaveChanges** method call.
   ```
   transaction.Complete();
   ```
6. Add a **try/catch**-block around the code inside the **using**-statement.
7. Add a call to the **Dispose** method on the transaction object variable (from the transaction scope) inside the **catch**-block to revert any changes that might have been made before the exception occured.
   ```
   transaction.Dispose();
   ```

The complete code for the **DeleteConfirmed** action:

```
[HttpPost, ActionName("Delete")]
[ValidateAntiForgeryToken]
public async Task<ActionResult> DeleteConfirmed(int id)
{
    Item item = await db.Items.FindAsync(id);
    using (var transaction = new TransactionScope(
        TransactionScopeAsyncFlowOption.Enabled))
    {
        try
        {
            var prodItems = db.ProductItems.Where(
                pi => pi.ItemId.Equals(id));
            db.ProductItems.RemoveRange(prodItems);
            db.Items.Remove(item);
```

```
            await db.SaveChangesAsync();
            transaction.Complete();
        }
        catch { transaction.Dispose(); }
    }

    return RedirectToAction("Index");
}
```

Adding a transaction to the Product's DeleteConfirmed action

Now we will add a transaction to the **ProductController**'s **DeleteConfirmed** action. Apart from removing the product itself from the **Product** table, we also have to remove any entry in the **ProductItem** table with that item id, as well as any entry in the **Susbcription-Product** table; and to be certain that both the product and the entries in the **ProductItem** and **SusbcriptionProduct** tables are removed as an atomic action where all or nothing is removed, then a transaction has to surround the database calls.

1. Open the **ProductController** class.
2. Locate the **DeleteConfirmed** acation.
3. Add a **using**-block with a **TransactionScope** instance around the **Remove** and **SaveChanges** method calls.
   ```
   using (var transaction = new TransactionScope(
   TransactionScopeAsyncFlowOption.Enabled))
   {
       db.Products.Remove(product);
       await db.SaveChangesAsync();
   }
   ```
4. Fetch all records in the **ProductItem** table matching the product id passed into the **DeleteConfirmed** action above the **Remove** method call. Then remove those records from the **ProductItem** table.
   ```
   var prodItems = db.ProductItems.Where(
       pi => pi. ProductId.Equals(id));
   db.ProductItems.RemoveRange(prodItems);
   ```
5. Fetch all records in the **SubscriptionProduct** table matching the product id passed into the **DeleteConfirmed** action above the **Remove** method call. Then remove those records from the **ProductItem** table.
   ```
   var prodSubscr = db.SubscriptionProducts.Where(
   ```

```
        sp => sp.ProductId.Equals(id));
    db.SubscriptionProducts.RemoveRange(prodSubscr);
```

6. Add a call to the **Complete** method on the transaction object variable (from the transaction scope) below the **SaveChanges** method call.
   `transaction.Complete();`

7. Add a **try/catch**-block around the code inside the **using**-statement.

8. Add a call to the **Dispose** method on the transaction object variable (from the transaction scope) inside the **catch**-block to revert any changes that might have been made before the exception occured.
   `transaction.Dispose();`

The complete code for the **DeleteConfirmed** action:

```
[HttpPost, ActionName("Delete")]
[ValidateAntiForgeryToken]
public async Task<ActionResult> DeleteConfirmed(int id)
{
    Product product = await db.Products.FindAsync(id);
    using (var transaction = new TransactionScope(
        TransactionScopeAsyncFlowOption.Enabled))
    {
        try
        {
            var prodItems = db.ProductItems.Where(
                pi => pi.ProductId.Equals(id));
            var prodSubscr = db.SubscriptionProducts.Where(
                sp => sp.ProductId.Equals(id));
            db.ProductItems.RemoveRange(prodItems);
            db.SubscriptionProducts.RemoveRange(prodSubscr);
            db.Products.Remove(product);

            await db.SaveChangesAsync();
            transaction.Complete();
        }
        catch { transaction.Dispose(); }
    }

    return RedirectToAction("Index");
}
```

Adding a transaction to the Subscription's DeleteConfirmed action

Now we will add a transaction to the **SubscriptionController**'s **DeleteConfirmed** action. Apart from removing the product itself from the **Subscription** table, we also have to remove any entry in the **SusbcriptionProduct** table; and to be certain that both the subscription and the entries in the **SusbcriptionProduct** table are removed as an atomic action where all or notihng is removed then a transaction has to surround the database calls.

1. Open the **SubscriptionController** class.
2. Locate the **DeleteConfirmed** acation.
3. Add a **using**-block with a **TransactionScope** instance around the **Remove** and **SaveChanges** method calls.
   ```
   using (var transaction = new TransactionScope(
   TransactionScopeAsyncFlowOption.Enabled))
   {
       db.Subscriptions.Remove(product);
       await db.SaveChangesAsync();
   }
   ```
4. Fetch all records in the **SubscriptionProduct** table matching the product id passed into the **DeleteConfirmed** action above the **Remove** method call. Then remove those records from the **ProductItem** table.
   ```
   var prodSubscr = db.SubscriptionProducts.Where(
       sp => sp.SubscriptionId.Equals(id));
   db.SubscriptionProducts.RemoveRange(prodSubscr);
   ```
5. Add a call to the **Complete** method on the transaction object variable (from the transaction scope) below the **SaveChanges** method call.
   ```
   transaction.Complete();
   ```
6. Add a **try/catch**-block around the code inside the **using**-statement.
7. Add a call to the **Dispose** method on the transaction object variable (from the transaction scope) inside the **catch**-block to revert any changes that might have been made before the exception occured.
   ```
   transaction.Dispose();
   ```

The complete code for the **DeleteConfirmed** action:

```
[HttpPost, ActionName("Delete")]
[ValidateAntiForgeryToken]
public async Task<ActionResult> DeleteConfirmed(int id)
{
    Subscription subscription = await db.Subscriptions.FindAsync(id);
    using (var transaction = new TransactionScope(
        TransactionScopeAsyncFlowOption.Enabled))
    {
        try
        {
            var prodSubscr = db.SubscriptionProducts.Where(
                sp => sp.SubscriptionId.Equals(id));
            db.SubscriptionProducts.RemoveRange(prodSubscr);
            db.Subscriptions.Remove(subscription);

            await db.SaveChangesAsync();
            transaction.Complete();
        }
        catch { transaction.Dispose(); }
    }

    return RedirectToAction("Index");
}
```

Adding the delete check to the DeleteConfirmed actions

Let's start by adding the delete check to the **SectionController**'s **DeleteConfirmed** action. Before removing the record from the **Section** table, you will have to check that it isn't in use by any item in the **Item** table.

1. Open the **SectionController** class.
2. Locate the **DeleteConfirmed** acation.
3. Use a LINQ query to find out if the section is referenced by any item in the **Item** table and store the result in a variable called **IsUnused**.
   `var isUnused = await db.Items.CountAsync(i => i.SectionId.Equals(id)) == 0;`
4. Add an if-block checking the IsUnused variablre's value around the **Remove** and **SaveChanges** merthods.

```
    if (isUnused)
    {
        db.Sections.Remove(section);
        await db.SaveChangesAsync();
    }
```

5. Now, do the same in the **DeleteConfirmed** actions in the **Part** and **ItemType** controllers.
6. Now, do the same in the **DeleteConfirmed** actions in the **ProductType** and **ProductLinkText** controllers. Replace the **Item** table with the **Product** table in the LINQ query.
```
    var isUnused = await db.Products.CountAsync(i =>
        i.ProductTypeId.Equals(id)) == 0;
```

The complete code for the **SectionController**'s **DeleteConfirmed** action:

```
[HttpPost, ActionName("Delete")]
[ValidateAntiForgeryToken]
public async Task<ActionResult> DeleteConfirmed(int id)
{
    Section section = await db.Sections.FindAsync(id);
    var isUnused = await db.Items.CountAsync(i =>
        i.SectionId.Equals(id)) == 0;

    if (isUnused)
    {
        db.Sections.Remove(section);
        await db.SaveChangesAsync();
    }

    return RedirectToAction("Index");
}
```

The complete code for the **PartController**'s **DeleteConfirmed** action:

```
[HttpPost, ActionName("Delete")]
[ValidateAntiForgeryToken]
public async Task<ActionResult> DeleteConfirmed(int id)
{
    Part part = await db.Parts.FindAsync(id);
    var isUnused = await db.Items.CountAsync(i =>
        i.PartId.Equals(id)) == 0;
```

```
    if (isUnused)
    {
        db.Parts.Remove(part);
        await db.SaveChangesAsync();
    }

    return RedirectToAction("Index");
}
```

The complete code for the **ItemTypeController**'s **DeleteConfirmed** action:

```
[HttpPost, ActionName("Delete")]
[ValidateAntiForgeryToken]
public async Task<ActionResult> DeleteConfirmed(int id)
{
    ItemType itemType = await db.ItemTypes.FindAsync(id);
    var isUnused = await db.Items.CountAsync(i =>
        i.ItemTypeId.Equals(id)) == 0;

    if (isUnused)
    {
        db.ItemTypes.Remove(itemType);
        await db.SaveChangesAsync();
    }
    return RedirectToAction("Index");
}
```

The complete code for the **ProductLinkTextController**'s **DeleteConfirmed** action:

```
[HttpPost, ActionName("Delete")]
[ValidateAntiForgeryToken]
public async Task<ActionResult> DeleteConfirmed(int id)
{
    ProductLinkText productLinkText = await
        db.ProductLinkTexts.FindAsync(id);
    var isUnused = await db.Products.CountAsync(i =>
        i.ProductLinkTextId.Equals(id)) == 0;

    if (isUnused)
    {
        db.ProductLinkTexts.Remove(productLinkText);
        await db.SaveChangesAsync();
    }
```

```
        return RedirectToAction("Index");
    }
}
```

The complete code for the **ProductTypeController**'s **DeleteConfirmed** action:

```
[HttpPost, ActionName("Delete")]
[ValidateAntiForgeryToken]
public async Task<ActionResult> DeleteConfirmed(int id)
{
    ProductType productType = await db.ProductTypes.FindAsync(id);
    var isUnused = await db.Products.CountAsync(i =>
        i.ProductTypeId.Equals(id)) == 0;

    if (isUnused)
    {
        db.ProductTypes.Remove(productType);
        await db.SaveChangesAsync();
    }

    return RedirectToAction("Index");
}
```

8. Users & Subscriptions

Introduction
In this chapter you will create a controller and views which will handle users and their subscriptions from the **Admin** menu. You will also fix the broken **Registration** action and **RegistrationViewModel**; as you might recall, new columns were added to the **AspNet-User** table earlier, these columns were not reflected in the **Registration** action.

To ensure that only users in a specific **Admin** role have access to the **Admin** menu, you will add the **Admin** role to the **AspNetRoles** table and connect a user to that role through the **AspNetUserRoles** table. To ensure that no user malliciously can be granted admin privileges through the UI, admin privileges will be added manually in the **AspNetUser-Roles** table.

Technologies used in this chapter
3. **C#** - Creating controller actions and view models to handle users and subscriptions.
4. **Razor** - To incorporate C# in the views where necessary.
5. **HTML 5** - To build the views.
6. **Bootstrap** - To style the HTML 5 components.
7. **Database** - To add and chane role and user data.

User Registration
In an earlier chapter you added columns to the **AspNetUser** table to store additional information about the user. This change broke the registration action because the new information hasn't been added to the **ApplicationUser** entity model defining a user in the **AspNetUser** table. In this section, you will add the necessary data to the **Application-User** entity model and update the **RegisterViewModel** and **Register** view with a field for the **FirstName** property.

Alter the RegisterViewModel

Because the customer wants to be able to store the user's first name in the database, a new **string** propery called **FirstName** has to be added to the **RegisterViewModel** class.

1. Open the **AccountViewModels.cs** file in the **Models** folder in the main project.
2. Locate the **RegisterViewModel** class.
3. Add a **string** property called **FirstName**.
4. Apply the **Required** attribute to force the user to enter a value in the textbox.
5. Apply the **Display** attribute to change the descriptive lable text "First Name".

The new **FirstName** property:

```
[Required]
[Display(Name = "First Name")]
public string FirstName { get; set; }
```

Alter the Register action

Four values have to be added to the **ApplicationUser** entity model object in the **Register** action in the **AccountController** when registering a new user.

The value for the **FirstName** column is fetched from the **FirstName** property in the **RegisterViewModel** object sent into the **Register** action from the **Register** view when the user clicks the **Register** submit button.

The value for the **IsActive** column is assigned **true** since the user will be active once registered. The value for the **Registered** column is assigned the current date since that is the date the user registered. The value for the **EmailConfirmed** column is assigned **true** because otherwise the system will wait indefinately for email confirmation that never will arrive because no email was sent in the first place.

1. Open the **AccountController** class located in the **Controllers** folder in the main project.
2. Locate the **Register** action method.
3. Assign the **FirstName** property from the model parameter to the **FirstName** property in the **ApplicationUser** instance.
4. Assign **true** to the **IsActive** and **EmailConfirmed** properties in the **ApplicationUser** instance.

5. Assign the current date to the **Registered** property in the **ApplicationUser** instance.

The changes to the **ApplicationUser** instance:

```
var user = new ApplicationUser {
   UserName = model.Email,
   Email = model.Email,
   FirstName = model.FirstName,
   IsActive = true,
   Registered = DateTime.Now,
   EmailConfirmed = true
};
```

Alter the Register view

Since the **RegisterViewModel** model has a new required **FirstName** property, the **Register** view has to be altered to display a textbox for that value. The easiest way to alter the view is to copy the email address **form-group <div>** and change the **Email** property to **FirstName**.

Add yourself as a user with your email address using the **Register** view when it has been altered to display a first name textbox.

The image below show the **Register** view after it has been altered.

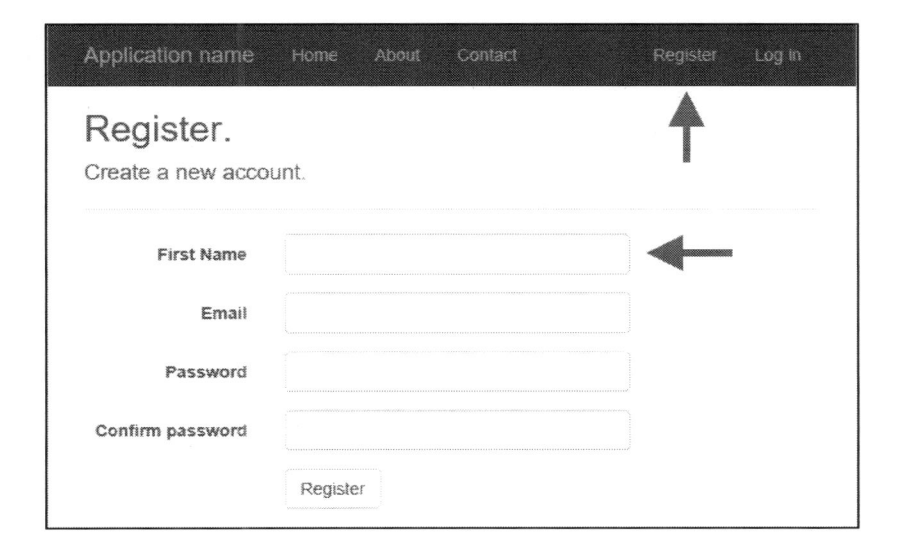

1. Open the **Register** view located in the **Views-Account** folder.
2. Copy the **form-group <div>** for the email address and paste it in above the email **form-group**.
3. Change the **Email** property to **FirstName** in the pasted in code.
4. Run the application and click the **Register** link in the upper right corner of the navigation bar.
5. Add a user named **Admin** with email **admin@company.com**.
6. Note that the user has access to the **Admin** menu even though the **Admin** role has not been assigned to the user. The reason for this is that the **Admin** menu hasn't been restricted for regular users yet.

The changes to the **ApplicationUser** instance:

```
<div class="form-group">
   @Html.LabelFor(m => m.FirstName,
       new { @class = "col-md-2 control-label" })
   <div class="col-md-10">
       @Html.TextBoxFor(m => m.FirstName,
           new { @class = "form-control" })
   </div>
</div>
```

The Admin role

The **Admin** role is meant to limit access to the **Admin** menu and the controllers associated with that menu. Only users added to the **Admin** role through the **AspNetUserRoles** table will be able to see and access the **Admin** menu.

The first thing you need to do is to add the **Admin** role to the **AspNetRoles** table and copy the **UserId** value for the user you added in the previous section, then add a record in the **AspNetUserRoles** table with the user **Id** and **Admin** role **Id**; this connects the user to the role. This connection table makes it possible to give users belonging to a specifc role access to certain features of the application though conditional logic.

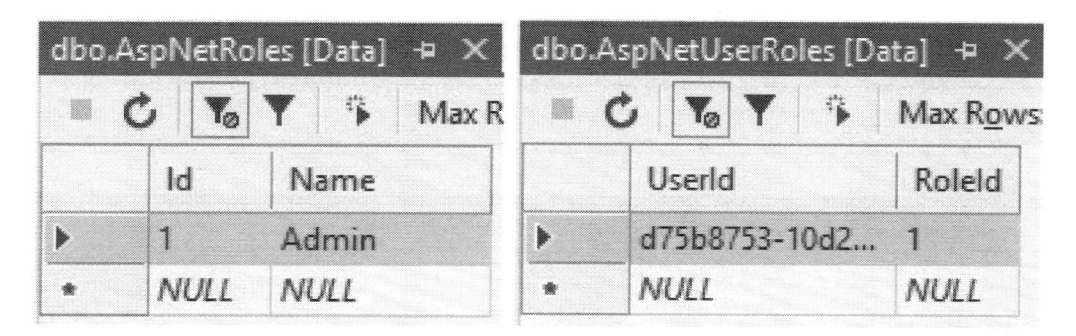

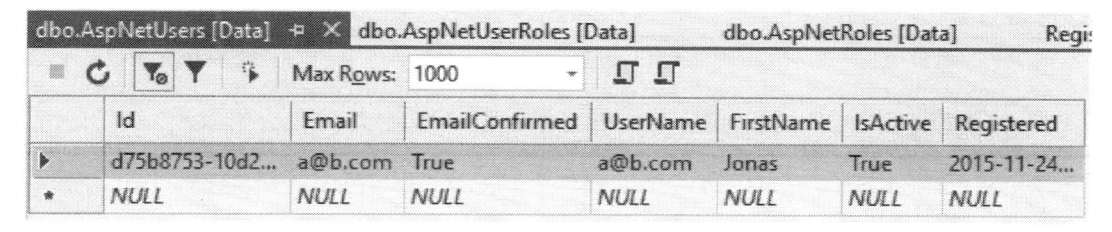

1. Open the **AspNetRoles** table in the Sever Explorer.
2. Add a new role called **Admin** with **Id** 1.
3. Open the **AspNetUsers** table in the Sever Explorer.
4. Copy the value in the **Id** column for the **Admin** user you added.
5. Open the **AspNetUserRoles** table in the Sever Explorer.
6. Add a new record with the user **Id** you copied and the **Admin** role **Id**.

Restict access to the Admin menu and its controllers

Now that the **Admin** role has been added, it's time to restrict access to the **Admin** menu. You will restrict access in two ways; the first is by using the **Request.IsAuthenticated** property to check if a user is logged in and authenticated. The other second check is to see if the authenticated user is associated with the **Admin** role. This can be achieved by calling the **User.IsInRole("Admin")** method.

To restrict access to the **Admin** menu you open the **_AdminMenuPartial** view and surround the code with an if-block checking the **IsAuthenticated** property and call the **IsInRole** method.

It's not enough to restrict access to the **Admin** menu; you also have to restrict access to the controllers which are called when a menu item is clicked. If you don't do this, any user can access the **Admin** actions by entering a correct URL in the browser. You can restrict access to all actions in a controller by adding the **Authorize** attribute with the **Admin** role specified to the class.

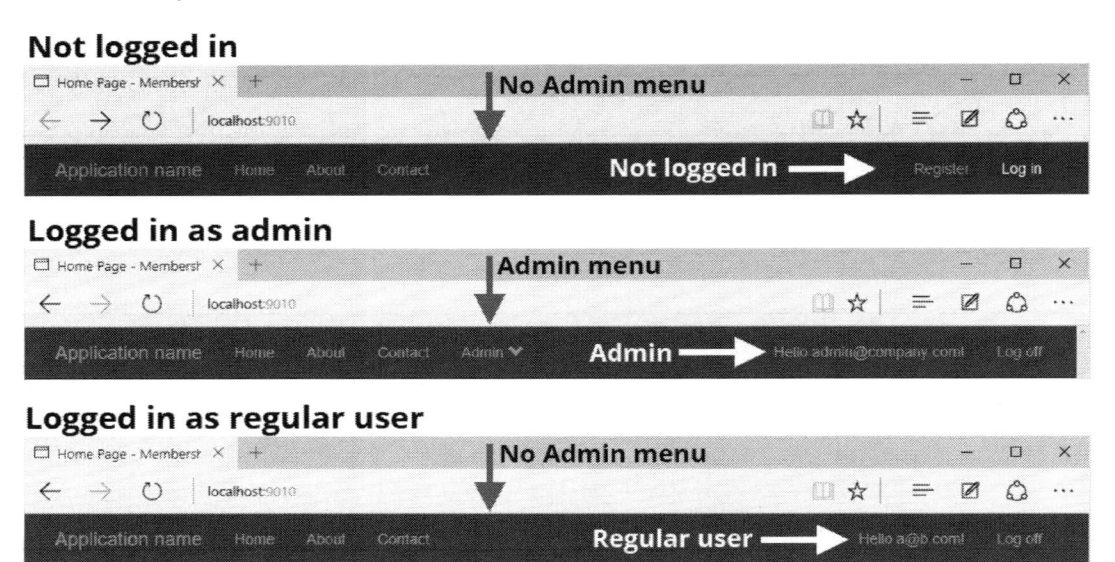

Not logged in

Logged in as admin

Logged in as regular user

1. Open the **_AdminMenuPartial** view located in the **Views-Shared** folder in the main project.
2. Add an if-block aound the code in the view and have it check the **IsAuthenticated** property and call the **IsInRole** method. If both return **true,** then the view should be rendered and the menu displayed in the navigation bar.

   ```
   @if (Request.IsAuthenticated && User.IsInRole("Admin"))
   {
       //... View code ...
   }
   ```
3. Open the **SectionController** in the **Controllers** folder in the **Admin** area.
4. Add the **Authorize** attribute and specify that only users with the **Admin** role will have access to the controller.

   ```
   [Authorize(Roles = "Admin")]
   public class SectionController : Controller
   {
   }
   ```
5. Now do the same for all controllers in the **Controllers** folder in the **Admin** area.

6. Run the application and logout.
7. Register a new user called **Joe** with email **joe@company.com** which is not added to the **Admin** role.
8. Note that the new user doesn't have access to the **Admin** menu because he's not an admin.
9. Logout **Joe** and login as the **Admin** user and check that the **Admin** menu is accessible.
10. Logout the **Admin** user and check that the menu isn't displayed.

Modify user information

In this section you will add actions to the **AccountController** and views to the **Views-Account** folder which will help maintain your user information; the **Index** view will be reachable from the **Users & Subscriptions Admin** menu option. The new views will make it possible for admins to add, change and delete users in the **AspNetUsers** table.

The views will need a model called **UserViewModel** containing **UserId, Email, FirstName** and **Password string** properties.

To make it easier to fetch the user's first name and to fill a list with users, a new **static** class called **IdentityExtensions** with two extension methods **GetUserFirstName** and **GetUsers** has to be added to a new folder called **Extensions**. The **GetUserFirstName** should act on a parameter of the **IIdentity** interface and the **GetUsers** sould act on a parameter of **List<UserViewModel>**.

Four views called **Index, Create, Edit** and **Delete** will have to be added to the **Views-Account** folder to list and alter user data.

Create the UserViewModel class

You can't use any of the existing models in the **AcountViewModels** file because none of them contain all the data needed in the model for the view you are about to create. Instead, you will create a new class called **UserViewModel** in the **Models** folder in the main project.

The properties needed are **Id**, **Email**, **FirstName** and **Password;** where the **Email** property is decorated with the **Required** and **EmailAddress** attributes, the **FirstName** property will allow a maximum of 30 characters and the **Password** property should be decorated with the **Required**, have a maximum string length of 100 characters and be declared as a password field.

1. Add a class called **UserViewModel** to the **Models** folder in the main project.
2. Add a **string** property called **Id** decorated with the **Display** attribute with the text "User Id".

   ```
   [Display(Name = "User Id")]
   public string Id { get; set; }
   ```

3. Add a **string** property called **Email** decorated with the **Display** attribute with the text "Email", the **Required** attribute and the **EmailAddress** attribute.
4. Add a **string** property called **FirstName** decorated with the **Display** attribute with the text "First Name" and the **StringLenght** attribute specifying that a maximum of 30 characters are allowed.

   ```
   [Display(Name = "First Name")]
   [StringLength(30, ErrorMessage = "The {0} must be at least {2} characters long.", MinimumLength = 2)]
   public string FirstName { get; set; }
   ```

5. Add a **string** property called **Password** decorated with the **Display** attribute with the text "Password", the **Required** attribute, the **DataType** attribute set to **Password** and the **StringLenght** attribute specifying that a maximum of 100 characters are allowed.

   ```
   [Required]
   [StringLength(100, ErrorMessage = "The {0} must be at least {2} characters long and have 1 non letter, 1 digit, 1 uppercase ('A'-'Z').", MinimumLength = 6)]
   [DataType(DataType.Password)]
   [Display(Name = "Password")]
   public string Password { get; set; }
   ```

The complete code for the **UserViewModel** class:

```
public class UserViewModel
{
    [Display(Name = "User Id")]
    public string Id { get; set; }
```

```
    [Required]
    [EmailAddress]
    [Display(Name = "Email")]
    public string Email { get; set; }

    [Display(Name = "First Name")]
    [StringLength(30, ErrorMessage = "The {0} must be at least {1}
        characters long.", MinimumLength = 2)]
    public string FirstName { get; set; }

    [Required]
    [StringLength(100, ErrorMessage = "The {0} must be at least {1}
        characters long and have 1 non letter, 1 digit, 1 uppercase
        ('A'-'Z').", MinimumLength = 6)]
    [DataType(DataType.Password)]
    [Display(Name = "Password")]
    public string Password { get; set; }
}
```

Create the extension methods

The first extension method is called **GetUserFirstName** and will act on an **IIdEntity** instance parameter containing the currently logged in user's identity and return a **string** with the user's first name. Because the **IIdentity** instance doesn' contain the **FirstName** property you added in a previous chapter, the first name has to be fetched from the **AspNetUsers** table in the database with the **Users** collection. Use an instance of the **ApplicationDbContext** to access the **AspNetUsers** table.

The first name will then be used in the **_LoginPartial** view to display the user's name instead of email in the navigation bar after they have successfully logged in.

The second extension method is called **GetUsers** and act on a **List<UserViewModel>** which is filled with a list of all the users in the **AspNetUsers** table. Three of the four properties in the model are filled with data, the **Password** property is meaningless to display for a list in the **Index** view since it contains a hashed value that has no meaning to the viewer.

Use an asynchronous LINQ query to fetch the users from the table and sort them by email.

ASP.NET MVC 5 - How to build a Membership Website

Adding the IdentityExtension class
1. Add a folder named **Extensions** to the main project.
2. Add a class called **IdentityExtensions** to the **Extensions** folder.
3. Because the class will contain extension methods, it has to be declared as **public static**.

The **IdentityExtensions** class:

```
public static class IdentityExtensions { }
```

Adding the GetUserFirstName extension method
1. Add a **public static** method called **GetUserFirstName** which returns a **string** to the **IdentityExtensions** class. It should have one **IIdentity** paramter called **identity**. Remember that the first parameter of an extension method has to be decorated with the **this** keyword denoting that it is the parameter the extension method acts on.
   ```
   public static string GetUserFirstName(this IIdentity identity)
   {
   }
   ```
2. Create an instance of the **ApplicationDbContext** called **db** inside the method to get access to the database.
   ```
   var db = ApplicationDbContext.Create();
   ```
3. Use the **FirstOrDefault** method on the **db.Users** collection to fetch the user where the **Name** property in the **identity** instance match the **UserName** field in the **Users** collection which represent the **AspNetUsers** table.
   ```
   var user = db.Users.FirstOrDefault(u =>
       u.UserName.Equals(identity.Name));
   ```
4. Return the value in the **FirstName** field if a match was found, otherwise return an empty string.
5. Open the **_LoginPartial** view.
6. Add a **@using** statement to the **Extensions** folder under the **@model** directive.
7. Replace the **User.Identity.GetUserName()** method call with a call to the **User.Identity.GetUserFirstName()** method you just created.
8. Run the application and logout and login again, the first name should be displayed to the left of the **Logout** button where the email was displayed before.

The code for the **GetUserFirstName** extension method:

```
public static string GetUserFirstName(this IIdentity identity)
{
    var db = ApplicationDbContext.Create();
    var user = db.Users.FirstOrDefault(u =>
        u.UserName.Equals(identity.Name));

    return user != null ? user.FirstName : string.Empty;
}
```

Adding the GetUsers extension method

This method will be called from the **Account** controller to display the users in the **Index** view you will create.

1. Add a **public static** method called **GetUsers** which returns a **Task** to the **IdentityExtensions** class. It should have one **List<UserViewMode>** parameter called **users**. Remember that the first parameter of an extension method has to be decorated with the **this** keyword denoting that it is the parameter the extension method act on.
2. Create an instance of the **ApplicationDbContext** called **db** inside the method to get access to the database.
3. Use an asynchronous LINQ query to fetch all the users and add them to the **users** collection parameter using the **AddRange** method. Order the users by email.

The code for the **GetUsers** extension method:

```
public static async Task GetUsers(this List<UserViewModel> users)
{
    var db = ApplicationDbContext.Create();
    users.AddRange(
        await (from u in db.Users
               select new UserViewModel
               {
                   Id = u.Id,
                   Email = u.Email,
                   FirstName = u.FirstName,
               }).OrderBy(o => o.Email).ToListAsync());
}
```

Adding the Index view

To display all the users, you need to add an **Index** view to the **Views-Account** folder with the associated **Index** action in the **ActionsController** class. The easiest way to add the **Index** view is to scaffold it and then remove the **Password** table header and table data from the view. Displaying the password is pointless since it is a hashed value that is meaningless to the user.

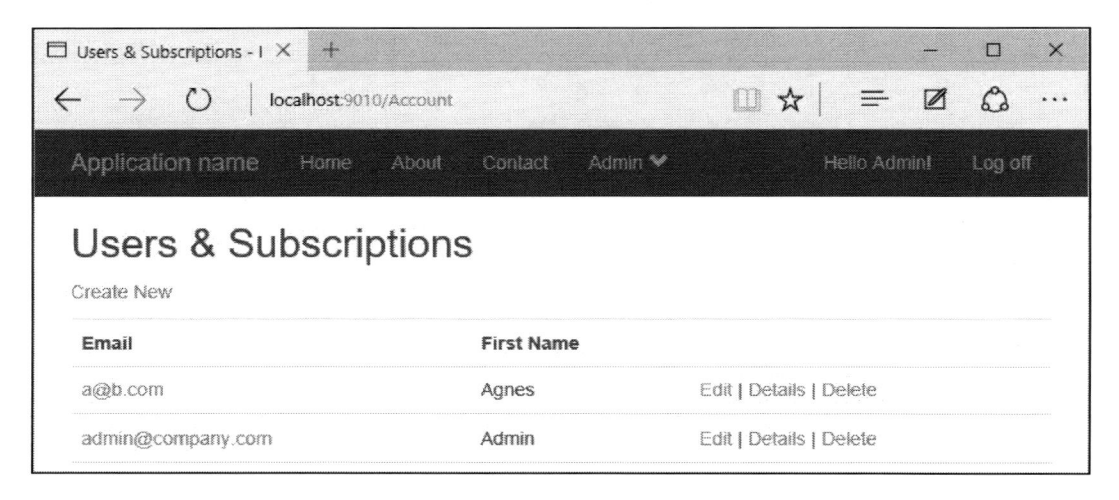

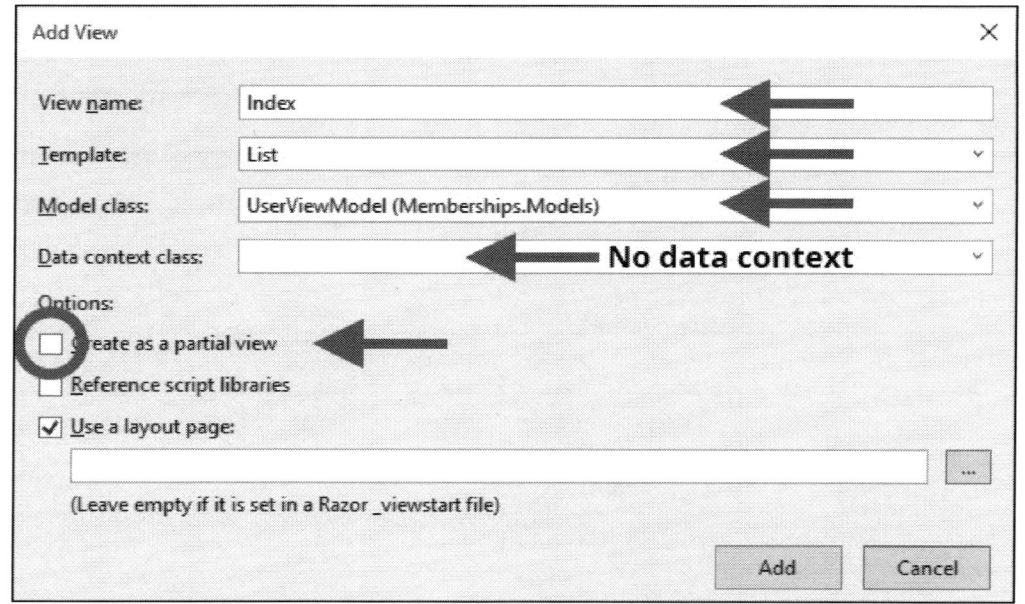

ASP.NET MVC 5 - How to build a Membership Website

1. Right-click on the **Views-Account** folder and fill in the controls according to the dialog above.
2. Change the **ViewBag.Title** property and the **<h2>** header to "Users & Subscriptions".
3. Delete the **<th>** displaying the header for the **Password** property.
4. Delete the **<td>** displaying the value in the **Password** property.
5. You can delete the **ActionLink** to the **Details** view because there will not be a **Details** view.
6. Check that the user is authenticated and belongs to the **Admin** role with an if-block below the **<h2>** element around the rest of the view markup.

```
<h2>Users & Subscriptions</h2>
@if (Request.IsAuthenticated && User.IsInRole("Admin"))
{
    //The rest of the view's HTML markup goes here
}
```

The **Index** view markup:

```
@model IEnumerable<Memberships.Models.UserViewModel>

@{ ViewBag.Title = "Users & Subscriptions"; }
<h2>Users & Subscriptions</h2>
@if (Request.IsAuthenticated && User.IsInRole("Admin"))
{
    <p>@Html.ActionLink("Create New", "Create")</p>
    <table class="table">
    <tr>
        <th>@Html.DisplayNameFor(model => model.Email)</th>
        <th>@Html.DisplayNameFor(model => model.FirstName)</th>
        <th></th>
    </tr>

    @foreach (var item in Model)
    {
        <tr>
            <td>@Html.DisplayFor(modelItem => item.Email)</td>
            <td>@Html.DisplayFor(modelItem => item.FirstName)</td>

            <td>@Html.ActionLink("Edit", "Edit", new { id = item.Id }) |
                @Html.ActionLink("Delete", "Delete", new { id = item.Id })
            </td>
        </tr>
```

```
    }
    </table>
}
```

Adding the Index action

An action method called **Index** has to be added to the **AccountController** class for the **Index** view to be rendered correctly. Don't forget to add the **Authorize** attribute to the action and limit the access to only users in the **Admin** role.

1. Open the **AccountController** class in the main project's **Controllers** folder.
2. Add a **using** statement to the **Memberships.Extensions** folder to get access to the **GetUsers** extension method you added earlier.
   ```
   using Memberships.Extensions;
   ```
3. Add an asynchronous paramter-less **Index** action method returning a **Task<ActionResult>**.
   ```
   public async Task<ActionResult> Index()
   {
   }
   ```
4. Create variable called **users** as a **List<UserViewModel>** which will hold the users' account data.
5. Call the **GetUsers** extension method asynchronously on the users variable to fill it.
   ```
   await users.GetUsers();
   ```
6. Pass in the **users** variable with the call to the **Views** method to render the view.
7. Run the application and navigate to **Users & Subscriptions** with the **Admin** menu. The users should be listed in a table.

The **Index** action code:

```
[Authorize(Roles = "Admin")]
public async Task<ActionResult> Index()
{
    var users = new List<UserViewModel>();
    await users.GetUsers();

    return View(users);
}
```

Styling the Index view

Let's style the **Index** view to make it more appealing and add a button partial view with buttons to the **Edit**, **Delete** and **Subscriptions** views.

Because the **_CreateNewButtonPartial**, **_SmallButtonPartial** and **_TableButtonsPartial** partial views will be used from views in the **Admin** area and the **Account** views in the main project, they have to be moved to the **Views-Shared** folder in the main project to be available in the whole project.

The image below shows the altered **Index** view:

1. Locate the **_CreateNewButtonPartial**, **_SmallButtonPartial** and **_TableButtonsPartial** partial views in the **Views-Shared** folder in the **Admin** area and move them to the **Views-Shared** folder in the main project. You can do this by selecting them and dragging them to the folder or use the *Cut-Paste* approach.
2. Open the **Index** view in the **Account** folder.
3. Add the **table**, **table-condensed** and **table-striped** Bootstrap classes to the **<table>** element to remove some padding on the rows and to display every other row wth a light gray color.
4. Add the **success** Bootstrap class to the **<tr>** element to give the header row a (green) background color.

5. Replace the *Create new* **ActionLink** with a call to the **_CreateNewButtonPartial** view you moved to the **Views-Shared** folder.
   `@Html.Partial("_CreateNewButtonPartial")`

Modifying the SmallButtonModel

The **SmallButtonModel** class must be altered to handle user id's for the buttons in the **Index** view in the **Views-Account** folder. A new **string** property called **UserId** has to be added and it also has to be added to the logic in the **ActionParameters** property.

1. Open the **SmallButtonModel** class in the **Models** folder in the **Admin** area.
2. Add a **string** property called **UserId**.
   `public string UserId { get; set; }`
3. Append the **UserId** to the paramter list if it isn't **null** and not an empty string.
   ```
   if (UserId != null && !UserId.Equals(string.Empty))
       param.Append(string.Format("{0}={1}&", "userId", UserId));
   ```

Modifying the _TableButtonsPartial view

To display the buttons correctly on each row, you will have to alter the **_TableButtons-Partial** view. It contains buttons for **Edit**, **Delete** and **Details** and must be altered to have a **Subscriptions** buttons. The **Details** button should only be visible if the **UserId** property is **null** or an empty string meaning that no **UserId** has been provided and the **Subscriptions** button should only be visible if the **UserId** property contains a value other than **null** or an empty string.

The easiest way to add the **Subscriptions** button is to copy the **Details** button partial view declaration in the **_TableButtonsPartial** view, paste it in below the **Details** button declaration and change the values. The following property values have to be changed: Action = "Subscriptions", ButtonType = "btn-info", Text = "Subscriptions".

The **UserId** property has to be added to all the button partial view declarations in the **_TableButtonsPartial** view.

1. Open the **_TableButtonsPartial** view in the **Views-Shared** folder where you copied it to.
2. Copy the **_SmallButtonPartial** view declaration for the **Details** button and paste it in below the **Details** button code.

3. Change the **Action** property to "Subscription", the **ButtonType** to "btn-info" and **Text** to "Subscriptions".
4. Add an if-block around the **Details** button declaration which checks if the **UserId** property is **null** or an empty string.
   ```
   @if (Model.UserId == null || Model.UserId.Equals(string.Empty)){ }
   ```
5. Add an if-block around the **Subscriptions** button declaration which checks that the **UserId** property contains a value other than **null** or an empty string.
   ```
   @if (Model.UserId != null && !Model.UserId.Equals(string.Empty)){}
   ```
6. Add the **UserId** property to all the button declarations.
   ```
   UserId = Model.UserId
   ```

The alterations of the **Details** button and the addition of the **Subscription** button:

```
@if (Model.UserId == null || Model.UserId.Equals(string.Empty))
{
    @Html.Partial("_SmallButtonPartial",
        new SmallButtonModel
        {
            Action = "Details",
            ButtonType = "btn-success",
            Glyph = "list",
            Text = "Details",
            Id = Model.Id,
            ItemId = Model.ItemId,
            ProductId = Model.ProductId,
            SubscriptionId = Model.SubscriptionId,
            UserId = Model.UserId
        })
}

@if (Model.UserId != null && !Model.UserId.Equals(string.Empty))
{
    @Html.Partial("_SmallButtonPartial",
        new SmallButtonModel
        {
            Action = "Subscriptions",
            ButtonType = "btn-info",
            Glyph = "list",
            Text = "Subscriptions",
            Id = Model.Id,
            ItemId = Model.ItemId,
            ProductId = Model.ProductId,
```

```
            SubscriptionId = Model.SubscriptionId,
            UserId = Model.UserId
        })
}
```

Adding the _TableButtonsPartial view to the Index view
1. Open the **Index** view in the **Account** folder.
2. Remove the **<td>** element and its content for the **<td>** containing the **ActionLinks** to the other views.
3. Add a partial view call to the **_TableButtonsPartial** view and pass in an instance of the **SmallButtonModel** with the **UserId** assigned. The buttons will not work yet because you haven't added the necessary views and actions.
   ```
   @Html.Partial("_TableButtonsPartial", new SmallButtonModel {
   UserId = item.Id })
   ```

Adding the Create view

To add the possibility for admins to add new users, you have to add a **Create** view belonging to the **AccountController** using the **UserViewModel** class as its model.

You add the **Create** view to the **Views-Account** folder and add its actions to the **Account-Controller** in the **Controllers** folder.

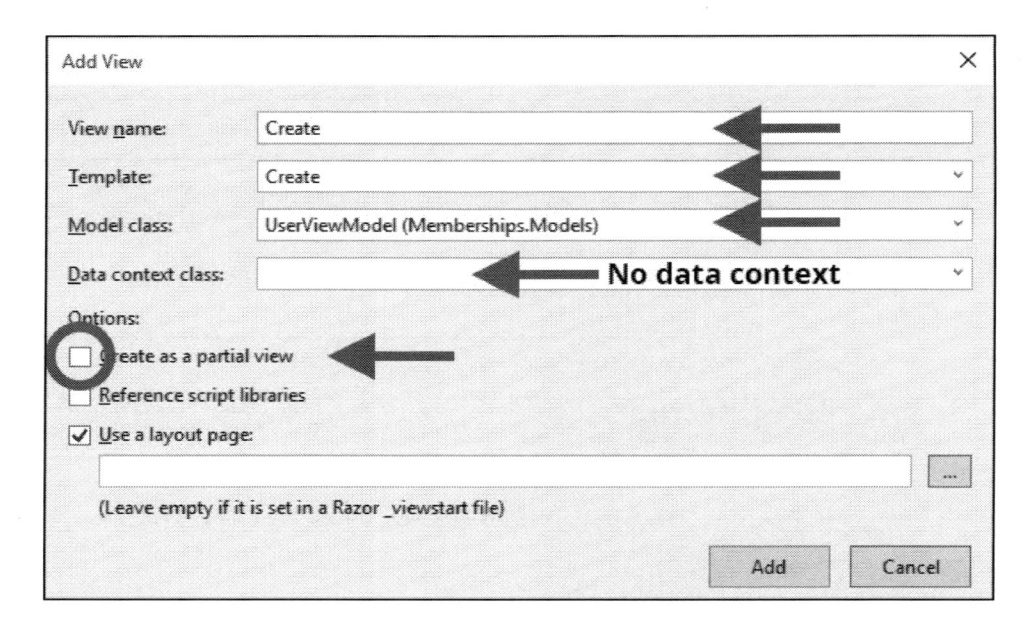

1. Right-click on the **Views-Account** folder and add the **Create** view with the values specified in the image above.
2. Change the **btn-default** Bootstrap class to **btn-success** on the **Create** button to give it (green) color.
   `<input type="submit" value="Create" class="btn btn-success" />`
3. Move the **_BackToListButtonPartial** partial view from the **Views-Shared** folder in the **Admin** area to the **Views-Shared** folder in the main project to make it accessible in the whole project.
4. Replace the *Back to List* **ActionLink** with the **_BackToListButtonPartial** partial view.
   `@Html.Partial("_BackToListButtonPartial")`

The image below displays the **Create** view after it has been altered.

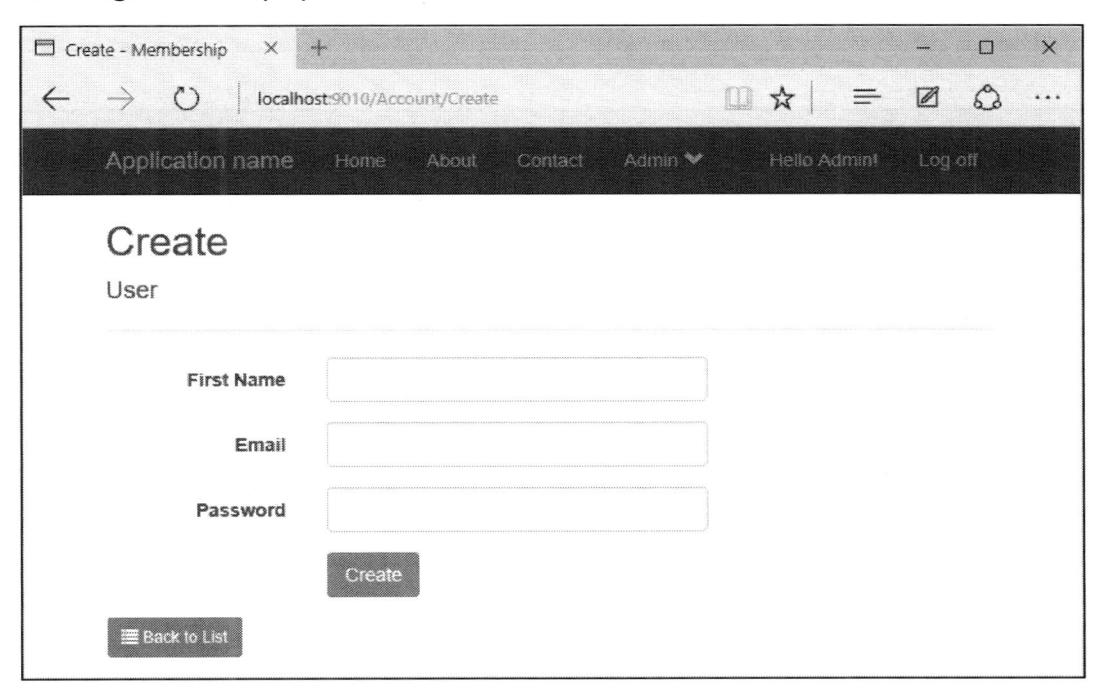

The complete code for the **Create** view:

```
@model Memberships.Models.UserViewModel

@{
    ViewBag.Title = "Create";
}

<h2>Create</h2>

@using (Html.BeginForm())
{
    @Html.AntiForgeryToken()

    <div class="form-horizontal">
        <h4>Create User</h4>
        <hr />
        @Html.ValidationSummary(true, "", new { @class = "text-danger" })
        <div class="form-group">
            @Html.LabelFor(model => model.Email, htmlAttributes:
                new { @class = "control-label col-md-2" })
            <div class="col-md-10">
                @Html.EditorFor(model => model.Email, new {
                    htmlAttributes = new { @class = "form-control" } })
                @Html.ValidationMessageFor(model => model.Email, "",
                    new { @class = "text-danger" })
            </div>
        </div>

        <div class="form-group">
            @Html.LabelFor(model => model.FirstName, htmlAttributes:
                new { @class = "control-label col-md-2" })
            <div class="col-md-10">
                @Html.EditorFor(model => model.FirstName, new {
                    htmlAttributes = new { @class = "form-control" } })
                @Html.ValidationMessageFor(model => model.FirstName,
                    "", new { @class = "text-danger" })
            </div>
        </div>

        <div class="form-group">
            @Html.LabelFor(model => model.Password, htmlAttributes:
                new { @class = "control-label col-md-2" })
            <div class="col-md-10">
```

```
                @Html.EditorFor(model => model.Password, new {
                    htmlAttributes = new { @class = "form-control" } })
                @Html.ValidationMessageFor(model => model.Password, "",
                    new { @class = "text-danger" })
            </div>
        </div>

        <div class="form-group">
            <div class="col-md-offset-2 col-md-10">
                <input type="submit" value="Create"
                    class="btn btn-success btn-sm" />
            </div>
        </div>
    </div>
}
<div>
    @Html.Partial("_BackToListButtonPartial")
</div>
```

Adding the Create actions

For the **Create** view to work, you have to add two action methods called **Create** to the **AccountController** class: one for displaying the view and one to handle submitted form values and save them to the **AspNetUsers** table in the database.

The HttpGet Create action

This action is called when the controller serves up the **Create** view to the user and displays it in the browser. This is a very simple action since it only serves up an empty view and therefore doesn't have model data to render.

The method returns an **ActionResult** and takes no parameters. Don't forget to add the **Authorize** attribute to restrict access only to users in the **Admin** role.

1. Open the **AccountController** class in the **Controllers** folder and navigate to the end of the class.
2. Add a method called **Create** which returns an **ActionResult** and takes no parameters.
3. The only call in the method is to the **View** method to render the **Create** view.
4. Add the **Authorize** attribute to the method.
   `[Authorize(Roles = "Admin")]`

The complete **HttpGet Create** action:

```
[Authorize(Roles = "Admin")]
public ActionResult Create()
{
    return View();
}
```

The HttpPost Create action

This action is called when the user clicks the **submit** button in the **Create** view's form.

This method is asynchronous and return an **Task<ActionResult>** and takes a **UserView-Model** as its only parameter. Don't forget to add the **Authorize** attribute to restrict access only to users in the **Admin** role. It also must be decorated with the **ValidateAntiForgeryToken** attribute which ensures that the call originated from your server.

If any exception occurs or if the **ModelState** is invalid, the model should be returned, keeping the user in the form they were without losing any data.

If the model is **null,** then return a **BadRequest**.

```
return new HttpStatusCodeResult(HttpStatusCode.BadRequest);
```

If the **ModelState** is valid, then create an instance of the **ApplicationUser** class and fill it with data from the model parameter. Also assign **true** to the **IsActive** and **EmailConfirmed** properties and the current date to the **Registred** property. The **ApplicationUser** class is the entity used when working with user data in the **AspNetUsers** table.

Call the **UserManager.CreateAsync** and **await** the result. If successful, the user will be added to the **AspNetUser** table in the database. Store the return value from the method call in a variable called **result**.

```
var result = await UserManager.CreateAsync(user, model.Password);
```

If the **Succeeded** property in the **result** variable is **true,** then redirect to the **Index** view that belongs to the **AccountController,** else call the **AddErrors** method to add the errors to the response sent back to the view.

```
return RedirectToAction("Index", "Account");
```

1. Open the **AccountController** class in the **Controllers** folder and navigate to the end of the class.
2. Add an asynchronous action method called **Create,** which returns a **Task<ActionResult>** and has a **UserViewModel** parameter. Decorate the action with the three attributes **HttpPost, ValidateAntiForgeryToken** and **Authorize**.
```
[HttpPost]
[ValidateAntiForgeryToken]
[Authorize(Roles = "Admin")]
public async Task<ActionResult> Create(UserViewModel model)
{
}
```
3. Add a **try/catch**-block to the action and leave the **catch**-block empty. Return the view with the model originally sent into the action to keep the user on the same form with the values preserved. The rest of the code will be aded inside the **try**-block.
```
try { }
catch { }

return View(model);
```
4. Return a **BadRequest** to the client if the model is **null**.
```
if (model == null)
{
    return new HttpStatusCodeResult(HttpStatusCode.BadRequest);
}
```
5. Add an if-block that check if the model state is valid. The rest of the code will be added inside this if-block.
```
if (ModelState.IsValid) { }
```
6. Create an instance of the **ApplicationUser** entity and fill it with data form the passed in model (the values from the controls in the **Create** view).
```
var user = new ApplicationUser
{
    UserName = model.Email,
    Email = model.Email,
    FirstName = model.FirstName,
    IsActive = true,
    Registered = DateTime.Now,
    EmailConfirmed = true
};
```

7. Call the **UserManager.CreateAsync** method with the user instance you just created. If the result is successful, then redirect to the **Index** view belonging to the **AccountController;** else, store the errors in the response sent to the client by calling the **AddErrors** method with the **result** object.

```
var result = await UserManager.CreateAsync(user, model.Password);
if (result.Succeeded)
{
    return RedirectToAction("Index", "Account");
}

AddErrors(result);
```

8. Run the application and navigate to the **Index** view beloning to the **AccountController**. Click the **Create new** button and add a new user. If successful, the new user should appear in the **Index** view which is loaded automatically after the user has been added to the **AspNetUsers** table in the database.

The complete **HttpPost Create** action:

```
[HttpPost]
[ValidateAntiForgeryToken]
[Authorize(Roles = "Admin")]
public async Task<ActionResult> Create(UserViewModel model)
{
    try
    {
        if (model == null)
        {
            return new HttpStatusCodeResult(HttpStatusCode.BadRequest);
        }

        if (ModelState.IsValid)
        {
            var user = new ApplicationUser
            {
                UserName = model.Email,
                Email = model.Email,
                FirstName = model.FirstName,
                IsActive = true,
                Registered = DateTime.Now,
                EmailConfirmed = true
```

```
            };

            // EmailConfirmed = true is a prerequisite for
            // sending "Forgot Password" email

            var result = await UserManager.CreateAsync(
                user, model.Password);

            if (result.Succeeded)
            {
                return RedirectToAction("Index", "Account");
            }

            AddErrors(result);
        }
    }
    catch { }

    // If we got this far something failed, re-display the form
    return View(model);
}
```

Adding the Edit view

To add the possibility for admins to chage user data, you have to add an **Edit** view belonging to the **AccountController** using the **UserViewModel** class as its model.

You add the **Edit** view to the **Views-Account** folder and add its actions to the **AccountController** in the **Controllers** folder.

Add View

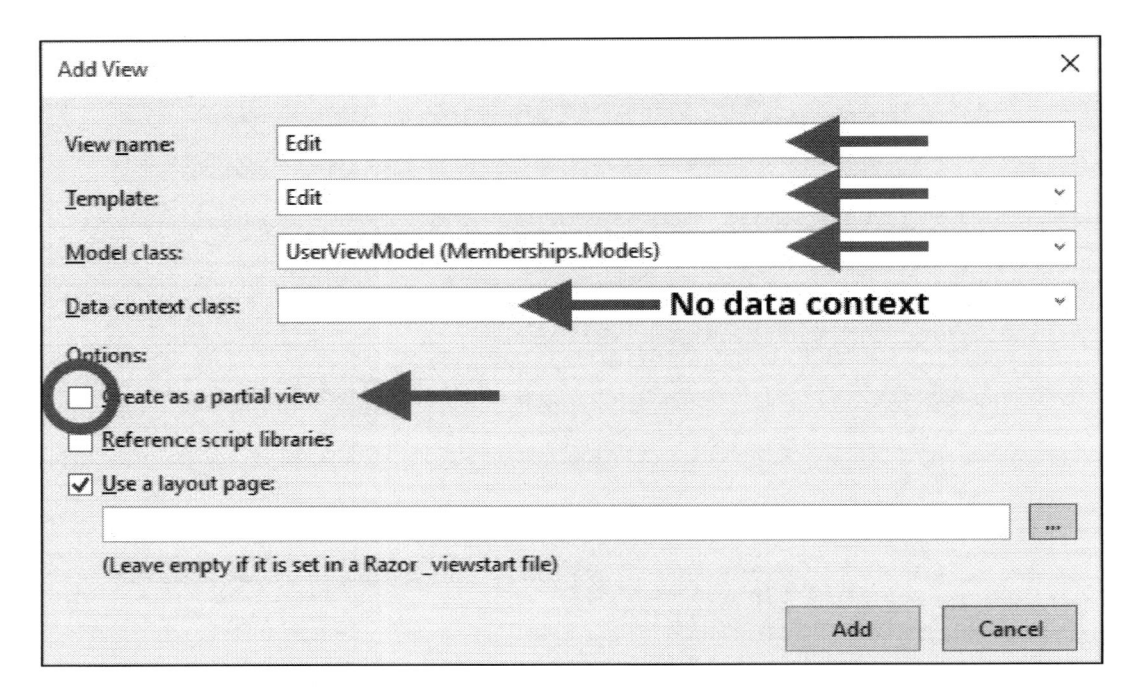

View name:	Edit
Template:	Edit
Model class:	UserViewModel (Memberships.Models)
Data context class:	← No data context

Options:
- ☐ Create as a partial view ←
- ☐ Reference script libraries
- ☑ Use a layout page:

(Leave empty if it is set in a Razor _viewstart file)

1. Right-click on the **Views-Account** folder and add the **Edit** view with the values specified in the image above.
2. Change the **btn-default** Bootstrap class to **btn-success** on the **Save** button to give it (green) color.
   `<input type="submit" value="Save" class="btn btn-success" />`
3. Replace the *Back to List* **ActionLink** with the **_BackToListButtonPartial** partial view.
   `@Html.Partial("_BackToListButtonPartial")`

The image below shows the **Edit** view after it has been altered.

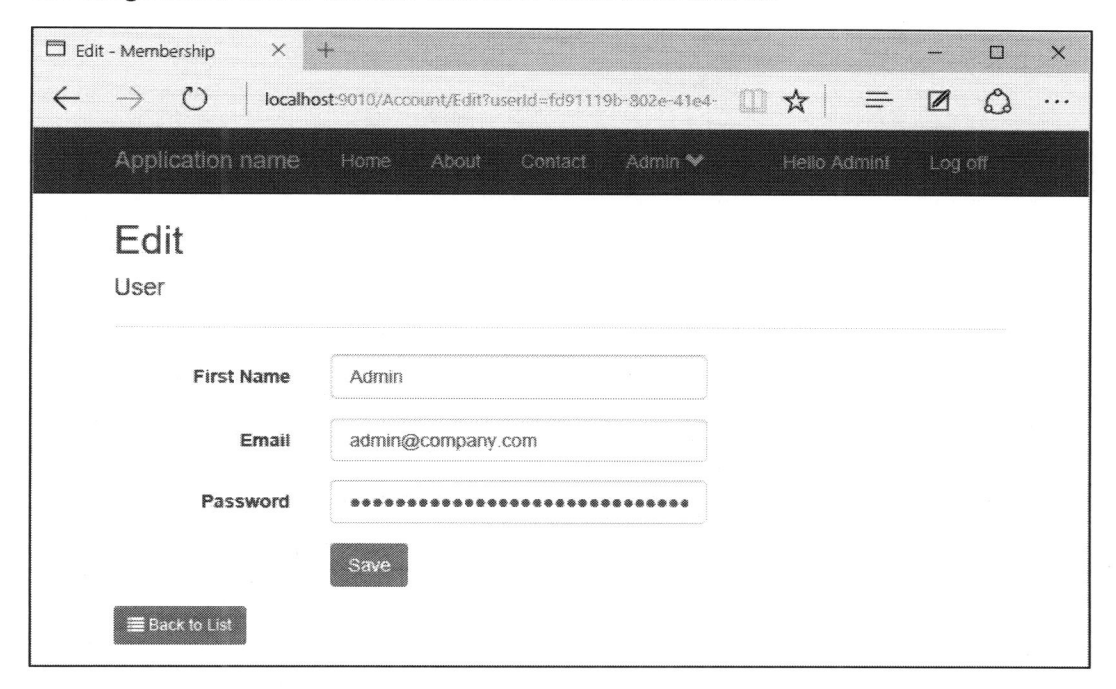

The complete code for the **Edit** view:

```
@model Memberships.Models.UserViewModel

@{
    ViewBag.Title = "Edit";
}

<h2>Edit</h2>

@using (Html.BeginForm())
{
    @Html.AntiForgeryToken()

    <div class="form-horizontal">
        <h4>Edit User</h4>
        <hr />
        @Html.ValidationSummary(true, "", new { @class = "text-danger" })
        @Html.HiddenFor(model => model.Id)
```

```html
            <div class="form-group">
                @Html.LabelFor(model => model.Email, htmlAttributes:
                    new { @class = "control-label col-md-2" })
                <div class="col-md-10">
                    @Html.EditorFor(model => model.Email, new {
                        htmlAttributes = new { @class = "form-control" } })
                    @Html.ValidationMessageFor(model => model.Email, "",
                        new { @class = "text-danger" })
                </div>
            </div>

            <div class="form-group">
                @Html.LabelFor(model => model.FirstName, htmlAttributes:
                    new { @class = "control-label col-md-2" })
                <div class="col-md-10">
                    @Html.EditorFor(model => model.FirstName, new {
                        htmlAttributes = new { @class = "form-control" } })
                    @Html.ValidationMessageFor(model => model.FirstName,
                        "", new { @class = "text-danger" })
                </div>
            </div>

            <div class="form-group">
                @Html.LabelFor(model => model.Password, htmlAttributes:
                    new { @class = "control-label col-md-2" })
                <div class="col-md-10">
                    @Html.EditorFor(model => model.Password, new {
                        htmlAttributes = new { @class = "form-control" } })
                    @Html.ValidationMessageFor(model => model.Password, "",
                        new { @class = "text-danger" })
                </div>
            </div>

            <div class="form-group">
                <div class="col-md-offset-2 col-md-10">
                    <input type="submit" value="Save"
                        class="btn btn-success btn-sm" />
                </div>
            </div>
        </div>
}
<div>
    @Html.Partial("_BackToListButtonPartial")
</div>
```

Adding the Edit actions

For the **Edit** view to work, you have to add two action methods called **Edit** to the **AccountController** class: one for displaying the view and one to handle submitted form values and save them to the **AspNetUsers** table in the database.

The HttpGet Edit action

This asynchronous action is called when the controller serves up the **Edit** view to the user and displays it in the browser. It is slightly more complex than the **Create** action in that it has to look up the user in the database before serving up the data to the view. It therefore needs a **string** parameter called **userId**.

The method returns a **Task<ActionResult>**. Don't forget to add the **Authorize** attribute to restrict access only to users in the **Admin** role.

Return a **BadRequest** to the client if the **userId** parameter is **null** or contain an empty string.

Fetch the user with the passed in **userId** by calling the **UserManager.FindByIsAsync** method ad store the awaited result in a variable called **user**.

Return *Http Not Found* if the **user** variable is **null** by calling the **HttpNotFound** method.

If the user exists, then create an instance of the **UserViewModel** class in a variable called **model** and assign the values from the fetched user to its properties before passing the object to the **View** method for rendering.

1. Open the **AccountController** class in the **Controllers** folder and navigate to the end of the class.
2. Add an **async** action method called **Edit** which returns a **Task<ActionResult>** and takes a **string** parameter called **userId**. Only **Admin** users should have access to this action.
   ```
   [Authorize(Roles = "Admin")]
   public async Task<ActionResult> Edit(string userId)
   {
   }
   ```
3. Return **BadRequest** if **userId** is **null** or an empty string.

```
if (userId == null || userId.Equals(string.Empty))
{
    return new HttpStatusCodeResult(HttpStatusCode.BadRequest);
}
```

4. Fetch the user asynchronously with the **userId** parameter and store the result in a variable called **user**.
   ```
   ApplicationUser user = await UserManager.FindByIdAsync(userId);
   ```

5. Return *Http Not Found* if the **user** variable is **null** by calling the **HttpNotFound** method.
   ```
   if (user == null)
   {
       return HttpNotFound();
   }
   ```

6. Create an instance of the **UserViewModel**, assign values from the fetched user and return the model with the **View** method.
   ```
   var model = new UserViewModel
   {
       Email = user.Email,
       FirstName = user.FirstName,
       Id = user.Id,
       Password = user.PasswordHash
   };

   return View(model);
   ```

The complete **HttpGet Edit** action:

```
[Authorize(Roles = "Admin")]
public async Task<ActionResult> Edit(string userId)
{
    if (userId == null || userId.Equals(string.Empty))
    {
        return new HttpStatusCodeResult(HttpStatusCode.BadRequest);
    }

    ApplicationUser user = await UserManager.FindByIdAsync(userId);

    if (user == null)
    {
        return HttpNotFound();
    }
```

```
    var model = new UserViewModel
    {
        Email = user.Email,
        FirstName = user.FirstName,
        Id = user.Id,
        Password = user.PasswordHash
    };

    return View(model);
}
```

The HttpPost Edit action
This action is called when the user clicks the **submit** button in the **Edit** view's form.

It is basically the same as the corresponding **Create** method; you only have to make a few minor modifications. Instead of creating a new instance from the **ApplicationUser** class, you will fetch the user from the database and assign values to that instance. The **catch**-block will also be modified to return an empty view.

1. Open the **AccountController** class in the **Controllers** folder and navigate to the **HttpPost Create** action and copy the method and its three attributes.
2. Navigate to the end of the class and paste in the code.
3. Chage the name of the action to **Edit**.
4. Remove the following variable and its assignments.
   ```
   var user = new ApplicationUser
   {
       // ... Assignments ...
   }
   ```
5. Call the **UserManager.FindByIdAsync** method asynchronously to fetch the user matching the **userId** parameter value and store the user in a variable called **user**.
   ```
   var user = await UserManager.FindByIdAsync(model.Id);
   ```
6. Assign the values from the **Email** and **FirstName** properties in the model to the **Email**, **UserName** and **FirstName** properties in the fetched **user** object.
7. The value in the model's **Password** property has to be hashed before it can be stored in the **PasswordHash** property. But it should only be assigned if the value

in the **PasswordHash** property isn't equal to the value in the model's **Password** property.

```
user.Email = model.Email;
user.UserName = model.Email;
user.FirstName = model.FirstName;
// Hash the password if a new password has been entered
// before saving the edited user to the database
if (!user.PasswordHash.Equals(model.Password))
user.PasswordHash = UserManager.PasswordHasher.HashPassword(
    model.Password);
```

8. Change the **CretateAsync** method call to **UpdateAsync** to update the user instead of creating a new user.
   ```
   var result = await UserManager.UpdateAsync(user);
   ```

9. Return an empty view from the **catch**-block.
   ```
   return View();
   AddErrors(result);
   ```

10. Run the application and navigate to the **Index** view belonging to the **AccountController**. Click the **Edit** button on one of the user rows and update some info about the user. If successful, the updated user information should appear in the **Index** view which is loaded automatically after the user has been updated in the **AspNetUsers** table in the database.

The complete **HttpPost Edit** action:

```
[HttpPost]
[ValidateAntiForgeryToken]
[Authorize(Roles = "Admin")]
public async Task<ActionResult> Edit(UserViewModel model)
{
    try
    {
        if (model == null)
        {
            return new HttpStatusCodeResult(HttpStatusCode.BadRequest);
        }

        if (ModelState.IsValid)
        {
            var user = await UserManager.FindByIdAsync(model.Id);
```

```
            if (user != null)
            {
                user.Email = model.Email;
                user.UserName = model.Email;
                user.FirstName = model.FirstName;
                // Hash the password if a new password has been entered
                // before saving the edited user to the database
                if (!user.PasswordHash.Equals(model.Password))
                    user.PasswordHash = UserManager.PasswordHasher
                        .HashPassword(model.Password);

                var result = await UserManager.UpdateAsync(user);
                if (result.Succeeded)
                {
                    return RedirectToAction("Index", "Account");
                }

                AddErrors(result);
            }
        }
    }
    catch { }

    return View(model);
}
```

Adding the Delete view

To add the possibility for admins to delete a user, you have to add a **Delete** view belonging to the **AccountController** using the **UserViewModel** class as its model.

You add the **Delete** view to the **Views-Account** folder and add its actions to the **AccountController** in the **Controllers** folder.

Add View

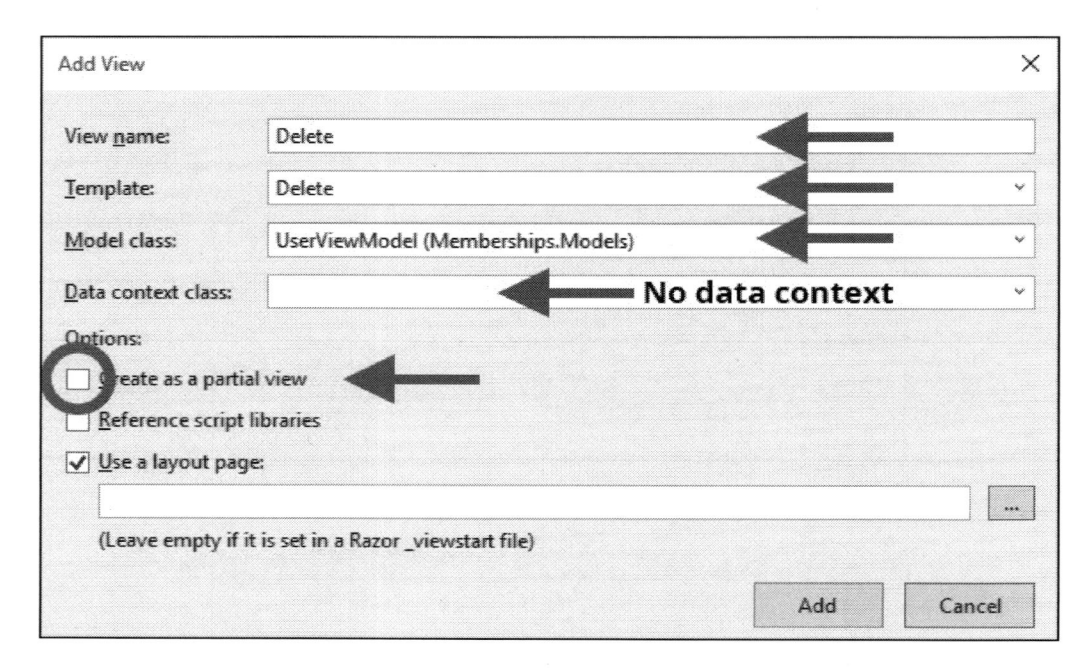

View name:	Delete
Template:	Delete
Model class:	UserViewModel (Memberships.Models)
Data context class:	← No data context

Options:
- ☐ Create as a partial view
- ☐ Reference script libraries
- ☑ Use a layout page:

(Leave empty if it is set in a Razor _viewstart file)

[Add] [Cancel]

1. Right-click on the **Views-Account** folder and add the **Delete** view with the values specified in the image above.
2. Delete the **<dt>** and **<dd>** elements for the **Password** property.
3. Add all the model properties as hidden form fields inside the form below the **@html.AntiForgeryToken()** method call using **@Html.HiddenFor**. You need to do this for the model to be valid in the **HttpPost Delete** action.
   ```
   @Html.HiddenFor(model => model.FirstName)
   @Html.HiddenFor(model => model.Email)
   @Html.HiddenFor(model => model.Id)
   @Html.HiddenFor(model => model.Password)
   ```
4. Change the **btn-default** Bootstrap class to **btn-danger** on the **Save** button to give it (green) color.
   ```
   <input type="submit" value="Delete" class="btn btn-success" />
   ```
5. Replace the *Back to List* **ActionLink** with the **_BackToListButtonPartial** partial view.
   ```
   @Html.Partial("_BackToListButtonPartial")
   ```

The image below shows the **Delete** view after it has been altered.

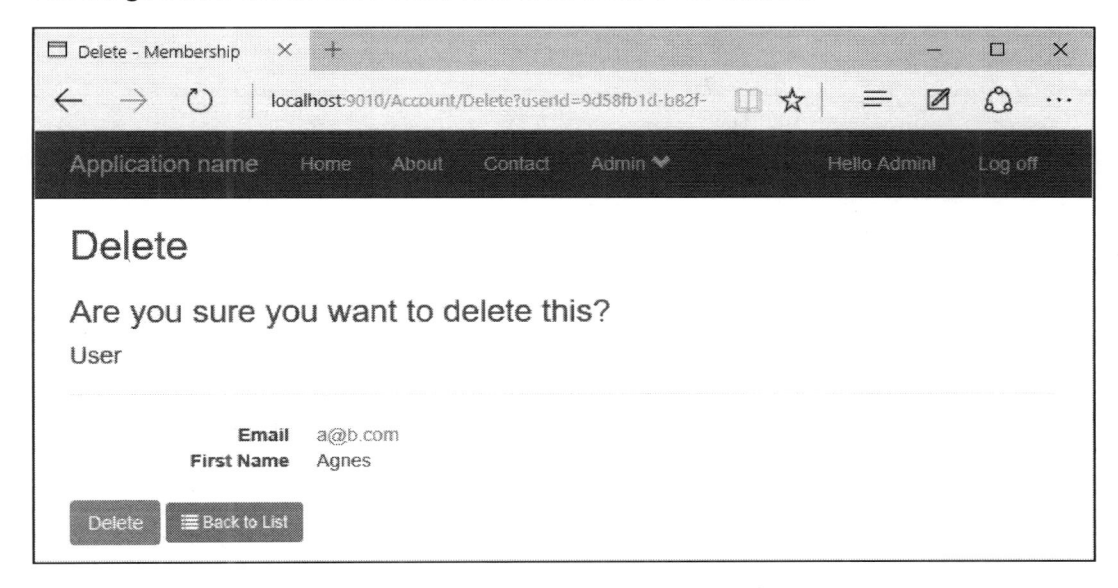

The complete code for the **Delete** view:

```
@model Memberships.Models.UserViewModel

@{
    ViewBag.Title = "Delete";
}

<h2>Delete</h2>

<h3>Are you sure you want to delete this?</h3>
<div>
    <h4>UserViewModel</h4>
    <hr />
    <dl class="dl-horizontal">
        <dt>@Html.DisplayNameFor(model => model.Email)</dt>
        <dd>@Html.DisplayFor(model => model.Email)</dd>
        <dt>@Html.DisplayNameFor(model => model.FirstName)</dt>
        <dd>@Html.DisplayFor(model => model.FirstName)</dd>
    </dl>

    @using (Html.BeginForm()) {
        @Html.AntiForgeryToken()
        @Html.HiddenFor(model => model.Password)
```

```
            @Html.HiddenFor(model => model.Email)
            @Html.HiddenFor(model => model.FirstName)
            @Html.HiddenFor(model => model.Id)

            <div class="form-actions no-color">
                <input type="submit" value="Delete"
                    class="btn btn-danger btn-sm" />
                @Html.Partial("_BackToListButtonPartial")
            </div>
    }
</div>
```

Adding the Delete actions

For the **Delete** view to work, you have to add two action methods called **Delete** to the **AccountController** class: one for displaying the view and one to handle submitted form values and delete the corresponding user from the **AspNetUsers** table in the database.

The HttpGet Delete action

This asynchronous action is called when the controller serves up the **Delete** view to the user and displays it in the browser. It is very similar to the **Edit** action in that it has to look up the user in the database before serving up the data to the view; it therefore need a **string** parameter called **userId**.

The method returns a **Task<ActionResult>**. Don't forget to add the **Authorize** attribute to restrict access only to users in the **Admin** role.

Return a **BadRequest** to the client if the **userId** parameter is **null** or contains an empty string.

Fetch the user with the passed in **userId** by calling the **UserManager.FindByIsAsync** method ad store the awaited result in a variable called **user**.

Return *Http Not Found* if the **user** variable is **null** by calling the **HttpNotFound** method.

If the user exists, then create an instance of the **UserViewModel** class in a variable called **model** and assign the values from the fetched user to its properties, except the password which you assign the value "Fake password" before passing the object to the **View** method for rendering. You use the text "Fake password" because it is pointless to send the password to the client in this scenario, but the model needs a value other than **null** or empty string to validate the model when the user clicks the **Delete** button and the **HttpPost Delete** action is called.

The easiest way to add this action is to copy the corresponding **Edit** action and alter it.

1. Open the **AccountController** class in the **Controllers** folder and navigate to the **HttpGet** version of the **Edit** action and copy the method and its attributes.
2. Navigate to the end of the **AccountController** class and paste in the code.
3. Change the action name to **Delete**.
4. Assign "Fake password" to the **Password** property in the **UserViewModel** instnace.
   Password = "Fake password"

The complete **HttpGet Delete** action:

```
[Authorize(Roles = "Admin")]
public async Task<ActionResult> Delete(string userId)
{
    if (userId == null || userId.Equals(string.Empty))
    {
        return new HttpStatusCodeResult(HttpStatusCode.BadRequest);
    }

    ApplicationUser user = await UserManager.FindByIdAsync(userId);

    if (user == null)
    {
        return HttpNotFound();
    }

    var model = new UserViewModel
    {
        Email = user.Email,
        FirstName = user.FirstName,
        Id = user.Id,
        Password = "Fake password"
    };

    return View(model);
}
```

ASP.NET MVC 5 - How to build a Membership Website

The HttpPost Delete action
This action is called when the user clicks the **submit** button in the **Delete** view's form.

It is basically the same as the corresponding **Edit** method; you only have to make a few minor modifications. Delete the property assignments and change the **UpdateAsync** method call to **DeleteAsync**. Delete all subscriptions beloning to the user from the **UserSubscriptions** table Inside the **result.Scucceeded** if-block before redirecting to the **Index** view. Don't return an empty view from the **catch**-block.

1. Open the **AccountController** class in the **Controllers** folder and navigate to the **HttpPost Edit** action and copy the method and its three attributes.
2. Navigate to the end of the class and paste in the code.
3. Chage the name of the action to **Delete**.
4. Remove the following code and assignments.
   ```
   user.Email = model.Email;
   user.UserName = model.Email;
   user.FirstName = model.FirstName;
   if (!user.PasswordHash.Equals(model.Password))
       user.PasswordHash = UserManager.PasswordHasher.HashPassword(
       model.Password);
   ```
5. Change the **UpdateAsync** method call to **DeleteAsync** to delete the user.
   ```
   var result = await UserManager.DeleteAsync(user);
   ```
6. Remove the empty view return from the **catch**-block.
   ```
   return View();
   ```
7. Add code to delete all the user's subscriptions from the **UserSubscriptions** table.
   ```
   var db = new ApplicationDbContext();
   var subscriptions = db.UserSubscriptions.Where(u =>
       u.UserId.Equals(user.Id));
   db.UserSubscriptions.RemoveRange(subscriptions);
   await db.SaveChangesAsync();
   ```
8. Run the application and navigate to the **Index** view belonging to the **AccountController**. Click the **Delete** button on one of the user rows and then click on the **Delete** button to remove that user from the database. If successful, the deleted user should not appear in the **Index** view.

The complete **HttpPost Delete** action:

```
[HttpPost]
[ValidateAntiForgeryToken]
[Authorize(Roles = "Admin")]
public async Task<ActionResult> Delete(UserViewModel model)
{
    try
    {
        if (model == null)
        {
            return new HttpStatusCodeResult(HttpStatusCode.BadRequest);
        }

        if (ModelState.IsValid)
        {
            var user = await UserManager.FindByIdAsync(model.Id);
            var result = await UserManager.DeleteAsync(user);
            if (result.Succeeded)
            {
                var db = new ApplicationDbContext();
                var subscriptions = db.UserSubscriptions.Where(u =>
                    u.UserId.Equals(user.Id));
                db.UserSubscriptions.RemoveRange(subscriptions);
                await db.SaveChangesAsync();

                return RedirectToAction("Index", "Account");
            }

            AddErrors(result);
        }
    }
    catch { }

    return View(model);
}
```

Adding subscriptions to a user

In this section, you will make it possible for an adimn to add and remove subscriptions to a user. The middle (light blue) button you modified earlier for the user rows will be connected to a new view called **Subscriptions** which will display a list of available subscriptions that can be assigned to the user for whom you opened the **Subscriptions** view. The view will also display a table with the already assigned subscriptions and a remove button per subscription row, making it possible to remove a specific subscription from the current user.

The image below shows the finished **Subscriptions** view.

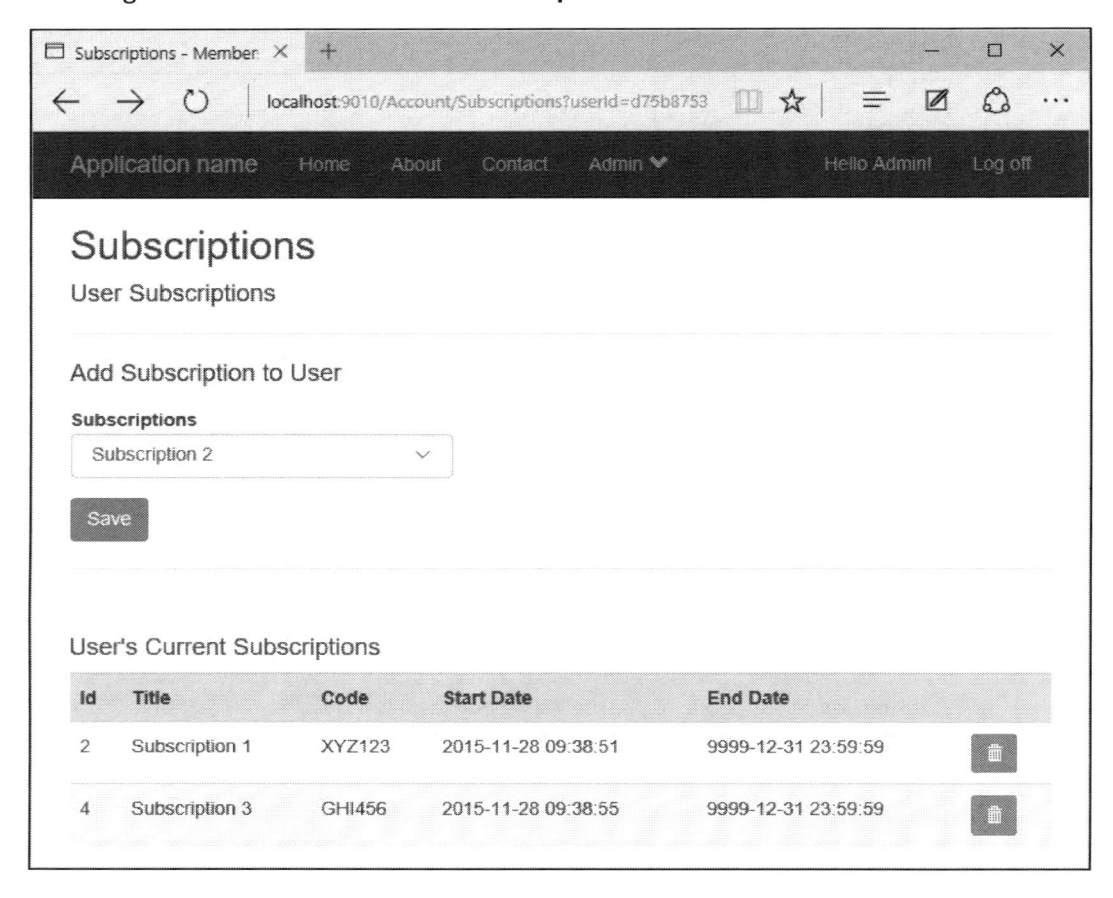

Adding the UserSubscriptionModel class

This class represents one subscription a user has access to and combines all columns from the **Subscription** table with the **StartDate** and **EndDate** columns from the **UserSubscription** table.

1. Add a class called **UserSubscriptionModel** to the **Models** folder in the main project.

2. Open the **Subscription** entity model in the **Entities** folder and copy all properties and their attributes except for the **DatabaseGenerate** attribute on the **Id** property.
3. Go back to the **UserSubscriptionModel** class and paste in the properties and their attributes.
4. Add two **DateTime?** propeties called **StartDate** and **EndDate**.
   ```
   public DateTime? StartDate { get; set; }
   public DateTime? EndDate { get; set; }
   ```
5. Save the class.

The **UserSubscriptionModel** class:
```
public class UserSubscriptionModel
{
    public int Id { get; set; }
    [MaxLength(255)]
    [Required]
    public string Title { get; set; }
    [MaxLength(2048)]
    public string Description { get; set; }
    [MaxLength(20)]
    public string RegistrationCode { get; set; }
    public DateTime? StartDate { get; set; }
    public DateTime? EndDate { get; set; }
}
```

Adding the UserSubscriptionViewModel class

This class is the view model used to send all the necessary data about available subscriptions and subscriptions associated with the selected user.

The class contains an **ICollection<Subscription>** property called **Subscriptions** which will hold all subscriptions not currently subscribed to by the selected user. The class also contains an **ICollection<UserSubscriptionModel>** property called **UserSubscriptions** which is a list of all subscriptions the selected user currently is subscribing to.

The data in the **Subscriptions** property will be displayed in a dropdown control where the admin can select a subscription and add it to the selected user by clicking a **Save** button.

The data in the **UserSubscriptions** property will be displayed in a table with one row per subscription the user currently subscribes to. Each row also has a **Delete** button to remove the subscription listed on that row.

The class also contains a **bool** property called **DisableDropDown** which is used to disable the subscriptions dropdown if there are no available subscriptions; one **int** property called **SubscriptionId** for the selected subscription and a **string** property for the selected user's id called **UserId**.

1. Add a class called **UserSubscriptionViewModel** to the **Models** folder in the main project.
2. Add an **ICollection<Subscription>** property called **Subscriptions**.
3. Add an **ICollection<UserSubscriptionModel>** property called **UserSubscriptions**.
4. Add a **bool** property called **DisableDropDown**.
5. Add a **string** property called **UserId**.
6. Add an **int** property called **SubscriptionId**.
7. Save the class.

The **UserSubscriptionViewModel** class:

```
public class UserSubscriptionViewModel
{
    public ICollection<Subscription> Subscriptions { get; set; }
    public ICollection<UserSubscriptionModel> UserSubscriptions
    { get; set; }
    public bool DisableDropDown { get; set; }
    public string UserId { get; set; }
    public int SubscriptionId { get; set; }
}
```

Adding the Subscriptions view

To add the possibility for admins to assign and remove subscriptions from a user selected in the **Account-Index** view, a **Subscriptions** view has to be added using a view model called **UserSubscriptionViewModel** for sending the necessary data to the view and another model called **UserSubscriptionModel** describing subscription data associated with a user.

Add the **Subscriptions** view to the **Views-Account** folder and add its actions to the **AccountController** in the **Controllers** folder.

Displaying subscriptions in a dropdown

The **Subscriptions** view has to be altered after you have scaffolded it with the **Edit** template and the **UserSubscriptionViewModel** class as its model. The first thing you need to do is to add a **@using** statement to the **Extensions** folder in the **Admin** area below the **@model** directive. The **using** statement makes it possible to call the **ToSelect-ListItem** extension method to convert items in a collection to items that can be displayed in a dropdown.

Add a hidden form field for the **UserId** property below the **@html.AntiForgeryToken** method call; this value will be used when a subscription is added to a user by calling the **HttpPost** version of the **Subscriptions** actions.

Remove two first **form-group <div>** elements for the **DisableDropDown** and **UserId**. Change the ramianing **LabelFor** method call to use the **Subscriptions** collection. Replace the **EditFor** method call with an if/else-block checkig if the **DisableDropDown** property is **true**. If it is **true,** then hide the dropdown and display the message "*User has all subscriptions*". Otherwise display the dropdown. You can look at the **Create** view in the **Views-ProductItem** folder in the **Admin** area to see how to implement the dropdown.

Style the **Save** button with the **btn-success** Bootstrap class and disable it if the **DisableDropDown** property is **true**. You can use the **disable** attribute in the input element to enable/disable the button.

ASP.NET MVC 5 - How to build a Membership Website

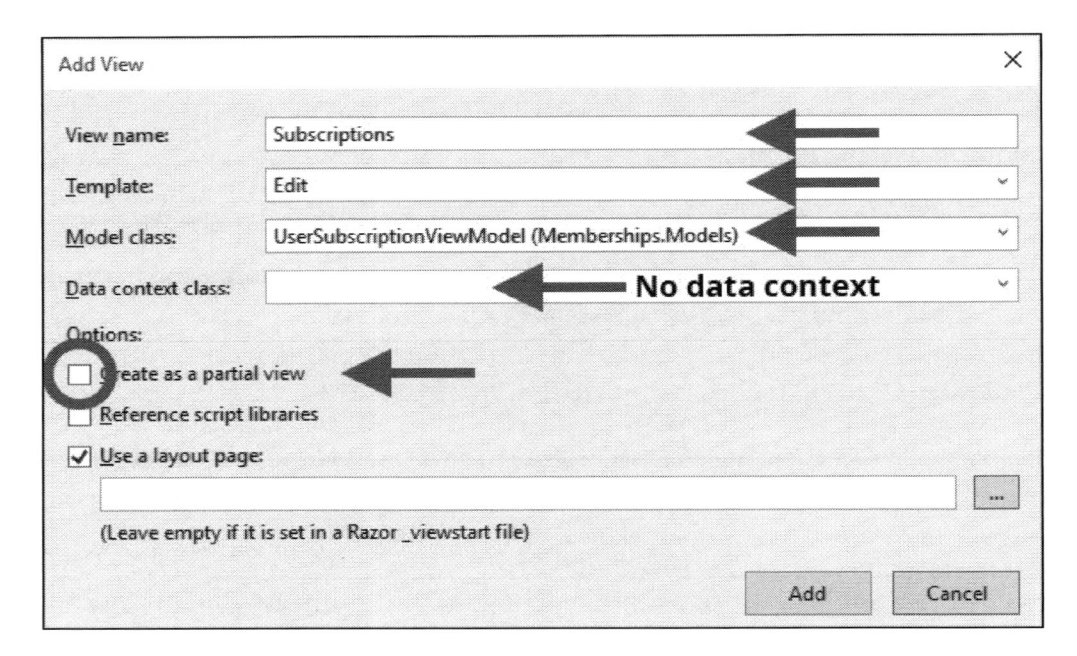

Add View dialog:
- View name: Subscriptions
- Template: Edit
- Model class: UserSubscriptionViewModel (Memberships.Models)
- Data context class: (empty) ← **No data context**
- Options:
  - ☐ Create as a partial view ←
  - ☐ Reference script libraries
  - ☑ Use a layout page:
  - (Leave empty if it is set in a Razor _viewstart file)

1. Right-click on the **Views-Account** folder and select **Add-View** in the menu.
2. Fill in the dialog with the data from the image above.
3. Add a **@using** statement to the **Extensions** folder in the **Admin** area.
   @using Memberships.Areas.Admin.Extensions
4. Add a hidden form field for the **UserId** property.
   @Html.Hidden("userId", Model.UserId)
5. Remove the **form-group <div>** elements for **DisableDropDown** and **UserId**.
6. Change the ramianing **LabelFor** method call to use the **Subscriptions** collection.
   @Html.LabelFor(model => model.Subscriptions, htmlAttributes: new { @class = "control-label col-md-2" })
7. Replace the **EditFor** method call with an if/else-block checkig if the **DisableDropDown** property is **true**. If it is **true** then hide the dropdown and display the message "User has all subscriptions" otherwise display the dropdown.
   ```
   @if (Model.DisableDropDown)
   {
       <span><strong>User has all subscriptions</strong></span>
   }
   else
   {
   ```

274

```
@Html.DropDownListFor(model => model.SubscriptionId,
    Model.Subscriptions.ToSelectListItem(Model.SubscriptionId),
    new { @class = "form-control" })
}
```

8. Style the **Save** button with the **btn-success** Bootstrap class and disable it if the **DisableDropDown** property is **true**.

```
<input type="submit" value="Save" class="btn btn-success" disabled="@Model.DisableDropDown" />
```

Displaying a user's subscriptions in a table

To be able to remove subscriptions from a user, a table with the selected user's subscriptions must be displayed below the ending curly brace for the **BeginForm** in the **Subscriptions** view, where each suscription row has a **Delete** button.

Add a table with the columns for **Id**, **Title**, **Code**, **StartDate**, **EndDate** and a column at the end without a title for the **Delete** button and fill it with data from the **UserSubscriptions** collection in the **Subscription** view's model.

Use a **@Url.Action** method call to the **RemoveUserSubscription** action and append the **UserId** and **SubscriptionId** property values as URL arguments to the button's **href** attribute.

1. Add a table below the ending curly brace for the **BeginForm** with the following column headers **Id**, **Title**, **Code**, **StartDate**, **EndDate** and a column at the end without a title.

```
<hr />
<br />
<h4>User's Current Subscriptions</h4>
<table class="table table-striped">
    <tr class="success">
        <th>Id</th>
        <th>Title</th>
        <th>Code</th>
        <th>Start Date</th>
        <th>End Date</th>
        <th></th>
    </tr>
    @*Iterate over the UserSubscriptions here*@
</table>
```

2. Add a foreach loop iterating over the items in the **UserSubscriptions** collection below the table header row (**<tr>**)

```
@foreach (var item in Model.UserSubscriptions)
{
    //Display individual subscriptions with delete button here
}
```

3. Add a table row for each item in the **UserSubscriptions** collection and display data for the corresponding table column headers and a **Delete** button.

```
<tr>
    <td>@Html.DisplayFor(modelItem => item.Id)</td>
    <td>@Html.DisplayFor(modelItem => item.Title)</td>
    <td>@Html.DisplayFor(modelItem => item.RegistrationCode)</td>
    <td>@Html.DisplayFor(modelItem => item.StartDate)</td>
    <td>@Html.DisplayFor(modelItem => item.EndDate)</td>
    <td>
        <a type="button" class="btn btn-danger btn-sm"
            href="@Url.Action("RemoveUserSubscription")
            ?subscriptionId=@item.Id&userId=@Model.UserId">
            <span class="glyphicon glyphicon-trash"
                aria-hidden="true"></span>
        </a>
    </td>
</tr>
```

4. Save the view.

The complete code for the **Subscriptions** view:

```
@model Memberships.Models.UserSubscriptionViewModel
@using Memberships.Extensions
@{
    ViewBag.Title = "Subscriptions";
}

<h2>Subscriptions</h2>

@using (Html.BeginForm())
{
    @Html.AntiForgeryToken()

    <div class="form-horizontal">
        <h4>Add Subscription to User</h4>
        <hr />
```

```
        @if (Model.DisableDropDown)
        {
            <div><strong>User has all the subscriptions</strong></div>
            <br />
        }
        else
        {
            @Html.ValidationSummary(true, "", new { @class =
                "text-danger" })

            <div class="form-group">
                @Html.LabelFor(model => model.Subscriptions,
                    htmlAttributes: new { @class = "control-label
                        col-md-2" })
                <div class="col-md-10">
                    @Html.DropDownListFor(model => model.SubscriptionId,
                        Model.Subscriptions.ToSelectListItem(
                        Model.SubscriptionId),
                        new { @class = "form-control" })
                    @Html.ValidationMessageFor(model =>
                        model.SubscriptionId, "", new { @class =
                        "text-danger" })
                </div>
            </div>

            <div class="form-group">
                <div class="col-md-offset-2 col-md-10">
                    <input type="submit" value="Save"
                        class="btn btn-success btn-sm" />
                </div>
            </div>
        }
    </div>
}

<div>
    @Html.Partial("_BackToListButtonPartial")
</div>

<hr />
<br />
<table class="table table-condensed table-striped">
    <tr class="success">
        <th>Id</th>
```

```
                <th>Title</th>
                <th>Code</th>
                <th>Start Date</th>
                <th>End Date</th>
                <th></th>
            </tr>
            @foreach(var item in Model.UserSubscriptions)
            {
                <tr>
                    <td>@Html.DisplayFor(modelItem => item.Id)</td>
                    <td>@Html.DisplayFor(modelItem => item.Title)</td>
                    <td>@Html.DisplayFor(modelItem => item.RegistrationCode)</td>
                    <td>@Html.DisplayFor(modelItem => item.StartDate)</td>
                    <td>@Html.DisplayFor(modelItem => item.EndDate)</td>
                    <td>
                        <a type="button" class="btn btn-danger btn-sm"
                            href="@Url.Action("RemoveUserSubscription")
                                ?subscriptionId=@item.Id&userId=@Model.UserId">
                            <span class="glyphicon glyphicon-trash"></span>
                        </a>
                    </td>
                </tr>
            }
</table>
```

Adding the Subscriptions actions

The Subscriptions view requires three asynchronous actions in the **AccountController**. The first is the **HttpGet Subscriptions** action which serves up the view to the user's browser. The second is the **HttpPost Subscriptions** action which is called when the admin clicks the **Save** button to add a subscription to a user. The third is the **RemoveUserSubscription** action which is called when the admin removes a subscription from a user.

Adding the HttpGet Subscriptions action

This action serves up the view to the user's browser and as such needs to fill the **UserSubscriptionViewModel** with data; fill the **UserSubscriptions** and **Subscriptions** collections with data, assign the **userId** parameter value to the **UserId** property and determine the value to be stored in the **DisableDropDown** property.

The action should be asynchronous, have a **string** parameter called **userId** and return a **Task<ActionResult>**.

A **BadRequest** error should be returned if the **userId** parameter is **null**.

Add a **UserSubscriptionViewModel** variable called **model** which you fill with the necessary data.

Use a LINQ query which joins the **Subscription** and **UserSubscription** tables on **SubscriptionId** and filters out those where the **UserId** property in the **UserSubscription** table match the **userId** parameter. Use the data to fill instances of the **UserSubscriptionModel** class and assign the list to the **UserSubscriptions** property.

To fill the **Subscriptions** collection with available subscriptions that the user doesn't already subscribe to, you need to use a LINQ query to extract only the id's from the **UserSubscriptions** property and use that list in the query which fetches the actual subscriptions from the **Subscription** table.

```
var ids = model.UserSubscriptions.Select(us => us.Id);
```

To figure out if the **DisableDropDown** property should be **true** or **false,** you can count the number of available subscriptions in the **Subscriptions** collection and return **true** if the count is 0.

Don't forget to add the **Authorize** attribute to the method, restricting it to only admin users.

Return the **model** variable with the **View** method call.

1. Open the **AccountController** class in the **Controllers** folder in the main project.
2. Locate the end of the class and add the **HttpGet Subscriptions** action.
   ```
   [Authorize(Roles = "Admin")]
   public async Task<ActionResult> Subscriptions(string userId)
   {
   }
   ```
3. Check if the **userId** parameter is **null** and return a **BadRequest** if it is.
4. Create the **UserSubscriptionViewModel model** variable.

```
var model = new UserSubscriptionViewModel();
```

5. Create an instance of the **ApplicatioDbContext** class in a variable called **db** to gain access to the database.
6. Fill the **UserSubscriptions** collection by joining the **UserSubscription** and **Subscription** tables and creating instances of the **UserSubscriptionModel** class. Use the **userId** parameter to filter out the subscriptions belonging to that user.

```
model.UserSubscriptions = await (
    from us in db.UserSubscriptions
    join s in db.Subscriptions on us.SubscriptionId equals s.Id
    where us.UserId.Equals(userId)
    select new UserSubscriptionModel
    {
        Id = us.SubscriptionId,
        StartDate = us.StartDate,
        EndDate = us.EndDate,
        Description = s.Description,
        RegistrationCode = s.RegistrationCode,
        Title = s.Title
    }).ToListAsync();
```

7. Extract the subscription id's from the **UserSubscriptions** collection and store them in a variable called **ids**.

```
var ids = model.UserSubscriptions.Select(us => us.Id);
```

8. Fetch the subscriptions from the **Subscriptions** table whose id's aren't in the **ids** collection.

```
model.Subscriptions = await db.Subscriptions.Where(s =>
    !ids.Contains(s.Id)).ToListAsync();
```

9. Assign a value to the **DisableDropDown** property.

```
model.DisableDropDown = model.Subscriptions.Count.Equals(0);
```

10. Assign the **userId** parameter to the **UserId** model property.
11. Return the **model** object with the **View** method.
12. Run the application and select **Users & Subscriptions** in the **Admin** menu. Click the (light blue) **Subscriptions** button for one of the users to display the list of available and subscribed to subscriptions. The **Save** and **Delete** buttons will not work until you have added the two remaining actions.

The complete code for the **HttpGet Subscriptions** action:

```
[Authorize(Roles = "Admin")]
public async Task<ActionResult> Subscriptions(string userId)
{
    if (userId == null)
    {
        return new HttpStatusCodeResult(HttpStatusCode.BadRequest);
    }

    var model = new UserSubscriptionViewModel();
    var db = new ApplicationDbContext();
    model.UserSubscriptions = await (
        from us in db.UserSubscriptions
        join s in db.Subscriptions on us.SubscriptionId equals s.Id
        where us.UserId.Equals(userId)
        select new UserSubscriptionModel
        {
            Id = us.SubscriptionId,
            StartDate = us.StartDate,
            EndDate = us.EndDate,
            Description = s.Description,
            RegistrationCode = s.RegistrationCode,
            Title = s.Title
        }).ToListAsync();

    var ids = model.UserSubscriptions.Select(us => us.Id);

    // SubscriptionModel
    model.Subscriptions = await db.Subscriptions.Where(s =>
        !ids.Contains(s.Id)).ToListAsync();
    model.DisableDropDown = model.Subscriptions.Count.Equals(0);
    model.UserId = userId;

    return View(model);
}
```

Adding the HttpPost Subscriptions action

This action assigns a subscription to a user storing a record in the **UserSubscription** table and redirects to the **HttpGet Subscription** action to display the changes. The method has a **UserSubscriptionViewModel** parameter called **model** which receives the form data from the client and returns a **Task<ActionResult>**.

Don't forget to add the **Authorize** attribute to the method, restricting it to only admin users.

Return **BadRequest** if the **model** parameter is **null** and redirect to the **HttpGet Subscriptions** action if the model state is invalid. Otherwise, create a new isntance of the **UserSubscription** class, fill it with data from the **model** parameter and save the record to the **UserSubscription** table in the database.

Any exception that occurs should be handled by an empty **catch**-block and redirect to the **HttpGet Subscriptions** action.

1. Open the **AccountController** class in the **Controllers** folder in the main project.
2. Locate the end of the class and add the **HttpPost Subscriptions** action.
   ```
   [HttpPost]
   [Authorize(Roles = "Admin")]
   public async Task<ActionResult>
   Subscriptions(UserSubscriptionViewModel model)
   {
   }
   ```
3. Add a try/catch-block to the action where the catch-block is empty and a redirect to the **HttpGet Subscriptions** action using a **RedirectToAction** method call.
   ```
   try
   {
   }
   catch { }

   return RedirectToAction("Subscriptions", "Account", new { userId = model.UserId });
   ```
4. The rest of the code should be added to the **try**-block. Return **BadRequest** if the **model** parameter is **null**.
5. Check if the model state is valid. If it is then create an instance of the **UserSubscription** entity class and populate it with data from the **model** parameter before saving it to the **UserSubscription** table in the database.
   ```
   var db = new ApplicationDbContext();
   db.UserSubscriptions.Add(new UserSubscription
   {
       UserId = model.UserId,
   ```

```
            SubscriptionId = model.SubscriptionId,
            StartDate = DateTime.Now,
            EndDate = DateTime.MaxValue
        });
        await db.SaveChangesAsync();
```

6. Run the application and add a subscription to one of the users. The list of subscriptions for that user should be updated automatically.

The complete code for the **HttpPost Subscriptions** action:

```
[HttpPost]
[Authorize(Roles = "Admin")]
[ValidateAntiForgeryToken]
public async Task<ActionResult> Subscriptions(UserSubscriptionViewModel model)
{
    try
    {
        if (model == null)
        {
            return new HttpStatusCodeResult(HttpStatusCode.BadRequest);
        }

        if (ModelState.IsValid)
        {
            var db = new ApplicationDbContext();
            db.UserSubscriptions.Add(new UserSubscription
            {
                UserId = model.UserId,
                SubscriptionId = model.SubscriptionId,
                StartDate = DateTime.Now,
                EndDate = DateTime.MaxValue
            });
            await db.SaveChangesAsync();
        }
    }
    catch { }

    return RedirectToAction("Subscriptions", "Account",
        new { userId = model.UserId });
}
```

Adding the RemoveUserSubscription action

This action removes a subscription from a user in the **UserSubscription** table and redirects to the **HttpGet Subscription** action to display the changes to the admin. The method has two parameters: a **string** parameter called **UserId** and an **int** parameter called **SubscriptionId**. The action should return a **Task<ActionResult>**.

As with the previous action, this has a **try/catch**-block where the **catch**-block is empty and the **return** statement redirect to the **HttpGet Subscriptions** action.

The if-statement detrmining if a **BadRequest** should be returned must check both the **userId** and **subscriptionId** parameters.

Inside the **ModelState.IsValid** if-block, the record for the subscription belonging to the user is fetched from the **UserSubscription** table with a LINQ expression. Then the record is removed from the table.

Don't forget to add the **Authorize** attribute to the method, restricting it to only admin users.

1. Open the **AccountController** class in the **Controllers** folder in the main project.
2. Locate the end of the class and add the **RemoveUserSubscription** action.
   ```
   [Authorize(Roles = "Admin")]
   public async Task<ActionResult> RemoveUserSubscription (string userId, int subscriptionId)
   {
   }
   ```
3. Add a **try/catch**-block to the action where the **catch**-block is empty and a redirect to the **HttpGet Subscriptions** action using a **RedirectToAction** method call.
   ```
   try
   {
   }
   catch { }

   return RedirectToAction("Subscriptions", "Account", new { userId = userId });
   ```
4. The rest of the code should be added to the **try**-block. Return **BadRequest** if the **userId** parameter is **null** or emty or the **subscriptionId** parameter is less than 1.

5. Check if the model state is valid. If it is then create an instance of the **ApplicationDbContext** class to fetch the record matching the **userId** and **subscriptionId** from the **UserSubscription** table in the database.
   ```
   var db = new ApplicationDbContext();
   var subscriptions = db.UserSubscriptions.Where(u =>
       u.UserId.Equals(userId) &&
       u.SubscriptionId.Equals(subscriptionId));
   ```
6. Remove the record from the **UserSubscription** table.
   ```
   db.UserSubscriptions.RemoveRange(subscriptions);
   await db.SaveChangesAsync();
   ```
7. Run the application and remove a subscription from a user. The list of subscriptions for that user should be updated automatically.

The complete code for the **RemoveUserSubscription** action:

```
[Authorize(Roles = "Admin")]
public async Task<ActionResult> RemoveUserSubscription(string userId,
int subscriptionId)
{
    Try {
        if (userId == null || userId.Length.Equals(0) ||
            subscriptionId <= 0)
        {
            return new HttpStatusCodeResult(HttpStatusCode.BadRequest);
        }

        if (ModelState.IsValid)
        {
            var db = new ApplicationDbContext();
            var subscriptions = db.UserSubscriptions.Where(u =>
                u.UserId.Equals(userId) &&
                u.SubscriptionId.Equals(subscriptionId));

            db.UserSubscriptions.RemoveRange(subscriptions);
            await db.SaveChangesAsync();
        }
    }
    catch { }

    return RedirectToAction("Subscriptions", "Account",
        new { userId = userId });
}
```

9. Application Layout

Introduction
In this chapter you will create the layout for the application grid and the navigation bar which will give it a cleaner look.

Technologies used in this chapter
1. **MVC** - To create the grid used by all upcoming exercises.
2. **HTML 5** - To create the grid.
3. **Bootstrap** - To create rows and columns in the grid.
4. **CSS** - To style HTML elements.

Use case
Create the foundational layout for the whole application using Bootstrap and CSS and add a logo in two sizes to the navigation bar – a large icon displayed on large, medium and small devices and a small icon displayed on extra small (mobile) devices.

In the upcoming chapters you will use Bootstrap *Glyphicons* library to decorate components.

Alter the navigation bar
To give the navigation bar a cleaner and airier look, you will remove the **navbar-inverse** Bootstrap class from the navigation bar. Because the "hamburger" menu displayed on extra small devices should be displayed in the inverse of the navigation bar, the **navbar-inverse** class has to be added to the **icon-bar <span>** elements.

Adding a nice logo to the site lifts the overall look of the site and makes it appear more professional. Keep in mind that images can take time to load on mobile devices. It's therefore advisable to have a smaller version of the logo for that scenario.

Add a CSS file named **navbar.css** to the **Content** folder and add it to the **BundleConfig.cs** file in the **App_Start** folder and the **_Layout** view. This CSS file will be used to style the navigation bar links.

Adding the navbar.css file

There are three steps to adding the CSS file. The first is to add it to the **Content** folder, the second is to add it to the **BundleConfig** file in the **App_Start** folder and and the third is to add a link to the bundle in the **_Layout** view.

1. Right-click on the **Content** folder and select **Add-Style Sheet** in the menu.
2. Name the file **navbar.css** in the dialog and click the **OK** button.
3. Open the **BundleConfig** file in the **App_Start** folder.
4. Add a new **StyleBundle** called *membership* for the **navbar.css** file at the end of the **RegisterBundles** method. You can copy and alter one of the existing bundles.
   bundles.Add(new StyleBundle("~/Content/membership").Include(
   "~/Content/navbar.css"));
5. Open the **_Layout** view and link in the *membership* bundle you just created. Copy one of the existing **Styles.Render** method calls and alter it.
   @Styles.Render("~/Content/membership")
6. Open the **navbar.css** file and remove the **body** class.

The navigation bar

Remove the **navbar-inverse** class from the **navbar <div>** element and add it to the three **icon-bar <span>** elements. This will change the background color of the navigation bar and the "hamburger" menu. If you don't make the background color white in the CSS file, the "hamburger" menu will be transparent.

Add a border at the bottom of the navigation bar to make it look more like a separate menu area.

The image below show the original navigation bar.

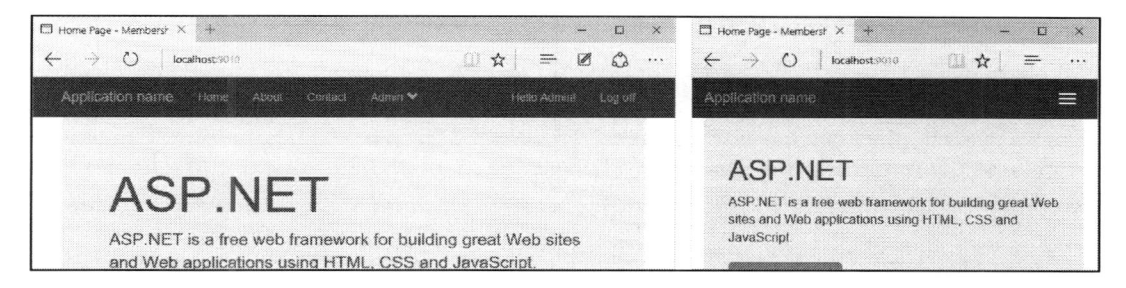

The image below shows the altered navigation bar.

1. Open the **_Layout** view.
2. Cut out the **navbar-inverse** class from the **navbar <div>** element.
   ```
   <div class="navbar navbar-fixed-top">
   ```
3. Paste in the **navbar-inverse** class to the three **icon-bar <span> class** attributes.
   ```
   <span class="icon-bar navbar-inverse"></span>
   ```
4. Open the **navbar.css** file and add a definition for the **navbar** class. Add **border-bottom** and **background-color** properties where the **border-bottom** is **1px** and **gray** and the **background-color** is **white**.
   ```
   .navbar {
       border-bottom: 1px solid #C8C8C8;
       background-color: #fff;
   }
   ```
5. Run the application and observe the changes.

ASP.NET MVC 5 - How to build a Membership Website

The navigation links

Let's change the default blue link color to a gray color and change the color to green when hovering over a link. To achieve this, you will have to target specific element types in the **navbar.css** file.

To change the link color, the **<a>** elements residing in an element decorated with the **nav** class have to be trageted; if you look at how the navigation links are added they reside in an **<ul>** element which is decorated with that class.

```
<ul class="nav navbar-nav">
    <li>@Html.ActionLink("Home", "Index", "Home")</li>
    <li>@Html.ActionLink("About", "About", "Home")</li>
    <li>@Html.ActionLink("Contact", "Contact", "Home")</li>
    @Html.Partial("_AdminMenuPartial")
</ul>
```

To change the background color of the link that the user hovers over, the **:hover** pseudo class has to be added to the targeted **<a>** element.

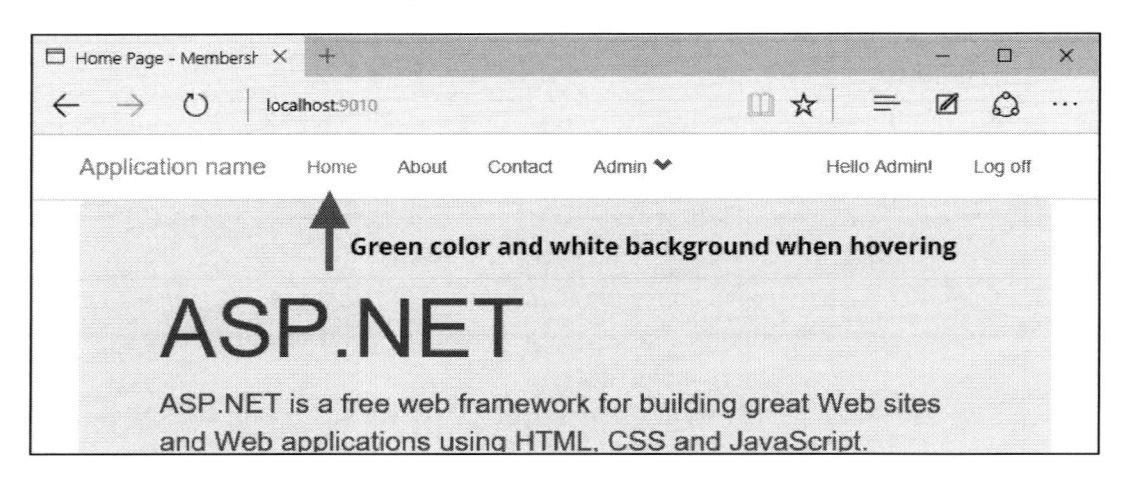

1. Open the **navbar.css** file and target **<a>** elements located in an element decorated with the **nav** class and a **color** property changing the color to gray.
   ```
   .nav a {
       color: #555;
   }
   ```

2. Target **<a>** elements located in an element decorated with the **nav** class and add the **:hover** pseudo class. Add a **color** property changing the color to a light green.
   ```
   .nav a:hover {
       color: #72C02C;
   }
   ```

3. To change the link background color to white when hovering over it, you want to be very specific in your targeting, because if you target all **<a>** elements, the menu items in the **Admin** menu will be affected also. To affect only the link, or rather the **<li>** element containing the link the user hovers over, you have to include only the **<li>** element that are direct decendants of the **<ul>** element decorated with the **nav** class.
   ```
   .nav > li > a:hover {
       background-color: white;
   }
   ```

4. Run the application and hover over the links. Note that the color changes when entering or leaving a link and that the link background is white.

Adding a Logo

Adding a logo can seem like a straightforward thing, but you must take into consideration that the logo can be viewed on devices with different screen sizes. You might for instance want a larger logo when users are viewing the site on a laptop compared to when viewing it on a smart phone. To solve this dilemma, you can have two or more logos of different sizes which are served up depending on the device size.

In this section, you will add two logos and use the **hidden-xs** and **visible-xs** Bootstrap classes to determine which should be displayed.

You will replace the **ActionLink** method call described below with an anchor tag **<a>** which contain the two logos. To place the logo in the correct position in the navigation bar the **<a>** element has to be decorated with the Bootstrap class **navbar-brand**. The reason you place the logos in an **<a>** element is to take advantage of its **href** attribute turning the image into a link; you can use the **href** attribute to redirect to any view but let's reditect to the **Index** view of the **HomeController**.

```
@Html.ActionLink("Application name", "Index", "Home", new { area = "" },
new { @class = "navbar-brand" })
```

As you can see in the image below, the logo messes up the links in the menu and hide part of the **body-content** element. The reason for this is that the default navigation bar is not as high as the one with the logo. To counteract this, you can add one CSS rule taregting the **<a>** elements residing in the **navbar-nav <ul>** element adding a few pixels to its top margin and another rule targeting the **body-content** element adding a few pixels to its top margin.

Adding the logo image
1. Add a folder named **Logos** to the **Content** folder.
2. Add the logo images to the **Logos** folder. You can drag them to the folder from a Windows Explorer window or right-click on the **Logos** folder and select **Add Existing** item in the menu.
3. Open the **_Layout** view in the **Admin** area and make sure that the following **ActionLink** is present; alter the existing **AlctionLink** if it differs. The **area** property set to an empty string will target the main project where the */Home/Index* view is located omitting this property will cause an error when clicking the link while in the **Admin** area.
   ```
   @Html.ActionLink("Application name", "Index", "Home", new { area = "" }, new { @class = "navbar-brand" })
   ```
4. Open the **_Layout** view in the main project and delete the following **ActionLink**.
   ```
   @Html.ActionLink("Application name", "Index", "Home", new { area = "" }, new { @class = "navbar-brand" })
   ```

5. Add an **<a>** element where the **ActionLink** was located. Add the **navbar-brand** class to its class attribute and */Home/Index* to its **href** attribute.
   ```
   <a class="navbar-brand" href="/Home/index">
      @*Add logo images here*@
   </a>
   ```
6. You can drag the logos from the **Logos** folder to the **<a>** element to add them.
7. Add the **height** attribute to the **<image>** elements and assign 45 to the large image and 30 to the small image.
8. Add the **hidden-xs** Bootstrap class to the large image and **visible-xs** to the small image.
   ```
   <img src="~/Content/Logo/membership-icon-large.png" height="45" class="hidden-xs" />
   <img src="~/Content/Logo/membership-icon-small.png" height="30" class="visible-xs" />
   ```

The complete code for the navigation bar:

```
<div class="navbar navbar-fixed-top">
    <div class="container">
        <div class="navbar-header">
            <button type="button" class="navbar-toggle"
                data-toggle="collapse" data-target=".navbar-collapse">
                <span class="icon-bar navbar-inverse"></span>
                <span class="icon-bar navbar-inverse"></span>
                <span class="icon-bar navbar-inverse"></span>
            </button>
            <a class="navbar-brand" href="/Home/index">
                <img src="~/Content/Logo/membership-icon-large.png"
                    height="45" class="hidden-xs" />
                <img src="~/Content/Logo/membership-icon-small.png"
                    height="30" class="visible-xs" />
            </a>
        </div>
        <div class="navbar-collapse collapse">
            <ul class="nav navbar-nav">
                <li>@Html.ActionLink("Home", "Index", "Home")</li>
                <li>@Html.ActionLink("About", "About", "Home")</li>
                <li>@Html.ActionLink("Contact", "Contact", "Home")</li>
                @Html.Partial("_AdminMenuPartial")
            </ul>
            @Html.Partial("_LoginPartial")
```

```
        </div>
    </div>
</div>
```

Styling the menu items

Because the logo changed the height of the navigation bar, the menu items have to be moved down by adding a top margin. The **body-content** element also has to be given a top margin to move it down and display the hidden part.

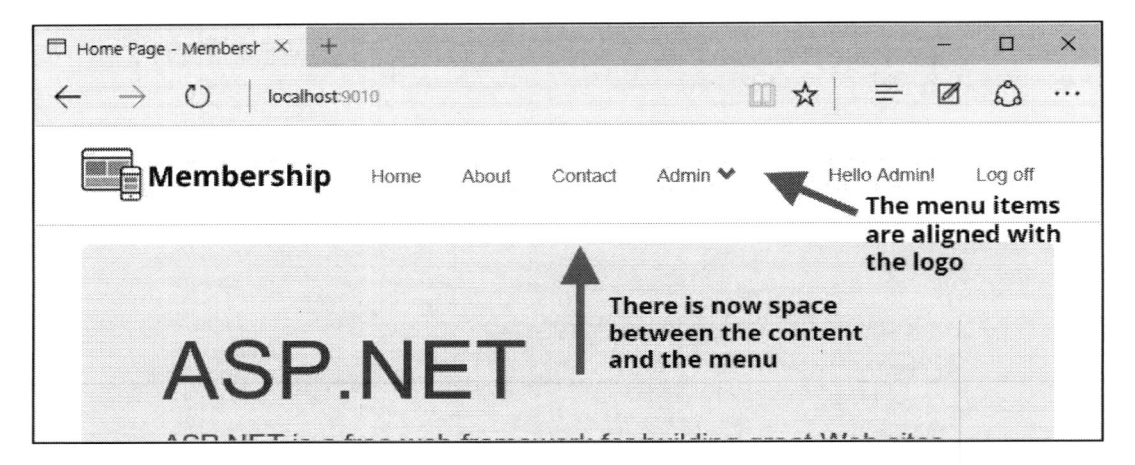

1. Open the **navbar.css** style sheet.
2. Add a CSS selector targeting all the menu items in the navigation bar and add 25px top margin, 5px top padding and a maximum height of 30px to them.
   ```
   .navbar-nav > li > a {
       margin-top: 25px;
       padding-top: 5px;
       max-height: 30px;
   }
   ```
3. Add a CSS selector targeting the **body-content** class and add a **40px** top margin property to it to move down the content hidden by the navigation bar and add some space between the navigation bar and the content.
   ```
   .body-content {
       margin-top: 40px;
   }
   ```
4. Run the application and look at the changes.

Fonts

When designing a website, it is important to have well-balanced fonts to display information. One site that provides free fonts is Google with their *Open Sans* fonts. You don't have to install them as font files; to use them, you simply add a link to your **_Layout** view. To create the font link, you can visit *https://www.google.com/fonts*. The site helps keep the page load down by showing how large the font is that you have included; you can select different versions of the font, like a certain thickness or if italic should be included. By excluding font settings not used on the site, you can achieve a faster load time.

When you have created the link, you add it to the **<head>** section of the **_Layout** view as an **href** of a **<link>** element.

Add the link described below, or the one you have created, to the **<head>** section.

Below is an example of a font link:

```
<link
href='http://fonts.googleapis.com/css?family=Open+Sans:400,600,700'
rel='stylesheet' type='text/css'>
```

1. Open a browser and navigate to *https://www.google.com/fonts* if you want to create your own font link, or use the one above.
2. Open the **_Layout** view and add the link at the end of the **<head>** section.

Alter the layout of the Index view

The default layout of the **Index** view belonging to the **HomeController** has to be altered to fit your layout. It must have a grid that changes with the device screen size to look good on any device. In order to achieve this, it must have different grid column settings for large, medium and small devices; the column setting for extra small devices can use the default setting.

In this application, you need two separate layouts: one for when the user is logged in and one for visitors who haven't logged in. In an upcoming chapter you will add a registration component to display when a visitor hasn't logged in; but for now, it will simply display the text "I'm not logged in". To begin with, the layout for a logged in user will display the text "I'm logged in" but you will change that in an upcoming chapter.

The layout for logged in users can simply be one column taking up all the space on the row (**col-xs-12**) for now; you will change this later. The layout for the other scenario will require two columns to palce the registration component to the far right and take up a certain amount of column segments depending on the device size. For large devices, the column ratio should be 9 and 3, for medium devices 8 and 4, and for small devices 7 and 5. Use Bootstrap **col-** classes to set the column widths. Remove all the HTML markup in the **Index** view before you add the new layouts.

You can use the **User.Identity.IsAuthenticated** property to check if the user is logged in.

The layout for a user that isn't logged in:

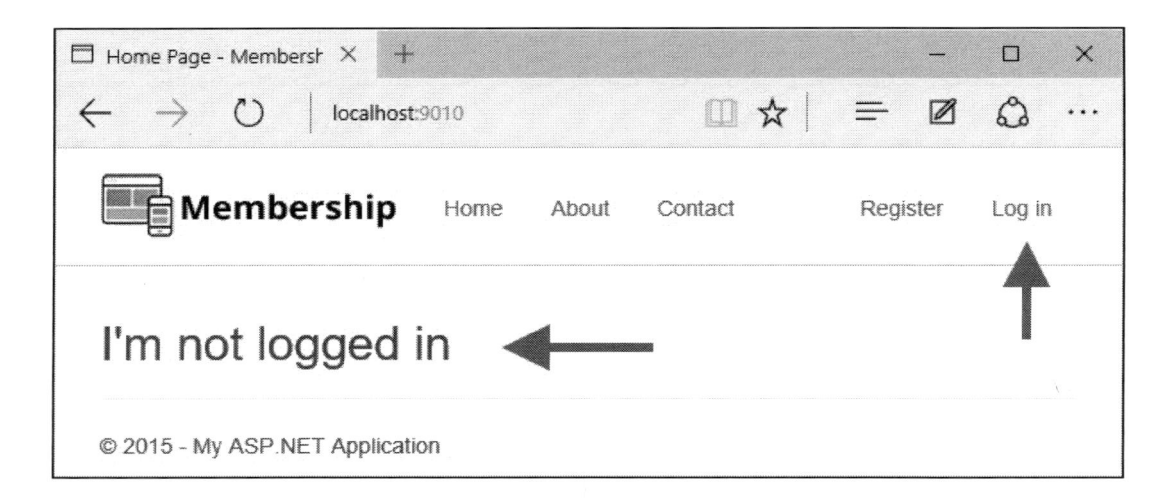

```
<!--left column-->
<div class="col-lg-9 col-md-8 col-sm-7">
    <h2>I'm not logged in</h2>
</div>
<!--right column-->
<div class="col-lg-3 col-md-4 col-sm-5">
</div>
```

1. Open the **Index** view in the **Views-Home** folder.
2. Delete all HTML markup below the Razor section containing the **ViewBag**.
3. Add a new **<div>** element decorated with the **row** class.
   ```
   <div class="row">
   </div>
   ```
4. Add an if/else-block inside the **<div>** element checking if the user is logged in.
   ```
   @if (User.Identity.IsAuthenticated)
   {
       // Displayed if the user is logged in
   }
   else
   {
       // Displayed if the user isn't logged in
   }
   ```
5. Add a **<div>** decorated with the **col-xs-12** Bootstrap class inside the if-block to make it take up all the avaialble room on the row. Add an **<h2>** element with the text *I'm logged in*.
   ```
   <div class="col-xs-12">
       <h2>I'm logged in</h2>
   </div>
   ```
6. Add a **<div>** element inside the else-block and decorate it with the following column classes: **col-lg-9, col-md-8, col-sm-7**. This will represent the left column of the grid layout defining specific column widths for different device sizes. Add an **<h2>** element with the text *I'm not logged in*.
   ```
   <!--left column-->
   ```

297

```
<div class="col-lg-9 col-md-8 col-sm-7">
    <h2>I'm not logged in</h2>
</div>
```

7. Add another **<div>** below the one you just added and decorate it with the following column classes: **col-lg-3**, **col-md-4**, **col-sm-5**. This will represent the right column of the grid.

```
<!--right column-->
<div class="col-lg-3 col-md-4 col-sm-5">
</div>
```

8. Run the application and logout and login to make sure that the text changes and the if/else-block is working.

The complete code in the **Index** view:

```
@{
    ViewBag.Title = "Home Page";
}

<div class="row">
    @if (User.Identity.IsAuthenticated)
    {
        // Displayed if the user is logged in
        <div class="col-xs-12">
            <h2>I'm logged in</h2>
        </div>
    }
    else
    {
        // Displayed if the user isn't logged in
        <!--left column-->
        <div class="col-lg-9 col-md-8 col-sm-7">
            <h2>I'm not logged in</h2>
        </div>
        <!--right column-->
        <div class="col-lg-3 col-md-4 col-sm-5">
        </div>
    }
</div>
```

10. Display products

Introduction

In this chapter you will add a subscription and display its products in the user interface to subscribing customers. The products will be displayed as Bootstrap **thumbnail** components in a partial view to keep the **Index** view as clean as possible.

Since there can be various types of products, you might want to display them in different areas; for instance, you might want an area at the top of the page dedicated to promotional content such as excerpts from books you are selling with links to a shopping cart. Then there might be content that you want to display ordered in different areas such as courses that belong togheter. Each row can hold four thumbnails where each thumbnail represent a product. In order to achieve this, a model called **ThumbnailAreaModel** has to be added to the project; the model will contain a **Title** property for the area and a collection containing the thumbnails for that area where each thumbnail is defined by a class called **ThumbnailModel**.

A **ThumbnailEqualityComparer** class must be implemented to make it possible to compare two **ThumbnailModel** objects on their **ProductId** properties. If this is not done, the default object comparer will be used comparing their object references.

An **IEnumerable<ThumbnailAreaModel>** will be used as the view model for the **Index** view and each area object in the **ThumbnailAreaModel's** collection will be passed to the **_ThumbnailAreaPartial** partial view to be rendered as thumbnails.

The thumbnail images will be animated, making the image rotate and zoom slightly and move the link text left when the user enters or exits the thumbnail. Below are examples of thumbnails in the user interface.

The thumbnail on the left is the inactive version, and the one on the right shows the thumbnail when a user is pointing to it with the mouse.

The top label on the thumbnail image shows what type of product the content belongs to. If, for instance, you are sharing content for a book, you use the **Book** label even though the book itself is not part of the content. The content could be related videos, downloads and PDF documents.

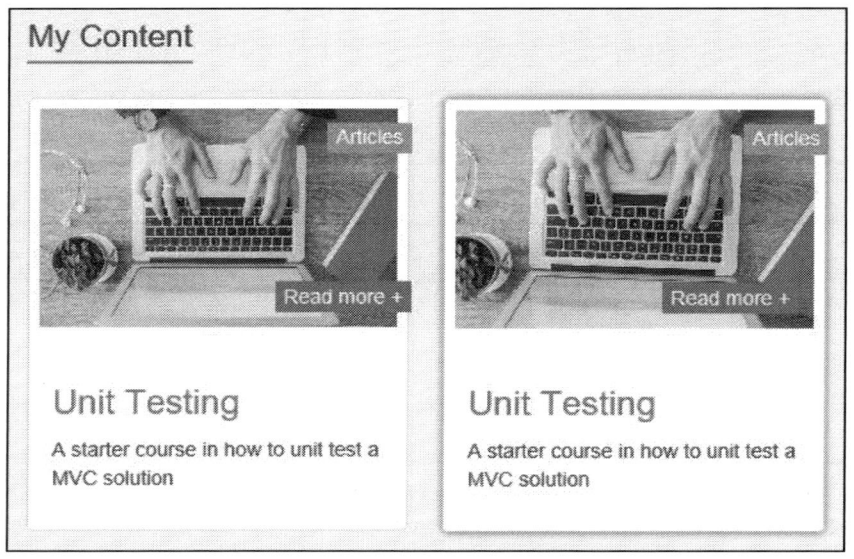

My Content

Book

C# For Beginners

Videos describing chapter 10-24 in the C# Programming book

Book

C# For Beginners

Videos describing chapter 10-24 in the C# Programming book

My Content

Articles

Unit Testing

A starter course in how to unit test a MVC solution

Articles

Unit Testing

A starter course in how to unit test a MVC solution

Adding a subscription

Before creating the thumbnail partial view, you have to add a product and a subscription. Let's use the example products from the thumbnails above. To add the two products *C# For Beginners* and *Unit Testing,* you will have to use the **Admin** user interface. Because the UI only will display the products and not their content at this stage, you will only be adding the product container and a subscription. In upcoming exercises you will add content items to the product.

The scenario is that you have written a book called *C# For Beginners* and want to share bonus content with the reader through this site. In order to do so, you add two products; one called *C# For Beginners* which can contain the zipped source code, videos and other content and another product called *Unit Testing* which is a couple of bonus articles they will receive when purchasing the book. The articles will be displayed on-line and stored as HTML in the database.

Adding a product link text

To be able to display the lower lable in the thumbnail image for products, you have to add product link texts to the **ProductLinkText** table in the database, which then can be selected in the **Create New** and **Edit** views for a product.

This label is in reality a link that can be clicked by the user to go to the product content.

1. Run the application and login as an admin.
2. Select **Product Link Text** in the **Admin** menu.
3. Click the **Create New** button.
4. Add the following product link text if it hasn't already been added: **Read more +**.
5. Click the **Create** button.

Adding the Product Type

The product type is used by the system to keep track of what type of product it is and is strored in the **ProductType** table in the database which then can be selected in the **Create New** and **Edit** views for a product.

1. Run the application and login as an admin.
2. Select **Product Type** in the **Admin** menu.

3. Click the **Create New** button.
4. Add the following product types if they haven't already been added: **Course**, **Book**, **Articles** and **Misc.**.
5. Click the **Create** button.

Adding the products

The product *C# For Beginners* is a collection of videos belonging to a book and the *Unit Testing* product is a collection of articels displayed as HTML. Both products will be displayed in the **Index** view of the **HomeController**.

1. Run the application and login as an admin.
2. Select **Product** in the **Admin** menu.
3. Click the **Create New** button.
4. Fill out the form with the following values:
    a. **Title:** *C# For Beginners*.
    b. **Description**: *Videos describing chapter 1-9 in the C# For Beginners book.*
    c. **Image Url:** Add a viable URL to a thumbnail image for instance: */Content/Images/csharp-for-beginners.png*.
    d. **Product Link Texts:** Select **Read more +** in the dropdown.
    e. **Product Types:** Select **Book** in the dropdown.
5. Click the **Create** button.
6. Click the **Create New** button again.
7. Fill out the form with the following values:
    a. **Title:** *Unit Testing*.
    b. **Description**: *A starter course in how to unit test a MVC solution.*
    c. **Image Url:** Add a viable URL to a thumbnail image for instance: */Content/Images/unit-testing.png*.
    d. **Product Link Texts:** Select **Read more +** in the dropdown.
    e. **Product Types:** Select **Articles** in the dropdown.
8. Click the **Create** button.

Adding the subscription

For users to be able to add products, they have to subscribe to one or more subscriptions in the **Subscription** table. To add a subscription to a user, an entry must be added to the **UserSubscription** table, and since you haven't added a subscription control to the site yet, you will have to do it manually through the **Admin** interface.

The value in the **Registration Code** field is the vaue the customer (user) has to enter in order to gain access to the products associated with the subscription.

Adding a subscription
1. Run the application and login as an admin.
2. Select **Subscription** in the **Admin** menu.
3. Click the **Create New** button.
4. Fill out the form with the following values:
    a. **Title:** *C# For Beginners Subscription*.
    b. **Description:** *Course materials for the C# For Beginners course*.
    c. **Registration Code:** *CSharp*
5. Click the **Create** button.

Adding a product to the subscription
1. Run the application and login as an admin.
2. Select **Subscription Product** in the **Admin** menu.
3. Click the **Create New** button.
4. Select a product and a subscription in the dropdowns and click the **Save** button. Add the two products *C# For Beginners*, and *Unit Testing* to the *C# For Beginners Subscription* subscription.

Adding a subscription to a user
This section describes how an admin can add a subscription to a user. Later, you will add a control to the **Index** view of the **HomeController** where the user will be able to enter a subscription code to get access to content.

1. Run the application and login as an admin.
2. Select **User & Subscriptions** in the **Admin** menu.
3. Click the **Create New** button.
4. Fill out the form with the following values:
    a. **First Name:** *Ray*.
    b. **Email**: *ray@company.com*.
    c. **Password**: Enter a password that is easy for you to remember.

5. Click the **Create** button.
6. Click the **Subscriptions** button (the middle button) on the row with Ray's credentials.
7. Select **C# For Beginners Subscription** in the dropdown.
8. Click the **Save** button. The subscription should be added to the list att the bottom of the page indicating that Ray now is subscribing to the content in the subscription.

Creating thumbnails

Now that you have added a subscription to a user, the user will automatically get access to all products belonging to that subscription.

The next step is to display the products to the subscribing users. In order to do that, the **Index** view has to be updated with a view model containing a **string** property called **Title** representing the thumbnail area title and an **IEnumerable<ThumbnailModel>** where every item in the collection is an instance of the **ThumbnailModel** class defining the content of a thumbnail.

The thumbnails in the collection will be rendered by a partial view called **_Thumbnail-Area**.

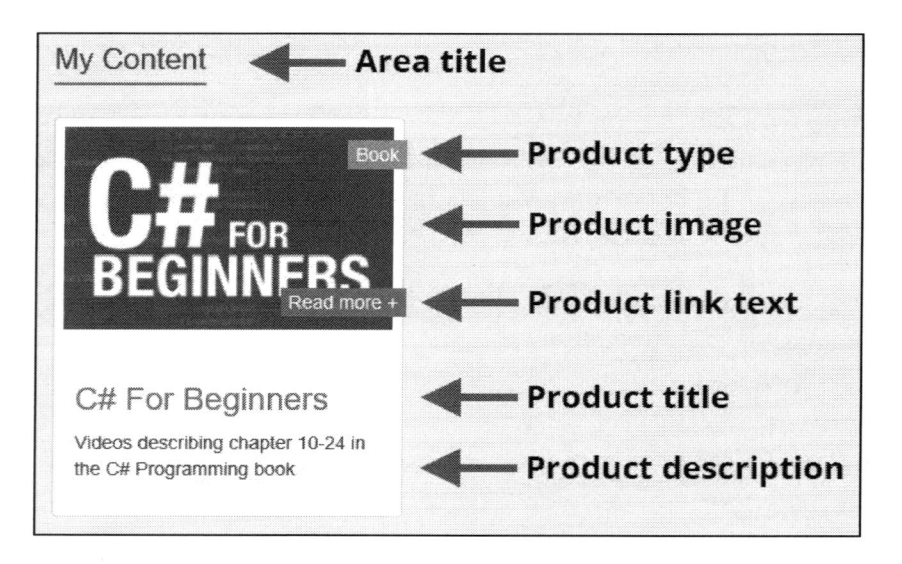

- Area title
  The area title is implemented as a **string** property called **Title** in the **ThumbnailAreaModel** class.
- Product type
  Shows the user what type of product the thumbnail represent. Because you might want to use the thimbnail in other scenarios, the property displaying the product type is a **string** proeprty called **ContentTag**.
- Product image
  Is a valid URL to an image that will be displayed as the product thumbnail. It's declared as a **string** property called **ImageUrl**.
- Product link text
  A link text enticing the user to click on the thumbnail. Because you might want to use the thumbnail in other scenarios, the property displaying the product link text is a **string** property called **TagText**. The **<a>** element displaying the text will also use a **string** property called **Link** containing the value (*/ProductContent/Index/*) in it's **href** attribute.
- Product title
  The product title is represented by an **<a>** element that uses a **string** property called **Title** and a **string** property called **Link** as the value (*/ProductContent/Index/*) in its **href** attribute.
- Product description
  The product description is represented by a **<p>** element that displays the text from a **string** property called **Description**.
- ProductId and SubscriptionId
  These two **int** id's must be present in the model to target the correct subscription and product.

Adding the ThumbnailModel class

Use the information in the list above to add a class called **ThumbnailModel**.

1. Right-click on the **Models** folder in the main project and select **Add-Class**.
2. Name the class **ThumbnailModel** and click on the **Add** button.
3. Add two **int** proerties called **ProductId** and **SubscriptionId**.

4. Add six **string** properties called **Title, Description, TagText, ImageUrl, Link** and **ContentTag**.
5. Save the class.

The complete code for the **ThumbnailModel** class:

```
public class ThumbnailModel
{
    public int ProductId { get; set; }
    public int SubscriptionId { get; set; }
    public string Title { get; set; }
    public string Description { get; set; }
    public string TagText { get; set; }
    public string ImageUrl { get; set; }
    public string Link { get; set; }
    public string ContentTag { get; set; }
}
```

Adding the ThumbnailAreaModel class

The **ThumbnailAreaModel** class is used as a view model for the **Index** and **_Thumbnail-AreaPartial** views to display products thumbnails to the user. It only has two properties; a **string** property caled **Title** which is displayed as a title above the thumbnail area and a collection of **ThumbnailModel** instances called **Thumbnails** where each instance represents a product thumbnail.

1. Right-click on the **Models** folder in the main project and select **Add-Class**.
2. Name the class **ThumbnailAreaModel** and click on the **Add** button.
3. Add a **string** property called **Title**.
4. Add an **IEnumerable<ThumbnailModel>** property called **Thumbnails**.
5. Save the class.

The complete code for the **ThumbnailAreaModel** class:

```
public class ThumbnailAreaModel
{
    public string Title { get; set; }
    public IEnumerable<ThumbnailModel> Thumbnails { get; set; }
}
```

Adding the thumbnails.css style sheet

The *thumbnails.css* style sheet will contain all styling associated with thumbnails. Add the style sheet to the **Content** folder.

1. Right-click on the **Content** folder in the main project and select **Add-Style Sheet**.
2. Name the style sheet **thumbnails** and click the **OK** button.
3. Remove the **body** definition.
4. Open the **BundleConfig** file in the **App_Start** folder.
5. Add the **thumbnails.css** file to the **memberships** bundle.
   ```
   bundles.Add(new StyleBundle("~/Content/membership").Include(
       "~/Content/navbar.css",
       "~/Content/thumbnails.css"));
   ```
6. Save the changes.

Adding the _ThumbnailAreaPartial partial view

This partial view represents a row of thumbnails where each thumbnail takes up 3 of the 12 available grid columns for a maximum of four thumbnails per row.

The view will have a **@model** directive to a single instance of the **ThumbnailAreaModel** class. The **Index** view will loop over its **IEnumerable<ThumbnailAreaModel>** model and create a thumbnail area for each item in the collection by rendering a **_ThumbnailArea-Partial** view.

Because each area is a separate row in the user interface, it must implement a **<div>** element decorated with the Bootstrap **row** class.

Let's start by dispalying one thumbnail with hard-coded default values just to see what it looks like right out of the box using the Bootstrap **thumbnail** component and an unstyled heading.

Add the title as a **<div>** element below the **@model** directive and add an **<h3>** element with the text *The area title* to the **<div>**.

The next **<div>** will be the thumbnail area which can contain up to four thumbnails. Add a **<div>** decorated with the Bootstrap **row** class.

Add a **<div>** decoreated with the **col-sm-3** Bootstrap class inside the previously added **<div>**; this **<div>** will determine the space a thumbnail is allowed to occupy, which in this instandce is 3 grid columns.

Add a third **<div>** decorated with the Bootstrap **thumbnail** class inside the previously added **<div>**. This **<div>** is the container for the Bootstrap **thumbnail** component and it will contain all the elements you want to display in the thumbnail.

Add an empty **<img>** element to the thumbnail **<div>** and make sure to add ... to the **src** attribute and leave the **alt** attribute empty.

```
<img src="..." alt="">
```

Add a **<div>** element decorated with the Bootstrap **caption** class below the image. This element will hold the thumbnail title and the description.

Add an **<h3>** element with the text *Thumbnail title* and a **<p>** element with the text *The thumbnail description* to the **caption <div>**.

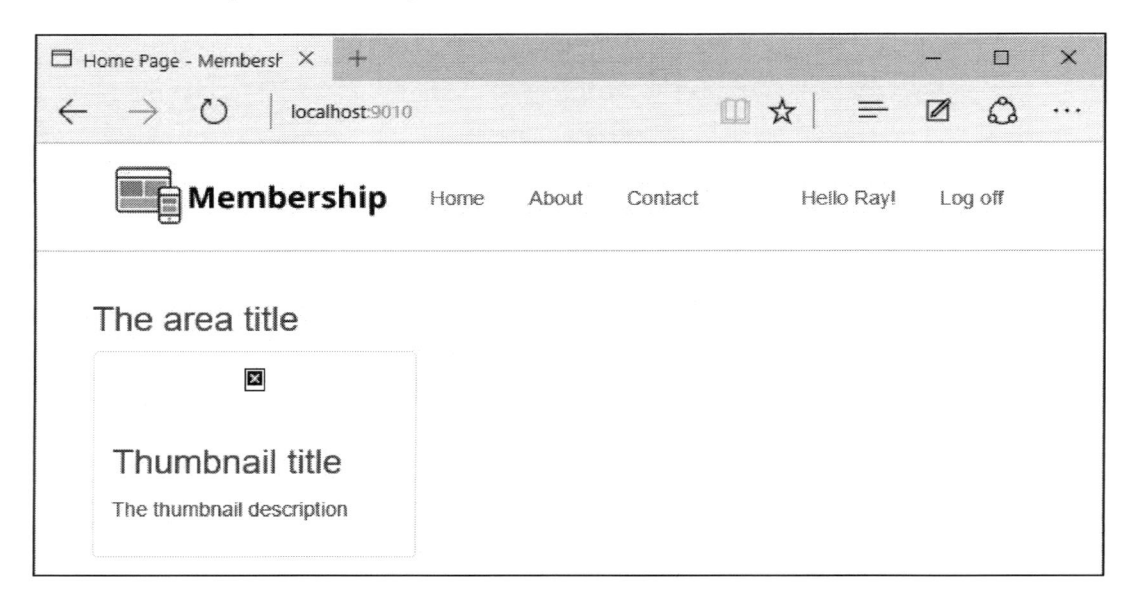

ASP.NET MVC 5 - How to build a Membership Website

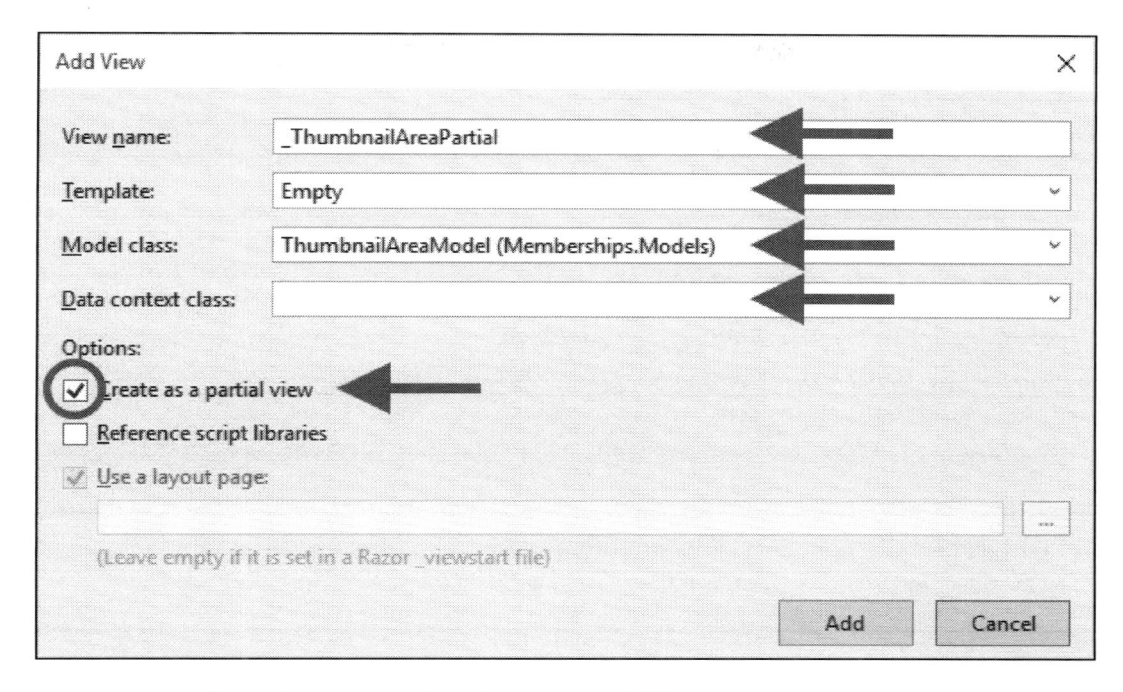

1. Open the **Index** view in the **Views-Home** folder.
2. Add an **IEnumerable<ThumbnailAreaModel> @model** directive.
   `@model IEnumerable<Memberships.Models.ThumbnailAreaModel>`
3. Add an **@Html.Partial** call inside the if-block in the **Index** view to render the **_ThumbnailAreaPartial** view. Pass in an new instance of the the **ThumbnailAreaModel** class; you will later change this code to loop over the model passed into the **Index** view.
   ```
   @if (User.Identity.IsAuthenticated)
   {
       @Html.Partial("_ThumbnailAreaPartial",
          new ThumbnailAreaModel())
   }
   ```
4. Right-click on the **Views-Shared** folder in the main project and select **Add-View**.
5. Name the view **_ThumbnailAreaPartial** and fill out the textboxes as described in the image above and click the **Add** button. It's important that you check the **Create as a partial view** checkbox.
6. Add a **<div>** element containing an **<h3>** header inside with the text *The area title*.

309

```
<div>
    <h3>The area title</h3>
</div>
```

7. Add a **<div>** element decorated with the **row** class below the previous **<div>**. This will be the thumbnail area for the thumbnails.
```
<div class="row">
</div>
```

8. Add a **<div>** decoreated with the **col-sm-3** Bootstrap class inside the **<div>** with the **row** class. This **<div>** will determine the space a thumbnail is allowed to occupy in the area row, which in this case is 3 grid columns.
```
<div class="col-sm-3">
</div>
```

9. Add a **<div>** decorated with the Bootstrap **thumbnail** class inside the previous **<div>**. This **<div>** is the container for the Bootstrap **thumbnail** component and will contain all the elements you want to display in the thumbnail.
```
<div class="thumbnail">
</div>
```

10. Add an empty **<img>** element to the thumbnail **<div>** and make sure to add ... to the **src** attribute and leave the **alt** attribute empty.
```
<img src="..." alt="">
```

11. Add a **<div>** element decorated with the Bootstrap **caption** class below the image. This element will hold the thumbnail title and the description. Add an **<h3>** element with the text *Thumbnail title* and a **<p>** element with the text *The thumbnail description* to the **caption <div>**.
```
<div class="caption">
    <h3>Thumbnail title</h3>
    <p>The thumbnail description</p>
</div>
```

12. Run the application and make sure that the title and thumbnail is displayed.

The code so far for the **_ThumbnailAreaPartial** view:

```
@model Memberships.Models.ThumbnailAreaModel

<div>
    <h3>The area title</h3>
```

```
        </div>

        <div class="row">
            <div class="col-sm-3">
                <div class="thumbnail">
                    <img src="..." alt="">
                    <div class="caption">
                        <h3>Thumbnail title</h3>
                        <p>The thumbnail description</p>
                    </div>
                </div>
            </div>
        </div>
```

Style the _ThumbnailAreaPartial view heading

Style the title to make it stand out more by adding a CSS class called **headline** to the **<div>** element surrounding the **<h3>** title element. Define a selector for the class in the **thumbnails.css** file which adds a green 2px solid line under the title and removes any margin except for a 15px bottom margin.

1. Open the **_ThumbnailAreaPartial** view.
2. Add a CSS class called **headline** to the **<div>** surrounding the **<h3>** heading.
3. Add a CSS selector for the **headline** class in the **thumbnails.css** file.
4. Add a CSS selector which removes any margin except for a 15px bottom margin.

5. Add a CSS selector which adds a green 2px solid line.
6. Save all files and run the application to see the changes.

The CSS **headline** class:

```
.headline {
    margin: 0px 0px 15px;
    border-bottom: 2px solid #72C02C;
}
```

The changes to the **_ThumbnailAreaPartial** view:

```
<div class="headline">
    <h3>The area title</h3>
</div>
```

Fetch the user id with Owin Context

The underlying ASP.NET foundational framework classes were completely rebuilt from the ground up for the Visual Studio 2015 release, and in doing so, they changed the way the Identity Framework handles authentication. To get to the user information, you go through the Owin Context on the current **HttpContext** object.

The user id is used when fetching the subscriptions the logged in user is subscribed to.

You will create an extension method called **GetUserId** acting on the current **HttpContext** to fetch the user id. Add the method to a **public static** class called **HttpContext-Extensions** in the **Extensions** folder.

The Owin Context works with *claims* when handling identities and the claim you are interested in for the user id is the *nameidentifier*.

Add a **string** constant called *nameidentifier* to the class which contains the path to the *nameidentifier* claim. It's important that the nameidentifier address is added exactly as displayed below for it to fetch the user information; remove any spaces.

```
private const string nameidentifier =
"http://schemas.xmlsoap.org/ws/2005/05/identity/claims/nameidentifier";
```

Add an extension method called **GetUserId** which acts on an instance of the **HttpContextBase** class called **ctx** and return a **string**.

Add a **string** variable called **uid** inside the method and assign an empty string to it. This variable will contain the user id if the user is logged in.

Add a **try/catch**-block where the **catch**-block is empty and return the **uid** variable below it.

Add a using statement to the **Owin** namespace above the class to get access to the Owin Context.

```
using Microsoft.AspNet.Identity.Owin;
```

Use the **ctx** instance variable inside the **try**-block to call the **GetOwinContext** method to get the Owin Context; call the generic **Get** method using the **ApplicationsSignInManager** class to get access to the **ApplicationManager** which contains the user's claims. Fetch the first claim matching the *nameidentifier* or return the default value of the **Claim** class in a variable called **claim**.

```
var claims = ctx.GetOwinContext()
   .Get<ApplicationSignInManager>()
   .AuthenticationManager.User.Claims
   .FirstOrDefault(claim => claim.Type.Equals(nameidentifier));
```

If the **claims** variable contains a claim, then assign the value of that claim to the **uid** variable by accessing the **claims** variable's **Value** property.

```
if (claims != default(Claim))
   uid = claims.Value;
```

1. Add a **public static** class called **HttpContextExtensions** to the **Extensions** folder.
2. Add a using statement to the **Owin** and **Claims** namespaces above the class.
   ```
   using Microsoft.AspNet.Identity.Owin;
   using System.Security.Claims;
   ```
3. Add a constant called *nameidentifier* to the class and assign the claims path to it.
   ```
   private const string nameidentifier = "http://schemas.xmlsoap.org/ws/2005/05/identity/claims/nameidentifier";
   ```

4. Add a **string** variable called **uid** to the class and assign an empty string to it.
5. Add a **try/catch**-block to the class where the **catch**-block is empty.
6. Return the **uid** variable below the **catch**-block.
7. Use the **ctx** instance variable inside the **try**-block to call the **GetOwinContext** method to get the Owin Context and call the generic **Get** method using the **ApplicationsSignInManager** class to get access to the **ApplicationManager** which contains the user's claims. Fetch the first claim matching the *nameidentifier* or return the default value of the **Claim** class and store the result in a variable called **claim**.

```
var claims = ctx.GetOwinContext()
   .Get<ApplicationSignInManager>()
   .AuthenticationManager.User.Claims
   .FirstOrDefault(claim => claim.Type.Equals(nameidentifier));
```

8. The user id is located in the **claims** object's **Value** property. Assign the user id to the **uid** variable if the claim contain a value.

```
if (claims != default(Claim))
   uid = claims.Value;
```

9. Open the **HomeController** class and locate the **Index** action.
10. Add a variable called **userId** to the **Index** action and assign the result from a call to the **GetUserId** method on the **HttpContext** instance if the user is authenticated, otherwise assign **null**.

```
var userId = Request.IsAuthenticated ?
   HttpContext.User.Identity.GetUserId() : null;
```

The complete code **HttpContextExtensions** class:

```
using Microsoft.AspNet.Identity.Owin; // Needed for Owin Context
using System.Security.Claims; // Needed for the Claims class

public static class HttpContextExtensions
{
   // Make sure that there are no spaces or line breaks in the string
   private const string nameidentifier = "http://schemas.xmlsoap.org/ws/2005/05/identity/claims/nameidentifier";
```

```
    public static string GetUserId(this HttpContextBase ctx)
    {
        string uid = String.Empty;
        try
        {
            var claims = ctx.GetOwinContext()
                .Get<ApplicationSignInManager>()
                .AuthenticationManager.User.Claims
                .FirstOrDefault(claim =>
                    claim.Type.Equals(nameidentifier));

            // Check that the user is logged in and a claim exist
            if (claims != default(Claim))
                uid = claims.Value;
        }
        catch { }

        return uid;
    }
}
```

Add the following using statements to the **HomeController**:

```
using Microsoft.AspNet.Identity; // Needed for HttpContext Identity
using Memberships.Extensions; // Needed for your extension methods
```

Add the following code to the **Index** action in the **HomeController**:

```
var userId = Request.IsAuthenticated ?
    HttpContext.User.Identity.GetUserId() : null;
```

The GetSubscriptionIdsAsync method

To fetch the user's products, you first have to fetch the user's subscription id's because without them you won't be able to get to the products. As you might recall, the user id can be used to fetch the user's subscription id's from the **UserSubscription** table which in turn is connected to the **SubscriptionProducts** table which has the product id's that can be used to fetch the products in the **Product** table.

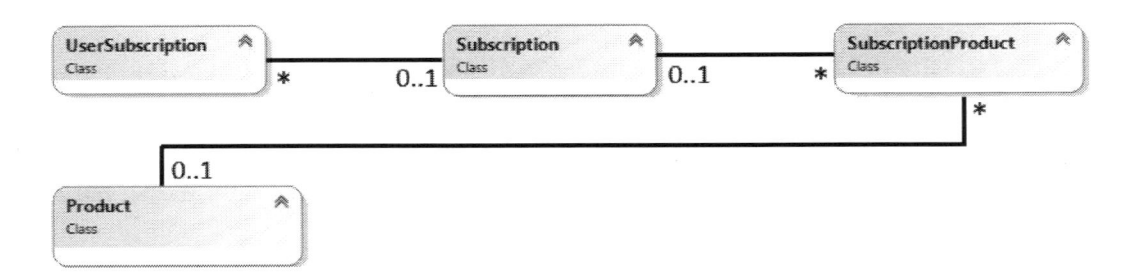

In this step, you will focus on fetching the subscription id's from the **UserSubscription** table and return them from the method. Add a **private** asynchronous method called **GetSubscriptionIdsAsync** which returns **Task<List<int>>** and has two parameters: one of type **string** called **userId** and one called **db** of type **ApplicationDbContext**. Both parameters should have a default value of **null**. The method will be called from a method called **GetProductThumbnailsAsync** which you will add later.

Add the two methods to a **public static** class called **ThumbnailExtensions** in the **Extensions** folder.

Add a **try/catch**-block to the method where the **catch**-block is empty.

Return an empty **List<int>** in the **try**-block if the **userId** parameter is **null**.

Create a new instance of the **ApplicationDbContext** in the **db** parameter if it is **null**. You can call the **Create** method on the **ApplicationDbContext** class to create the instance.

Fetch the subscription id's for the user asynchronously from the **UserSubscription** table and return them from the method using the value in the **userId** parameter.

Return an empty **List<int>** below the **catch**-block.

1. Add **a public static** class called **ThumbnailExtensions** to the **Extensions** folder.
2. Add a **private** asynchronous method called **GetSubscriptionIdsAsync** to the class which returns **Task<List<int>>** and has two parameters one of type **string** called **userId** and one called **db** of type **ApplicationDbContext**. Both parameters should have a default value of **null**.
```
Private static async Task<List<int>> GetSubscriptionIdsAsync(
string userId = null, ApplicationDbContext db = null)
```

3. Add a **try/catch**-block to the method where the **catch**-block is empty.
4. Check if the value in the **userId** parameter is **null** in the **try**-block and return an empty list if it is.
   ```
   If (userId == null) return new List<int>();
   ```
5. Create a new instance of the **ApplicationDbContext** in the **db** parameter if it is **null**.
   ```
   If (db == null) db = ApplicationDbContext.Create();
   ```
6. Fetch the subscription id's for the user asynchronously from the **UserSubscription** table and return them from the method using the value in the **userId** parameter.
   ```
   Return await (
       from us in db.UserSubscriptions
       where us.UserId.Equals(userId)
       select us.SubscriptionId).ToListAsync();
   ```
7. Return an empty list at the end of the method below the **catch**-block.

The complete code for the **GetSubscriptionIdsAsync** method:

```
private static async Task<List<int>> GetSubscriptionIdsAsync(string userId = null, ApplicationDbContext db = null)
{
    try
    {
        if (userId == null) return new List<int>();
        if (db == null) db = ApplicationDbContext.Create();

        return await (
            from us in db.UserSubscriptions
            where us.UserId.Equals(userId)
            select us.SubscriptionId).ToListAsync();
    }
    catch { }

    return new List<int>();
}
```

Add a ThumbnailEqualityComparer

To compare thumbnails on their product id's instead of on their references, you need to add a **public** comparer class called **ThumbnailEqualityComparer** which implements the **IEqualityComparer<ThumbnailModel>** interface to a new folder called **Comparers**.

The **IEqualityComparer** interface defines two methods called **Equals** and **GetHashCode**. The **Equals** method is used when you want to compare two objects with your logic and rules; in this case the objects should be compared on the **ProjectId** property. The **GetHashCode** method returns a unique id for an object – in this case, the **ProjectId**.

1. Add a new folder called **Comparers** to the main project.
2. Add a **public** class called **ThumbnailEqualityComparer** to the folder and have it implement the **IEqualityComparer** interface for the **ThumbnailModel** class.
   ```
   public class ThumbnailEqualityComparer
       : IEqualityComparer<ThumbnailModel> {
   }
   ```
3. Compare the **ProductId** properties in the **ThumbnailModel** parameters passed into the **Equals** method and return the result. The method should return **true** if the two **ProductId** properties are equal.
   ```
   return thumb1.ProductId.Equals(thumb2.ProductId);
   ```
4. Return the **ProductId** property value in the **GetHashCode** method.
   ```
   return thumb.ProductId;
   ```

The complete code for the **ThumbnailEqualityComparer** class:

```
public class ThumbnailEqualityComparer :
IEqualityComparer<ThumbnailModel>
{
    public bool Equals(ThumbnailModel thumb1, ThumbnailModel thumb2)
    {
        return thumb1.ProductId.Equals(thumb2.ProductId);
    }

    public int GetHashCode(ThumbnailModel thumb)
    {
        return thumb.ProductId;
    }
}
```

Fetch the thumbnails from the database

Add an asynchronous extension method called **GetProductThumbnailsAsync** in the **ThumbnailExtensions** class and have it fetch the thumbnail information from the database. The method should act on a **List<ThumbnailModel>** called **thumbnails** and have two additional parameters; a **string** parameter called **userId** and a **ApplicationDbContext** parameter called **db**. Both the **userId** and **db** parameters should have a default value of **null**. The method should return a **Task<IEnumerable<ThumbnailModel>>**.

Add a **try/catch**-block where the **catch**-block is empty.

Create a new instance of the **ApplicationDbContext** class inside the **try**-block if the **db** parameter if it is **null**. You can use the **Create** method on the **ApplicationDbContext** class to create the instance.

Call the **GetSubscriptionIdsAsync** method asynchronously and store the returned subscription id's in a variable called **subscriptionIds**.

Fetch the necessary information for **ThumbnailModel** instances from the database and store the result in the **thumbnails** parameter. You will have to join the **Product**, **ProductLinkText** and **ProductType** tables with the **SubscriptionProduct** table to get all the information. Add a **where** clause to the LINQ expression selecting only entries matching the subscription id's in the **subscriptionIds** collection, you can use the **Contains** method on the collection to achieve this.

Use the **ThumbnailEqualityComparer** class to select distinct **ThumbnailModel** instances to avoid duplicates in the user interface. Use the **Distinct** method on the **thumbnails** parameter to return the distinct instances sorted by title.

```
return thumbnails.Distinct(new ThumbnailEqualityComparer()).OrderBy(o =>
o.Title);
```

1. Open the **ThumbnailExtensions** class in the **Extensions** folder.
2. Add an asynchronous extension method called **GetProductThumbnailsAsync** which act on a **List<ThumbnailModel>** called **thumbnails** and have two additional parameters; a **string** parameter called **userId** and a **ApplicationDbContext** parameter called **db**. Both the **userId** and **db** parameters

should have a default value of **null**. The method should return a **Task<IEnumerable<ThumbnailModel>>**.

```
public static async Task<IEnumerable<ThumbnailModel>>
GetProductThumbnailsAsync(this List<ThumbnailModel> thumbnails,
string userId = null, ApplicationDbContext db = null)
```

3. Add a **try/catch**-block where the **catch**-block is empty.
4. Create a new instance of the **ApplicationDbContext** class inside the **try**-block if the **db** parameter if it is **null**.

```
if (db == null) db = ApplicationDbContext.Create();
```

5. Call the **GetSubscriptionIdsAsync** method asynchronously and store the returned subscription id's in a variable called **subscriptionIds**.

```
var subscriptionIds = await GetSubscriptionIdsAsync(userId, db);
```

6. Use a LINQ query to fetch the necessary data from the database asynchronously and create instances of the **ThumbnailModel** class. Make sure that only subscriptions in the **subscriptionIds** collection are fetched. Join in the necessary tables. Note that the **Link** property contain a path to a controller action that you will add in the next chapter.

```
thumbnails = await (
    from ps in db.SubscriptionProducts
    join p in db.Products on ps.ProductId equals p.Id
    join plt in db.ProductLinkTexts on p.ProductLinkTextId
        equals plt.Id
    join pt in db.ProductTypes on p.ProductTypeId equals pt.Id
    where subscriptionIds.Contains(ps.SubscriptionId)
    select new ThumbnailModel
    {
        ProductId = p.Id,
        SubscriptionId = ps.SubscriptionId,
        Title = p.Title,
        Description = p.Description,
        ImageUrl = p.ImageUrl,
        Link = "/ProductContent/Index/" + p.Id,
        TagText = plt.Title,
        ContentTag = pt.Title
    }).ToListAsync();
```

7. Use the **ThumbnailEqualityComparer** class to return distinct data from the **thumbnails** parameter below the **catch**-block.

```
return thumbnails.Distinct(new ThumbnailEqualityComparer())
    .OrderBy(o => o.Title);
```

8. Open the **Index** action in the **HomeController**.
9. Add a **using** statement to the **Tasks** namespace.
   ```
   using System.Threading.Tasks;
   ```
10. Make the **Index** action asynchronous by adding the **async** keyword, and have it return a **Task<ActionResult>**. You need to do this to **await** results.
    ```
    public async Task<ActionResult> Index()
    ```
11. Call the **GetProductThumbnailsAsync** method asynchronously on a new **List<ThumbnailModel>** instance and store the result in a variable called **thumbnails**.
    ```
    var thumbnails = await new List<ThumbnailModel>()
        .GetProductThumbnailsAsync(userId);
    ```
12. Place a breakpoint on the **View** method call in the **Index** action.
13. Run the application in debug mode and inspect the **thumbnails** variable. It should contain two products provided you are logged in as Roy.

The complete code for the **GetProductThumbnailsAsync** method:

```
public static async Task<IEnumerable<ThumbnailModel>>
GetProductThumbnailsAsync(this List<ThumbnailModel> thumbnails,
string userId = null, ApplicationDbContext db = null)
{
    try
    {
        if (db == null) db = ApplicationDbContext.Create();

        var subscriptionIds = await GetSubscriptionIdsAsync(userId, db);

        thumbnails = await (
            from ps in db.SubscriptionProducts
            join p in db.Products on ps.ProductId equals p.Id
            join plt in db.ProductLinkTexts on p.ProductLinkTextId
                equals plt.Id
            join pt in db.ProductTypes on p.ProductTypeId equals pt.Id
            where subscriptionIds.Contains(ps.SubscriptionId)
            select new ThumbnailModel
            {
                ProductId = p.Id,
```

```
                SubscriptionId = ps.SubscriptionId,
                Title = p.Title,
                Description = p.Description,
                ImageUrl = p.ImageUrl,
                Link = "/ProductContent/Index/" + p.Id,
                TagText = plt.Title,
                ContentTag = pt.Title
            }).ToListAsync();
    }
    catch { }

    return thumbnails.Distinct(new ThumbnailEqualityComparer())
        .OrderBy(o => o.Title);
}
```

The code so far for the **Index** action in the **HomeController**:

```
using Microsoft.AspNet.Identity; // Needed for HttpContext Identity
using Memberships.Extensions; // Needed for your extension methods
using System.Threading.Tasks; // Needed for Async Controller Action
using Memberships.Models;

namespace Memberships.Controllers
{
    public class HomeController : Controller
    {
        public async Task<ActionResult> Index()
        {
            var userId = Request.IsAuthenticated ?
                HttpContext.User.Identity.GetUserId() : null;
            var thumbnails = await new List<ThumbnailModel>()
                .GetProductThumbnailsAsync(userId);

            return View();
        }
    }
}
```

Modify the Index action

There are a couple of tweaks you have to add to the **Index** action in order to send the model to the **Index** view to be rendered.

The first thing you need to do is to find out how many areas should be displayed for the fetched products. Divide the total number of thumbnails in the **thumbnails** variable by 4 to get the number of areas needed. Store the result in a variable called **count**.

Add a **List<ThumbnailAreaModel>** variable called **model** which will hold all the areas generated for the thumbnails.

Add a **for** loop which iterate the number of times specified by the **count** variable. Create new instances of the **ThumbnailAreaModel** class inside the **for**-block and add them to the **model** variable. In this particular scenario, you only want one heading for all the areas and should therefore only assign a value to the **Title** property during the first iteration and assgin an empty string for the remaining iterations. Use the **Skip** and **Take** LINQ methods to fetch the next set of thumbnails from the **thumbnails** collection. Skip the value in the iteration variable multiplied by 4 and take the next 4 thumbnails in the loop and assign them to the **Thumbnails** propety of the **ThumbnailAreaModel** instance.

```
Thumbnails = thumbnails.Skip(i * 4).Take(4)
```

Return the **model** variable with the **View** method to render its data in the **Index** view.

1. Open the **Index** action in the **HomeController**.
2. Find out how many areas should be created by dividing the number of thumbnails by 4 and store the result in a variable called **count**.
   ```
   var count = thumbnails.Count() / 4;
   ```
3. Create the model variable.
   ```
   var model = new List<ThumbnailAreaModel>();
   ```
4. Add a **for** loop and Iterate the number of times specified by the **count** variable.
   ```
   for (int i = 0; i <= count; i++)
   ```

5. Create instances of the **ThumbnailAreaModel** class inside the **for**-block and add them to the **model** variable. Assign the thumbails in the thumbnails collection to the current **ThumbnailAreaModel** instance. Only assign a title to the first **ThumbnailAreaModel** instance.

```
        model.Add(new ThumbnailAreaModel
        {
            Title = i.Equals(0) ? "My Content" : String.Empty,
            Thumbnails = thumbnails.Skip(i * 4).Take(4)
        });
```

6. Return the **model** variable with the **View** method.
   ```
   return View(model);
   ```

The complete code for the **Index** action in the **HomeController**:

```
public async Task<ActionResult> Index()
{
    var userId = Request.IsAuthenticated ?
        HttpContext.User.Identity.GetUserId() : null;

    var thumbnails = await new List<ThumbnailModel>()
        .GetProductThumbnailsAsync(userId);

    var count = thumbnails.Count() / 4;
    var model = new List<ThumbnailAreaModel>();
    for (int i = 0; i <= count; i++)
    {
        model.Add(new ThumbnailAreaModel
        {
            Title = i.Equals(0) ? "My Content" : String.Empty,
            Thumbnails = thumbnails.Skip(i * 4).Take(4)
        });
    }

    return View(model);
}
```

Modify the Index view

Open the **Index** view in the **Views-Home** folder and add a **forech** loop around the **@Html.Partial** method call and change the parameter passed in to the method from **Model** to the loop variable.

The loop will iterate over all the areas sent to the view from the **Index** action.

If you run the application at this stage, you will still only see one thumbnail because the **_ThumbnailAreaPartial** hasn't been modified yet.

```
@if (User.Identity.IsAuthenticated)
{
    //Displayed if the user is logged in
    foreach (var area in Model)
    {
        @Html.Partial("_ThumbnailAreaPartial", area)
    }
}
```

Display data in the _ThumbnailAreaPartial view

Open the **_ThumbnailAreaPartial** view and add data from the view model sent in through the **@model** directive.

Add an if-block around the title **<div>** and **<h3>** elements which display the title only if the model's **Title** property contains text. If you recall, you only assigned a title to the first area. Also replace the hard-coded title with the value from the model's **Title** property.

Move the **<div>** decorated with the **row** class above the if-block to create the row for the area and not the thumbnail.

Add an if-block around the thumbnail HTML markup below the title if-block which checks that the **Thumbnails** collection property in the model isn't **null**. Note that the last closing **</div>** belong to the **<div>** decorated with the row class and should not be included in the if-block.

Add a foreach loop inside the if-block iterating over the thumbnails in the model's **Thumbnails** collection property.

The last thing to do before viewing the changes is to add data from the loop variable (the product) to the thumbnail.

Create a folder called **Images** in the **Content** folder and copy two thumbnail images (246x156) called *csharp-for-beginners.png* and *unit-testing.png* to the new folder. If you used different names for the thumbnail images, then name the images acordingly.

Replace the ... with the model's **ImageUrl** property in the **<img>** element's **src** attribute.

Replace the text *Thumbnail title* with an **<a>** element where the content is the value in the loop variable's **Title** property (the thumbnail title) and the **href** attribute is assigned the URL in the **Link** property. Note that the link won't work at the moment because the necessary controllers and views have not been added yet.

Replace the text *The Thumbnail Description* with in the the loop variable's **Decription** property (the thumbnail description).

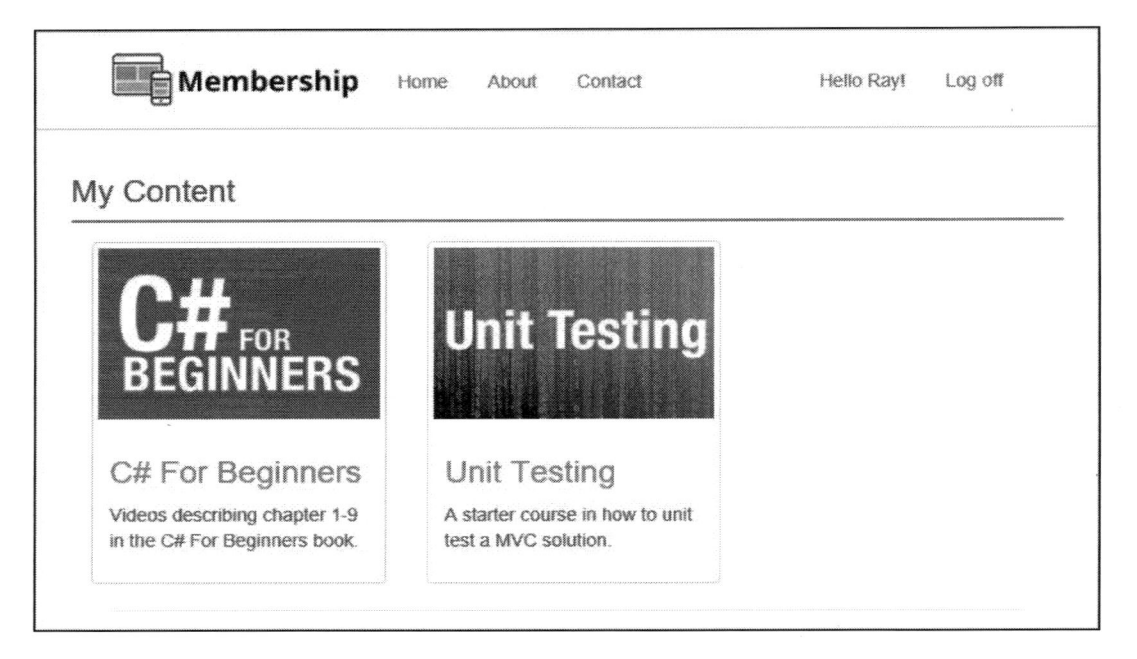

1. Open the **_ThumbnailAreaPartial** view.
2. Add an if-block around the title **<div>** and **<h3>** elements that display the title only if the model's **Title** property contains text. If you recall, you only assigned a title to the first area. Also change the hard-coded title with the value from the model's **Title** property.

```
@if (!Model.Title.Equals(String.Empty))
{
    <div class="headline">
        <h3>@Model.Title</h3>
    </div>
}
```

3. Move the **<div>** decorated with the **row** class above the if-block to create the row for the area and not the thumbnail.
4. Add an if-block around the thumbnail HTML markup below the title if-block which checks that the **Thumbnails** collection property in the model isn't **null**. Note that the last closing **</div>** belong to the **<div>** decorated with the **row** class and should not be included in the if-block.
   `@if (Model.Thumbnails != null)`
5. Add a foreach loop inside the if-block iterating over the thumbnails in the model's **Thumbnails** collection property.
   `foreach (var thumb in Model.Thumbnails)`
6. Create a folder called **Images** in the **Content** folder and copy two thumbnail images (246x156) called *csharp-for-beginners.png* and *unit-testing.png* to the new folder. If you used different names for the thumbnail images then name the images acordingly.
7. Replace the ... with the model's **ImageUrl** property in the **<img>** element's **src** attribute.
   `<img src="@thumb.ImageUrl" alt="">`
8. Replace the text *Thumbnail title* with an **<a>** element where the content is the value in the loop variable's **Title** property (the thumbnail title) and the **href** attribute is assigned the URL in the **Link** property. Note that the link won't work at the moment because the necessary controllers and views have not been added yet.
   `<h3><a href="@thumb.Link">@thumb.Title</a></h3>`
9. Replace the text *The Thumbnail Description* with in the the loop variable's **Decription** property (the thumbnail description).
   `<p>@thumb.Description</p>`
10. Run the application and view the thumbnails.

The complete code in the **_ThumbnailAreaPartial** view:

```
@model Memberships.Models.ThumbnailAreaModel

<div class="row">
    @if (!Model.Title.Equals(String.Empty))
    {
        <div class="headline">
            <h3>@Model.Title</h3>
        </div>
    }

    @if (Model.Thumbnails != null)
    {
        foreach (var thumb in Model.Thumbnails)
        {
            <div class="col-sm-3">
                <div class="thumbnail">
                    <img src="@thumb.ImageUrl" alt="">
                    <div class="caption">
                        <h3><a href="@thumb.Link">@thumb.Title</a></h3>
                        <p>@thumb.Description</p>
                    </div>
                </div>
            </div>
        }
    }
</div>
```

Add the labels

Because elements are positioned relative to their closest-positioned parent, you need to add a **<div>** element around the **<img>** element and decorate the **<div>** with a CSS class called **thumbnail-img-container**, which you later will add to the **thumbnails.css** file. The CSS rule for that class will position the element **realtive** to its parent to make it possible to position the labels **absolute** to their container. It will also hide any overflowing parts of the image, this will come in handy when you animate the image.

Add a CSS class called **thumbnail-img** to the **<img>** element, you will later add a selector to style the image from the **thumbnails.css** file.

Add another **<div>** decorated with a CSS class called **thumbnail-container** around the **<div>** decorated with the **thumbnail-img-container** class.

Add an **<a>** element below the **<div>** decorated with the **thumbnail-img-container** class and decorate it with two CSS classes called **tag** and **text-tag** which you will add to the **thumbnails.css** file later. This is the bottom label in the image. Also add the loop variable's **Link** property to the **href** and the **TagText** property as the content.

Add a **<div>** element below the **<a>** element and decorate it with two CSS classes called **tag** and **content-tag** which you will add to the **thumbnails.css** file later. This is the upper label in the image. Also add the loop variable's **ContentTag** property as its content.

1. Add the **thumbnail-img** class to the **<img>** element.
   ```
   <img class="thumbnail-img" src="@thumb.ImageUrl" alt="">
   ```
2. Add a **<div>** element around the **<img>** element and decorate it with a CSS class called **thumbnail-img-container**.
   ```
   <div class="thumbnail-img-container">
       <img class="thumbnail-img" src="@thumb.ImageUrl" alt="">
   </div>
   ```
3. Add an **<a>** element below the **<div>** decorated with the **thumbnail-img-container** class. Add two classes called **tag** and **text-tag** to the **<a>** element and assign the **Link** property to the **href** attribute and the **TagText** as its content.
   ```
   <a class="tag text-tag" href="@thumb.Link">
       @thumb.TagText</a>
   ```
4. Add a **<div>** element below the **<a>** element and decorate it with two CSS classes called **tag** and **content-tag**. Use the **ContentTag** property as its content.
   ```
   <div class="tag content-tag">@thumb.ContentTag</div>
   ```

The modified code in the **_ThumbnailAreaPartial** view:

```
@if (Model.Thumbnails != null)
{
    foreach (var thumb in Model.Thumbnails)
    {
        <div class="col-sm-3">
            <div class="thumbnail">
                <div class="thumbnail-container">
                    <div class="thumbnail-img-container">
```

```
                <img class="thumbnail-img"
                    src="@thumb.ImageUrl" alt="">
            </div>
            <a class="tag text-tag hover-effect" href="@thumb.Link">
                @thumb.TagText
            </a>
            <div class="tag content-tag">@thumb.ContentTag</div>
        </div>
        <div class="caption">
            <h3><a href="@thumb.Link">@thumb.Title</a></h3>
            <p>@thumb.Description</p>
        </div>
    </div>
</div>
}
```

Styling the thumbnail labels

The image shows what the thumbnails look like with the labels added and styled. I suggest that you make the changes one at a time and watch what happens with the thumbnails in the browser.

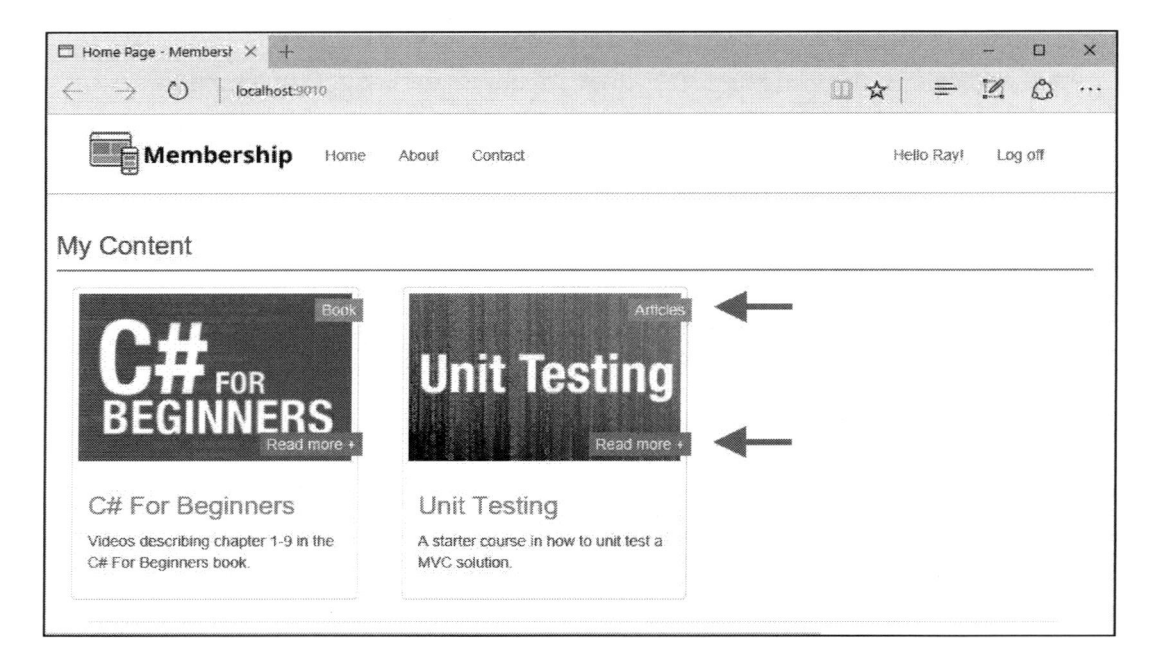

Open the **thumbnails.css** file and add a rule for the **thumbnail** class to add 5px padding around the thumbnail.

```
.thumbnail {
    padding: 5px;
}
```

Add a rule which targets elements with the **tag** class inside an element with the **thumbnail** class to style the two labels. Position them -10px from the right border of the container (this will make them apear as though they are sticking out) and make the text white. Add 1px padding to the top and bottom and 5px to the left and right sides. Position the labels with absolute positioning and display them as inline blocks.

```
.thumbnail .tag {
    right: -10px;
    color: #FFF;
    padding: 1px 6px;
    position: absolute;
    display: inline-block;
}
```

Add a rule which targets elements with the **thumbnail-img-container** class inside an element with the **thumbnail** class to style the `<div>` containing the thumbnail image. Hide any overflowing image parts; this will be useful when animating the image.

```
.thumbnail .thumbnail-img-container {
    overflow: hidden;
}
```

Add a rule which targets elements with the **thumbnail-container** class inside an element with the **thumbnail** class to give the `<div>` relative positioning making it possible to position its chilren with absolute positioning relative to the `<div>`.

```
.thumbnail .thumbnail-container {
    position: relative;
}
```

Add a rule which targets elements with the **text-tag** class inside an element with the **thumbnail** class to style the bottom label. Change the background color to green and position it 5px from the bottom of its closest-positioned parent which is the **<div>** decorated with the **thumbnail-container** class.

```
.thumbnail .text-tag {
    background-color: #72C02C;
    bottom: 5px;
}
```

Add a rule which targets elements with the **content-tag** class inside an element with the **thumbnail** class to style the top label. Change the background color to orange and position it 5px from the top of its closest-positioned parent which is the **<div>** decorated with the **thumbnail-container** class.

```
.thumbnail .content-tag {
    background-color: #f79a47;
    top: 5px;
}
```

Add a rule which targets elements with the **thumbnail-img** class inside an element with the **thumbnail** class to style the thumbnail image. Make the image scale to 100% of the width and use automatic scaling of the height. This will make the whole image fit inside its container even when the browser size changes.

```
.thumbnail .thumbnail-img {
    width: 100%;
    height: auto;
}
```

Add a rule which targets **<a>** elements inside an element with the **thumbnail** class to remove the outline and text under line in the links.

```
.thumbnail a, a:focus, a:hover, a:active {
    outline: 0px none !important;
    text-decoration: none;
}
```

Add a rule which targets **<a>** elements when hovering over the link, when it is active or has focus and it resides inside an element with the **thumbnail** class. Use the rule to change the text color to the same green color that is used when hovering over links in the main menu.

```
.thumbnail > a:focus, a:hover, a:active {
    color: #72C02C;
}
```

Use a media query which targets extra small devicees and add a rule which targets elements with the **thumbnail** class. The rule should set a maximum width of 260px to elements decorated with the class. The rule will make the thumbnail look better on smartphones and such devices.

```
@media screen and (min-width: 480px) {
    .thumbnail {
        max-width: 260px;
    }
}
```

Animating the thumbnail image and labels

Now let's make the thumbnails a bit more fun by animating the image to rotate and zoom. Move the lower label to the left and give the thumbnail a shadow when hovering over the image. All CSS rules are added to the **thumbnails.css** file.

I suggest that you add the CSS rules one by one and note the changes to the various elements involved in the animations.

Animating the lower label

To move the lower label 5px to the left from the image's right side and to make the label larger when hovering over it, you need to define three CSS rules.

The first rule is a class called **hover-effect** and will define an animation on the **<a>** element making it ease in and out over a period of 0.4 seconds when the mouse pointer enters or leaves the element. Add the CSS class to the **<a>** element and the rule to the **thumbnails.css** file.

```
.thumbnail .hover-effect {
    transition: all 0.4s ease-in-out 0s;
}
```

```
<a class="tag text-tag hover-effect" href="@thumb.Link">
    @thumb.TagText</a>
```

The second rule uses the already existing **text-tag** CSS class to target the **<a>** element when hovering over it and adds a box shadow to the **<a>** element making it appear larger.

```
.thumbnail a.text-tag:hover {
    box-shadow: 0px 0px 0px 2px #5FB611;
}
```

The third rule uses the already existing **text-tag** CSS class to target the **<a>** element when hovering over the thumbnail. This rule will be applied as soon as the mouse pointer enters the thumbnail and will move the label 5px from the parent container's right border.

```
.thumbnail:hover a.text-tag {
    right: 5px;
}
```

Add a shadow around the thumbnail

To add a shadow around the thumbnail container, the **:hover** pseudo class has to be used with the **thumbnail** CSS class to target the container with that class when hovering over it. Add a box shadow transition of 0.2 seconds and reset all other ease in and out transitions to add the animation.

```
.thumbnail:hover {
    box-shadow: 0px 0px 8px #555;
    transition: box-shadow 0.2s ease-in-out 0s;
}
```

Rotate and zoom the image

To rotate the image, a rule targeting the image the **:hover** pseudo class has to be used with the **thumbnail** CSS class to target the container with that class when hovering over it. Scale and rotate the image with the **scale** and **rotate** CSS methods.

```
.thumbnail:hover img {
    transform: scale(1.2) rotate(2deg);
}
```

You also need to add a 0.8 second transition and reset all other ease in and out transitions to the the already exisitng **.thumbnail .thumbnail-img** CSS rule.

```css
.thumbnail .thumbnail-img {
    width: 100%;
    height: auto;
    transition: all 0.8s ease-in-out 0s;
}
```

11. Display Product Page

Introduction

In this chapter you will add the page which displays a product's content. This page can contain several sections for sections/modules and a section for downloadable material. The sections will be displayed using collapsible Bootstrap **panel** components and the product items will be displayed as **<div>** elements containing a Bootstrap **grid** layout.

By the end of this chapter, the application will display the product items grouped by the section they belong to for a selected product. The sections can for instance be chapters or downloads. This view will be displayed when the user clicks on one of the product thumbnails you added in the previous chapter. The image below shows what the end result will look like.

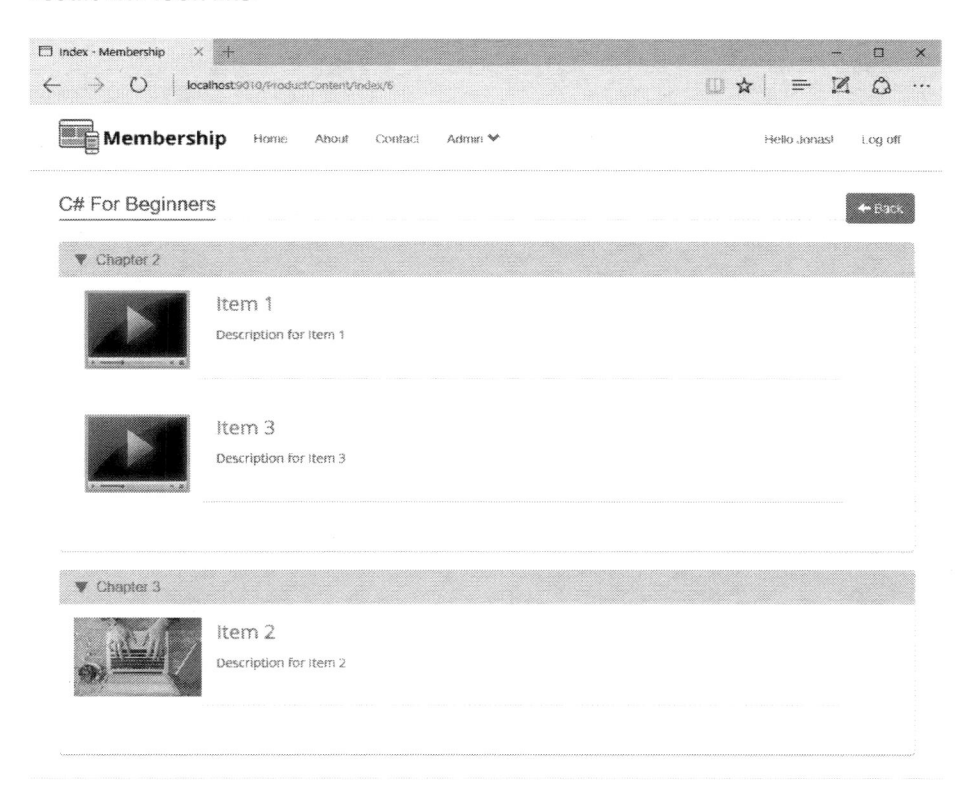

n will display a thumbnail, the item title and a description. In a future chapter, will add the views which will display the item content when on one of the item links is clicked.

In the previous chapter, you added an extension method called **GetProductThumbnails-Async** in the **ThumbnailExtensions** class to display the product thumbnails. In the LINQ query for the thumbnails, you populated a property called **Link** with a unique link to the product. This link will now be used to fetch the items belonging to the selected product and open a view to display the content.

The sections will be created using data from the **Section** table; note that this table can contain section names other than *Chapter xyz*, for instance *Downloads*.

Adding the ProductContent controller

To be able to render the product listings, you first have to add an empty controller named **ProductContent**.

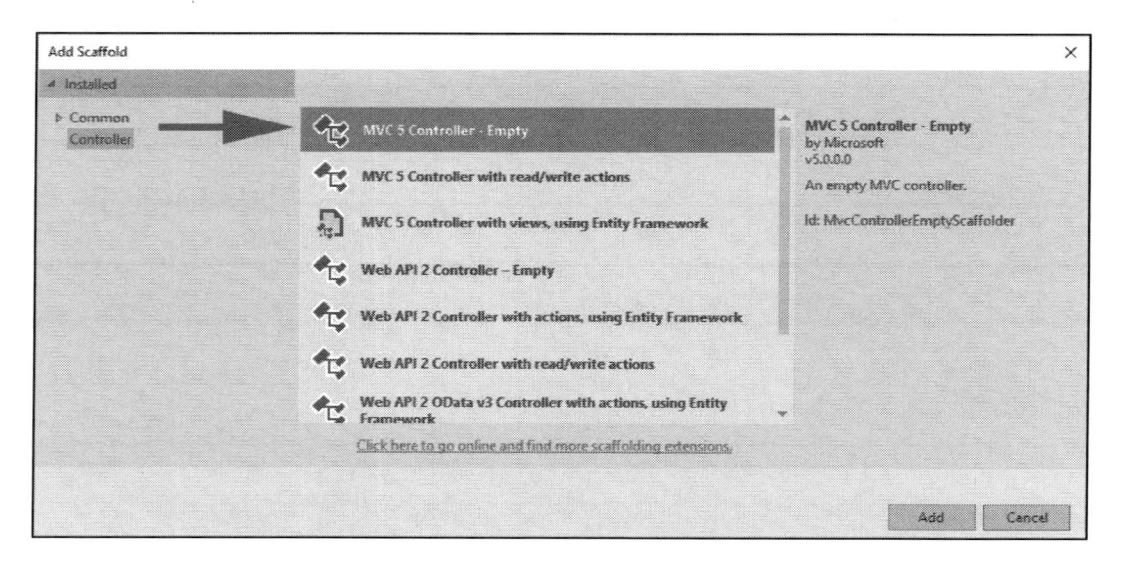

ASP.NET MVC 5 - How to build a Membership Website

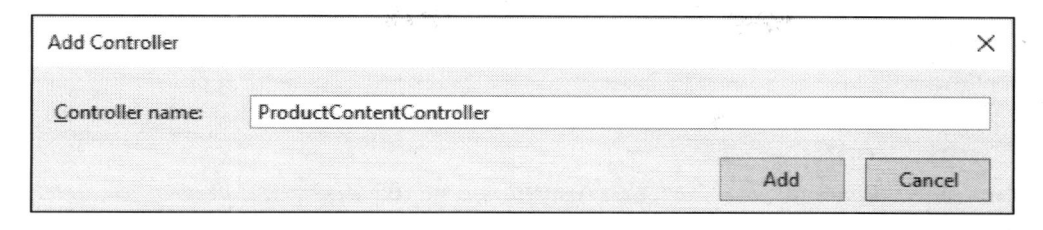

1. Right-click on the **Controllers** folder in the main project and select **Add-Controller** in the menu.
2. Make sure that the **MVC 5 Controller - Empty** option is selected and click the **Add** button.
3. Enter the name **ProductContentController** in the text field and click the **Add** button.
4. Add the **Authorize** attribute to the class to ensure that only logged in users can reach this controller.
   ```
   [Authorize]
   public class ProductContentController : Controller
   ```
5. Add a **using** statement to the **System.Threading.Tasks** namespace to enable asynchronous action methods.
6. Make the **Index** action asynchronous by adding the **Async** and **Task** keywords to its declaration. Also add an **id** parameter of type **int** which will hold the product id when the action is called.
   ```
   public async Task<ActionResult> Index(int id)
   ```

The code so far for the **ProductContentController** class:

```
using System.Threading.Tasks;
using System.Web.Mvc;
namespace Memberships.Controllers
{
    [Authorize]
    public class ProductContentController : Controller
    {
        public async Task<ActionResult> Index(int id)
        {
            return View();
        }
    }
}
```

Adding the model classes

To display the data in the **Index** view a few model classes must to be added.

The ProductItemRow class

This class will hold the necessary data to display and handle one product item in one of the sections. It must contain the following properties:

- **ItemId** of type **int**
- **ImageUrl** of type **string**
  For displaying the item thumbnail next to the title and description.
- **Link** of type **string**
  The URL to navigate to when the user clicks the tiltle link to see the content.
- **Title** of type **string**
- **Description** of type **string**
- **IsDownload** of type **bool**
  Determines if the data is a downloadable like a PDF or a Zip file. If it is then the content will be opened in a new tab.
- **ReleaseDate** of type **nullable DateTime**
- **IsAvailable** of type **bool**
  Determines if the content is available for consumption or if it should be disabled.

1. Right-click on the **Models** folder in the main project and select **Add-Class** in the menu.
2. Name the class **ProductItemRow** and click the **Add** button.
3. Add the properties according to the bullet list above.
4. Save the class.

The complete code for the **ProductItemRow** class:

```
public class ProductItemRow
{
    public int ItemId { get; set; }
    public string ImageUrl { get; set; }
    public string Link { get; set; }
    public string Title { get; set; }
    public string Description { get; set; }
```

```
    public bool IsDownload { get; set; }
    public DateTime? ReleaseDate { get; set; }
    public bool IsAvailable { get; set; }
}
```

The ProductSection class

This class will hold the necessary data to display the different product sections, like *Chapters xyz* and a *download* section. It must contain the following properties:

- **Id** of type **int**
- **Title** of type **string**
- **ItemTypeId** of type **int**
- **Items** of type **IEnumerable<ProductItemRow>**
  The list of product items for each section.

1. Right-click on the **Models** folder in the main project and select **Add-Class** in the menu.
2. Name the class **ProductSection** and click the **Add** button.
3. Add the properties according to the bullet list above.
4. Save the class.

The complete code for the **ProductSection** class:

```
public class ProductSection
{
    public int Id { get; set; }
    public string Title { get; set; }
    public int ItemTypeId { get; set; }
    public IEnumerable<ProductItemRow> Items { get; set; }
}
```

The ProductSectionEqualityComparer class

This class will be used when comparing **ProductSection** instances to make sure that only one instance of each available section will be in the list of product sections. To achieve this, the **ProductSectionEqualityComparer** class will have to implement the **IEquality-Comparer** interface using the **ProductSection** class as its data type. Implement the **Equals** method of the interface to compare the value of the **Id** properties of the two instances. Implement the **GetHashCode** method to return the hash value for the **Id** property.

1. Right-click on the **Comparers** folder in the main project and select **Add-Class** in the menu.
2. Name the class **ProductSectionEqualityComparer** and click the **Add** button.
3. Implement the **IEqualityComparer** interface using the **ProductSection** as its data type.
   ```
   public class ProductSectionEqualityComparer
       : IEqualityComparer<ProductSection>
   ```
4. Implement the methods by selecting **Implement Interface** from the **Quick Actions** button (the light bulb button that appears when hovering over the interface name). Two methods called **Equals** and **GetHashCode** are added to the class.
5. Change the **x** parameter to **section1** and **y** to **section2** for the **Equals** method.
6. Return the value from comapring the **Id** properties of the **section1** and **section2** parameters in the **Equals** method.
   ```
   public bool Equals(ProductSection section1, ProductSection section2)
   {
       return section1.Id.Equals(section2.Id);
   }
   ```
7. Change the **obj** parameter to **section** for the **GetHashCode** method.
8. Return the hash code of the **Id** property for the passed in **section** parameter.
   ```
   public int GetHashCode(ProductSection section)
   {
       return (section.Id).GetHashCode();
   }
   ```
9. Save the class.

The complete code for the **ProductSectionEqualityComparer** class:

```
public class ProductSectionEqualityComparer :
IEqualityComparer<ProductSection>
{
    public bool Equals(ProductSection section1, ProductSection section2)
    {
        return section1.Id.Equals(section2.Id);
```

```
    }
    public int GetHashCode(ProductSection section)
    {
        return (section.Id).GetHashCode();
    }
}
```

The ProductSectionModel class

This class will hold the product title and a list of the sections associated with that product. It must contain the following properties:

- **Title** of type **string**
  The product title.
- **Sections** of type **List<ProductSection>**
  The list of product sections associated with the product.

1. Right-click on the **Models** folder in the main project and select **Add-Class** in the menu.
2. Name the class **ProductSectionModel** and click the **Add** button.
3. Add the properties according to the bullet list above.
4. Save the class.

The complete code for the **ProductSectionModel** class:

```
public class ProductSectionModel
{
    public string Title { get; set; }
    public List<ProductSection> Sections { get; set; }
}
```

Adding the Index view for the ProductContent controller

Now that you have added the **ProductContent** controller, it is time to add the **Index** view which will be displayed when the user clicks on one of the product thumbnails.

Use the **ProductSectionModel**, **ProductSection** and **ProductItemRow** classes to display the product title, sections and product items in the view.

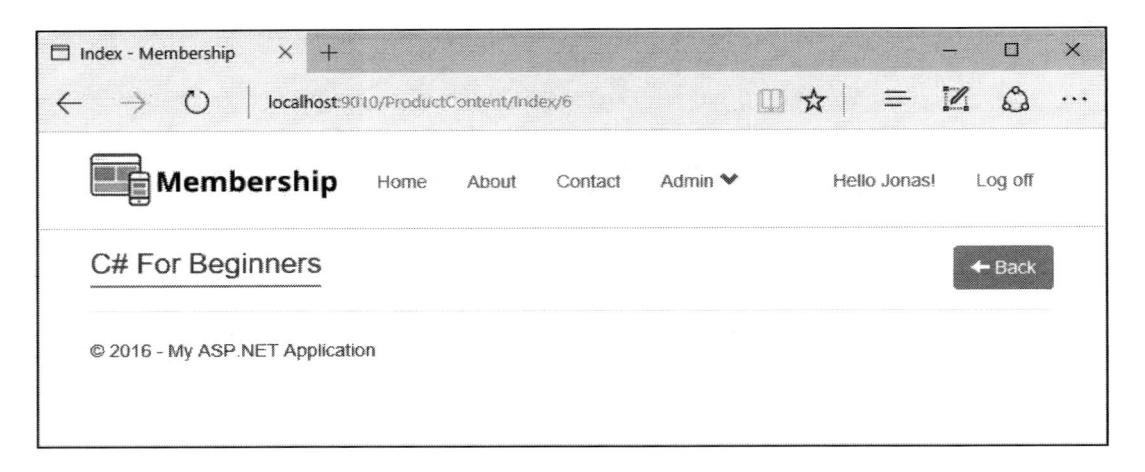

Add the **Index** view to the **Views-ProductContent** folder and select the empty template. Use the **ProductSectionModel** class as its model and remove the data context class. The image below shows the necessary settings.

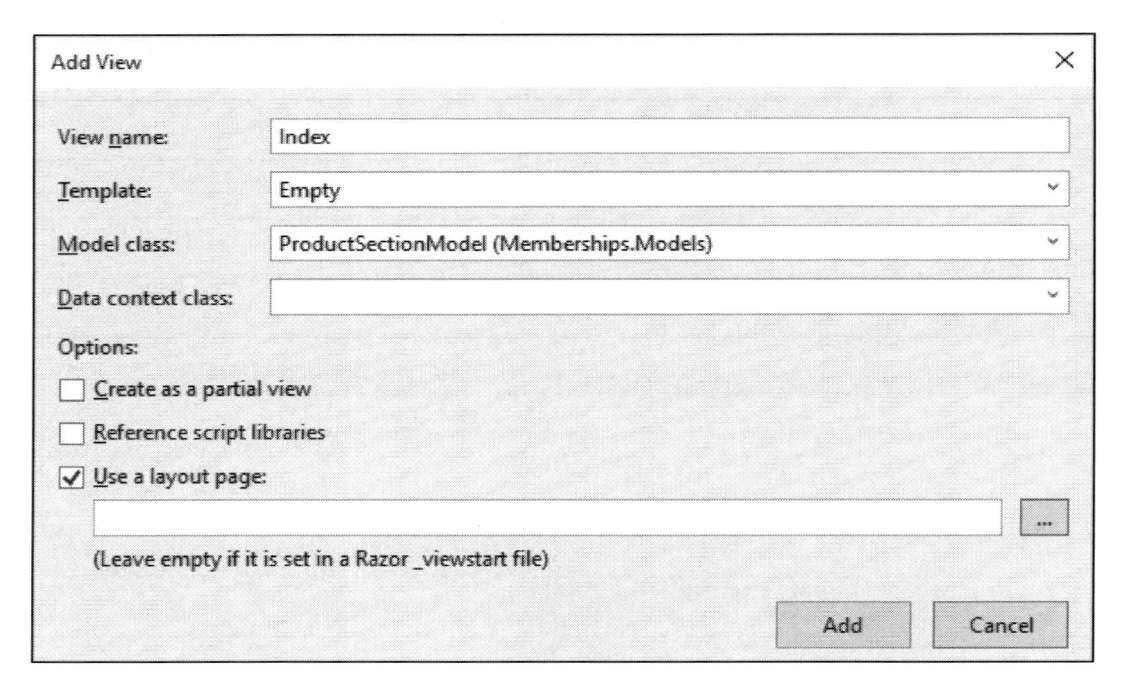

1. Right-click on the **Views-ProductContent** folder and select **Add-View**.
2. Name the view **Index** in the *View name* field.

3. Select **Empty** in the *Template* drop-down.
4. Select **ProductSectionModel** in the *Model class* drop-down.
5. Delete the text in the *Data context class* drop-down.
6. Make sure that the *Create as a partial view* checkbox is <u>unchecked</u>.
7. Click the **Add** button.
8. Delete the **<h2>** element.
9. Add a **<div>** element and asign the **headline** class to it.
10. Add a **<h2>** element inside the **<div>** which displays the **Title** property from the **@Model** object.
11. Add an **<a>** element with the **btn**, **btn-primary** and **pull-right** bootstrap classes assigned to it. Add the **href** attribute to it and assign */Home/Index* to it. Add a **<span>** element displaying the **glyphicon-arrow-left** glyphicon and the text *Back* inside the **<a>** element.

```
<a class="btn btn-primary pull-right" href="/Home/Index">
    <span class="glyphicon glyphicon-arrow-left"
        aria-hidden="true"></span> Back
</a>
```

12. Save the **Index** view.

The **Index** view markup so far:

```
@model Memberships.Models.ProductSectionModel

@{
    ViewBag.Title = "Index";
}

<div class="headline">
    <h2>
        @Model.Title
    </h2>
    <a class="btn btn-primary pull-right" href="/Home/Index">
        <span class="glyphicon glyphicon-arrow-left"
            aria-hidden="true"></span> Back
    </a>
</div>
```

Adding the GetProductSectionsAsync extension method

Now that you have added the **ProductContent** controller and the **Index** view, it is time to fill the view with data. In order to do that, you will have to add an asynchronous extension method called **GetProductSectionsAsync** which will fetch the sections and their data from the database and display them in the view.

You will create supporting methods to the **GetProductSectionsAsync** method, and to keep them together, you will add a **static** class called **SectionExtensions** to the **Extensions** folder.

The method should return an instance of the **ProductSectionModel** which is the model class for the **Index** view. Two parameters are needed to fetch the data; **productId** of type **int** and **userId** of type **string**.

The first thing you need to add to the the method is an instance of the **ApplicationDbContext** called **db** to be able to fetch the data from the database.

Then add a LINQ query to fetch the sections as **ProductSection** instances and store them in a variable called **sections**. Start with the **Product** table and join in the **ProductItem**, **Item** and **Section** tables when fetch the data. Only select products where the product id matches the value in the **productId** parameter. Order the data by section id. Use the **await** keyword to fetch the data asynchronously.

Pass in an instance of the **ProductSectionEqualityComparer** class to the **Distinct** list method to fetch a distinct list of sections, removing any duplicates. Store the list in a variable called **result**.

Create an instance of the **ProductSectionModel** class and assign the **result** list to its **Sections** proerty and fetch the product title asynchronously storing it in the **Title** property. Return the instance from the method.

1. Add a **static** class called **SectionExtensions** to the **Extensions** folder.
2. Add an asynchronous method called **GetProductSectionsAsync** which returns a Task<ProductSectionModel> to the class. The method must have two parameters called **productId** of type **int** and **userId** of type **string**.

```
public static async Task<ProductSectionModel>
GetProductSectionsAsync(int productId, string userId)
```

3. Create an instance of the **ApplicationDbContext** called **db**.
4. Add a LINQ query to fetch the sections as **ProductSection** instances and store them in a variable called **sections**.
    a. Start with the **Product** table and join in the **ProductItem**, **Item** and **Section** tables when fetch the data.
    b. Only select products where the product id match the value in the **productId** parameter.
    c. Order the data by section id.
    d. Use the **await** keyword to fetch the data asynchronously.
5. Remove any duplicates from the sections list using an instance of the **ProductSectionEqualityComparer** class.
    ```
    var result = sections.Distinct(
        new ProductSectionEqualityComparer()).ToList();
    ```
6. Create an instance of the **ProdcutSectionModel** class, fill it with data and return it from the method.

The code in the **GetProductSectionsAsync** method so far:

```
public static class SectionExtensions
{
    #region Product Methods for the ProductController
    public static async Task<ProductSectionModel>GetProductSectionsAsync(
        int productId, string userId)
    {
        var db = ApplicationDbContext.Create();

        var sections = await (from p in db.Products
            join pi in db.ProductsItems on p.Id equals pi.ProductId
            join i in db.Items on pi.ItemId equals i.Id
            join s in db.Sections on i.SectionId equals s.Id
            where p.Id.Equals(productId)
            orderby s.Id
            select new ProductSection
            {
                Id = s.Id,
                ItemTypeId = i.ItemTypeId,
                Title = s.Title
```

```
            }).ToListAsync();

        var result = sections.Distinct(
            new ProductSectionEqualityComparer())
            .ToList();

        var model = new ProductSectionModel
        {
            Sections = result,
            Title = await (from p in db.Products
                where p.Id.Equals(productId)
                select p.Title).FirstOrDefaultAsync()
        };

        return model;
    }
    #endregion
}
```

Altering the Index action

Now that you have created the extension method needed to fetch the product title and sections, it is time to add a call to it in the **Index** action method in the **ProductContent** controller.

Use the **GetUserId** method on the **HttpContext** class to fetch the user id and store it in a variable called **userId**.

Call the **GetProductSectionsAsync** method on the **SectionExtensions** class and pass in the product id from the **id** action parameter and the user id from the **userId** variable. Await the result and store it in a variable called **sections**.

Pass in the **sections** object to the **View** method.

1. Open the **ProductContentController** class.
2. Fetch the user id if the user is authenticated orherwise return **null**.
   ```
   var userId = Request.IsAuthenticated ? HttpContext.GetUserId() : null;
   ```

348

3. Call the **GetProductSectionsAsync** method on the **SectionExtensions** class and pass in the product id from the **id** action parameter and the user id from the **userId** variable.
   ```
   var sections = await SectionExtensions.GetProductSectionsAsync(id,
       userId);
   ```
4. Pass in the **sections** object to the **View** method.
   ```
   return View(sections);
   ```
5. Run the application and click on one of the product thumbnails.
   As you can see, the output doesn't contain any sections because you haven't created the necessary partial view. It is also badly formatted. In the next section, you will add some styling to fix the layout.

The code in the **Index** action so far:

```
public async Task<ActionResult> Index(int id)
{
    var userId = Request.IsAuthenticated ?
        HttpContext.GetUserId() : null;

    var sections = await SectionExtensions.GetProductSectionsAsync(id,
        userId);

    return View(sections);
}
```

Styling the Index view

As you saw in the previous section, the heading of the Index view is not well styled. In this section, you will add a style sheet called **ProductContent.css** and create the necessary CSS classes.

Add the **ProductContent.css** to the membership style bundle in the **BundleConfig** class to load it on start-up.

The upper image on the next page shows the view without any added styling.

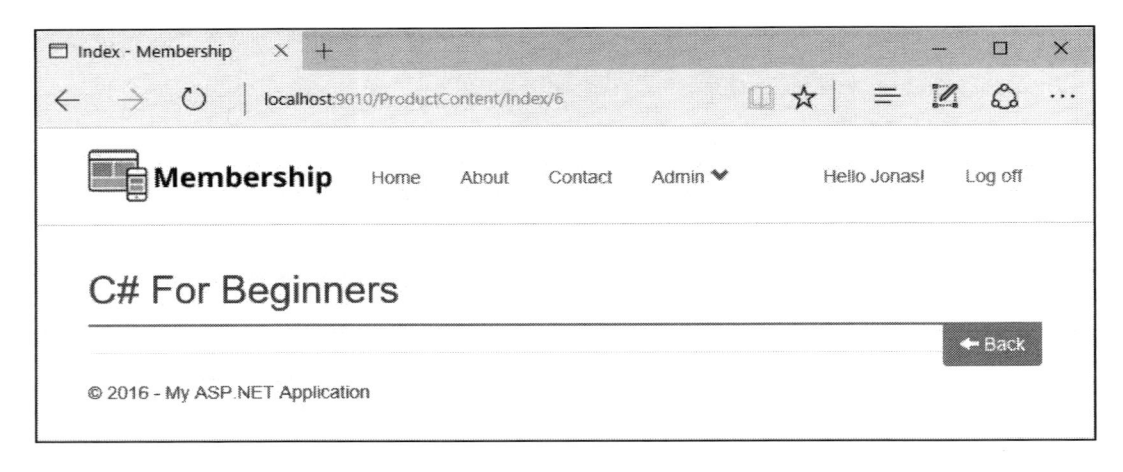

The **headline** CSS selector will only remove the bottom border from the **<div>** element.

The selector for the **<h2>**, **<h3>** and **<h4>** elements inside the **headline** selector will need a bit more styling. Add a -2px bottom margin to allign the heading with the **Back** button. Add a 2px solid green (#72C02C) bottom border and a 5px bottom padding to add some space between the text and the bottom border. Lastly display the heading as an **inline-block** to let the content flow on the same line.

Add a selector for **<h2>** elements inside the **headline** selector and change the font size to 22px.

The image below shows the styled view.

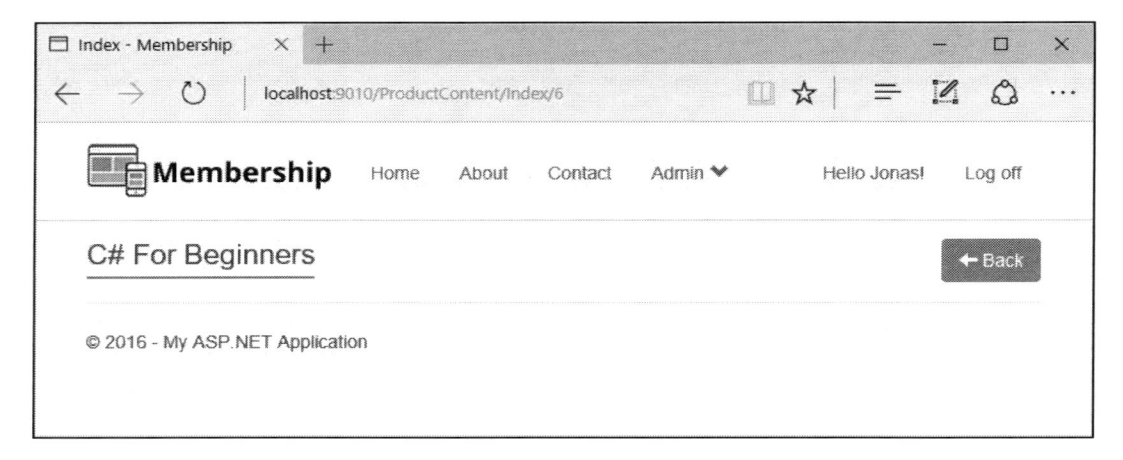

The complete code for the **headline** selectors:

```
.pc-headline
{
    border-bottom: none;
    margin-bottom: 10px;
}

. pc-headline h2, .pc-headline h3, .pc-headline h4
    {
        margin: 0px 0px -2px;
        border-bottom: 2px solid #72C02C;
        padding-bottom: 5px;
        display: inline-block;
    }

    .pc-headline h2
    {
        font-size: 22px;
    }
```

Adding the _ProductSection partial view

To display the actual sections in the **Index** view, you need to add a partial view called **_ProductSection**. The model for the view should be **IEnumerable<ProductSection>** passed in from the **Index** view's **Sections** model property.

Add the **_ProductSection** partial view to the **Views-Shared** folder and select the empty template. Use the **ProductSection** class as its model and remove the data context class. Check the *Create as a partial view* checkbox. The image below shows the necessary settings.

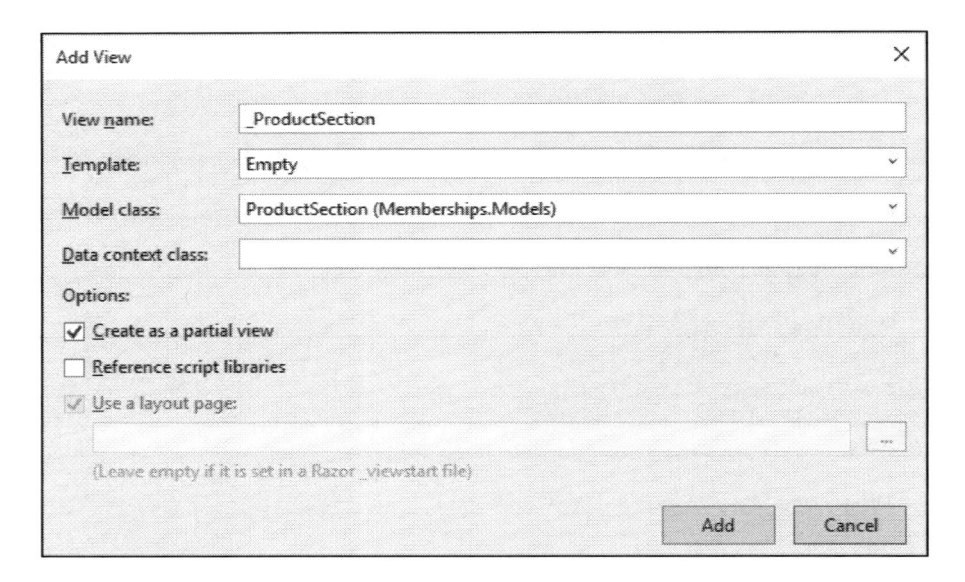

Add a foreach loop iterating over the **Model** and create a Bootstrap panel for each section. Add an **<a>** element to the **panel-title <h4>** element that can be used to collapse the **panel-body <div>** element to hide the section items. Display the section title and an empty **<span>** with a carret icon (**glyphicon-play**) in the **<a>** element. The carret should rotate 90 degrees when displaying and hiding a panel body.

Render the **_ProductSection** partial view at the end of the **Index** view.

The image below shows the finished result.

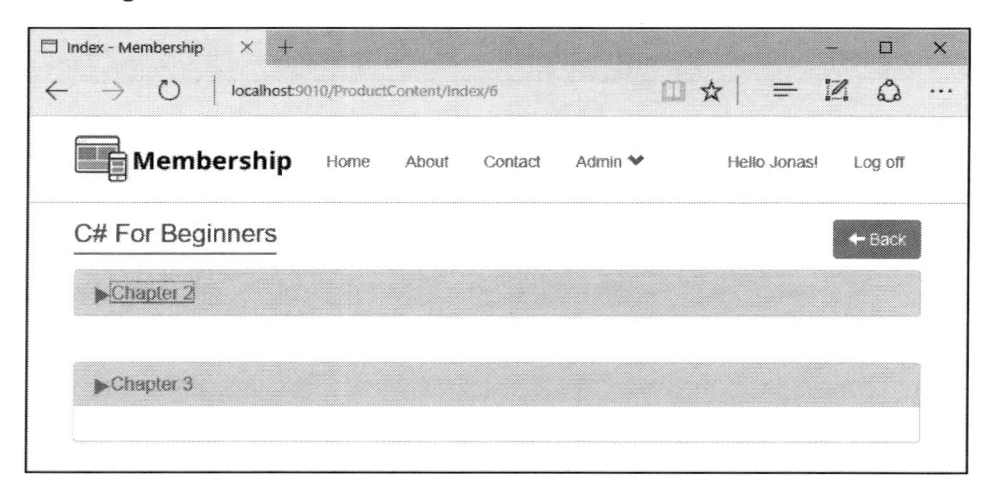

1. Right-click on the **Views-Shared** folder and select **Add-View**.
2. Name the view **_ProductSection** in the *View name* field.
3. Select **Empty** in the *Template* drop-down.
4. Select **ProductSection** in the *Model class* drop-down.
5. Delete the text in the *Data context class* drop-down.
6. Make sure that the *Create as a partial view* checkbox is checked.
7. Click the **Add** button.
8. Change the **@model** directive to **IEnumerable<ProductSection>**.
   ```
   @model IEnumerable <Memberships.Models.ProductSection>
   ```
9. Add a foreach loop iterating over the **Model**.
   ```
   @foreach (var s in Model) { // Add panel markup here }
   ```
10. Create a Bootstrap panel for each section in the loop and add the **panel-success** class to give the panel a (green) color. Also, add a line break after the panel's closing **</div>** element.
    ```
    <div class="panel panel-success">
    </div>
    <br />
    ```
11. Add a **<div>** element decorated with the Bootstrap **panel-heading** class inside the panel **<div>** element.
    ```
    <div class="panel-heading"></div>
    ```
12. Add a **<h4>** element decorated with the Bootstrap **panel-title** class inside the **panel-heading <div>** element.
    ```
    <h4 class="panel-title"></h4>
    ```
13. Add an **<a>** element to the **panel-title <h4>** element which can be used to collapse the **panel-body <div>** element to hide the section items.
    ```
    <a data-toggle="collapse" class="panel-carret"
    href="#collapse@{@s.Id}">@s.Title</a>
    ```
14. And an empty **<span>** with a carret icon (**glyphicon-play**) to the left of the title in the **<a>** element.
    ```
    <a data-toggle="collapse" class="panel-carret"
    href="#collapse@{@s.Id}">
       <span class="pull-left glyphicon glyphicon-play
          gly-rotate-90"></span>
       @s.Title
    </a>
    ```

15. Add a **<div>** element decorated with the necessary classes to make it collapsible when the **<a>** element in the header is clicked. Add the **panel-body <div>** to the **<div>**, the **panel-body <div>** will later contain the section items.
    ```
    <div id="collapse@{@s.Id}" class="panel-collapse collapse in">
        <div class="panel-body">
        </div>
    </div>
    ```
16. Save the **_ProductSection** partial view.
17. Open the **Index** view and add a call to the **@Html.Partial** extension method to render the **_ProductSection** partial view at the end of the **Index** view. Pass in the **Sections** collection from the model.
    ```
    @Html.Partial("_ProductSection", Model.Sections)
    ```
18. Save the **Index** view.

The complete **_ProductSection** view markup:

```
@model IEnumerable<Memberships.Models.ProductSection>

@foreach (var s in Model)
{
    <div class="panel panel-success">
        <div class="panel-heading">
            <h4 class="panel-title">
                <a data-toggle="collapse" class="panel-carret"
                href="#collapse@{@s.Id}">
                    <span class="pull-left glyphicon glyphicon-play
                    gly-rotate-90"></span>
                    @s.Title
                </a>
            </h4>
        </div>
        <div style="" id="collapse@{@s.Id}" class="panel-collapse
        collapse in">
            <div class="panel-body">
            </div>
        </div>
    </div>
    <br />
}
```

Styling the carret symbol

To transform the carret symbol, making it rotate when the panel body is displayed and hidden, you need to style the **glyphicon-play**. Add a new CSS style sheet called **carret.css** to the **Content** folder and add it to the **memebership** styles bundle in the **BindleConfig** class.

The image below shows the carret in rotated and default state.

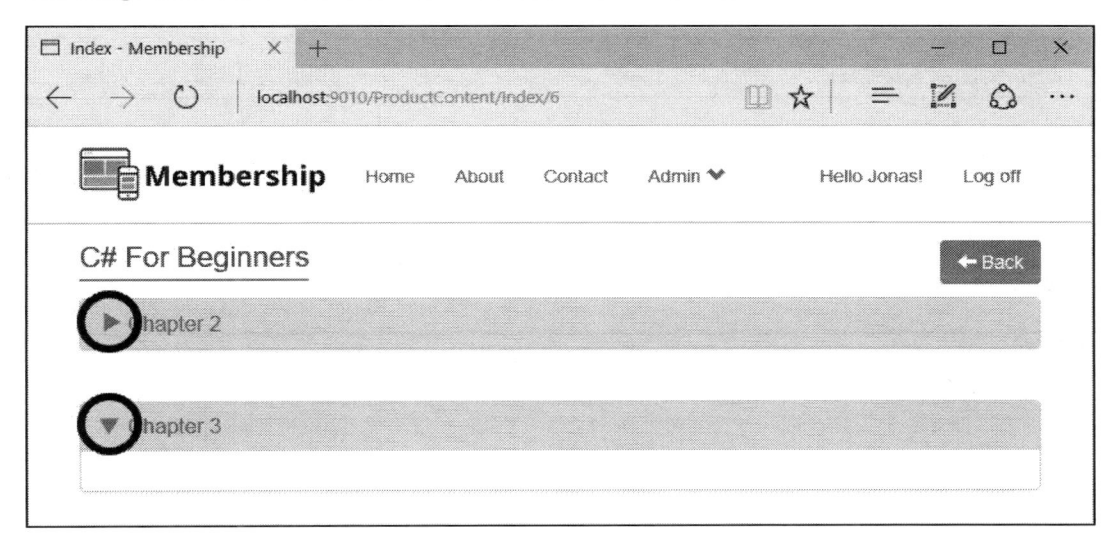

The gly-rotate-90 selector
This CSS selector configures the rotation transforms to 90 degreees for the different browsers.

```
.gly-rotate-90 {
    -webkit-transform: rotate(90deg);
    -moz-transform: rotate(90deg);
    -ms-transform: rotate(90deg);
    -o-transform: rotate(90deg);
    transform: rotate(90deg);
}
```

Alligning the carret to the top of the header text
You'll have to add two selectors to allign the carret (**glyphicon-play**) to the top of the panel header text. The first will allign the glyph when the panel body section is displayed and the second when it is hidden.

The first selector needs a top margin of -1px to be correctly alligned and the second needs a top margin of -4px and right margin of 4px.

```
.panel-carret .glyphicon-play.gly-rotate-90 {
    margin-top: -1px;
}

.panel-carret .glyphicon-play {
    margin-top: -4px;
    margin-right: 4px;
}
```

Rotating the carret
You'll have to add two selectors to rotate the carret (**glyphicon-play**) as well as a JavaScript method which is triggered when the user clicks the carret or the panel title.

The first selector will rotate the carret to its open position (90 degrees), which is its default state since the panle body sections are open by default. The rotation will be performed with a 0.3 second transition to make it rotate smoother. The second selector will rotate the carret to 0 degrees.

```
.panel-carret span {
    transition: all 0.3s ease 0s;
    transform: rotate(90deg);
}

.panel-carret.pressed span {
    transform: rotate(0deg);
}
```

The JavaScript
The **glyphicon-play** glyph will be transformed when an element decorated with the **panel-carret** class is clicked, which is the **<a>** element located inside the **<h4>** element

decoreated with the **panel-title** class. Add a JavaScript file called **carret.js** to the **Scripts** folder and add it to the **memebership** script bundle in the **BindleConfig** class.

The JavaScript will toggle the **pressed** CSS class on the clicked element. It will aslo toggle the **gly-rotate-90** CSS class on the clicked element's children, in this case the **<span>** inside the **<a>** element located inside the **<h4>** element decoreated with the **panel-title** class.

```
$(".panel-carret").click(function (e) {
    $(this).toggleClass("pressed");
    $(this).children(".glyphicon-play").toggleClass("gly-rotate-90");
    e.preventDefault();
});
```

Adding the GetProductItemRowsAsync extension method

To display the product items in the panel's body sections, you need to add an extension method called **GetProductItemRowsAsync** to the **SectionExtensions** class. The method needs five parameters to fetch the data; three **int** parameters called **sectionId**, **itemTypeId** and **productId** as well as a **string** parameter called **userId** and an **ApplicationDbContext** instance called **db**.

The method needs access to an instance of the **ApplicationDbContext** class to access the database.

Start with the **Item** table when building the LINQ query that will fetch the product items. Join in the **ItemType**, **ProductsItems**, **SubscriptionProducts** and **UserSubscriptions** tables. Add a **where** clause that limits the returned items to items where the section id is equal to the passed in **sectionId** parameter, the item type id is equal to the passed in **itemTypeId** parameter, the product id is equal to the passed in **productId** parameter and the user id is equal to the passed in **userId** parameter.

Order the result by **PartId** and return instances of the **ProductItemRow** class where each item represent one item in the product section.

The **Link** property of the **ProductItemRow** objects should target the **ProductContent** controller and pass along the **Title** from the **ItemType** table; this is the action method to call when the item is clicked. The product id and the item id also have to be part of the URL. Example URL: */ProductContent/Book/5/3*.

The method should be asynchronous.

1. Open the **SectionExtensions** class.
2. Add a new **static** method called **GetProductRowsAsync** which returns **Task<IEnumerable<ProductItemRow>>** and takes five parameters; three **int** parameters called **sectionId, itemTypeId** and **productId** as well as a **string** parameter called **userId** and an **ApplicationDbContext** instance called **db**.
   ```
   public static async Task<IEnumerable<ProductItemRow>>
   GetProductItemRowsAsync(int productId, int sectionId, int
   itemTypeId, string userId, ApplicationDbContext db = null)
   ```
3. Create an instance of the **ApplicationDbContext** if none has been passed in through the **db** parameter.
   ```
   if (db == null) db = ApplicationDbContext.Create();
   ```
4. Store the current date in a variable called **today**.
5. Await the result from a LINQ query that fetches the section items and store the result in a variable called **items**. Join in the **ItemType, ProductsItems, SubscriptionProducts** and **UserSubscriptions** tables with the **Item** table to get the correct data.
6. Use a **where** clause to limit the result to items where the **SectionId** in the **Item** table match the value in the **sectionId** parameter, the **ProductId** in the **ProductItem** table match the value in the **productId** parameter and the **UserId** in the **UserSubscription** table match the value in the **userId** parameter.
7. Order the result by **PartId** in the **Item** table.
8. Let the **select** statement return instances of the **ProductItemRow** where the **Link** property contain the URL to call in the **ProductContent** controller when a product item is clicked or the URL to the downloadable file like a PDF which should be opened in a separate tab; you can use the **ItemType** title or id to determine if it is a downloadable file. Use the **DbFunctions.CreateDateTime** method when assigning the **ReleaseDate** property and calculating the value for the **IsAvailable** property; the **DateTime** class cannot be used in LINQ queries.

```
Link = it.Title.Equals("Download") ? i.Url : 
"/ProductContent/Content/" + pi.ProductId + "/" + i.Id,

ReleaseDate = DbFunctions.CreateDateTime(us.StartDate.Value.Year, 
us.StartDate.Value.Month, us.StartDate.Value.Day + i.WaitDays, 0, 
0, 0),

IsAvailable = DbFunctions.CreateDateTime(today.Year, today.Month, 
today.Day, 0, 0, 0) >= DbFunctions.CreateDateTime(
us.StartDate.Value.Year, us.StartDate.Value.Month, 
us.StartDate.Value.Day + i.WaitDays, 0, 0, 0)
```

9. Assign a value to the **IsDownload** property that will determine if the link is to a downloadable file or an item in the database. This property will be used to determine if the item should be displayed in the **Downolads** section in the product items list. Use the **ItemType** title or id to determine if it's a downloadable.
10. Save the class.

The complete code for the **GetProductItemRowsAsync** method:

```
public static async Task<IEnumerable<ProductItemRow>> 
GetProductItemRowsAsync(int productId, int sectionId, string userId, 
ApplicationDbContext db = null)
{
    if (db == null) db = ApplicationDbContext.Create();
    var today = DateTime.Now.Date;

    var items = await (from i in db.Items
        join it in db.ItemTypes on i.ItemTypeId equals it.Id
        join pi in db.ProductsItems on i.Id equals pi.ItemId
        join sp in db.SubscriptionProducts on pi.ProductId 
            equals sp.ProductId
        join us in db.UserSubscriptions on sp.SubscriptionId 
            equals us.SubscriptionId
        where i.SectionId.Equals(sectionId) && 
            pi.ProductId.Equals(productId) && 
            us.UserId.Equals(userId)
        orderby i.PartId
        select new ProductItemRow
        {
            ItemId = i.Id,
            Description = i.Description,
```

```
            Title = i.Title,
            Link = it.Title.Equals("Download") ? i.Url :
                "/ProductContent/Content/" + pi.ProductId + "/" + i.Id,
            ImageUrl = i.ImageUrl,
            ReleaseDate = DbFunctions.CreateDateTime(
                us.StartDate.Value.Year, us.StartDate.Value.Month,
                us.StartDate.Value.Day + i.WaitDays, 0, 0, 0),
            IsAvailable = DbFunctions.CreateDateTime(today.Year,
                today.Month, today.Day, 0, 0, 0) >=
                DbFunctions.CreateDateTime(us.StartDate.Value.Year,
                    us.StartDate.Value.Month, us.StartDate.Value.Day +
                    i.WaitDays, 0, 0, 0),
            IsDownload = it.Title.Equals("Download")
        }).ToListAsync();

    return items;
}
```

Altering the GetProductSectionsAsync extension method

Now that you have added the **GetProductItemRowsAsync** method, it can be called from **GetProductSectionsAsync** method to fetch the items for each product section.

Add a foreach loop iterating over the sections in the **sections** variable immediately below the LINQ query in the **GetProductSectionsAsync** method and assign the result from calling the **GetProductItemRowsAsync** method to the **Items** property of the current loop object (section).

```
foreach (var section in sections)
    section.Items = await GetProductItemRowsAsync(productId, section.Id,
        section.ItemTypeId, userId);
```

Because the Downloads section should be displayed as the last section at the end of the view, you have to change the LINQ query to be ordered by the section **Title** property.

```
orderby s.Title
select new ProductSection
```

And create a union between the sections without the word *download* in the title and the once with the word *download* in the title.

```
var union = result.Where(r => !r.Title.ToLower().Contains("download"))
    .Union(result.Where(r => r.Title.ToLower().Contains("download")));
```

The finished code for the **GetProductSectionsAsync** method:

```
public static async Task<ProductSectionModel>
GetProductSectionsAsync(int productId, string userId)
{
    var db = ApplicationDbContext.Create();

    var sections = await (
        from p in db.Products
        join pi in db.ProductsItems on p.Id equals pi.ProductId
        join i in db.Items on pi.ItemId equals i.Id
        join s in db.Sections on i.SectionId equals s.Id
        where p.Id.Equals(productId)
        orderby s.Title
        select new ProductSection {
            Id = s.Id,
            ItemTypeId = i.ItemTypeId,
            Title = s.Title
        }).ToListAsync();

    foreach (var section in sections)
        section.Items = await GetProductItemRowsAsync(productId,
            section.Id, userId);

    var result = sections.Distinct(new ProductSectionEqualityComparer())
        .ToList();

    var union = result.Where(r => !r.Title.ToLower()
        .Contains("download")).Union(result.Where(r => r.Title.ToLower()
        .Contains("download")));

    var model = new ProductSectionModel {
        Sections = union.ToList(),
        Title = await (
            from p in db.Products
            where p.Id.Equals(productId)
            select p.Title).FirstOrDefaultAsync()
    };

    return model;
}
```

Adding the _ProductItemRow partial view

To display the product items, you have to add a partial view that renders a single product item and loop over the **Items** collection in the **ProductSection** model in the **_Product-Section** partial view.

The **_ProductItemRow** partial view should take a single instance of the **ProductItemRow** class as its model. The view should have a container **<div>** element decorated with the **product-item** and **row** classes; the former class will be used to target the intrinsic elements with CSS.

There should be two **<div>** elements acting as columns decorated with the **col-sm-2** and **col-sm-10** classes respectively inside the **row <div>**. Place an **<img>** element with a fixed width of 140px that will display the item thumbnail inside the first column **<div>**. Inside the second column **<div>,** you will have to perform some logic to determine if the item is available by checking the **IsAvailable** property; if it isn't available, then display a **<p>** element with a text telling the user that the item will be released on the date stored in the **ReleaseDate** property.

Add a second logic check if the item is available inside an **<h2>** element and display the value in the item **Title** as static text if it isn't 362vailable. Otherwise, add the **Title** as an **<a>** element with the **target** attribute set to **_blank** if it is a downloadable item or as an **<a>** element without a **target** attribute if it isn't downloadable. Use the model's **Link** property in the **<a>** element's **href** attribute to add the destination URL.

Add a **<p>** element displaying the value in the model's **Description** property below the **<h2>** element.

Add a line break (**
) below the **row <div> to add some space between the product items.

The image below shows the settings for the **_ProductItemRow** partial view.

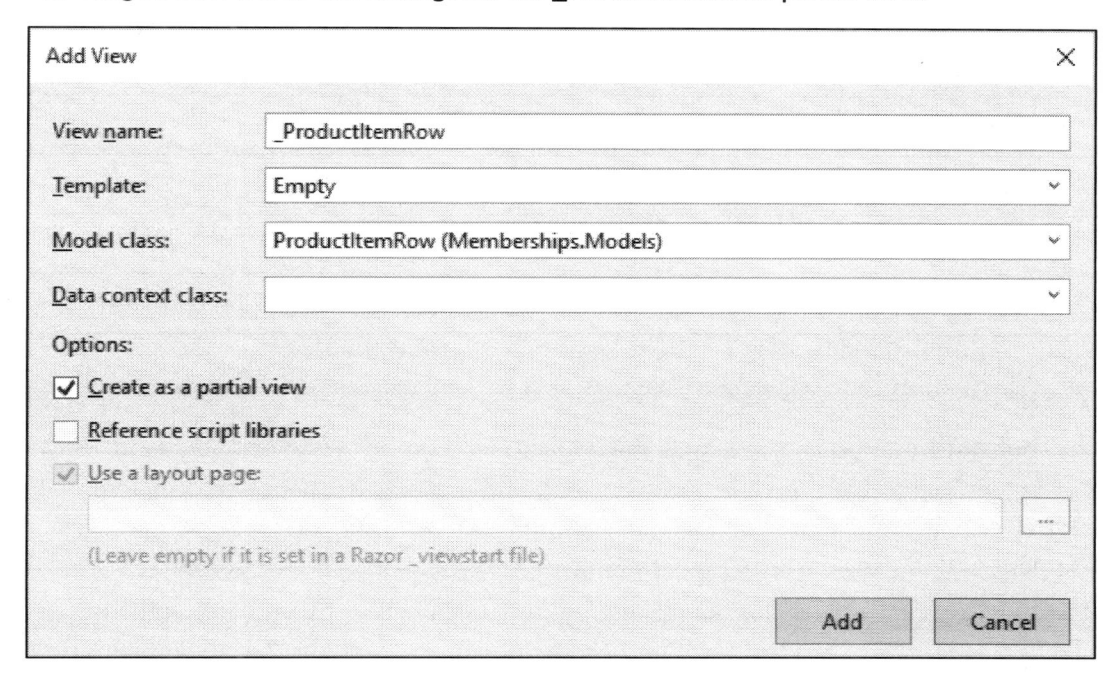

1. Right-click on the **Views-Shared** folder and select **Add-View**.
2. Name the view **_ProductItemRow** in the *View name* field.
3. Select **Empty** in the *Template* drop-down.
4. Select **ProductItemRow** in the *Model class* drop-down.
5. Delete the text in the *Data context class* drop-down.
6. Make sure that the *Create as a partial view* checkbox is checked.
7. Click the **Add** button.
8. Add a **<div>** element and decorate it with the **product-item** and **row** classes.
9. Add a **<div>** element inside the previous **<div>** and decorate it with the **col-sm-2** class.
10. Add an **<img>** element inside the previous **<div>** with a fixed width of 140px and has the model's **ImageUrl** property assigned to its **src** attribute.
    ```
    <img src="@Model.ImageUrl" width="140" />
    ```

11. Add a **<div>** element below the previous **<div>** and decorate it with the **col-sm-10** class as well as the **text-color, line-bottom, min-height** classes that will be used to style its content.
12. Add an if-block inside the previously added **<div>** that will display the text *Will be released:* followed by the date from the model's **ReleaseDate** property in a **<p>** element if the model's **IsAvailable** property is **false**.

```
@if (!Model.IsAvailable)
{
    <p>
        Will be released:
        @Model.ReleaseDate.Value.ToShortDateString()
    </p>
}
```

13. Add an **<h2>** element below the if-block.
14. Add an if-block inside the **<h2>** element that checks if the item is available.
    a. Add an if-block that checks if the item is downloadable inside the block of the previous if-statement.
        i. If it is downloadable, add an **<a>** element with the **target** attribute set to **_blank**, the **href** attribute set to the model's **Link** property and its text to the model's **Title** property.
        ii. Otherwise, add the same **<a>** element without the target attribute present.
    b. If the item isn't available, then display the model's **Title** property as static text.

```
<h2>
@if (Model.IsAvailable) {
    if (Model.IsDownload)
    {
        <a class="" href="@Model.Link" target="_blank">
            @Model.Title</a>
    }
    else
    {
        <a class="" href="@Model.Link">@Model.Title</a>
    }
}
else { @Model.Title }
</h2>
```

15. Add a **<p>** element displaying the model's **Diescription** property below the **<h2>** element.
16. Add a **
** below the last closing **</div>**.
17. Save the partial view.

The complete code for the **_ProductItemRow** partial view:

```
@model Memberships.Models.ProductItemRow

<div class="product-item row">
    <div class="col-sm-2">
        <img src="@Model.ImageUrl" width="140" />
    </div>
    <div class="col-sm-10 text-color line-bottom min-height">
        @if (!Model.IsAvailable)
        {
            <p>Will be released:
                @Model.ReleaseDate.Value.ToShortDateString()</p>
        }
        <h2>
            @if (Model.IsAvailable)
            {
                if (Model.IsDownload)
                {
                    <a class="" href="@Model.Link" target="_blank">
                        @Model.Title</a>
                }
                else
                {
                    <a class="" href="@Model.Link">@Model.Title</a>
                }
            }
            else
            {
                @Model.Title
            }
        </h2>
        <p>@Model.Description</p>
    </div>
</div>
<br />
```

Altering the _ProductSectionPartial view

To display only the sections that contain items, you have to place an if-block around all the markup inside the foreach loop, checking that there are items in the model's **Items** collection.

Add a foreach loop iterating over the items in the model's **Items** collection inside the **<div>** decorated with the **panel-body** class. Use the **@Html.Partial** extension method to render the the **_ProductItemRow** partial view for each item. Pass in the current item in the loop to the partial view.

The image below shows the product content page after the **_ProductSection** partial view has been activated.

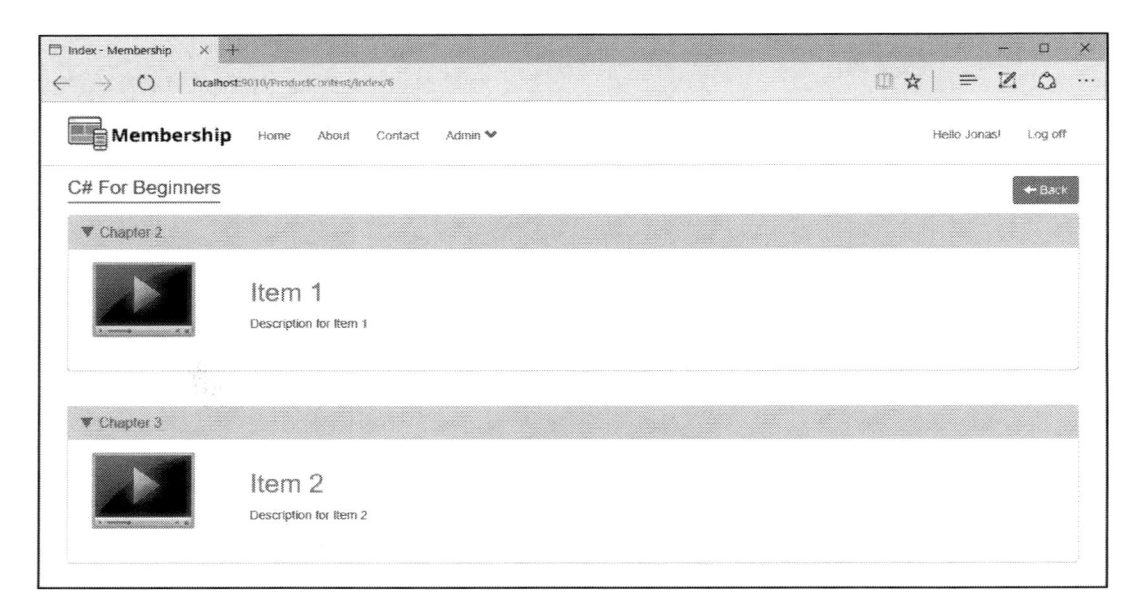

1. Open the **_ProductSection** partial view.
2. Add an if-block checking that there are items available in the model's **Items** collection around the markup inside the foreach loop.
   `if (s.Items.Count() > 0)`
3. Add a foreach loop iterating over the items in the model's **Items** collection inside the **<div>** decorate with the **panel-body** class and render the **_ProductItemRow**

partial view for each item. Pass in the current item in the loop to the partial view.

```
@foreach (var item in s.Items)
{
    @Html.Partial("_ProductItemRow", item)
}
```

4. Save all the files (**Ctrl+Shift+S**).
5. Run the application and make sure that the sections with items are displayed.

The complete altered code for the **_ProductSection** partial view:

```
@model IEnumerable<Memberships.Models.ProductSection>

@foreach (var s in Model)
{
    if (s.Items.Count() > 0)
    {
        <div class="panel panel-success">
            <div class="panel-heading">
                <h4 class="panel-title">
                    <a data-toggle="collapse" class="panel-carret"
                        href="#collapse@{@s.Id}">
                        <span class="pull-left glyphicon glyphicon-play
                            gly-rotate-90"></span>@s.Title
                    </a>
                </h4>
            </div>
            <div style="" id="collapse@{@s.Id}" class="panel-collapse
                collapse in">
                <div class="panel-body">
                    @foreach (var item in s.Items)
                    {
                        @Html.Partial("_ProductItemRowPartial", item)
                    }
                </div>
            </div>
        </div>
        <br />
    }
}
```

Styling the _ProductItemRowPartial view

Now that you have successfully displayed the product items listed by section/category, it is time to make it look nicer for a better user experience. Open the **ProductContent.css** file and add selectors for the **product-item** class and some of its child elements to display the heading, description and content in a more appealing way.

The image below shows the finished styling.

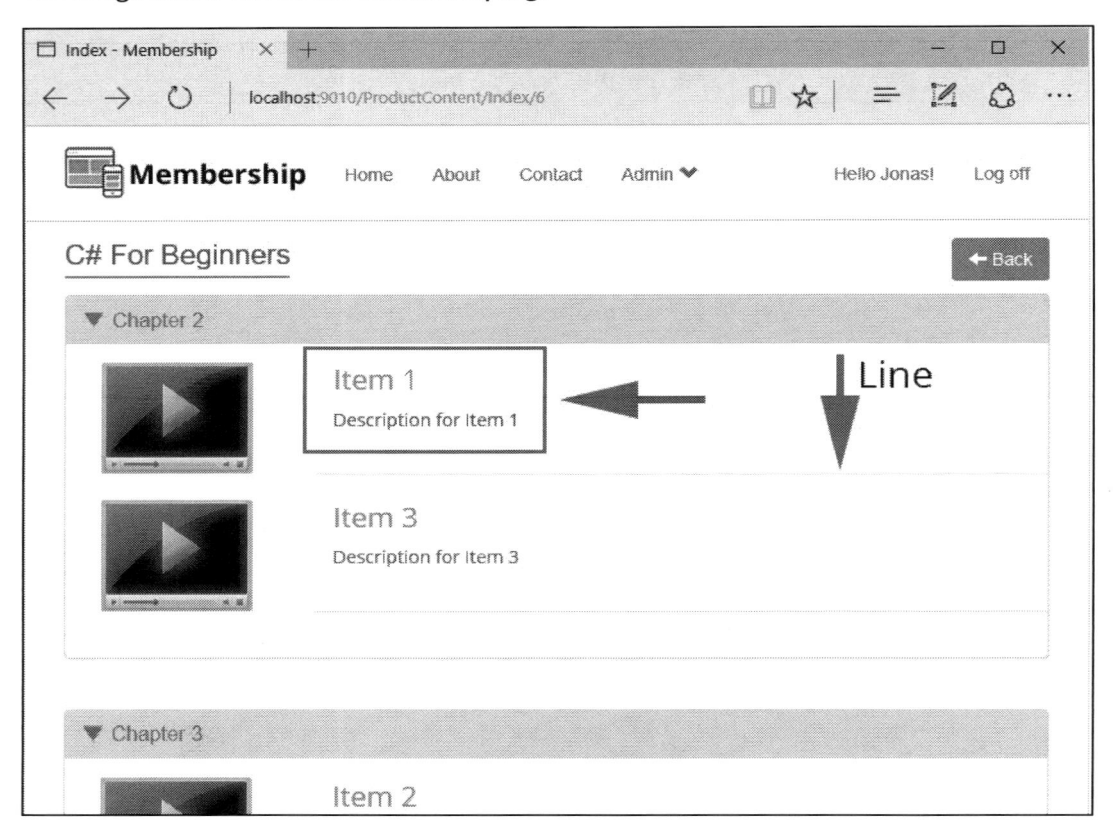

Change the font family to *Open Sans* (Google's font family) and use *Arial* and *sans-serif* as fall-back font families for all text elements that are children to the **<div>** decorated with the **product-item** class.

```
.product-item * {
    font-family: 'Open Sans',Arial,sans-serif;
}
```

Add a 2px top margin and change the font size to 22px for **<h2>** elements that are children to the **<div>** decorated with the **product-item** class.

```
.product-item h2 {
    margin-top: 2px;
    font-size: 22px;
}
```

Remove any text decoration, such as link underlines, for **<a>** elements that are children to the **<div>** decorated with the **product-item** class.

```
.product-item a {
    text-decoration: none;
}
```

Add the line separating the items to the **<div>** decorated with the **product-item** and **line-bottom** classes.

```
.product-item .line-bottom {
    border-bottom: 1px solid #E4E9F0;
}
```

Give the product item a min height of 90px.

```
.product-item .min-height {
    min-height: 90px;
}
```

12. Show Content

Introduction
In this chapter you will implement the final step to display the product items by adding a view called **Content** to the **ProductContent** folder. This view will be responsible for showing both HTML and Video content belonging to a specific product item.

The **@Html.Raw** extension method is used to display the HTML; note that this method only should be used when you are certain that the HTML being displayed comes from a secure source and does not contain any mallicious code.

JW Player is used to display video content, but you can implement any HTML5 compliant video player. The **<video>** element is not used since it, at the time of this writing, doesn't support YouTube videos and videos from many other external sources. To use the JW Player, you have to register with their site and retrieve a script link that you can include in the **<head>** section in the **_Layout** view, see example below. You'll need your own link because the one below won't work.

```
<script src="https://content.jwplatform.com/libraries/ArqgrS23.js">
</script>
```

JW Player
Visit the https://www.jwplayer.com/ site to sign up for JW Player and download the script code you need to play the video content.

Create a JW Player cloud player URL
1. Navigate to the https://www.jwplayer.com/ site and register for an account.
2. Click the **Players** tab in the navigation area.
3. Click the **Add Player** button.
4. Give the player a name in the top left text field.
5. Select the **Responsive** radio button and the **16:9** aspect ration in the **Basic Setup** section.
6. Click the **Save Changes** button.

7. Click the **Close** button.
8. Click on the **License Keys & Downloads** link.
9. Select the player in the **Player Title** drop-down.
10. Click the **Copy** button to the right of the **Cloud Player Url** text field.
11. Open the **_Layout** view in the main project.
12. Add a **<script>** element and paste in the copied URL in its **src** attribute.
    ```
    <script src="https://content.jwplatform.com/libraries/ArqgrS23.js">
    </script>
    ```

Adding the necessary JavaScript to play a video

In order to play a video, you need to add a JavaScript function that calls the cloud player with the necessary parameters.

1. Add a new JavaScript file called **JWPlayer.js** to the **Scripts** folder.
2. Add a function called **jwVideo** that takes one parameter:
    a. **video**: The path to the video to play.
    ```
    function jwVideo(video) { ... }
    ```
3. Call the **jwplayer** function in the JavaScript library you add to the **<head>** section. It takes one parameter which is the **id** of the **<div>** element where the video will be displayed.
4. Call the **setup** method on the **jwplayer** method to pass in setup information:
    a. **file**: The URL to the video.
5. Open the **BundleConfig** class and add the **JWPlayer.js** JavaScript file to the **membership** script bundle.

The complete **jwVideo** function:

```
function jwVideo(video) {
    //Play single video
    jwplayer("video").setup({
        file: video
    });
}
```

Register a ProductContent route

To be able to reach the new action method you are about to add to the **ProductContent** controller, you need to add a new route with two paramters to the **RouteConfig** class. The first parameter is the product id and the second the item id. Assign *ProductContent* to the **controller** and **name** properties and *Index* to the **action** property.

1. Open the **RouteConfig** class.
2. Copy the existing *default* route and paste it in above it.
3. Change the **name** and **controller** properties to *ProductContent*.
4. Remove the **id** property from the **defaults** object.
5. Rename the **id** placeholder **itemId**.
6. Add a **productId** placeholder to the **Url** property between the **action** and the **itemId** place holders.

The complete **ProductContent** route:

```
routes.MapRoute(
    name: "ProductContent",
    url: "{controller}/{action}/{productId}/{itemId}/",
    defaults: new
    {
        controller = "ProductContent",
        action = "Index"
    }
);
```

The ContentViewModel class

This class will contain the necessary data to display any piece of content, be it HTML or Video. The class must contain a **ProductId** property of type **int** for navigation purposes, **Title** and **Description** properties of type **string** to describe the content piece, a property called **HTML** of type **string** for article content in HTML markup and a **VideoUrl** proeprty of type **string** for a video URL.

1. Create a new class called **ContentViewModel** in the **Models** folder in the main project.
2. Add a public **int** property called **ProductId**.

3. Add four public **string** properties called **Title, Description, HTML** and **VideoUrl**.
4. Save the class.

The complete code for the **ContentViewModel** class:

```
public class ContentViewModel
{
    public int ProductId { get; set; }
    public string Title { get; set; }
    public string Description { get; set; }
    public string HTML { get; set; }
    public string VideoURL { get; set; }
}
```

The GetContentAsync extension method

In order to display a piece of content (item) to the user, a new extension method called **GetContentAsync** has to be added to the **SectionExtensions** class. It will take two **int** parameters called **productId** and **Itemid**.

Create an instance of the **ApplicationDbContext** called **db** in the method to make it possible to fetch the necessary data from the database.

Add an asynchronous LINQ query that join the **Item** and **ItemType** tables and filters on the **itemId** property. Have the query return a single object of the **ContentViewModel** class and the method a **Task<ContentViewModel>**.

1. Open the **SectionExtensions** class.
2. Add a new asynchronous extension method called **GetContentAsync** that returns a **Task<ContentViewModel>** and takes two **int** parametes called **productId** and **Itemid**.
   ```
   public static async Task<ContentViewModel> GetContentAsync(int productId, int itemId) { ... }
   ```
3. Create an instance of the **ApplicationDbContext** called **db**.
4. Add an awaited LINQ query that join the **Item** and **ItemType** tables. Add a **where** clause that filters on the **itemId** property. Have the query return a single object of the **ContentViewModel** class.

5. Use the **FirstOrDefaultAsync** method to return the first item matching the criteria in the query.

The complete code for the **GetContentAsync** method:

```
public static async Task<ContentViewModel> GetContentAsync(int productId, int itemId)
{
    var db = ApplicationDbContext.Create();

    return await (
        from i in db.Items
        join it in db.ItemTypes on i.ItemTypeId equals it.Id
        where i.Id.Equals(itemId)
        select new ContentViewModel
        {
            ProductId = productId,
            HTML = i.HTML,
            VideoUrl = i.Url,
            Title = i.Title,
            Description = i.Description
        }).FirstOrDefaultAsync();
}
```

Adding the Content Action

To be able to display a piece of content in a view, you have to add an asynchronous action method called **Content** to the **ProductContent** controller matching the route you added earlier.

The action must have two **int** parameters called **productId** and **itemId** where the **itemId** uniquely identifies an item in the **Item** tabe.

Call the **GetContentAsync** extension method with the product id and item id passed in to the action and store the result in a variable called **model**.

Pass in the name of the view (*Content*) to display along with the **model** variable to the **View** method to render the content.

1. Open the the **ProductContent** controller.

2. Add an **async** action method called **Content** that takes two **int** parameters called **productId** and **itemId**.
   ```
   public async Task<ActionResult> Content(int productId, int itemId)
   ```
3. Call the **GetContentAsync** extension method and store the result in a variable called **model**.
   ```
   var model = await SectionExtensions.GetContentAsync(productId, itemId);
   ```
4. Pass in the name of the view (*Content*) along with the **model** variable to the **View** method.
   ```
   return View("Content", model);
   ```

The complete code for the **Content** action method:

```
public async Task<ActionResult> Content(int productId, int itemId)
{
    var model = await SectionExtensions.GetContentAsync(
        productId, itemId);
    return View("Content", model);
}
```

Adding the Content view

To be able to display a piece of content, you will have to add a view called **Content** to the **Views-ProductContent** folder.

The view will have three sections: one for displaying title and description information and a **Back** button navigating to the product that the content belongs to. One for displaying HTML content if the **HTML** property isn't **null** and one for displaying a video if the **VideoUrl** property isn't **null**.

To display a video, the **jwVideo** javascript method has to be called when the DOM has been loaded. Fetch the video URL from a **<div>** with the id **hiddenUrl**.

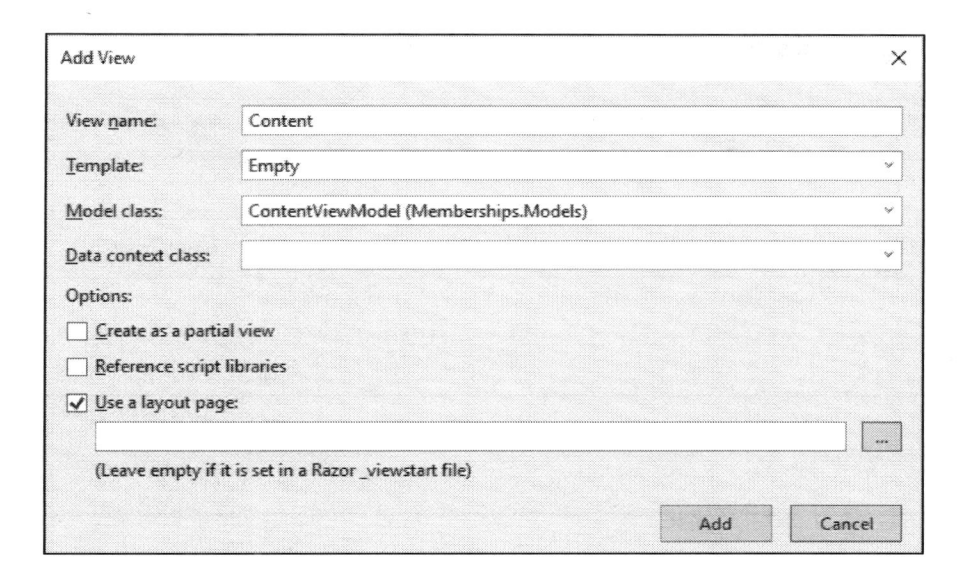

Adding the Content view
1. Right-click on the **Views-ProductContent** folder and select **Add-View**.
2. Name the view **Content** in the **View name** field.
3. Select the **Empty** template in the **Template** drop-down.
4. Select **ContentViewModel** in the **Model class** drop-down.
5. Delete the text in the **Data context class** drop-down.
6. Uncheck the **Create as a partial view** if it is checked.
7. Click the **Add** button.

Adding the title and header section
1. Add a **<div>** element decorated with the **headline** class to style it using an already existing CSS style with the same name.
2. Add an **<h2>** element that displays the content in the model's **Title** property inside the previous **<div>**.
3. Add an **<a>** element with the text *Back* and the **glyphicon-arrow-left** glyph. The **<a>** element must be decorated with the **btn** and **btn-primary** Botstrap classes to turn it into a blue button and the **pull-right** class to display it as far to the right in the display area as possible. The **href** attribute should navigate to the **Index** action in the **ProductContent** controller and pass along the product id.

```
<a class="btn btn-primary pull-right"
   href="/ProductContent/Index/@Model.ProductId">
   <span class="glyphicon glyphicon-arrow-left"
         aria-hidden="true"></span>
   Back
</a>
```

4. Add a **<div>** element below the **<div>** element decorated with the **headline** class. Display the content in the model's **Description** proeprty inside the **<div>**.
5. Add a line break after the last **<div>**.

Displaying HTML conent

1. Add an if-block checking that the model's **HTML** property isn't **null** below the line break.
2. Add a **<div>** element decorated with a class called **article** that will be used later to add styling to the HTML content. Use the **@Html.Raw** method to display the HTML markup in the model's **HTML** property.

```
<div class="article">@Html.Raw(Model.HTML)</div>
```

Displaying Video conent

1. Add an if-block checking that the model's **VideoUrl** property isn't **null** below the previous if-block.
2. Add a **<div>** element decorated with a class called **video-margin** that will be used to remove the margin around the video. Add the id **video** to the element; this id will be used by the JW Player to find the correct element to display the streamed video.

```
<div id="video" class="video-margin"> </div>
```

3. Add another **<div>** below the previous video inside the if-block and give it the id **hiddenUrl**. Add the content in the model's **VideoUrl** property to the element; the content will be fetched with JavaScript and sent to the **jwVideo** function to display the video when the view has finished loading. Use the **hidden** attribute to hide the content.

```
<div id="hiddenUrl" hidden="hidden">@Model.VideoUrl</div>
```

4. Add a **scripts** section below the last if-block for the necessary JavaScript.

```
@section scripts { ... }
```

5. Call the **jwVideo** function from the **Document Ready** function inside the **scripts** section. Pass in the hidden url and the string *Video* to the method.
   jwVideo($("#hiddenUrl").text(), 'Video');

The complete markup for the **Conetnt** view:

```
@model Memberships.Models.ContentViewModel

@{
    ViewBag.Title = Model.Title;
}

<div class="headline">
    <h2>@Model.Title</h2>
    <a class="btn btn-primary pull-right" href="/ProductContent/Index/
        @Model.ProductId">
        <span class="glyphicon glyphicon-arrow-left">
        </span>
        Back
    </a>
</div>
<div>@Model.Description</div>
<br/>

@if (Model.HTML != null)
{
    <div class="article">@Html.Raw(Model.HTML)</div>
}

@if (Model.VideoUrl != null)
{
    @*place holder for the video player*@
    <div id="video" class="video-margin"> </div>
    <div id="hiddenUrl" hidden="hidden">@Model.VideoUrl</div>
}

@section scripts
{
    <script type="text/javascript">
        $(function () {
            // Call the video player function in the JWPlayer.js file.
            jwVideo($("#hiddenUrl").text());
        });
    </script>
```

}

Styling the Video element
1. Open the **ProductContent.css** file.
2. Add a selector for the **video-margin** class.
3. Remove the left margin.

The complete styling for the **video-margin** class:

```
.video-margin {
    margin-left: 0px;
}
```

Styling the article HTML markup
Add a new CSS stylesheet called **html.css** in the **Content** folder to style the HTML content displayed with the **@Html.Raw** method.

Give the **<h1>**, **<H2>** and **<H3>** elements inside the **<div>** decoretad with the **article** class a top margin of 10px, change the line hight to 150% and the text color to gray (#555).

```
.article h1, .article h2, .article h3 {
    margin-top: 10px;
    line-height: 150%;
    color: #555;
}
```

Override the text color for the **<H2>** and **<H3>** elements and give them a light blue color (#0094ff) .

```
.article h2, .article h3 {
    color: #0094ff;
}
```

Add the **html.css** style sheet to the **membership** style bundle in the **BundleConfig** class.

13. Register Subscription Code

Introduction

In this chapter you will add a panel for entering a subscription code. The idea is that when customers purchase a product from you, you send them a code that they then enter in this panel to unlock access to the products associated with that subscription. The images below show what the panel will look like when finished; it will contain a text field, a submit button and an alert label where a success or fail message can be delivered.

The registration panel should only be displayed to logged in users.

If a code is registered successfully, the text field should be cleared and a success message should be displayed. If no code or a non-exisiting code is entered, different error messages should be displayed.

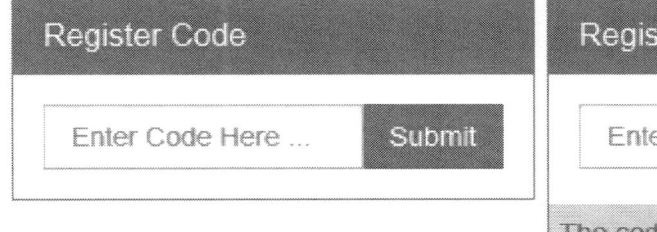

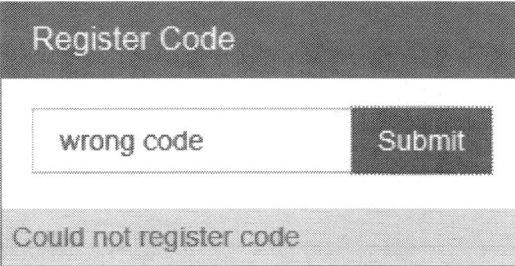

Adding the _RegisterCodePartial view

To keep the markup clean in the **Index** view, the pannel will be added as a partial view called **_RegisterCodePartial** to the **Views-Shared** folder. Adding it as a partial view will make it possible to update only that portion of the **Index** view when the **Register** action of the **RegisterCode** controller renders its content.

Create the partial view as an empty view without a model.

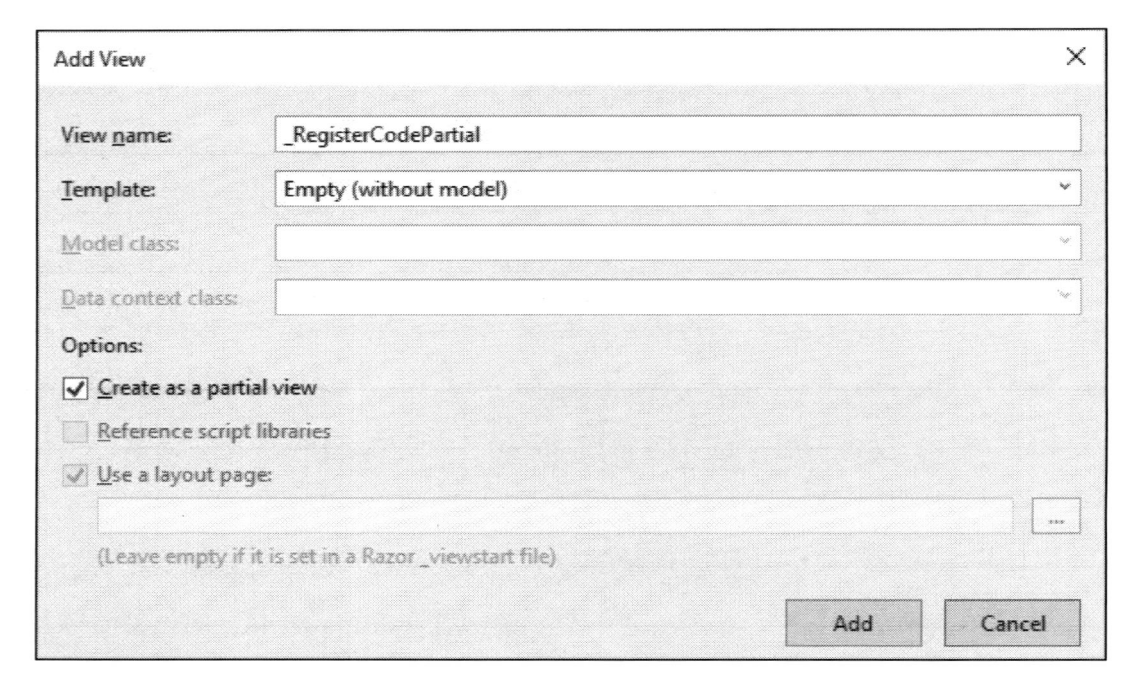

1. Right-click on the **Views-Shared** folder in the main project.
2. Select **Add-View** in the menu.
3. Name the view **_RegisterCodePartial** in the **View name** field.
4. Select **Empty (without model)** in the **Template** drop-down.
5. Make sure that the **Create as a partial view** checkbox is checked.
6. Click the **Add** button.

Adding the Register Code panel content

You will have to start by adding an if-block checking that the user is logged in and authenticated. This can be done by checking the value in the **Request.IsAuthenticated** property. Place all the markup inside the if-block.

Add a Bootstrap panel to the if-block and the **panel-primary** and **register-code-panel** classes to it; the former class will give it a blue color and the latter will be used to style the panel using CSS.

Use an **<h4>** heading with the text *Register Code* for the panel title.

Add the Bootstrap **input-group** class to the panel body **<div>** to group the controls used in it and to make them look nicer. Add a text field decorated with the **form-control** class to make the field behave like a form control and look more aesthetically pleasing. Also add a **<button>** element decorated with the **btn**, **btn-primary** and **input-group-btn** Bootstrap classes; the latter class will place the button flush to the left side of the text field making them look like a single control.

Add a **<div>** element decorated with the **alert**, **alert-danger** and **hidden** classes below the panel body **<div>**; the first class will make it look and behave as a Bootstrap **alert** component, the second class will give it a red background color and the third will hide the **<div>**. The **alert-danger** and **hidden** classes will be accessed with JavaScript depending on if the asynchronous action call to the controller fails or is successful.

1. Open the **_RegisterCodePartial** partial view if it's not already open.
2. Add an if-block checking that the user is authenticated.
   `@if (Request.IsAuthenticated) { /* Add the HTML here */ }`
3. Add a **<div>** decorated with the **panel**, **panel-primary** and **register-code-panel** classes.
4. Add a **<div>** decorated with the **panel-heading** class inside the previous **<div>**.
5. Add an **<h4>** element decorated with the **panel-title** class inside the previous **<div>**. Add the text *Register Code* to the element.
6. Add a **<div>** decorated with the **panel-body** and **input-group** classes below the **<div>** decorated with the **panel-heading** class.

7. Add an **<input>** element decorated with the **form-control** class and has its **type** attribute set to **text** to the panel body **<div>**. Also add the **placeholder** attribute with the text *Enter code here ...*; the text will be displayed in the text field to help the user understand what the input is expected to be.
   ```
   <input type="text" class="form-control" placeholder="Enter Code Here "...">
   ```

8. Add a **<button>** element decorated with the **btn**, **btn-primary** and **input-group-btn** Bootstrap classes. Have the button display the text *Submit*. The but'on's **Click** event will later be wired up with JavaScript.
   ```
   <button cla"s="btn btn-primary input-group-"tn" ty"e="but"on">Submit</button>
   ```

9. Add a **<div>** decorated with the **alert, alert-danger** and **hidden** classes. Also add the default text *Could not register code* to the **<div>**.
   ```
   <div cla"s="alert alert-danger hid"en">Could not register code</div>
   ```

The complete markup for the **_RegisterCodePartial** partial view:

```
@if (Request.IsAuthenticated)
{
    <div cla"s="panel panel-primary register-code-pa"el">
        <div cla"s="panel-head"ng">
            <h4 cla"s="panel-ti"le">
                Register Code
            </h4>
        </div>
        <div cla"s="panel-body input-gr"up">
            <input ty"e="t"xt" cla"s="form-cont"ol"
                placehold"r="Enter Code Here "..">
            <button cla"s="btn btn-primary input-group-"tn"
                ty"e="but"on">Submit</button>
        </div>
        <div cla"s="alert alert-danger hid"en">Could not register
            code</div>
    </div>
}
```

Styling the Register Code panel

You will move the whole panel to the left, aligning it with the product panels, and add a top margin of 20px to it. Then you will remove the border radius, making the corners sharp rather than rounded. The **alert <div>** will have to be styled the most, adding 5px padding all around it, removing any bottom margin, adding a 3px top margin, removing the border radius and hiding the border.

Add the style changes to a CSS style sheet called **RegisterCode.css** in the **Content** folder and add it to the **membership** style bundle in the **BundleConfig** class.

Changing the left margin:

```
.register-code-area {
    margin-left: -15px;
}
```

Adding a top margin:

```
.register-code-panel {
    margin-top: 20px;
}
```

Removing the border radius from the panel and its elements:

```
.register-code-panel,
.register-code-panel .panel-heading,
.register-code-panel * {
    border-radius:0px;
}
```

Altering the alert **<div>**:

```
.register-code-panel .alert {
    padding: 5px;
    margin-bottom: 0px;
    margin-top:3px;
    border:hidden;
    border-radius: 0px;
}
```

Adding the Register Code panel to the Index view

To display the Register Code panel, it has to be rendered as a partial view below the already existing **<div>** in the **Index** view. Display the panel in a Bootstrap grid row and in a **col-sm-3** column **<div>** decorated with the **register-code-area** class. The class will be used to position the panel (see previous section).

Use the **@Html.Partial** extension method to render the **_RegisterCodePartial** partial view.

The complete markup for the **_RegisterCodePartial** partial view in the **Index** view:

```
<div class="row">
    <div class="col-sm-3 register-code-area">
        @Html.Partial("_RegisterCodePartial")
    </div>
    <div class="col-sm-9">
    </div>
</div>
```

The GetSubscriptionIdByRegistrationCode extension method

Add an asynchronous extension method called **GetSubscriptionIdByRegistrationCode** to a **static** class called **SubscriptionExtensions** that you add to the **Extensions** folder.

The purpose of this method is to fetch the first subscription whose **RegistrationCode** value matches the value from the text field in the Register Code panel. The method will act on a **IDbSet<Subscription>** and take a **string** parameter called **code** which is the code the user entered in the text field. It will return a **Task<int>**.

Before querying the **IdbSet<Subscription>,** it has to be checked to make sure that the collection isn't **null** and that the **code** parameter isn't **null** or an empty string; if any of these criteria aren't met, then return **Int32.MinValue** to signal that no matching subscription could be found.

Also return **Int32.MinValue** if an exception occurs.

1. Add a **static** class called **SubscriptionExtensions** to the **Extensions** folder.

2. Add an asynchronous extension method called **GetSubscriptionIdBy-RegistrationCode** to the class. It should return a **Task<int>**, act on **IDbSet <Subscription>** and take a **string** parameter called **code**.
   ```
   public static async Task<int> GetSubscriptionIdByRegistrationCode(
       this IDbSet<Subscription> subscription, string code)
   ```
3. Add exception handling to the method and return **Int32.MinValue** from the **catch**-block.
4. Return **Int32.MinValue** if the **IDbSet<Subscription>** parameter is **null** or the code **string** parameter is **null** or an empty string.
   ```
   if (subscription == null || code == null || code.Length <= 0)
       return Int32.MinValue;
   ```
5. Fetch the subscription matching the value in the code parameter asynchronously and return its subscription id.
   ```
   var subscriptionId = await (
       from s in subscription
       where s.RegistrationCode.Equals(code)
       select s.Id).FirstOrDefaultAsync();
   ```

The complete code for the **GetSubscriptionIdByRegistrationCode** extension method:

```
public static async Task<int> GetSubscriptionIdByRegistrationCode(
this IDbSet<Subscription> subscription, string code)
{
    try
    {
        if (subscription == null || code == null || code.Length <= 0)
            return Int32.MinValue;

        var subscriptionId = await (
            from s in subscription
            where s.RegistrationCode.Equals(code)
            select s.Id).FirstOrDefaultAsync();

        return subscriptionId;
    }
    catch
    {
        return Int32.MinValue;
    }
}
```

The Register extension method

The purpose of this method is to register the subscription id matching the code entered in the Register Code panel to the logged in user; this is done by adding a new entry in the **UserSubscription** table.

The method will act on a **IDbSet<UserSubscription>** and take an **int** paremater called **subscriptionId** and a **string** paraemter called **userId**. This method will not return a value and will therefore return a **Task** in accordance with best practices for asynchronous methods.

Return from the method if the **userSubscription** parameter is **null**, the **subscriptionId** parameter is equal to **Int32.MinValue** or the **userId** parameter is an empty **string**.

Use an awaited **Task** to check if the combination of subscription id and user id already exists in the **UserSubscription** table; store the result in a variable called **exist**.

If no entry exists, then **await** another **Task** that enters the data into the **UserSubscription** table. Store the current date and time in the **StartDate** column, the max value for a date in the **EndDate** column, the **userId** parameter's value in the **UserId** column and the **subscriptionId** parameter's value in the **SubscriptionId** column.

1. Add an asynchronous method called **Register** to the **SubscriptionExtensions** class that return a **Task**. The method should act on a **IDbSet<UserSubscription>** and take an **int** parameter called **subscriptionId** and a **string** parameter called **userId**.
   ```
   public static async Task Register(this IDbSet<UserSubscription> userSubscription, int subscriptionId, string userId)
   ```
2. Add exception handling and leave the **catch**-block empty.
3. Return from the method if the **userSubscription** parameter is **null**, the **subscriptionId** parameter is equal to **Int32.MinValue** or the **userId** parameter is an empty **string**.
   ```
   if (userSubscription == null ||
      subscriptionId.Equals(Int32.MinValue) ||
      userId.Equals(String.Empty))
      return;
   ```

4. Check if the combination of subscription id and user id already exists in the **UserSubscription** table.
   ```
   var exist = await Task.Run<int>(() => userSubscription.CountAsync(
       s => s.SubscriptionId.Equals(subscriptionId) &&
       s.UserId.Equals(userId))) > 0;
   ```
5. Add the **userId** and **subscriptionId** values asynchronously as a new record in the **UserSubscription** table.

The complete code for the **Register** extension method:

```
public static async Task Register(this IDbSet<UserSubscription>
userSubscription, int subscriptionId, string userId)
{
    try
    {
        if (userSubscription == null ||
            subscriptionId.Equals(Int32.MinValue) ||
            userId.Equals(String.Empty))
            return;

        // Check if user already has the subscription
        var exist = await Task.Run<int>(() => userSubscription.CountAsync(
            s => s.SubscriptionId.Equals(subscriptionId) &&
            s.UserId.Equals(userId))) > 0;

        if (!exist)
            await Task<UserSubscription>.Run(() =>
                userSubscription.Add(
                    new UserSubscription
                    {
                        UserId = userId,
                        SubscriptionId = subscriptionId,
                        StartDate = DateTime.Now,
                        EndDate = DateTime.MaxValue
                    }));

    }
    catch { }
}
```

The RegisterUserSubscriptionCode method

To keep the **Register** action method as clean possible, you will create an asynchronous method called **RegisterUserSubscriptionCode** in the **SubscriptionExtensions** class which will attempt to register the code entered in the Register Code panel. If successful, the user will gain access to the products associated with that subscription.

The method will return a **Task<bool>** signalling if the code was successfully registered or not for the logged in user. It will take two parameters of type **string** called **code** and **userId**.

This method will in turn call the two **GetSubscriptionIdByRegistrationCode** and **Register** extension methods to attempt to register the code with the logged in user.

Use the **ChangeTracker.HasChanged** method on the **ApplicationDbContext** instance to check if there are any changes to save to the database, and only call the **SaveChanges** method to persist the data to the database if there are changes.

1. Add an asynchronous method called **RegisterUserSubscriptionCode** to the **SubscriptionExtensions** class. The method should return **Task<bool>** and take two parameters of type **string** called **code** and **userId**.
   ```
   public static async Task<bool> RegisterUserSubscriptionCode(string code, string userId)
   ```
2. Add exception handling and return **false** in the **catch**-block.
3. Create an instance of the **ApplicationDbContext** class called **db**.
4. **Await** the result from a call to the **GetSubscriptionIdByRegistrationCode** extension method and store the result in a variable called **id**.
   ```
   var id = await db.Subscriptions
       .GetSubscriptionIdByRegistrationCode(code);
   ```
5. Return **false** if the value in the **id** variable is less than or equal to 0.
6. **Await** a call to the **Register** method.
7. Save the changed to the database if there are any.
   ```
   if (db.ChangeTracker.HasChanges())
       db.SaveChanges();
   ```
8. Return **true** from the method.

The complete code for the **RegisterUserSubscriptionCode** method:

```
public static async Task<bool> RegisterUserSubscriptionCode(string code,
string userId)
{
    try
    {
        var db = ApplicationDbContext.Create();

        // Make sure that the code is a valid code
        var id = await db.Subscriptions
            .GetSubscriptionIdByRegistrationCode(code);
        if (id <= 0) return false;

        // Register the code with the user if it is valid
        await db.UserSubscriptions.Register(id, userId);

        if (db.ChangeTracker.HasChanges())
            db.SaveChanges();

        return true;
    }
    catch { return false; }
}
```

The RegisterCode controller

To be able to add a registration code, you have to add a controller called **RegisterCode** which has an asynchronous action called **Register** which can be called from the client with JavaScript.

The **RegisterUserSubscriptionCode** in the **SubscriptionExtensions** class will only be called if the user is authenticated, otherwise the view will be returned as is.

You can fetch the user id on the **HttpContext** object with the **GetUserId** extension method that you added in a previous chapter.

Throw a new **ApplicationException** if the code registration was unsuccessful; this exception will then be handled by the Ajax call in the client by displaying an appropriate message.

Use the **PartialView** method to return the **_RegisterCodePartial** partial view upon successful code registration.

Note: *The Register action is made asynchronous to be able to call necessary methods asynchronously on the server side. This has nothing to do with the asynchronous Ajax call which is made from the client.*

Adding the RegisterCode Controller
1. Right-click on the **Controllers** folder and select **Add-Controller**.
2. Select **MVC 5 Controller - Empty** and click the **Add** button.
3. Delete the comment and the **Index** action.

Adding the Register action method
1. Add an asynchronous action called **Register** to the **RegisterCode** controller class. It should take a **string** parameter called **code**; it will contain the value from the text field in the Register Code panel sent in from the client's Ajax call.
   `public async Task<ActionResult> Register(string code)`

2. Add an if-block which is executed if the user is authenticated.
   `if (Request.IsAuthenticated)`

3. Return the view as it was sent in below the if-block.
   `return View();`

4. Fetch the user id and store it in a variable called **userId**. by calling the **GetUserId** extension method on the **HttpContext** object.
   `var userId = HttpContext.GetUserId();`

5. Call the **RegisterUserSubscriptionCode** in the **SubscriptionExtensions** class and store the awaited result in a variable called **registered**.
   `var registered = await SubscriptionExtensions.RegisterUserSubscriptionCode(code, userId);`

6. Throw a new **ApplicationException** if the code registration was unsuccessful.
7. Use the **PartialView** method to return the **_RegisterCodePartial** partial view.
   `return PartialView("_RegisterCodePartial");`

The complete code for the **Register** action method:

```
public class RegisterCodeController : Controller
{
    public async Task<ActionResult> Register(string code)
    {
        if (Request.IsAuthenticated)
        {
            // Extension method for fetching the user id
            var userId = HttpContext.GetUserId();

            // Extension method for registering a code with a user
            var registered = await SubscriptionExtensions
                .RegisterUserSubscriptionCode(code, userId);

            if (!registered) throw new ApplicationException();

            return PartialView("_RegisterCodePartial");
        }

        return View();
    }
}
```

The JavaScript functions

To be able to call the **Register** action in the **RegisterCode** controller from the client, you have to add a couple of JavaScript functions to a new JavaScript file called **RegisterCode** which you create in the **Scripts** folder. Add it to the **membership** sctipt bundle in the **BundleConfig** class.

The first thing you will need to add to the JavaScript file is a variable called **code** that stores the value from the **<input>** element in the Register Code panel.

```
var code = $(".register-code-panel input");
```

Next, you will add a function called **displayMessage,** which takes two parameters called **success** and **message**. Replace the text in the **<div>** decorated with the **alert** class with the text in the **message** parameter.

393

If the **success** parameter is **true,** then remove the **alert-danger** class and add the **alert-success** class giving the **alert** element a green background color, else remove the **alert-success** class and add the **alert-danger** class giving the **alert** element a red background color.

Remove the **hidden** class from the **alert** element, making it visible.

```
function displayMessage(success, message) {
   var alert_div = $(".register-code-panel .alert");
   alert_div.text(message);

   if (success)
      alert_div.removeClass('alert-danger').addClass('alert-success');
   else
      alert_div.removeClass('alert-sucess').addClass('alert-danger');

   alert_div.removeClass('hidden');
}
```

Wire up the **click** event for the panel's button.

```
$(".register-code-panel button").click(function (e) { ... }
```

Add the **hidden** class to the **alert** element.

Call the **displayMessage** function with **false** and the message *Enter a code* if the **<input>** element is empty and then return from the function.

Make an asynchronous call to the server with an Ajax call to the **Register** action in the **RegisterCode** controller using the **post** method. Pass the value from the **<input>** element as a parameter named **code**.

```
$.post('/RegisterCode/Register', { code: code.val() },
   function (data) { ... })
```

Call the **displayMessage** function with **true** and the message *The code was successfully registered. \n\r Please reload the page. \n\r* will add a line break to the text. Then clear the text in the **<input>** element.

Chain on the **fail** method and call the **displayMessage** function with **false** and the message *Could not register code*.

The complete code for the **click** event:

```
$(".register-code-panel button").click(function (e) {
    $(".register-code-panel .alert").addClass('hidden');

    if (code.val().length == 0) {
        displayMessage(false, "Enter a code");
        return;
    }

    $.post('/RegisterCode/Register', { code: code.val() },
    function (data) {
        displayMessage(true, "The code was successfully registered. \n\r
            Please reload the page.");
        code.val('');
    }).fail(function (xhr, status, error) {
        displayMessage(false, "Could not register code");
    });
});
```

14. Register User

Introduction

In this chapter you will create a partial view called **_RegisterUserPartial** which can be used by site visitors to register with the site. It should be rendered as part of the **Home** controller's **Index** view and Ajax will be used to make an asynchronous call to the controller when the user clicks the **Sign me Up!** button. The response from the server will be used to update only the partial view.

To confirm that the visitor has read the *User Agreement,* they have to check the **I accept the User Agreement** checkbox to enable the submit button.

A new view model called **RegisterUserModel** has to be created with the correct validation and data annotation attributes with its properties.

If you don't want to use Bootstrap *Glyphicons* to decorate the textboxes with icons, you can use the *Font Awesome* library. Browse to the following link to learn more about installing the http://fontawesome.github.io/Font-Awesome/ library. You should be aware that it can be tricky to get Font Awesome to work with Azure if you plan to host your web applications in the cloud.

Technologies used in this chapter

1. **MVC** - To create the partial view controller and action needed to register a user.
2. **C#** - Creating a view model with validation attributes used to register a user.
3. **Razor** - To incorporate C# in the views where necessary.
4. **HTML 5** - To build the partial view.
5. **Bootstrap** - To style the HTML 5 components.
6. **Glyphicons** - To decorate the textboxes with icons.
7. **CSS** - To style the registration panel.
8. **JavaScript/JQuery** - To hook in to component events and make Ajax calls.
9. **Ajax** - To make an asynchronous call to the server and use the response to update a partial view.

Use case

Create a partial view which can be used to register a user with the site. The form should be visible for non-logged in users and hidden when the user has logged in successfully.

The user's first name, email and encrypted password will be stored in the database when a user registers with the site. The password should be stored using one-way encryption where the stored encrypted password (not an unecrypted version of it) will be compared to an encrypted version of the password submitted on subsequent logins.

The textboxes should have descriptive icons and descriptive placeholder texts.

The **Sign me Up!** submit button should be disabled (unclickable) until the user checks the **I accept the User Agreement** checkbox.

When clicked, the submit button will call a JavaScript function making an asynchronous Ajax call to the server and use the response to update the register panel with any error messages in a validation summary above the textboxes.

This is what the finished register panel will look like:

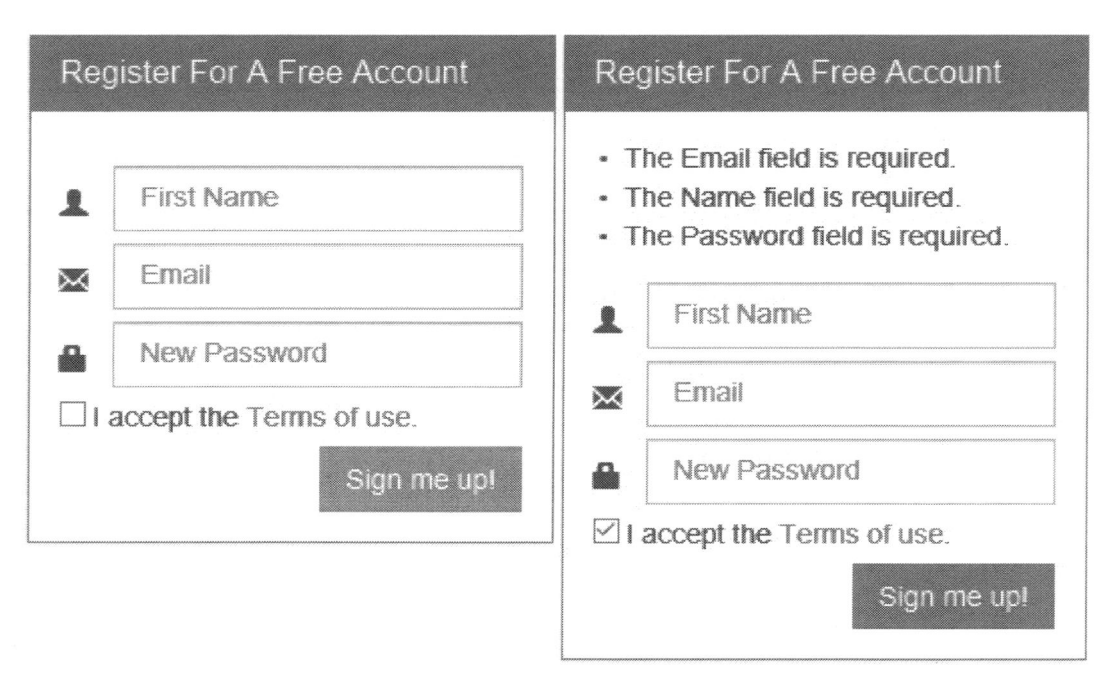

Adding the RegisterUserModel

The **Index** view needs a model to display user information in the register panel and send that information to the controller. When the view renders the first time, it will need an empty model, but if erroneous data is sent back to the controller, you want to retain the already entered data in the text fields to make it faster to fill out the form a second time by changing the already provided information.

Create a class called **RegisterUserModel** in a the **Models** folder. The model's properties will be mapped to specific components in the register panel and display validation messages if the data is erroneous. The validation rules are added to the model as property attributes. You can provide you own error messages for the validation attributes or rely on the default messages provided by .NET framework.

Since the registration form asks the visitor to enter a first name, email address and password, you need to add properties for these values in the model class. You also need to add a **bool** property for the checkbox value to keep track of whether it has been checked or not. This saves the visitor the hassle of checking it again if erroneous data was entered.

You will add the following validation attributes to the properties where applicable:

- **Required** - The field must have content.
- **EmailAddress** - Checks that a valid email address has been entered in the textbox.
- **Display** - The text to be displayed in the control's label. It can be left out if you want to use the property name instead.
- **StringLength** - Determines the maximum and minimum number of characters allowed in the textbox. It can also hold an error message which is displayed if too few or too many characters have been entered in the textbox.
- **DataType** - Can be used to check that the password meets the set standard for passwords as well as display the entered text as dots.

Add the RegisterUserModel
1. Right-click on the **Models** folder and select **Add-Class** in the context menu.
2. Name the class **RegisterUserModel** and click the **Add** button.

3. Add a **string** property called **Email** and decorate it with the **Required**, **EmailAddress**, and **Display** attributes.
   ```
   [Required]
   [EmailAddress]
   [Display(Name = "Email")]
   public string Email { get; set; }
   ```

4. Now do the same for a property called **Name** but use the **StringLength** attribute instead of the **EmailAddress** attribute. The **StringLength** attribute should specify a maximum of 30 characters and a minimum of 2.
   ```
   [Required]
   [Display(Name = "Name")]
   [StringLength(30, ErrorMessage = "The {0} must be at least {2} characters long.", MinimumLength = 2)]
   public string Name { get; set; }
   ```

5. Add a third property called **Password** using the **Required**, **DataType**, **StringLength** and **Display** attributes. The **StringLength** attribute should specify a maximum of 100 characters and a minimum of 6.
   ```
   [Required]
   [StringLength(100, ErrorMessage = "The {0} must be at least {2} characters long. Have 1 non letter, 1 digit, 1 uppercase ('A'-'Z').", MinimumLength = 6)]
   [DataType(DataType.Password)]
   [Display(Name = "Password")]
   public string Password { get; set; }
   ```

6. The last property, of type **bool**, is called **AcceptUserAgreement** and is decorated with the **Required** attribute.
   ```
   [Required]
   public bool AcceptUserAgrrement { get; set; }
   ```

The complete code for the **RegisterUserModel** class:

```
public class RegisterUserModel
{
    [Required]
    [EmailAddress]
    [Display(Name = "Email")]
    public string Email { get; set; }

    [Required]
    [Display(Name = "Name")]
```

```
    [StringLength(30, ErrorMessage =
        "The {0} must be at least {2} characters long.",
        MinimumLength = 2)]
    public string Name { get; set; }

    [Required]
    [StringLength(100, ErrorMessage =
        "The {0} must be at least {2} characters long. Have 1 non letter,
        1 digit, 1 uppercase ('A'-'Z').", MinimumLength = 6)]
    [DataType(DataType.Password)]
    [Display(Name = "Password")]
    public string Password { get; set; }

    [Required]
    public bool AcceptUserAgrrement { get; set; }
}
```

Authentication check and calling the partial view

Because this panel should only be visible for non-logged in users, you have to perform an authentication check before rendering the partial view. You can achieve this by checking the **IsAuthenticated** property on the **User.Identity** object. The call to the partial view should be surrounded by an if-statement checking that property.

So far, the **_ThumbnailAreaPartial** partial view is displayed if the user is logged in and a the text *Please register or login* is displayed if the visitor hasn't logged in.

```
<div class="row">
    @if (User.Identity.IsAuthenticated)
    {
        foreach (var area in Model)
        {
            @Html.Partial("_ThumbnailAreaPartial", area)
        }
    }
    else
    {
        <!--left column-->
        <div class="col-lg-9 col-md-8 col-sm-7">
            <h2>Please register or login</h2>
        </div>
        <!--right column-->
```

```
        <div class="col-lg-3 col-md-4 col-sm-5">
            <!--Add the Register User Panel here-->
        </div>
    }
</div>
```

1. Locate the *right column* in the **else**-block close to the end of the of the **Index** view in the **Home** folder.
2. Use Razor syntax to render a partial view called **_RegisterUserPartial** which you will create shortly.
   ```
   <!--right column-->
   <div class="col-lg-3 col-md-4 col-sm-5">
       @Html.Partial("_RegisterUserPartial", new RegisterUserModel {
           Email = "", Name = "", Password = "" })
   </div>
   ```

Add the _RegisterUserPartial view

Separating the register user functionality from the rest of the **Index** view using a partial view will make it easier to update only that specific area; Add a partial view for the register panel called **_RegisterUserPartial** to the **Views-Shared** folder.

The first thing you will do in the partial view is to add and style the panel which will hold the input controls. In upcoming sections, you will add the panel's intrinsic controls and style them.

You can do your own styling if you like or you can stick with the styling described in this chapter.

The panel you add has to be placed inside a **<div>** decorated with a class called **register-user-panel** class. The **<div>** will be used when populating the partial view with a server response from the asynchronous Ajax call made to the server (will be implemented in an upcoming section).

You can go to the Bootstrap web site and copy the code for a *panel component with a header and title* and paste it in to the **<div>** element you just created. This panel will be the start of the register panel. The only class you have to change is **panel-default** to **panel-primary**. Then change the title to *Register For A Free Account* or whatever you want the heading to say. Add the text *Panel Content* to the **<div>** element decorated with the **panel-body** class.

The image below shows what the panel looks like so far:

Register For A Free Account

Panel Content

Add the partial view
1. Right-click on the **Views-Shared** folder and select **Add-View** in the context menu.
2. Enter the name **_RegisterUserPartial** in the **View name** textbox.
3. Select **Empty** in the **Template** drop-down.
4. Select **RegisterUserModel** in the **Model class** drop-down.
5. Delete the text from the **Data context class** drop-down.
6. Check the **Create as a partial view** checkbox.
7. Click on the **Add** button.

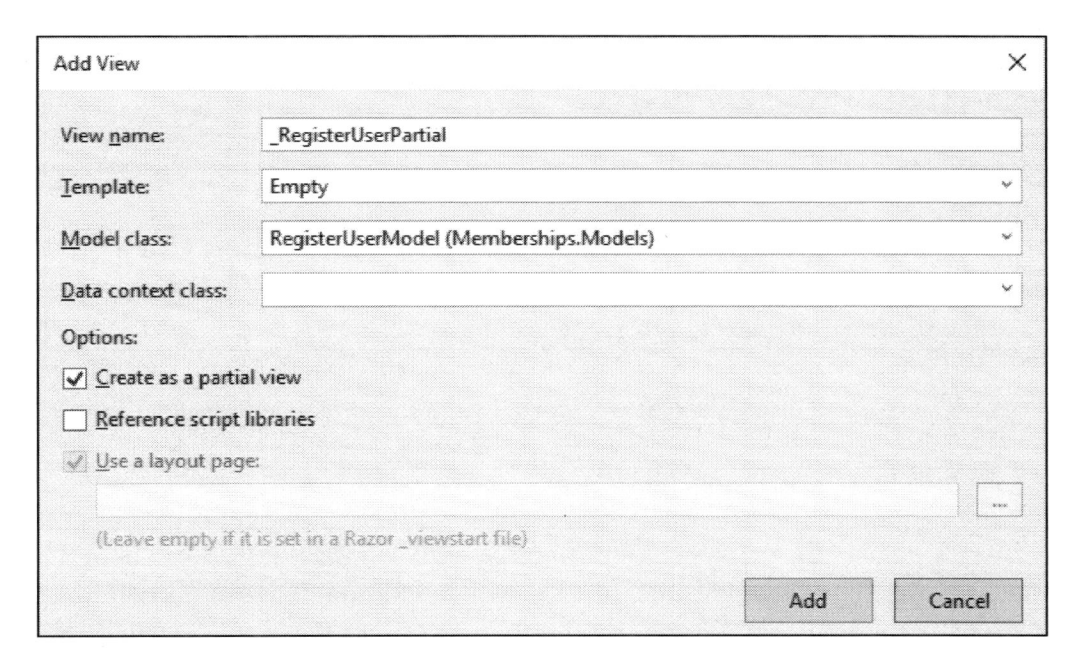

403

Add the panel to the view

1. Add a **<div>** element decorated with a class called **register-user-panel** to the partial view below the **@model** directive.
2. Either type in the code for a *panel with a header and title* by hand or copy the code from the Bootstrap web site and paste it into the **<div>**. Change the **panel-default** class to **panel-primary**. Change the panel title to *Register For A Free Account* and the panel title to a **<h4>** element. Add the text *Panel Content* to the **panel-body** element.
3. Run the application and log out to view the result.

The **_RegisterUserPartial** view markup so far:

```
@model Memberships.Models.RegisterUserModel

<div class="register-user-panel">
    <div class="panel panel-primary">
        <div class="panel-heading">
            <h4 class="panel-title">
                Register For A Free Account
            </h4>
        </div>
        <div class="panel-body">
            Panel Content
        </div>
    </div>
</div>
```

Adding controls to the Register User panel

Now it's time to make the panel useful to the user by adding controls to it. Since you will make an Ajax call to the **Account** controller's **RegisterUserAsync** action, you can add the panel controls in a form. If you look at the image of the panel, you can see that it holds three textboxes decorateds with glyph icons, a checkbox, some text with a link and a button. The first textbox is for the user's first name, the second is for an email and the third for a password.

The checkbox must be checked by the user to enable the button; this ensures that he or she has read and agree to the user agreement reachable by the link. In this example, the link is unused but you could easily redirect the user to a separate page or tab in the browser when clicked.

Glyph icons are used to decorate the textboxes with descriptive icons and placeholders instead of space-consuming labels. Glyph icons have to be added as classes to an empty **<span>** element.

Adding the controls

1. Open the **_RegisterUserPartial** view and replace the *Panel Content* text with a postable form.
   ```
   @using (Html.BeginForm("RegisterUserAsync", "Account",
   FormMethod.Post, new { @class = "form-horizontal", role = "form"
   })) { ... }
   ```
2. The first thing you need to add inside the form is an **AntiForgeryToken** to make it harder to send fraudulent data to the server.
   ```
   @Html.AntiForgeryToken()
   ```
3. Add a summary of any errors and validation violations that occurs; an example would be that data is left out from one or more of the textboxes or if the data does not conform to the validation for a particular control.
   ```
   @Html.ValidationSummary(false, "", new { @style = "" })
   ```
4. Place the first textbox for the user's first name below the validation summary. In order to display an icon with the textbox, you have to wrap it and the icon in a **<div>** element decorated with the **input-group** class. You can use the **@Html.TextBoxFor** extension method along with the **Name** property of the model to add the textbox inside the **<div>** element. You can decorate the textbox with the **form-control** class to make it look nicer. Add the placeholder attribute to display the text "First Name" as descriptive text inside the textbox. The glyphicon **<span>** must be decorated with the **input-group-addon** class to place it beside the textbox. Lastly you need to add a class called **first-name** to the textbox to makeit easier to target it from CSS and JavaScript.
   ```
   <div class="input-group input-group-md">
       <span class="input-group-addon glyphicon
           glyphicon-user"></span>

       @Html.TextBoxFor(m => m.Name, new { @class = "form-control
           first-name", @placeholder = "First Name" })
   ```

            </div>

5. Repeat step 4 and 5 for the **Email** property in the model and change the icon to **glyphicon-envelope**, the placeholder text to *Email* and the **class** to **email**.
6. Repeat step 4 and 5 for the **Password** property in the model and change the icon to **glyphicon-lock**, the placeholder text to *New Password* and the **class** to **password**.
7. Add a checkbox which will enable and disable the registration button below the three textboxes. By checking the checkbox, the user agrees to the user agreement available through the link placed in the text beside the checkbox. Use the **@Html.CheckBoxFor** extension method to add the checkbox targeting the **AcceptUserAgreement** property of the model.

    ```
    <div class="register-checkbox">
       @Html.CheckBoxFor(m => m.AcceptUserAgreement,
          new { @data_register_user_agreement_click = "" })

       <span>I accept the @Html.ActionLink("Terms of use",
          "TermsOfUse", "Legal").</span>
    </div>
    ```

8. The last control in the panel is the register button. Add the **pull-right** class (to send the button to the right side of the container), the **btn** and **btn-success** classes to style it as a Bootstrap success (green) button and the **disabled** class to disable the button when the **Index** page loads.

    ```
    <button type="button" class="pull-right btn btn-success disabled">
       Sign me up!
    </button>
    ```

The complete code for the **_RegisterUserPartial** view:

```
@model Memberships.Models.RegisterUserModel

<div class="register-user-panel">
   <div class="panel panel-primary">
      <div class="panel-heading">
         <h4 class="panel-title">Register for a free account</h4>
      </div>
      <div class="panel-body">
         @Html.AntiForgeryToken()
         @Html.ValidationSummary(false, "", new { @style = "" })
```

```
            <div class="input-group input-group-sm">
                <span class="input-group-addon glyphicon
                    glyphicon-user"></span>
                @Html.TextBoxFor(m => m.Name, new {
                    @class = "form-control first-name",
                    @placeholder = "First Name"
                })
            </div>

            <div class="input-group input-group-sm">
                <span class="input-group-addon glyphicon
                    glyphicon-envelope"></span>
                @Html.TextBoxFor(m => m.Email, new
                {
                    @class = "form-control email",
                    @placeholder = "Email"
                })
            </div>

            <div class="input-group input-group-sm">
                <span class="input-group-addon glyphicon
                    glyphicon-lock"></span>
                @Html.PasswordFor(m => m.Password, new
                {
                    @class = "form-control password",
                    @placeholder = "Password"
                })
            </div>

            <div class="register-checkbox">
                @Html.CheckBoxFor(m => m.AcceptUserAgreement,
                    new { @data_register_user_agreement_click = "" })

                <span>I Accept the @Html.ActionLink("Terms of use",
                    "TermsOfUse", "Legal")</span>
            </div>

            <button type="button" class="pull-right btn btn-success
                disabled">
                Sign me up!
            </button>
        </div>
    </div>
</div>
```

Styling the panel and the controls

While the controls are nicely styled, a bit of space between the controls will make the design even nicer – and removing the rounded corners takes it to the next level. Let's add a couple of CSS selectors to a stylesheet called **RegisterUser.css** to put it all together.

Add the CSS file to the **membership** style bundle in the **BundleConfig** class.

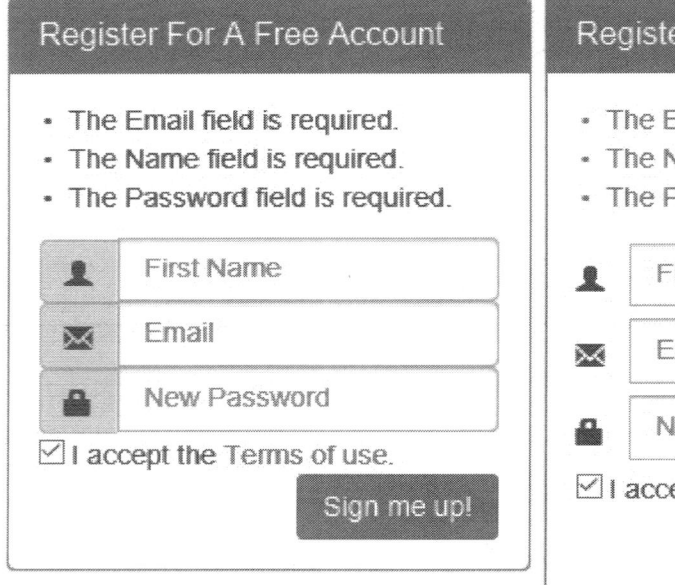

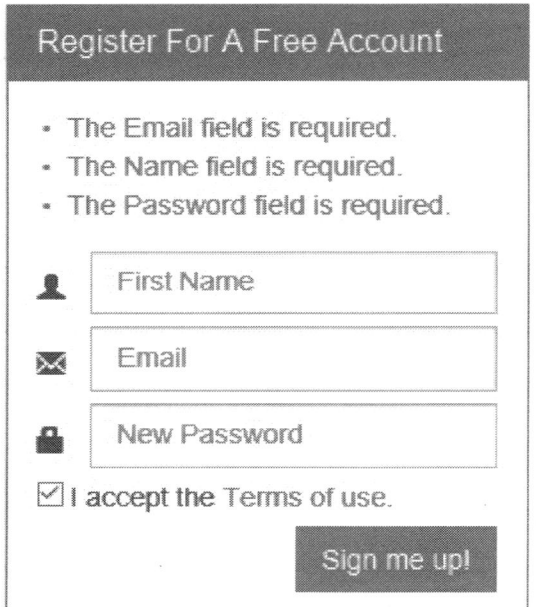

Styling the validation error summary

A red color will make the validation error text pop, and giving it 15px left padding will align the text with the other controls. The validation **<div>** element has a class called **validation-summary-errors** you can use.

```
.validation-summary-errors > ul{
    padding-left: 15px;
    color:red;
}
```

Removing the rounded corners

Assign 0 to the **border-radius** to remove the rounded corners from the textboxes and the panel. Use the ***** selector in combination with the **register-user-panel** class decorating the **<div>** surrounding the panel to target all elements in the panel.

```
.register-user-panel *,
.input-group-sm > .form-control,
.input-group-sm > .input-group-addon,
.input-group-sm > .input-group-btn > .btn {
    border-radius: 0px;
}
```

Adding space between the textboxes

Add 3px top and bottom margin to all textboxes in the panel.

```
.register-user-panel input[type="text"].form-control,
.register-user-panel input[type="password"].form-control {
    margin-bottom:3px;
    margin-top:3px;
}
```

Styling the icons

To position the icons, give them a white background and remove the border around them. You have to add selectors for the three glypicons **glyphicon-user**, **glyphicon-envelope** and **glyphicon-lock**.

```
.register-user-panel .glyphicon-user,
.register-user-panel .glyphicon-envelope,
.register-user-panel .glyphicon-lock {
    background-color:white;
    border:none;
    padding-left:0px;
}
```

Styling the button

To add some space between the button and the checkbox, you can add a top margin of 5px. Use the **button** element selector with the **register-user-panel** class to target the registration button.

```
.register-user-panel button { margin-top:5px; }
```

Adding the RegisterUserAsync action

You can copy the **HttpPost** version of the **Register** action (and all of its attributes), the one with the **RegisterViewModel** parameter, and paste it into a new region at the end of the **AccountController** class.

Note: *The **Register** action method is declared using the **Async** keyword to make it asynchronous on the server, it is important to know that this has nothing to do with asynchronous Ajax calls which are handled by the client. An asynchronous action method can temporarily relinquish control of the current thread while doing a long-running task, freeing it up for the server to use it for other work. The asynchronous task is then handled by a background thread pool which gives the task a thread when one is available in the pool.*

Some changes have to be made to the **Register** action for it to work in this registration scenario. First, rename it **RegisterUserAsync** and then replace the **RegisterViewModel** parameter with the **RegisterUserModel** class. Then you have to add values for the **FirstName, Registered** and **IsActive** properties in the **ApplicationUser** instance. You also need to set the **EmailConfirmed** property of the same instance variable to **true** since you are not using email confirmation in this exercise.

If you haven't added the fields to the table yet, then read this section to find out how: Modifying the AspNetUser class.

```
Var user = new ApplicationUser { FirstName = model.Name, UserName =
model.Email, Email = model.Email, EmailConfirmed = true, Registered =
DateTime.Now, IsActive = true };
```

Replace the **RedirectToAction** return with the **_RegisterUserPartial** view you created earlier in this chapter, use the **PartialView** method to render the partial view.

```
Return PartialView("_RegisterUserPartial", model);
```

Since you only want to render the partial view and not the whole **Index** view, you have to replace the **View** method call at the end of the **RegisterUserAsync** action to the same **PartialView** call as described above.

Copy the **AddErrors** method, paste the copy into the region you created earlier in this section and rename the method **AddUserErrors**.

You want to exclude the check for errors stating that the *Name ... is already taken* in the method since that does not apply to this solution. To achieve this, you have to add an if-statement ignoring these validation errors in the **AddUserErrors** method; the default implementation does not allow the same name twice.

```
if (error.StartsWith("Name") && error.EndsWith("is already taken."))
    continue;
ModelState.AddModelError("", error);
```

You can also delete all the comments in the **RegisterUserAsync** action since you won't be using email confirmation.

The AddUserErrors method

The **AddUserErrors** method is used to create a list of all errors that occur during a call to the **RegisterUserAsync** action call. You can modify it to exclude errors that have to do with the name in the **UserName** column, since it always will contain the user's email; earlier you added a non-unique field called **FirstName** to store the first name of the user during registration.

1. Locate and copy the **AddErrors** method in the **AccountController** class.
2. Paste in the region you created for the **RegisterUserAsync** action and change its name to **AddUserErrors**.
3. Add an if-statement excluding errors containing the text "Name" and "is already taken" above the **ModelState.AddModelError** method call. You can simply call the **continue** command to skip to the next error in the loop.
    ```
    if (error.StartsWith("Name") && error.EndsWith("is already taken.")) continue;
    ModelState.AddModelError("", error);
    ```
4. Build the solution to make sure that it works properly.

This is the complete code for the **AddUserErrors** method:

```
private void AddUserErrors(IdentityResult result)
{
```

```
        foreach (var error in result.Errors)
        {
            if (error.StartsWith("Name") &&
                error.EndsWith("is already taken.")) continue;

            ModelState.AddModelError("", error);
        }
    }
```

The Register action

1. Open the **AccountController** class.
2. Add a new region with the text *Register User*.
3. Copy the **HttpPost** version of the **Register** method along with its attributes and paste it into the region you just added. Rename the method **RegisterUserAsync**.
4. You can clean up the code a bit by removing all comments.
5. Change the **RegisterViewModel** parameter to **RegisterUserModel** which is the model used in the **_RegisterUserPartial** view.
6. Change the **ApplicationUser** instance to include assigning values to the **FirstName** property from the **model** parameter, the **EmailConfirmed** and **IsActive** properties to **true**, and the **Registered** property to the current date.
   ```
   var user = new ApplicationUser { FirstName = model.Name, UserName
   = model.Email, Email = model.Email, EmailConfirmed = true,
   Registered = DateTime.Now, IsActive = true };
   ```
7. If you want to assign default subscriptions to every registered user, then you can call the **RegisterUserSubscriptionCode** in the **SubscriptionExtensions** class that you added in a previous chapter.
   ```
   await SubscriptionExtensions.RegisterUserSubscriptionCode("Free",
   user.Id);
   ```
8. Replace the **RedirectToAction** call to a **PartialView** method call, rendering the **_RegisterUserPartial** view passing in the **model** as its parameter.
   ```
   return PartialView("_RegisterUserPartial", model);
   ```
9. Replace the call to the **AddErrors** method with a call to the **AddUserErrors** method.
10. Change the **View** call to a call to **PartialView** rendering the **_RegisterUserPartial** view passing in the **model** as its parameter.
    ```
    return PartialView("_RegisterUserPartial", model);
    ```

The complete code for the **RegisterUserAsync** action:

```
[HttpPost]
[AllowAnonymous]
[ValidateAntiForgeryToken]
public async Task<ActionResult> RegisterUserAsync(RegisterUserModel model)
{
    model.AcceptUserAgreement = true;

    if (ModelState.IsValid)
    {
        var user = new ApplicationUser
        {
            FirstName = model.Name,
            UserName = model.Email,
            Email = model.Email,
            EmailConfirmed = true,
            Registered = DateTime.Now,
            IsActive = true
        };

        var result = await UserManager.CreateAsync(user, model.Password);
        if (result.Succeeded)
        {
            await SignInManager.SignInAsync(user, isPersistent: false,
                rememberBrowser: false);

            // Add a default subsctiption called "Free" to all users.
            await SubscriptionExtensions.RegisterUserSubscriptionCode(
                "Free", user.Id);

            return PartialView("_RegisterUserPartial", model);
        }

        AddUserErrors(result);
    }

    // If we get this far something failed and we re-display the form
    return PartialView("_RegisterUserPartial", model);
}
```

Adding JavaScript click events

To keep the HTML Markup clean and separated from the JavaScript code, you will create a new JavaScript file for the Register User panel called **RegisterUser.js** in the **Scripts** folder in the main project.

In the JavaScript file, you will create **click** events for the checkbox and the button as well as a method for the asynchronous Ajax call to the **AccountController**'s **RegisterUser-Async** action which will add new user to the **AspNetUser** database table.

When wiring up the **click** events for the checkbox and the button, you can cache it in a variable for easy access and reuse in the **onRegisterUserClick** function where you have to wire up the **click** events again after the Ajax call. If you don't do that, the button and checkbox will stop working.

Create two functions separate from the actual **click** event functions which are called from the two **click** events respectively. The first function called **onToggleRegisterUser-DisabledClick** will toggle the **disabled** CSS class for the button enabling/disabling it. The second function called **onRegisterUserClick** will make the asynchronous Ajax call to the controller's action method and is called from the button's **click** event function.

Fetch the values from the textboxes and the **__RequestVerificationToken** value from the hidden field In the **onRegisterUserClick** function and pass them along as parameters to the controller action. Create a variable called **url** which hold the URL to the action method.

Redirect to the **Index** view of the **Home** controller to update the page when a user loggs in successfully.

If an error has been thrown in the action, then display a validation summary to the user in the panel, retain the textbox values and keep the checkbox checked.

Regardless of a successful or unsuccessful call, the **click** events have to be re-wired after the Ajax call.

Add the JavaScript file

1. Right-click on the **Scripts** folder and select **Add-JavaScript File** in the context menu.
2. Name the file **RegisterUser.js** in the dialog and click the **OK** button.
3. Open the **BundleConfig** file in the **App_Start** folder and add it to the **membership** bundle.
   ```
   bundles.Add(new ScriptBundle("~/bundles/membership").Include(
       "~/Scripts/RegisterUser.js"));
   ```
4. Open the **_Layout** view and locate the last **@Scripts.Render** method call at the end of the view and add a new one below that one for the **membership** bundle if it does not already exist.
   ```
   @Scripts.Render("~/bundles/membership")
   ```

Wire up the checkbox click event function

1. The first thing you will have to add in the JavaScript file is the **Document Ready** function; its content will be loaded when the web page (view) is loaded into the browser but before the page is displayed to the user. The short-hand JQuery notation is used for the **Ready** function. Note that this JavaScript file has to be loaded after the JQuery library in the **_Layout** view, more on that later.
   ```
   $(function () {
       /*Your JavaScript code goes here*/
   });
   ```
2. Next, you will wire up the **click** event for the checkbox which will toggle the button's enabled/disabled state. You cache it in a variable for easy access and reuse in the **onRegisterUserClick** method which you will add later.
   ```
   var registerUserCheckBox = $("#AcceptUserAgreement").click(
   onToggleRegisterUserDisabledClick);
   ```
3. Add the **onToggleRegisterUserDisabledClick** method in the JavaScript file and toggle between the disabled and enabled button states. You can target the button by the **register-user-panel** class and the **button** element selector. Use the **toggleClass** method to toggle the **disabled** CSS class on and off.
   ```
   function onToggleRegisterUserDisabledClick() {
       $(".register-user-panel button").toggleClass("disabled");
   }
   ```

4. If you run the application and click the checkbox, the button should toggle between being disabled and enabled. If you click the button, nothing will happen because you haven't implemented the Ajax call to the controller action yet.

The complete code for the checkbox:

```
var registerUserCheckBox = $("#AcceptUserAgreement").click(
onToggleRegisterUserDisabledClick);

/* User Agreement Check Box */
function onToggleRegisterUserDisabledClick() {
    $(".register-user-panel button").toggleClass("disabled");
}
```

Adding the Ajax action call

This is what you have been working towards in this chapter – making the button actually perform a task. Here, you will wire up the button's **click** event function and make the call to the **AccountController**'s **RegisterUserAsync** action which will add a new user to the **AspNetUser** database table.

Wire up the button click event function

1. Add a new variable called **registerUserButton** below the previously added variable, assign the button **click** event function for easy access and reuse. Make the **click** event function call a function called **onRegisterUserClick,** which you will add shortly. Use the **register-user-panel** class and the **button** element selector to target it.

   ```
   var registerUserButton = $(".register-user-panel button").click(
   onRegisterUserClick);
   ```

2. Add a function called **onRegisterUserClick** below the other function you created earlier.

   ```
   function onRegisterUserClick() {
        /*Your JavaScript code and Ajax call goes here*/
   };
   ```

3. Add a variable called **url** inside the function which stores the URL used when navigating to the action method with Ajax.

   ```
   var url = "/Account/RegisterUserAsync";
   ```

4. Next fetch the anti-forgery token from the hidden field created by the **@Html.AntiForgeyToken** method call in the panel HTML markup.
   ```
   var antiforegry = $('[name="__RequestVerificationToken"]').val();
   ```
5. Target the input boxes in the panel with their respective name classes to fetch their values and store them in variables.
   ```
   var name = $('.register-user-panel .first-name').val();
   var email = $('.register-user-panel .email').val();
   var pwd = $('.register-user-panel .password').val();
   ```
6. Add the Ajax call to the controller action using the **$.post** method passing in the **url** variable as the first parameter and the other variables as named parameters in an anonymous object as the second parameter.
   ```
   $.post(url, { __RequestVerificationToken: antiforegry, email: email, name: name, password: pwd, acceptUserAgrrement: true },
   function (data) {
       //Code executed when returning from a successful action call
   }).fail(function (xhr, status, error) {
       //Error code goes here
   });
   ```
7. The **data** parameter in the "success" function of the Ajax call will contain the rendered partial view returned from the action. To search for potential errors in the returned HTML, you first have to parse the data to HTML markup using the **pasrseHTML** JQuery method.
   ```
   var parsed = $.parseHTML(data);
   ```
8. You can then use the parsed data to find out if it contains any errors using a regular expression to remove line breaks from the **[data-valmsg-summary]** attribute and then checking its length. If the length is greater than 0, the view has errors.
   ```
   hasErrors = $(parsed).find("[data-valmsg-summary]").text()
   .replace(/\n|\r/g, "").length > 0;
   ```
9. Use an if-else statement to check if the view has errors. If it does, then replace the HTML markup in the partial view **<div>** element with the **register-user-panel** class to re-display the partial view and its errors. Then wire up the button and checkbox **click** event functions again and remove the **disabled** CSS class from the button to make it clickable.

```
    If (hasErrors == true) {
        $(".register-user-panel").html(data);

        registerUserButton = $(".register-user-panel button").click(
            onRegisterUserClick);

        registerUserCheckBox = $("#AcceptUserAgreement").click(
            onToggleRegisterUserDisabledClick);

        $(".register-user-panel button").removeClass("disabled");
    }
```

10. If no errors were found, then re-register the **click** event functions for the button and the checkbox and redirect to the */Home/Index* action to update the page for the logged in user (a registered user automatically gets logged in by the framework).

```
    else {
        registerUserButton = $(".register-user-panel button").click(
            onRegisterUserClick);

        registerUserCheckBox = $("#AcceptUserAgreement").click(
            onToggleRegisterUserDisabledClick);

        location.href = '/Home/Index';
    }
```

11. If you run the application, you should now be able to register a user using the panel controls. Note that the panel disappears when the **Index** view is re-rendered after successful registration.

The complete code for the **RegisterUser.js** JavaScript file:

```
$(function () {
    var registerUserButton = $(".register-user-panel button").click(
        onRegisterUserClick);

    var registerUserCheckBox = $("#AcceptUserAgreement").click(
        onToggleRegisterUserDisabledClick);

    /* User Agreement Check Box */
    function onToggleRegisterUserDisabledClick() {
        $(".register-user-panel button").toggleClass("disabled");
    }
```

```js
        /* Register User Button*/
        function onRegisterUserClick() {
            var url = "/Account/RegisterUserAsync";
            var antiforegry = $('[name="__RequestVerificationToken"]').val();
            var name = $('.register-user-panel .first-name').val();
            var email = $('.register-user-panel .email').val();
            var pwd = $('.register-user-panel .password').val();

        $.post(url, { __RequestVerificationToken: antiforegry, email:
            email, name: name, password: pwd, acceptUserAgrement: true },
            function (data) {
                var parsed = $.parseHTML(data);
                hasErrors = $(parsed).find("[data-valmsg-summary]").text()
                    .replace(/\n|\r/g, "").length > 0;

                if (hasErrors == true) {
                    $(".register-user-panel").html(data);

                    registerUserButton = $(".register-user-panel button")
                        .click(onRegisterUserClick);

                    registerUserCheckBox = $("#AcceptUserAgreement").click(
                        onToggleRegisterUserDisabledClick);

                    $(".register-user-panel button").removeClass(
                        "disabled");
                }
                else {
                    registerUserButton = $(".register-user-panel button")
                        .click(onRegisterUserClick);

                    registerUserCheckBox = $("#AcceptUserAgreement").click(
                        onToggleRegisterUserDisabledClick);

                    location.href = '/Home/Index';
                }
            }).fail(function (xhr, status, error) {
                //Error handling code goes here
            });
        }
    });
```

15. Login

Introduction

In this chapter you will add a login panel made visible when hovering over the **Log in** link. The panel should have a close button defined by the **glyphicon-remove** icon in the upper right corner, two textboxes for email and password, a checkbox for the option to keep the user logged in and a **Log in** button calling the **LoginAsync** action you will add to the **Account** controller. The textboxes should change background color if the log in is unsuccessful.

Change the panel's header and the **Log in** button's background color to a dark blue (#4765A0). Make the button's background color 75% opaque when hovering over the button by changing its alpha channel to 0.75 using the rgba CSS function.

```
background-color:rgba(71, 101, 160, 0.75);
```

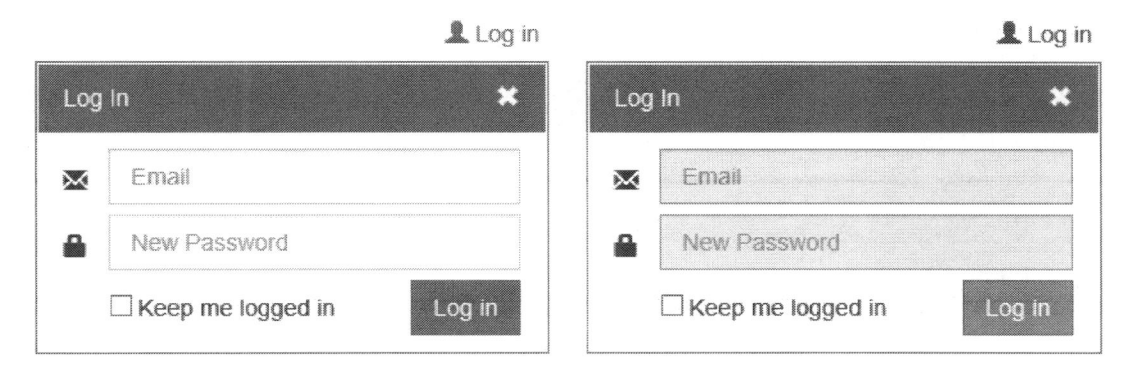

Instead of using a partial view to create an anchor tag with a glyphicon for the **Log in** link, you will create an extension method that can be used with **@Html** helper; it should render an **<a>** element containing a **<span>** for the glyphicon and a link text. The extension method should act on object of the **HtmlHelper** class.

The login panel should be created as a partial view rendered from the **_LoginPartial** view when the visitor hovers over the **Log in** link and hasn't logged in.

The call to the server should be done using Ajax and the necessary events for the panel's intrinsic controls should be wired up using JavaScript. Wire up the **hover** and **click** events in a JavaScript file called **login.js** and add any JavaScript necessary for the log in panel to it.

All CSS should be added to a style sheet called **login.css**.

When the user has successfully logged in, the **Log in** and **pwd** links will be relpaced by the user's first name and a red **Log off** button.

The GlyphLink extension method

This extension method will render an anchor tag (**<a>**) containing a **<span>** element for the glyphicon and the link text. The method must take one **HtmlHelper** declared with the **this** keyword and six **string** prameters called **controller**, **action**, **text**, **glyphicon**, **cssClasses** and **id** where the two last parameters have empty strings as default values.

Name the method **GlyphLink** and have it return a **MvcHtmlString** and act on the **HtmlHelper** class which makes it possible to access it through the **@Html** helper class.

Use the **TagBuilder** class to create the **<a>** element inside the method.

1. Add a **public static** class called **HtmlExtensions** to the **Extensions** folder.
2. Add a **public static** method called **GlyphLink** to the class. It should take one **HtmlHelper** parameter declared with the **this** keyword and six **string** prameters.
   ```
   public static MvcHtmlString GlyphLink(this HtmlHelper htmlHelper,
   string controller, string action, string text, string glyphicon,
   string cssClasses = "", string id = "") { ... }
   ```
3. Use **String.Format** to create a variable called **glyph** for the **<span>** element with its glyph CSS classes.
   ```
   var glyph = string.Format("<span class='glyphicon glyphicon-{0}'></span>", glyphicon);
   ```
4. Add a variable called **anchor** for the **<a>** element.

```
var anchor = new TagBuilder("a");
```

5. Add the **href** attribute to the **<a>** element and use the **controller** and **action** parameters to create a destination URL.
   ```
   anchor.MergeAttribute("href", string.Format("/{0}/{1}/",
       controller, action));
   ```

6. Use **String.Format** to add the **<span>** and the link text to the **InnerHtml** property of the **<a>** element making it part of its content. Use the **glyph** variable and the **text** parameter.
   ```
   anchor.InnerHtml = string.Format("{0} {1}", glyph, text);
   ```

7. Add the CSS classes in the **cssClasses** parameter to the **<a>** element.
   ```
   anchor.AddCssClass(cssClasses);
   ```

8. Add an id to the **<a>** element using the **id** parameter and the **GenerateId** method.
   ```
   anchor.GenerateId(id);
   ```

The code so far for the **GlyphLink** extension method:

```
public static class HtmlExtensions
{
    public static MvcHtmlString GlyphLink(this HtmlHelper htmlHelper,
    string controller, string action, string text, string glyphicon,
    string cssClasses = "", string id = "") {
        // declare the span for the glyphicon
        var glyph = string.Format("<span class='glyphicon
            glyphicon-{0}'></span>", glyphicon);

        // declare the anchor tag
        var anchor = new TagBuilder("a");
        anchor.MergeAttribute("href", string.Format("/{0}/{1}/",
            controller, action));
        anchor.InnerHtml = string.Format("{0} {1}", glyph, text);
        anchor.AddCssClass(cssClasses);
        anchor.GenerateId(id);

        // Create the helper
        return MvcHtmlString.Create(anchor.ToString(
            TagRenderMode.Normal));
    }
}
```

Adding the login styles heet and JavaScript files

To style the login panel and wire up events to its elements, you have to add a CSS style sheet called **login.css** to the **Content** folder and a JavaScript file called **login.js** to the **Scripts** folder. Add links to the files to the **BundleConfig** class.

1. Right-click on the **Content** folder and select **Add-Style Sheet** in the menu.
2. Name it **login.css** and click the **OK** button.
3. Right-click on the **Scripts** folder and select **Add-JavaScript** in the menu.
4. Name it **login.js** and click the **OK** button.
5. Open the the **BundleConfig** class.
6. Add the style sheet to the style bundle and the JavaScript file to the script bundle.

Altering the _LoginPartial view

Change the **Log off** link to a "danger" button using Bootstrap classes and add a **data-** attribute for targeting. You have previously used element descriptors, unique id's and classes to target elements with CSS and JavaScript, but in this chapter, you will learn how to use attributes to target elements.

Attributes beginning with **data-** will be ignored by the browser and can be used for targeting or specifying element attribute values. Add an attribute called **data-logout-button** to the **Log off <a>** link; you will use this attribute to style the link.

```
<li><a class="btn btn-danger" data-logout-button href="javascript:
document.getElementById('logoutForm').submit()">Log off</a></li>
```

Remove the **Register** link; it is no longer needed since new users can register with the registration panel you added in a previous chapter.

Add two **using** statements to the view one for the **Extensions** folder and one for the **Models** folder. You need the first **using** to get access to the **GlyphLink** extension and the second to get access to the **LoginViewModel**.

Replace the **Log in** action link with a call to the **GlyphLink** extension method; pass in *Account* for the **controller** parameter, *Login* for the **action** parameter, *Log in* for the **text** parameter, *user* for the **glyphicon** parameter, an empty string for the **cssClasses** parameter and *loginLink* for the **id** parameter.

Add a **<div>** element which is hidden for extra small devices below the **GlyphLink** method call. Add a **data-** attribute called **login-panel-partial** to the **<div>**; this attribute will be used to repopulate the **_LoginPanelPartial** partial view which will contain the login panel.

You will create the **_LoginPanelPartial** partial view in the next section, but you will add the markup to render it now. Use the **Partial** extension method in the last **<div>** you added to render the partial view. Pass an instance of the **LoginViewModel** with empty string values as a second parameter to the **Partial** method.

1. Open the **_LoginPartial** view in the **Views-Shared** folder.
2. Add two **using** statements to the view one for the **Extensions** folder and one for the **Models** folder.
   ```
   @using Memberships.Extensions
   @using Memberships.Models
   ```
3. Add the **area** property to the form's **routeValues** parameter and assign an empty string to it. This will target the main project's route and make it possible to logout from both user interfaces; the user interface and the admin user interface located in the **Admin** area.
   ```
   using (Html.BeginForm("LogOff", "Account", new { area = "" },
   FormMethod.Post, new { id = "logoutForm", @class = "navbar-right" }))
   ```
4. Add the **area** property to the manage link's **routeValues** parameter and assign an empty string to it.
   ```
   @Html.ActionLink("Hello " + User.Identity.GetUserFirstName() +
   "!", "Index", "Manage", routeValues: new { area = "" },
   htmlAttributes: new { title = "Manage" })
   ```
5. Change the **Log off** link to a "danger" button using Bootstrap classes and add a **data-** attribute for targeting.
   ```
   <li><a class="btn btn-danger" data-logout-button href="javascript:
   document.getElementById('logoutForm').submit()">Log off</a></li>
   ```
6. Comment out or remove the **Register** link.

```
     <li>@Html.ActionLink("Register", "Register", "Account",
     routeValues: null, htmlAttributes: new { id = "registerLink"
     })</li>
```

7. Comment out or remove the **Log in** link.
   ```
   @Html.ActionLink("Log in", "Login", "Account", routeValues: null,
   htmlAttributes: new { id = "loginLink" })
   ```

8. Add a call to the **GlyphLink** extension method to create a **Log in** link with a glyphicon where the previous **Log in** link was located.
   ```
   @Html.GlyphLink("Account", "Login", "Log in", "user", "",
   "loginLink")
   ```

9. Add a **<div>** element which is hidden for extra small devices below the **GlyphLink** method call and add a **data-** attribute called **login-panel-partial** to it.
   ```
   <div class="hidden-xs" login-panel-partial>
   ```

10. Use the **Partial** extension method to render the partial view. Pass in an instance of the **LoginViewModel** with empty string property values.
    ```
    @Html.Partial("_LoginPanelPartial", new LoginViewModel { Email =
    "", Password = "", RememberMe = false })
    ```

The code so far for the **_LoginPartial** view:

```
@using Microsoft.AspNet.Identity
@using Memberships.Extensions @*Add this row*@
@using Memberships.Models @*Add this row*@

@if (Request.IsAuthenticated)
{
    using (Html.BeginForm("LogOff", "Account",
        new { area = "" }, FormMethod.Post,
        new { id = "logoutForm", @class = "navbar-right" }))
    {
        @Html.AntiForgeryToken()

        <ul class="nav navbar-nav navbar-right">
            <li>
                @Html.ActionLink("Hello " +
                    User.Identity.GetUserFirstName() + "!", "Index",
                    "Manage", routeValues: new { area = "" },
                    htmlAttributes: new { title = "Manage" })
            </li>
```

```
            <li><a class="btn btn-danger" data-logout-button
                href="javascript:document.getElementById('logoutForm')
                    .submit()">Log off</a>
            </li>
        </ul>
    }
}
else
{
    <ul class="nav navbar-nav navbar-right">
        <li>
            @Html.GlyphLink("Account", "Login", "Log in", "user", "",
                "loginLink")
            <div class="hidden-xs" login-panel-partial>
                @Html.Partial("_LoginPanelPartial", new LoginViewModel
                    { Email = "", Password = "", RememberMe = false })
            </div>
        </li>
    </ul>
}
```

Styling the Log off link

When creating CSS selectors for attributes, you place the attribute name inside square brackets (**[]**) in the style sheet.

Earlier, you changed the **Log off** link to a red Bootstrap button. To make the text eaiser to read, you will change its text color to white. Target **<a>** elements that have a **data-logout-button** attribute when changing the color.

```
a[data-logout-button] { color:white; }
```
Change the button's background color to **orangered** when the user hovers over it with the mouse. To achieve this, you will have to use a much more specific targeting to out-rank CSS classes added by Bootstrap.

```
.nav > li > a[data-logout-button]:hover {
    color:white;
    background-color:orangered;
    border-color:orangered;
}
```

Adding the _LoginPanelPartial view

To display the login panel as a pop-up, you will create it as a patial view called **_Login-PanelPartial** which is rendered when the user hovers over the **Log in** link and stays open either until the user closes it with the close button or when a successful login has been achieved.

The view should have two textboxes; one for the email address and one for the password. It should also have a checkbox that the user can check to remain logged in the next time he or she visits the site. A close button displaying the **glyphicon-remove** icon should be available in the top right corner of the panel's **heading** area. When the **Log in** button located in the lower right corner of the panel body is clicked, an action called **LoginAsync** in the **Account** controller should be called using Ajax.

The panel **body** needs to contain an **AntiForgeryToken** to make secure calls to the server and a **ValidationSummary** to handle any errors that might occur.

Use the **TextBoxFor**, **PasswordFor** and **CheckBoxFor** helper methods to create the controls in the panel's **body** area and sync them with the corresponding properties in the **LoginViewModel** model object in the view.

Creating the view
The image below shows the view settings for creating the **_LoginPanelPartial** view.

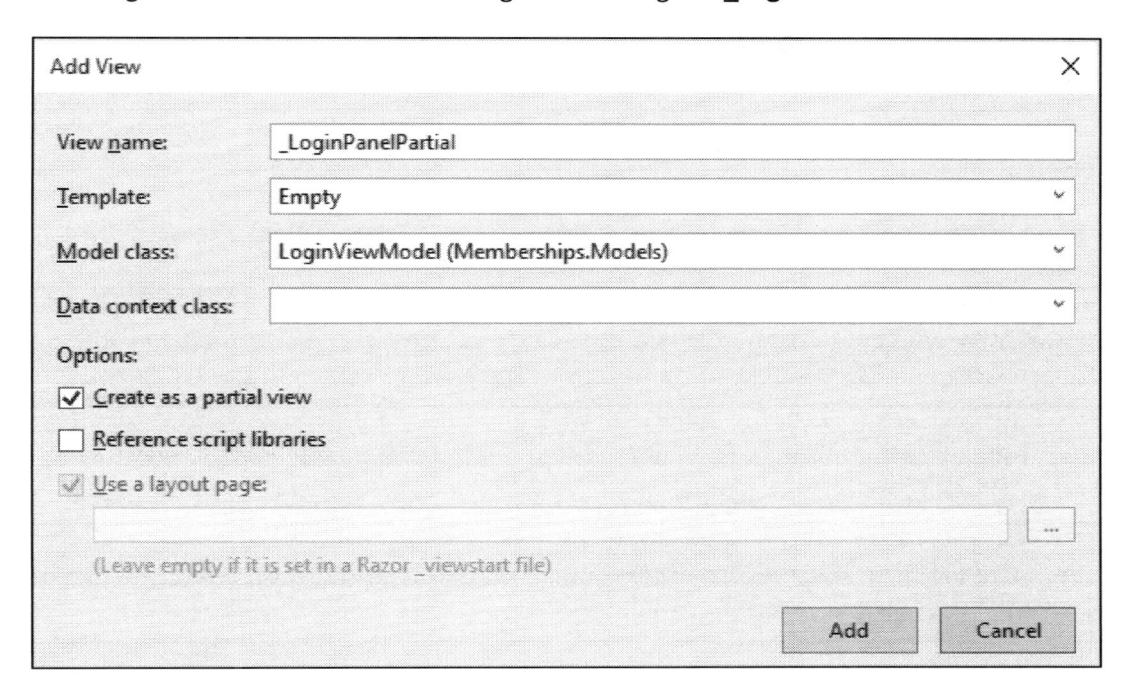

1. Right-click on the **Views-Shared** folder and select **Add-View**.
2. Name the view **_LoginPanelPartial** in the **View name** field.
3. Select the **Empty** template.
4. Select the **LoginViewModel** class as the model class.
5. Delete any text in the **Data context class** drop-down.
6. Make sure the **Create as a partial view** checkbox is checked.
7. Click the **Add** button.

Adding the login panel
Add a Bootstrap panel with a heading and a body inside a **<div>** element decorated with an attribute called **data-login-user-area** and **dropdown-menu dropdown-panel** classes.

Add the text *Log in* followed by an **<a>** element with the id **close-login** which is decorated with the **pull-right** class to move it to the far right of the container. Place a **<span>** element inside the **<a>** element and have it display the **glyphicon-remove** icon.

Add **AntiForgeryToken** and **ValidationSummary** elements to the panel body, add the **hidden** class to the **ValidationSummary** element.

Use **<div>** elements decorated with the **input-group** class to act as containers for the individual textboxes and their icons. Use the **glyphicon-envelope** and **glyphicon-lock** icons to decorate the textboxes and add the **input-group-addon** class to the **<span>** elements to make them look as though they belong to the textboxes.

Add a class called **email** to the email textbox and a class called **password** to the **password** textbox.

Add a **<div>** element decorated with a class called **remember-me-checkbox** and add the checkbox element to it followed by the text *Keep me logged in* and the **Log in** button. Decorate the button with the **pull-right** class and make it a default Bootstrap button. Give it the id **login-button** and add one attribute called **data-login-action** which will hold the destinaltion URL for the controller action and one called **data-login-return-url** which will hold the URL to the **Index** view in the **Home** controller that will be used upon successful log in. The values from these two attributes will be fetched with JavaScript when the Ajax call is made to the server.

1. Add a **<div>** element decorated with an attribute called **data-login-user-area** and the classes **dropdown-menu dropdown-panel** to the view.
   ```
   <div class="dropdown-menu dropdown-panel" data-login-user-area>
   ```
2. Add a Bootstrap panel with a heading and a body inside the **<div>** element.
   ```
   <div class="panel">
       <div class="panel-heading"></div>
       <div class="panel-body"></div>
   </div>
   ```
3. Add the text *Log In* and an **<a>** element with a **<span>** element for the **glyphicon-remove** icon to the panel heading **<div>**.
   ```
   Log In<a id="close-login" class="pull-right">
   <span class="glyphicon glyphicon-remove"></span></a>
   ```
4. Add **AntiForgeryToken** and **ValidationSummary** elements to the panel body.
   ```
   @Html.AntiForgeryToken()
   @Html.ValidationSummary(false, "", new { @class = "text-danger
       hidden" })
   ```

5. Add a **<div>** element decorated with the **input-group** class.
6. Add a **<span>** element decorated with the **glyphicon, glyphicon-envelope** and the **input-group-addon** classes to the previous **<div>**. The latter class will make the icon and the textbox visually look like one control.
7. Use the **@Html.TextBoxFor** helper method to add the email textbox to the previous **<div>** below the **<span>**.

   ```
   <div class="input-group">
       <span class="input-group-addon glyphicon
       glyphicon-envelope"></span>
       @Html.TextBoxFor(m => m.Email, new { @class = "form-control
           email", @placeholder = "Email" })
   </div>
   ```

8. Repeat step 5-7 for the password textbox. Don't forget to change the icon to **glyphicon-lock**, the class to **password** and the property to **m.Password**.
9. Add a **<div>** element decorated with a class called **remember-me-checkbox** and add the checkbox element to it followed by the text *Keep me logged in* and the **Log in** button.

   ```
   <div class="remember-me-checkbox">
       @Html.CheckBoxFor(m => m.RememberMe)
       <span>Keep me logged in</span>
       <button id="login-button" type="button" class="pull-right
           btn btn-default" data-login-action="/Account/LoginAsync"
           data-login-return-url="/Home/Index">
           Log in
       </button>
   </div>
   ```

The image on the next page shows what the panel would look like if displayed without any additional CSS styling. Needless to say, it could do with a make-over, which you will provide in the next section.

ASP.NET MVC 5 - How to build a Membership Website

The complete markup for the **_LoginPanelPartial** view:

```
@model Memberships.Models.LoginViewModel

<div class="dropdown-menu dropdown-panel" data-login-user-area>
    <div class="panel">
        <div class="panel-heading">
            Log In<a id="close-login" class="pull-right">
            <span class="glyphicon glyphicon-remove"></span></a>
        </div>
        <div class="panel-body">
            @Html.AntiForgeryToken()
            @Html.ValidationSummary(false, "", new { @class = "text-danger
                hidden" })

            <div class="input-group">
                <span class="input-group-addon glyphicon
                    glyphicon-envelope"></span>
                @Html.TextBoxFor(m => m.Email, new { @class = "form-control
                    email", @placeholder = "Email" })
            </div>

            <div class="input-group">
                <span class="input-group-addon glyphicon
                    glyphicon-lock"></span>
                @Html.PasswordFor(m => m.Password, new { @class =
                    "form-control password", @placeholder = "New Password"})
            </div>

            <div class="remember-me-checkbox">
```

```
            @Html.CheckBoxFor(m => m.RememberMe)
            <span>Keep me logged in</span>
            <button id="login-button" type="button" class="pull-right
                btn btn-default" data-login-action="/Account/LoginAsync"
                data-login-return-url="/Home/Index">
                Log in
            </button>
        </div>
    </div>
  </div>
</div>
```

Adding JavaScript and CSS to display the login panel

To make the login panel pop-up, you'll have to wire up the **hover** event for the **Log in** link in the **login.js** file. The panel will be displayed when the **open** class has been added to the **<div>** surrounding the panel and a CSS selector for the **open** class has been added to the **login.css** file and the **display** property has been added to it displaying the **<div>** as a **block**.

Wire up the **hover** event to the **Log in** link and have it call a function named **onLogin-LinkHover** which adds the **open** class to the **<div>** decorated with the **[data-login-user-area]** attribute. Store the delegate in a variable called **loginLinkHover**.

```
$(function () {
    // Wire up the hover event
    var loginLinkHover = $("#loginLink").hover(onLoginLinkHover);

    // The function called by the hover event
    function onLoginLinkHover() {
        $('div[data-login-user-area]').addClass('open');
    };
});
```

Now that the **hover** event is wired up, you have to add a CSS selector for the **<div>** with the **open** class added.

Open the **login.css** style sheet and add a selector for the **<div>** with the **open** class and display it as a **block**. Also remove the top padding, add 3px bottom padding and a 10px right margin.

```
[data-login-user-area].open {
    display:block;
    padding-top: 0px;
    padding-bottom: 3px;
    margin-right:10px;
}
```

The login panel will look like this when opened:

Adding JavaScript to close the login panel

To make the login panel close when the **glyphicon-remove** link is clicked, its **click** event has to be wired up in the **login.js** file. The panel will be hidden when the **open** class is removed from the **<div>** surrounding the panel.

Store the **click** event in a variable called **loginCloseButton** below the **loginLinkHover** variable and have it call a method named **onCloseLogin** which removes the **open** class from the **<div>**.

```
// Wire up the click event
var loginCloseButton = $("#close-login").click(onCloseLogin);
```

```
// The function called by the click event
function onCloseLogin()
{
    $('div[data-login-user-area]').removeClass('open');
}
```

Run the application and hover over the **Log in** link to open the panel. Close the panel again using the **X**-button in the upper right corner of the panel. You don't have to close the application when adding new styles; keep it running and the changes will be visible as soon as they are added.

Styling the login panel

The form is a bit lackluster as it stands right now, but with a few styling modifications that can be remedied. Open the **login.css** file and let's add some CSS selectors and properties to make the login panel pop.

The panel

Add a selector to the **<div>** surrounding the panel and change the border color to a dark blue (#4765A0).

```
[data-login-user-area] {
    border-color:#4765A0;
}
```

Remove any rounded corners on the surrounding **<div>** and its intrinsic controls. The asterisk (*) targets all elements within the **<div>**.

```
[data-login-user-area], [data-login-user-area] * {
    border-radius: 0px;
}
```

Remove the box shadow, add a 3px bottom margin and make the panel **<div>** element at least 300px wide.

```
[data-login-user-area] .panel {
    box-shadow: none;
    margin-bottom: 3px;
    min-width: 300px;
}
```

The image below is a before/after comparison of the login panel. Note that all elements have sharp corners after the border radius has been removed.

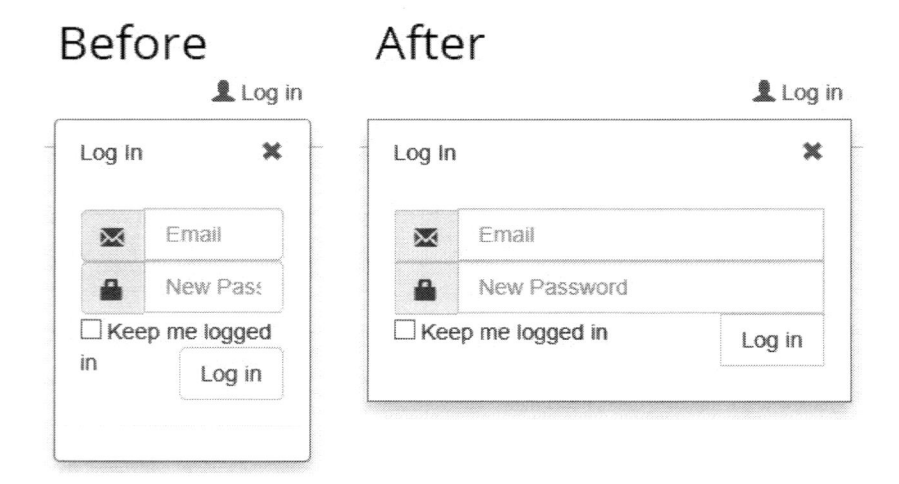

The panel heading and body

Add a selector for the **panel-heading <div>** and change the background color to a dark blue (#4765A0). Also change the text color to white to contrast it with the dark blue background and add a 7px bottom margin.

```
[data-login-user-area] .panel-heading {
    margin-bottom: 7px;
    background-color:#4765A0;
    color:white;
}
```

Change the cursor to a hand when hovering over the **glyphicon-remove** icon and change the icon color to white.

```
[data-login-user-area] .glyphicon-remove {
    cursor: pointer;
    color:white;
}
```

Add a selector to the **panel-body <div>** and change the top and bottom padding to 7px.

```
[data-login-user-area] .panel-body {
    padding-top: 7px;
    padding-bottom: 7px;
}
```

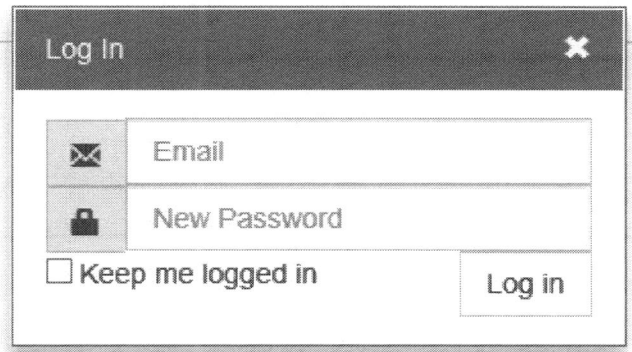

The textboxes

First, let's allign the icons with the textboxes and remove the background color behind the icons and their borders.

```
[data-login-user-area] .glyphicon-envelope,
[data-login-user-area] .glyphicon-lock {
    background-color:white;
    border:none;
    padding-left:0px;
}
```

Add a 3px top and bottom margin to the textboxes to add some space between them.

```
[data-login-user-area] input[type="text"].form-control,
[data-login-user-area] input[type="password"].form-control {
    margin-bottom:3px;
    margin-top:3px;
}
```

Add a selector for class called **data-login-error** that can be added to the textboxes with JavaScript, changing their background color to a light red if the login fails when the user clicks the **Log in** button. This style will not be applied before the Ajax call to the server has been implemented.

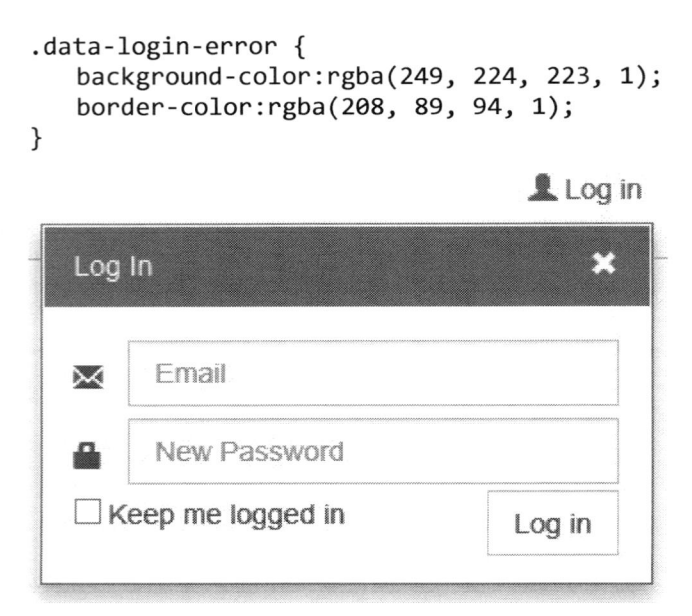

```
.data-login-error {
   background-color:rgba(249, 224, 223, 1);
   border-color:rgba(208, 89, 94, 1);
}
```

The Log in button

The **Log in** button need a 3px top margin to add a little more space between it and the **password** textbox. Also change its background and border color to the same blue color used in the panel heading (#4765A0) and its text color to white.

```
#login-button {
   margin-top: 3px;
   background-color:#4765A0;
   border-color:#4765A0;
   color:white;
}
```

Use the RGBA function to make the button's background less opaque when hovering over it. Change the alpha channel to 0.75 (75%).

```
#login-button:hover {
   background-color:rgba(71, 101, 160, 0.75);
}
```

The checkbox
The checkbox could do with a 27px left margin to align it with the textboxes and a 12px top margin to align it vertically with the **Log in** button.

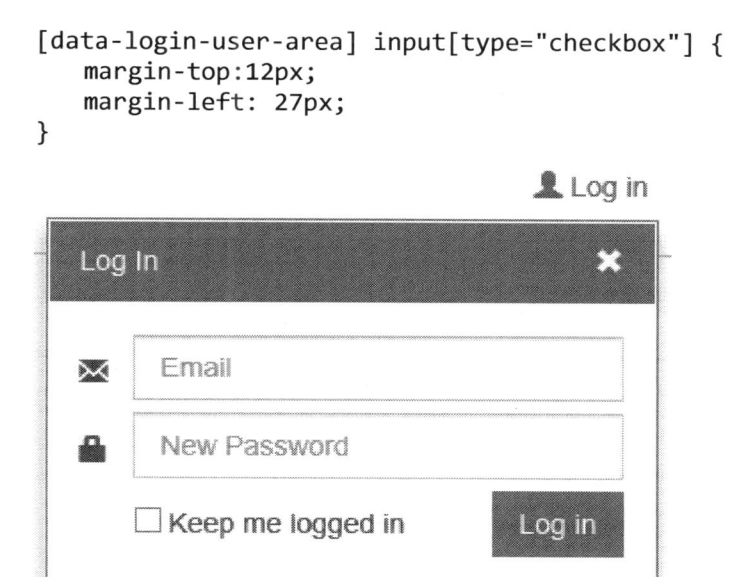

```
[data-login-user-area] input[type="checkbox"] {
    margin-top:12px;
    margin-left: 27px;
}
```

The LoginAsync action
You need to add a new asynchronous action called **LoginAsync** to the **Account** controller which will be called asynchronously from the client using Ajax when the user clicks the **Log in** button.

Note: *The **async** keyword on the action has nothing to do with calling it asynchronously with Ajax; it is added to be able to use the **await** keyword to temporarily give back the main thread to the application during long-running tasks.*

The action should be decorated with the **HttpPost, AllowAnonymous** and **ValidateAntiForgeryToken** attributes. The first attribute makes it possible to call the action during posts from the client. The second attribute makes it possible for non-logged in visitors to use the action. The third attribute validates the anti forgery token sent with the Ajax call to the server to verify that the call originated on the same sever.

Two parameters are needed where the first is the **LoginViewModel** that will be filled with data on the client and the second is a **string** holding the URL that will be called upon successful login.

Add an if-block which is executed if the model state is valid. Add the error message *Invalid login attempt* to the model state if the model state is invalid and return the **_LoginPanelPartial** view with the model.

You need to use the **UserManager** class inside the if-block to fetch the user matching the supplied email if it exists in the database and store the result in a variable called **user**.

Add an if-block below the **user** variable inside the previous if-block which checks that the **user** variable contains a user name.

Await a call to the **PasswordSignInAsync** method on the **SinInManager** class and store the result in a variable called **result** inside the inner if-block. Pass in the user name from the **user.UserName** property, the model's **Password** and **RememberMe** properties and a parameter called **shouldLockout** set to **false** to prevent the user from being locked out if providing wrong login credentials.

Return the **_LoginPanelPartial** view with the model if the **result** variable contains the value **SignInStatus.Success**.

1. Open the **AccountController** class.
2. Add a region called *Log in* at the bottom of the class.
3. Add an **async** action called **LoginAsync** decorated with the **HttpPost**, **AllowAnonymous** and **ValidateAntiForgeryToken** attributes and takes one **LoginViewModel** parameter called **model** and a **string** parmeter called **returnUrl**.

```
#region Log in
[HttpPost]
[AllowAnonymous]
[ValidateAntiForgeryToken]
public async Task<ActionResult> LoginAsync(LoginViewModel model,
string returnUrl)
{

}
#endregion
```

4. Add an if-block which is executed if the model state is valid.
5. Add the error message *Invalid login attempt* to the model state if the model state is invalid.
   ```
   ModelState.AddModelError("", "Invalid login attempt.");
   ```
6. Return the **_LoginPanelPartial** view with the model.
   ```
   return PartialView("_LoginPanelPartial", model);
   ```
7. Use the **UserManager** class to fetch the user matching the supplied email if it exists in the database inside the if-block. Store the result in a variable called **user**.
   ```
   var user = UserManager.Users.FirstOrDefault(u => u.Email.Equals(model.Email));
   ```
8. Add an if-block below the **user** variable inside the previous if-block which checks that the **user** variable contains a user name.
9. Try to sign in to the site using the **PasswordSignInAsync** method on the **SinInManager** class inside the inner if-block. Store the result in a variable called **result**.
   ```
   var result = await SignInManager.PasswordSignInAsync(
   user.UserName, model.Password, model.RememberMe, shouldLockout: false);
   ```
10. Return the **_LoginPanelPartial** view with the model if the **result** variable contains the value **SignInStatus.Success**.
    ```
    if (result.Equals(SignInStatus.Success))
        return PartialView("_LoginPanelPartial", model);
    ```

The complete code for the **LoginAsync** action:

```
#region Log in
[HttpPost]
[AllowAnonymous]
[ValidateAntiForgeryToken]
public async Task<ActionResult> LoginAsync(LoginViewModel model, string returnUrl)
{
    if (ModelState.IsValid)
    {
```

```
        var user = UserManager.Users.FirstOrDefault(u =>
            u.Email.Equals(model.Email));
        if (user != null && user.UserName.Length > 0)
        {
            var result = await SignInManager.PasswordSignInAsync(
                user.UserName, model.Password, model.RememberMe,
                shouldLockout: false);

            if (result.Equals(SignInStatus.Success))
                return PartialView("_LoginPanelPartial", model);
        }
    }

    // If we get this far something has failed and we re-display the form
    ModelState.AddModelError("", "Invalid login attempt.");
    return PartialView("_LoginPanelPartial", model);
}
#endregion
```

The Log in button JavaScript

You need to wire up the **click** event for the **Log in** button in the **login.js** JavaScript file and then use Ajax to call the **LoginAsync** action in the **Account** controller.

Wire up the **click** event for the **Log in** button and have it call a function named **onLoginClick** where the Ajax call is made. Store the **click** event delegate in a variable called **loginButton**.

Fetch the action and return URL's from the button's **data-login-action** and **data-login-return-url** atributes and store them in variables called **url** and **return_url** inside the **onLoginClick** method.

Fetch the email, password and remember me values from the corresponding elements and store them in variables called **email**, **pwd** and **remember_me**.

Fetch the anti-forgery token from the hidden element called **__RequestVerification-Token** and store it ina variable named **antiforgery**.

```
var antiforegry = $('[name= "__RequestVerificationToken"]').val();
```

Make the Ajax call to the server using the **$.post** method passing in the values from the variables.

Check if any errors have been reported by the server by parsing the **data** function parameter with the **parseHTML** function and check if the **[data-valmsg-summary]** attribute is empty and store the result in variable called **hasErrors**.

```
var parsed = $.parseHTML(data);
var hasErrors = $(parsed).find("[data-valmsg-summary]").text().replace(
    /\n|\r/g, "").length > 0;
```

Keep the log in panel open if there are errors by adding the conent of the data function parameter, which contain the panel, to the **<div>** with the **[data-login-panel-partial]** attribute surrounding the panel calling the **html** method on the element.

```
$("div[data-login-panel-partial]").html(data);
```

Add the **open** class to the **<div>** with the **[data-login-user-area]** attribute to keep the log in panel open.

Add the **data-login-error** class to the textboxes to change their background color to a light red if there are errors.

If no errors have occurred and the login was successful, then remove the **open** class on the panel's container **<div>** and the **data-login-error** class from the textboxes.

Redirect to the URL in the **return_url** variable (/Home/Index).

```
location.href = return_url;
```

Regardless if the log in was successful or not, the link and button events have to be wired up again using the variables you added at the beginning of this section.

```
loginButton = $("#login-button").click(onLoginClick);
loginLinkHover = $("#loginLink").hover(onLoginLinkHover);
loginCloseButton = $("#close-login").click(onCloseLogin);
```

Chain on the **fail** function on the **success** function to handle errors that might occur. Add the **data-login-error** class to the textboxes and wire up the events again.

1. Open the **login.js** file.
2. Add a variable called **loginButton**, below the already defined variables, which is used to wire up the **click** event to the **Log in** button in the panel. Have the event call a function named **onLoginClick**.
   ```
   var loginButton = $("#login-button").click(onLoginClick);
   ```
3. Add a function called **onLoginClick** below the already existing functions.
4. Fetch the values from attributes and element values and store them in variables as described above.
   ```
   var url = $('#login-button').attr('data-login-action');
   var return_url = $('#login-button').attr('data-login-return-url');
   var email = $('#Email').val();
   var pwd = $('#Password').val();
   var remember_me = $('#RememberMe').prop('checked');
   var antiforegry = $('[name= "__RequestVerificationToken"]').val();
   ```
5. Add an Ajax call, below the variable declarations, which calls the **LoginAsync** action in the **Account** controller.
   ```
   $.post(url, { __RequestVerificationToken: antiforegry, email: email, password: pwd, RememberMe: remember_me },
   function (data) {
       // Success function
   }).fail(function (xhr, status, error) {
       // Fail function
   });
   ```
6. Check if any errors have been reported by the server by parsing the **data** function parameter with the **parseHTML** function
   ```
   var parsed = $.parseHTML(data);
   ```
7. Check if the **[data-valmsg-summary]** attribute is empty and store the result in variable called **hasErrors**.
   ```
   var hasErrors = $(parsed).find("[data-valmsg-summary]").text()
   .replace(/\n|\r/g, "").length > 0;
   ```
8. Keep the log in panel open if there are errors by adding the content of the **data** function parameter to the **<div>** with the **[data-login-panel-partial]** attribute.
   ```
   $("div[data-login-panel-partial]").html(data);
   ```
9. Open the panel by adding the **open** class to the **<div>** with the **[data-login-user-area]** attribute.

```
$('div[data-login-user-area]').addClass('open');
```

10. Add the **data-login-error** class to the textboxes to change their background color to a light red.
    ```
    $('#Email').addClass("data-login-error");
    $('#Password').addClass("data-login-error");
    ```

11. Remove the **open** and **data-login-error** classes if the login was successful.
    ```
    $('div[data-login-user-area]').removeClass('open');
    $('#Email').removeClass("data-login-error");
    $('#Password').removeClass("data-login-error");
    ```

12. Redirect to the URL in the **return_url** variable (/Home/Index).
    ```
    location.href = return_url;
    ```

13. Regardless if the log in was successful or not, the link and button events have to tbe wired up again.
    ```
    loginButton = $("#login-button").click(onLoginClick);
    loginLinkHover = $("#loginLink").hover(onLoginLinkHover);
    loginCloseButton = $("#close-login").click(onCloseLogin);
    ```

14. If an error occurs and the fail function is executed, then add the **data-login-error** class to the textboxes and wire up the events again.
    ```
    $('#Email').addClass("data-login-error");
    $('#Password').addClass("data-login-error");
    /* Wire up events */
    loginButton = $("#login-button").click(onLoginClick);
    loginLinkHover = $("#loginLink").hover(onLoginLinkHover);
    loginCloseButton = $("#close-login").click(onCloseLogin);
    ```

15. Run the application and try to log in using a non-existing email and make sure that the login panel stays open and the background color of the textboxes are changed to a light red.

16. Try to login using an exisitng email and password. The user should be logged in and the **Index** view in the **Home** controller should be displayed. The **Log in** link should be replaced with a red **Log out** button; clicking the button should log out the user.

The complete code for the **Log in** button:

```
var loginButton = $("#login-button").click(onLoginClick);

function onLoginClick() {
    var url = $('#login-button').attr('data-login-action');
    var return_url = $('#login-button').attr('data-login-return-url');
    var email = $('#Email').val();
    var pwd = $('#Password').val();
    var remember_me = $('#RememberMe').prop('checked');
    var antiforegry = $('[name= "__RequestVerificationToken"]').val();

    $.post(url, { __RequestVerificationToken: antiforegry, email: email,
    password: pwd, RememberMe: remember_me },
    function (data) {
        var parsed = $.parseHTML(data);
        var hasErrors = $(parsed).find("[data-valmsg-summary]").text()
            .replace(/\n|\r/g, "").length > 0;

        if (hasErrors == true) {
            $("div[data-login-panel-partial]").html(data);
            $('div[data-login-user-area]').addClass('open');
            $('#Email').addClass("data-login-error");
            $('#Password').addClass("data-login-error");
        }
        else {
            $('div[data-login-user-area]').removeClass('open');
            $('#Email').removeClass("data-login-error");
            $('#Password').removeClass("data-login-error");
            location.href = return_url;
        }
        /* Wire up events */
        loginButton = $("#login-button").click(onLoginClick);
        loginLinkHover = $("#loginLink").hover(onLoginLinkHover);
        loginCloseButton = $("#close-login").click(onCloseLogin);

    }).fail(function (xhr, status, error) {
        $('#Email').addClass("data-login-error");
        $('#Password').addClass("data-login-error");
        /* Wire up events */
        loginButton = $("#login-button").click(onLoginClick);
        loginLinkHover = $("#loginLink").hover(onLoginLinkHover);
        loginCloseButton = $("#close-login").click(onCloseLogin);
    });
};
```

16. Forgot Password

Introduction
In this chapter you will implement a password recovery mechanism whereby the user can request a password rest link to his or her mailbox. This is a more secure way of resetting a password compared to dispalying a form with a password textbox directly.

There are a few steps that you have to go through to unlock this functionality, among which are implementing a method that sends the recovery email and defining the correct SMTP data in the **Web.Config** file. Get any of these wrong and the email will not be sent.

It's impossible to list SMTP settings for all the providers, so you will have to contact your email provider and ask them or Google it to find the answer. You will need a **from** email address and its **password**, the the email provider's **host** name and the **port** they use for SMTP traffic.

When testing the password recovery, you should use an email which isn't connected in any way to the **from** email address you specified in the **Web.Config** file. If the **from** email address is set to forward emails to the email address you try to change the password for, it will likely not work.

A modal dialog will be used to display the textbox and button needed to send a password reset request and in the background JavaScript will be used to make an Ajax call to the **ForgotPassword** action in the **Account** controller.

You'll need to call the **Send** extension method you implement from the **SendAsync** method in the **EmailService** class. This method is called by the framework to send the reset email when a new password is requested.

The **ForgotPassword** action in the **Account** controller has some commented out code at the end of the method that you need to uncomment in order to activate the password recovery process.

The **GlyphLink** extension method you created in a previous chapter must be modified to take a list of attributes which are added to the **<a>** element it generates.

The recovery process:

1. The user clicks the **pwd** link in the navigation area which opens the modal form where the email is entered.
2. When the **Reset Password** button is clicked an Ajax call is made to the **ForgotPassword** action in the **Account** controller.
3. After the model is verified as valid, the user is fetched from the database to make sure that a user with that email exists.
    a. If the user doesn't exist, the user is redirected to the **ForgotPasswordConfirmation** view. It's a security measure, not to show that the password recovery failed.
    b. If the user exists, an email with a recovery link is sent to the provided email address.
4. When the user clicks the link in the recovery email, the **ResetPassword** view is displayed where the user enters the email address and the new password.
5. When the user clicks the **Reset** button in the **ResetPassword** view the new password is stored in the database and the **ResetPasswordConfirmation** view is displayed.
6. The user can now login with the new password.

Sending email

The first thing you need to do is to get the SMTP settings for the email address you want to send the email from. Contact the provider or Google it. You need the following information:

- The email address to send the emails from.
- The password for the email address.
- The host name; it usually starts with smtp like **smtp**.gmail.com.
  You can read more about Gmail's SMTP settings here (https://support.google.com/a/answer/176600?hl=en) or search for *Gmail SMTP* to find the proper settings outlined.

- The port number used by the provider to send email, which as of this writing is port 587 for Gmail and many other providers.

Web.Config

Add the information to the **Web.Config** file's **<appSettings>** element.

```
<appSettings>
  ...
  <!--Email settings-->
  <add key="from" value="noreply@mydomain.com" />
  <add key="host" value="smtp01.prvider.com" />
  <add key="port" value="587" />
  <add key="password" value="--the email password--" />
  <!--End Email settings-->
</appSettings>
```

The Send extension method

This method is called when the recovery email is sent. One way to send emails will be described in this section, it is however possible to implement it differently if you are so inclined.

You will implement the **Send** method as an extension of the **IdentityMessage** class which is used to define an email message.

Read the email settings from the **Web.Config** file's **<appSettings>** element and store them in variables called **from**, **pasword**, **host** and **port**.

```
var password = ConfigurationManager.AppSettings["password"];
```

Use an instance of the **MailMessage** class to create the email that will be sent and call the **Send** method on an instance of the **SmtpClient** to send the email.

1. Right-click on the **Extensions** folder and select **Add-Class**.
2. Name the class **EmaiExtensions**.
3. Add the following **using** statements.
   ```
   using Microsoft.AspNet.Identity;
   using System.Configuration;
   using System.Net.Mail;
   ```

4. Make the class **static** and add a **static void** method called **Send** that uses the **this** keyword to target instances of the **IdentityMessage** class.
   ```
   public static void Send(this IdentityMessage message) { ... }
   ```
5. Fetch the four settings for the email from the **Web.Config** file.
   ```
   var password = ConfigurationManager.AppSettings["password"];
   var from = ConfigurationManager.AppSettings["from"];
   var host = ConfigurationManager.AppSettings["host"];
   var port = Int32.Parse(ConfigurationManager.AppSettings["port"]);
   ```
6. Use an instance of the **MailMessage** class and the data in the **message** parameter to create the email that will be sent.
   ```
   var email = new MailMessage(from, message.Destination,
   message.Subject, message.Body);
   email.IsBodyHtml = true;
   ```
7. Create the **SmtpClient** instance that will send the email to the recipient.
   ```
   var client = new SmtpClient(host, port);
   client.EnableSsl = true;
   client.Credentials = new System.Net.NetworkCredential(from,
   password);
   ```
8. Add a **try/catch**-block around the code in the method to prevent any errors from crashing the application. I suggest that you add an **Exception** parameter and a breakpoint to the **catch**-block during debugging for easy access to the error messages.
   ```
   try
   {
       ...
       client.Send(email);
   }
   catch(Exception ex)
   {
   }
   ```

The complete code for the **Send** extension method:

```
public static class EmailExtensions
{
    public static void Send(this IdentityMessage message)
    {
        try
        {
```

```csharp
        // Read settings from Web.Config
        var password = ConfigurationManager.AppSettings["password"];
        var from = ConfigurationManager.AppSettings["from"];
        var host = ConfigurationManager.AppSettings["host"];
        var port = Int32.Parse(ConfigurationManager
           .AppSettings["port"]);

        // Create the email to send
        var email = new MailMessage(from, message.Destination,
           message.Subject, message.Body);
        email.IsBodyHtml = true;

        // Create the SmtpClient that will send the email
        var client = new SmtpClient(host, port);
        client.EnableSsl = true;
        client.Credentials = new System.Net.NetworkCredential(
           from, password);

        // Send the email
        client.Send(email);
     }
     catch(Exception ex)
     {
     }
   }
}
```

The Account controller

1. Open the **AccountController** class and locate the **ForgotPassword** action method.
2. Uncomment the four commented out code lines at the end of the action to enable sending emails.
3. Make sure that the **EmailConfirmed** property on the **ApplicationUser** instance is set to **true** in the **Register** and **RegisterAsync** actions.

```csharp
var user = new ApplicationUser {
   UserName = model.Email,
   Email = model.Email,
   FirstName = model.FirstName,
   IsActive = true,
   Registered = DateTime.Now,
   EmailConfirmed = true
};
```

The complete code for the **ForgotPassword** action:

```
[HttpPost]
[AllowAnonymous]
[ValidateAntiForgeryToken]
public async Task<ActionResult> ForgotPassword(ForgotPasswordViewModel
model)
{
    if (ModelState.IsValid)
    {
        var user = await UserManager.FindByEmailAsync(model.Email);
        if (user == null || !(await UserManager.IsEmailConfirmedAsync(
            user.Id)))
        {
            // To avoid revealing that the user does not exist
            // or is not confirmed
            return View("ForgotPasswordConfirmation");
        }

        /* --- Uncomment these four code lines --- */
        string code = await UserManager.GeneratePasswordResetTokenAsync(
            user.Id);

        var callbackUrl = Url.Action("ResetPassword", "Account",
            new { userId = user.Id, code = code },
            protocol: Request.Url.Scheme);

        await UserManager.SendEmailAsync(user.Id, "Reset Password",
            "Please reset your password by clicking <a href=\"" +
            callbackUrl + "\">here</a>");

        return RedirectToAction("ForgotPasswordConfirmation", "Account");
    }

    // If we got this far, something failed, redisplay form
    return View(model);
}
```

The SendAsync method

To send emails, the **Send** extension method that you implemented earlier in this chapter has to be called from the **SendAsync** method in the **EmailService** class in the **IdentityConfig.cs** file.

1. Open the **IdentityConfig.cs** file located in the **App_Start** folder.
2. Locate the **SendAsync** method in the **EmailService** class.
3. Add a call to the **Send** extension method that you implemented earlier above the **return** statement.
   ```
   message.Send();
   ```

The complete code for the **SendAsync** method:

```
public class EmailService : IIdentityMessageService
{
    public Task SendAsync(IdentityMessage message)
    {
        message.Send(); /* Add this row to send the email */
        return Task.FromResult(0);
    }
}
```

The modal reset password form

In this section, you will create the modal password reset form and add an Ajax call to the **Reset Password** button's **click** event which calls the **ForgotPassword** action of the **Account** controller asynchronously to send an email with a password reset link to the email specified in the textbox.

The modal form will have two buttons; one to reset the password and one to close the form. The close button should be decoreated with the **glyphicon-remove** icon and be located in the upper right corner of the form's heading.

A link with the company's support email should be placed below the textbox. Clicking the link should open the default email software. Add the email address prefixed with **mailto:** in the **<a>** element's **href** attribute.

You'll need to add a CSS style sheet called **forgot-password.css** and a JavaScript file with the same name. Create the modal form in a partial view called **_ForgotPaswordPanel-Partial** in the **Views-Shared** folder.

The **GlyphLink** extension method in the **HtmlExtensions** class must be updated to receive a list of attributes which are added to the **<a>** element rendered by the method. Use a **Dictionary<string, string>** collection for the attribute parameter.

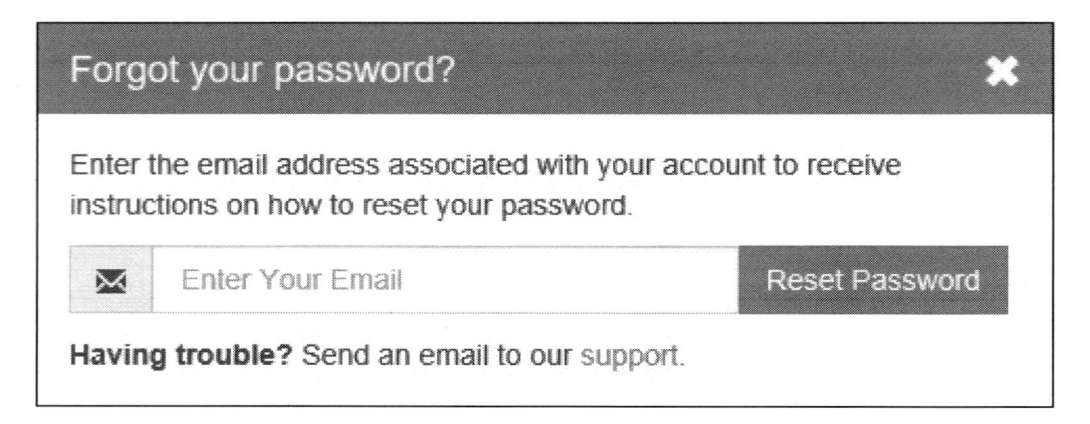

Adding the CSS and Javbascript files
1. Right-click on the **Content** folder and select **Add-Style Sheet**.
2. Name the style sheet **forgot-password.css**.
3. Right-click on the **Scripts** folder and select **Add-JavaScript File**.
4. Name the JavaScript file **forgot-password.js**.
5. Open the **BundleConfig** class located in the **App_Start** folder.
6. Add the style sheet file to the style bundle.
7. Add the JavaScript file to the script bundle.
8. Save all the files.

Modifying the GlyphLink extension method
The **pwd** link that will open the modal form, which you will add to the application's navigation area, must have certain attributes. To be able to add these attributes to the **<a>** element, that the **GlypLink** extension method renders, it has to be updated to take a **Dictionary<string, string>** as a parameter for the attributes and add the supplied attributes to the element.

1. Open the **HtmlExtensions** class and locate the **GlyphLink** method.
2. Add a **Dictionary<string, string>** parameter called **attributes** with a default value of **null** to the method definition.

```
public static MvcHtmlString GlyphLink(this HtmlHelper htmlHelper,
string controller, string action, string text, string glyphicon,
string cssClasses = "", string id = "", Dictionary<string, string>
attributes = null)
```

3. Add an if-statement before the **href** attribute assignment which checks that the **controller** parameter contains a value. Add an else-statement after the previous **href** assignment and assign # to the **href**.

```
if(controller.Length > 0)
    anchor.MergeAttribute("href", string.Format("/{0}/{1}/",
        controller, action));
else
    anchor.MergeAttribute("href", "#");
```

4. Add an if-statement below the **href** assignment which checks if the **attributes** parameter is not **null** and iterate over the attributes in the **attributes** parameter adding them one at a time to the **<a>** element.

```
if(attributes != null)
    foreach(var attribute in attributes)
        anchor.MergeAttribute(attribute.Key, attribute.Value);
```

The complete code for the **GlyphLink** method:

```
public static MvcHtmlString GlyphLink(this HtmlHelper htmlHelper,
string controller, string action, string text, string glyphicon,
string cssClasses = "", string id = "", Dictionary<string, string>
attributes = null)
{
    // Declare the span for the glyphicon
    var glyph = string.Format("<span class='glyphicon
        glyphicon-{0}'></span>", glyphicon);

    // Declare the anchor tag
    var anchor = new TagBuilder("a");

    // Add the href attribute to the <a> element
    if(controller.Length > 0)
        anchor.MergeAttribute("href", string.Format("/{0}/{1}/",
            controller, action));
    else
        anchor.MergeAttribute("href", "#");
```

```
    // Add the attributes to the <a> element
    if(attributes != null)
        foreach(var attribute in attributes)
            anchor.MergeAttribute(attribute.Key, attribute.Value);

    // Add the <span> element and the text to the <a> element
    anchor.InnerHtml = string.Format("{0} {1}", glyph, text);
    anchor.AddCssClass(cssClasses);
    anchor.GenerateId(id);

    // Create the helper
    return MvcHtmlString.Create( anchor.ToString(TagRenderMode.Normal));
}
```

Adding the password link

The **pwd** (password) link must have the **data-toggle** attribute with the value **modal** in order to be able to open the modal form specified in the **data-target** attribute. The **data-target** attribute should contain the **id** of the form, which in this case is **#pwdModal**. These two attributes are added with the new **Dictionary** parameter of the **GlyphLink** method.

Add the **pwd** link in a new list item **<li>** element below the previous **GlyphLink** in the **_LoginPartial** view. The link should not specify any controller or action since the call will be handled by Ajax.

1. Open the **_LoginPartial** view.
2. Add a new **<li>** element below the previous one calling the **GlyphLink** method.
3. Add a call to the **GlyphLink** method inside the new **<li>** element. Specify the link text *pwd*, the glyphicon *lock*, the id *pwdLink* and add the two attributes to the **Dictionary** parameter.
   ```
   <li>
      @Html.GlyphLink("", "", "pwd", "lock", "", "pwdLink",
          new Dictionary<string, string>{ { "data-toggle", "modal" },
          { "data-target", "#pwdModal" } })
   </li>
   ```
4. Run the application and make sure that he **pwd** link is displayed properly with its lock icon.

Building the modal form

To create the modal form, you need to add two **<div>** elements where the first defines the modal dialog and the second specifies where the form area begins. The first element should be decorated with the **modal** class and have the **role** attribute set to **dialog**. It can also be decorated with the **fade** class to make the dialog fade in and out. The second element should be decorated with the **modal-dialog** class to specify that it is the container for the dialog content.

Within the **modal-dialog** container, you add the elements that will be part of the dialog. In this exercise, you will use a Bootstrap panel to which you add a link decorated with the **glyphicon-remove** which will close the dialog, a textbox for the email address, the **Reset Password** button which will send a password recover email to the user and a support email link at the bottom.

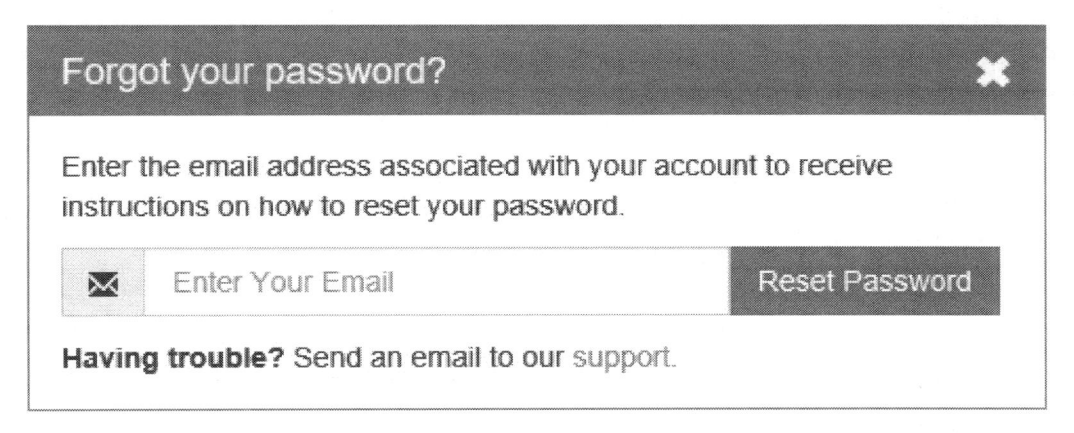

Forgot your password?

Enter the email address associated with your account to receive instructions on how to reset your password.

✉ Enter Your Email   Reset Password

Having trouble? Send an email to our support.

Create the modal dialog as a partial view called **_ForgotPasswordPanelPartial** in the **Views-Shared** folder. Use the **ForgotPasswordViewModel** class as the view model. Render the view using the **@Html.Partial** method below the **_RegisterUserPartial** view in the **Index** view for the **Home** controller.

Adding the _ForgotPasswordPanelPartial view

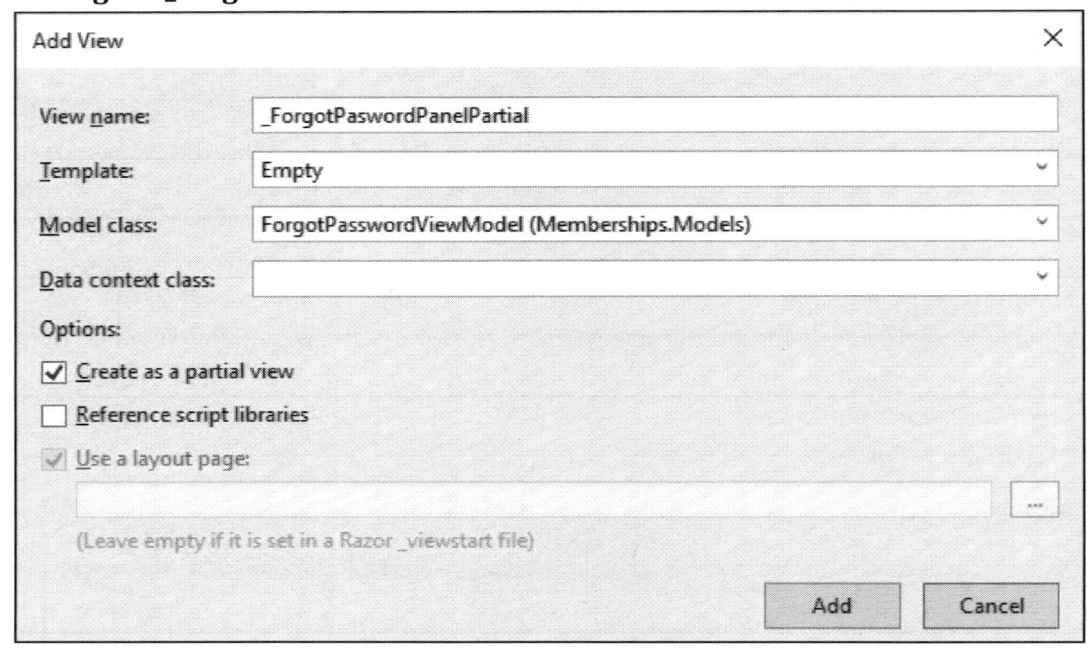

(Add View dialog)
- View name: _ForgotPaswordPanelPartial
- Template: Empty
- Model class: ForgotPasswordViewModel (Memberships.Models)
- Data context class: *(empty)*
- Options:
  - ☑ Create as a partial view
  - ☐ Reference script libraries
  - ☑ Use a layout page: *(empty)*
  - (Leave empty if it is set in a Razor _viewstart file)

1. Right-click on the **Views-Shared** folder and select **Add-View**.
2. Use the following settings for the view:
    a. View name: **_ForgotPasswordPanelPartial**
    b. Tempate: **Empty**
    c. Model class: **ForgotPasswordViewModel**
    d. Data context class: Remove any text in this field
    e. Check the **Create as a partial view** checkbox.
    f. Click the **Add** button.

Adding the modal dialog to the view

1. Add a **<div>** decorated with the **modal** and **fade** classes and have the **role** attribute set to **dialog**. Give the element an **id** of **pwdModal**.
   ```
   <div class="modal fade" id="pwdModal" role="dialog">
   ```

2. Add a **<div>** decorated with the **modal-dialog** class inside the previous **<div>**.
   ```
   <div class="modal-dialog">
   ```

3. Add a Bootstrap **panel-primary** panel with heading and body elements to the inner **<div>**.

   ```
   <div class="panel panel-primary">
       <div class="panel-heading">
       </div>
       <div class="panel-body">
       </div>
   </div>
   ```

4. Add an **<h4>** element containing the text *Forgot your password?* and an **<a>** element displaying a **glyphicon-remove** icon using a **<span>**. The **<a>** element should be pulled to the far right of the panel heading by decorating it with the **pull-right** class. It also should have a **data-dismiss** attribute set to **modal** to close the dialog when clicked and an **id** of **close-forgot-password**.

   ```
   <h4>Forgot your password?
       <a id="close-forgot-password" class="pull-right"
           data-dismiss="modal">
           <span class="glyphicon glyphicon-remove"></span>
       </a>
   </h4>
   ```

5. Create an anti-forgery token in the **panel-body** element.
   @Html.AntiForgeryToken()

6. Add a paragraph below the anti-forgery token with the text: *Enter the email address associated with your account to receive instructions on how to reset your password.*

7. Add a **<div>** decorated with the **input-group** class which encompasses the **envelope** glypicon, the textbox and the **Reset Password** button. The **<span>** for the glyphicon must also be decorated with the **input-group-addon** for it to stick to the textbox as If they were one control. The textbox should be decorated with the **form-control** and **reset-email** classes, the latter for CSS and JavaScript targeting. The **<button>** element should have an **id** of **resetPwd**.

   ```
   <div class="input-group">
       <span class="input-group-addon glyphicon
           glyphicon-envelope"></span>

       @Html.TextBoxFor(m => m.Email, new { @class = "form-control
           reset-email", @placeholder = "Enter Your Email" })
   ```

```
            <button id="resetPwd" class="btn btn-primary" type="button">
                Reset Password
            </button>
        </div>
```

8. Add a **<div>** decorated with a class called **support-text** for CSS targeting.
9. Add the text *Having trouble? send an email to our support* followed by a link to an email address.
10. Open the **Index** view in the **Home** folder. Render the view using the **@Html.Partial** method below the **_RegisterUserPartial** view.

    ```
    @Html.Partial("_ForgotPaswordPanelPartial",
        new ForgotPasswordViewModel { Email = "" })
    ```

The complete code for the **_ForgotPasswordPanelPartial** view:

```
@model Memberships.Models.ForgotPasswordViewModel

<div class="modal fade" id="pwdModal" role="dialog">
    <div class="modal-dialog">
        <div class="panel panel-primary">
            <div class="panel-heading">
                <h4>Forgot your password?
                    <a id="close-forgot-password" class="pull-right"
                        data-dismiss="modal">
                        <span class="glyphicon glyphicon-remove"></span>
                    </a>
                </h4>
            </div>
            <div class="panel-body">
                @Html.AntiForgeryToken()

                <p>Enter the email address associated with your account to
                    receive instructions on how to reset your password.</p>

                <div class="input-group">
                    <span class="input-group-addon glyphicon
                        glyphicon-envelope"></span>

                    @Html.TextBoxFor(m => m.Email, new { @class =
                        "form-control reset-email", @placeholder =
                        "Enter Your Email" })
```

```html
                <button id="resetPwd" class="btn btn-primary"
                    type="button">Reset Password
                </button>
            </div>

            <div class="support-text">
                <strong>Having trouble?</strong> Send an email
                    to our <a href="mailto:info@csharpschool.com">
                    support</a>.
            </div>
        </div>
    </div>
  </div>
</div>
```

Styling the modal dialog

Apply the following CSS styles in the **forgot-password.css** style sheet.

Remove the rounded corners on the all the controls in the dialog, you can use the * selector to target all elements.

```
.modal-dialog * {
    border-radius:0px;
}
```

Assign a fixed width of 485px to the panel.

```
.modal-dialog .panel {
    width:485px;
}
```

The panel heading need the top margin removed and less top- and bottom padding.

```
.modal-dialog .panel-heading {
    margin-top: 0px;
    padding-top: 1px;
    padding-bottom: 1px;
}
```

The close button must have 100% opacity to be displayed as white. It could also benefit from the same font size as the heading (18px) and a negative 2px top margin for vertical positioning. Also, change the mouse pointer to a hand pointer.

```
#close-forgot-password {
    opacity: 1;
    font-size:18px;
    margin-top:-2px
    color: white;
    cursor: pointer;
}
```

To align the **glyphicon-envelope** icon background with the textbox, it needs a 0px top positioning.

```
.modal-dialog .glyphicon-envelope {
    top:0px;
}
```

The **Reset Password** button needs a -4px left margin to be displayed flush to the right side of the textbox.

```
#resetPwd{
    margin-left:-4px;
}
```

The support text needs a 10px top margin to get some space from the controls above it.

```
.modal-dialog .support-text {
    margin-top:10px;
}
```

Add this CSS if the backdrop blocks the modal input form.

```
.modal-backdrop {
    position: static;
}
```

Adding JavaScript to the modal dialog

Apply the following JavaScript in the **forgot-password.js** file.

Add the document ready function to the script file and add the subsequent code to it.

```
$(function () {
});
```

Hook up the **hover** event to the **pwd** link to close the **Log in** pop-up if it is open.

```
var pwdLinkHover = $("#pwdLink").hover(onCloseLogin);

function onCloseLogin() {
    $('div[data-login-user-area]').removeClass('open');
}
```

Hook up the click event for the **Reset Password (#resetPwd)** button and have it call the **/Account/ForgotPassword** action with the anti-forgery token and the email address. When the Ajax call to the server returns to the client, redirect to the **/Account/ForgotPasswordConfirmation** action even if an error has ocurred. This will take the the user to a page displaying a confirmation message.

On the server side, an attempt is made to send an email to the email address provided to the **ForgotPassword** action. Below the code is a sequence of images showing what happens when a successful password reset is completed.

The complete code for the **forgot-password.js** file:

```
$(function () {
    var pwdLinkHover = $("#pwdLink").hover(onCloseLogin);
    var resetPwd = $("#resetPwd").click(onResetPassword);

    function onCloseLogin() {
        $('div[data-login-user-area]').removeClass('open');
    }

    function onResetPassword() {
        var email = $(".modal-dialog .reset-email").val();
        var antiforegry = $('[name= "__RequestVerificationToken"]').val();
        var url = "/Account/ForgotPasswordConfirmation";

        $.post("/Account/ForgotPassword", { __RequestVerificationToken:
            antiforegry, email: email },
        function (data) {
            location.href = url;
        }).fail(function (xhr, status, error) {
            location.href = url;
        });
    }
});
```

The Forgot Password Confirmation view
When the email has been sent, whether or not it was delivered, the **Forgot Password Confirmation** view is displayed to the user. It is always displayed to prevent the user from knowing if it was successful or not. Knowing if it failed could help coders with malicious intent to hack the system.

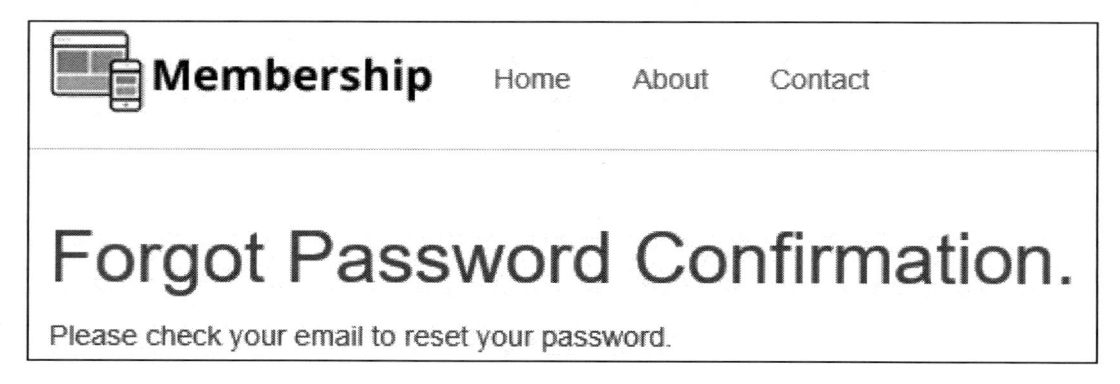

The Reset Password email
If the email is sent successfully from the server, an email with a reset link will appear in the inbox of the provided email address.

The expanded email with the link circled.

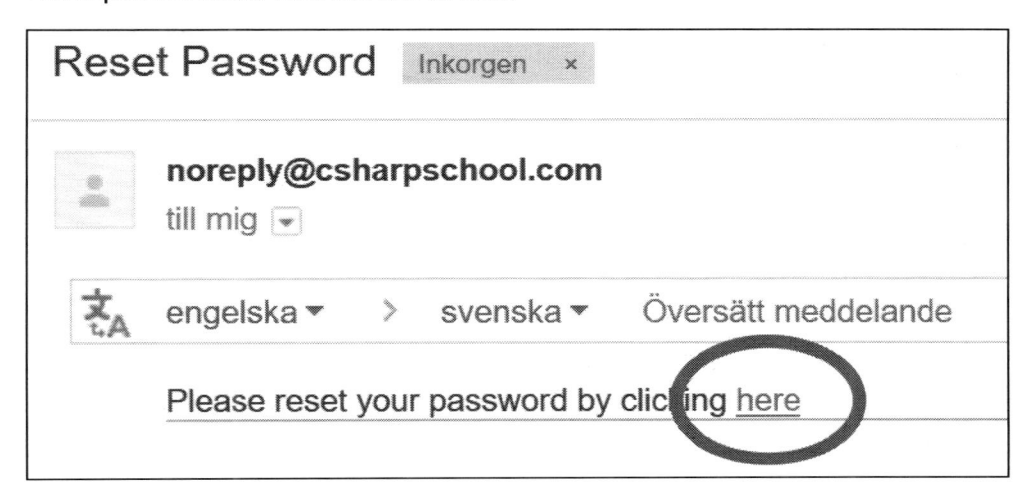

The Reset Passsword view
When the user clicks the link in the email, the following view is opened in a browser where a new password can be entered.

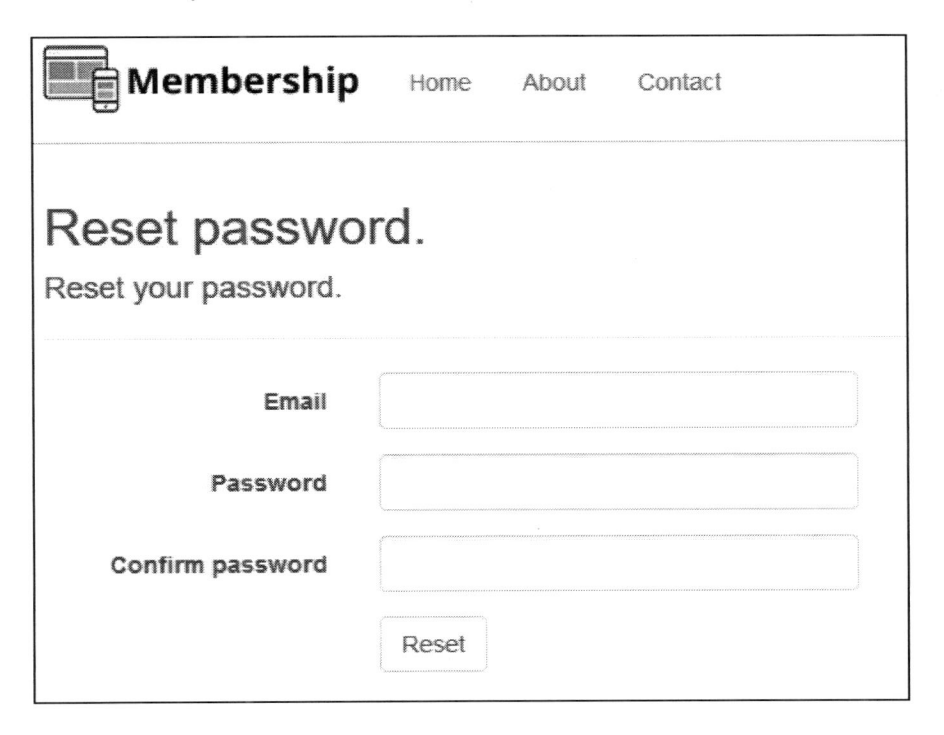

465

When the user clicks the **Reset** button, the new password will be stored for the provided email and the user is redirected to the **Reset Password Confiormation** view where he or she can log in.

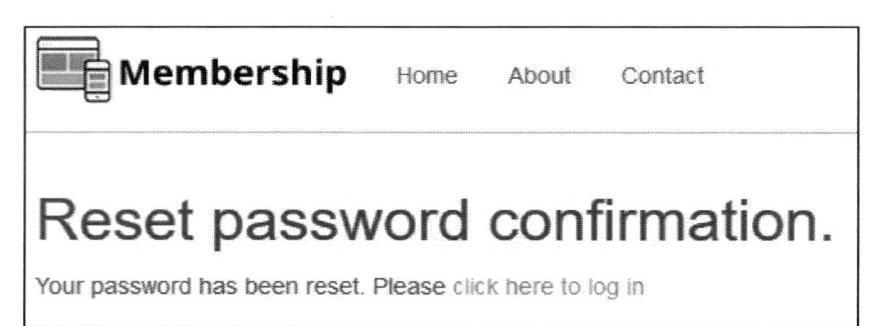

Reset password confirmation.

Your password has been reset. Please click here to log in

17. Useful Tools & Links

Tools

This is not a content chapter per se. It contains useful tools and links which can help you greatly in your day-to-day work as a developer.

Microsoft Web Platform Installer 5.0

The Microsoft Web Platform Installer (Web PI) is a free tool that makes getting the latest components of the Microsoft Web Platform, including Internet Information Services (IIS), SQL Server Express, .NET Framework and Visual Web Developer easy.

Link: http://www.microsoft.com/web/downloads/platform.aspx

Bootstrap

Bootstrap is the most popular HTML, CSS, and JavaScript framework for developing responsive, mobile first projects on the web. It helps bring your website to life and give it a professional look and feel. Bootstrap makes front-end web development faster and easier. It's made for folks of all skill levels, devices of all shapes, and projects of all sizes.

Bootstrap is automatically installed with all Visual Studio web projects.

Link: http://getbootstrap.com/

CodeLens

Is a quality and diagnostic tool which helps you keep track of what is happening to your code while your focus remains on the code window. This tool is only available for Visual Studio Ultimate. It helps you find code references, changes to your code, linked bugs, work items, code reviews, and unit tests.

Link: https://msdn.microsoft.com/en-us/library/dn269218.aspx

Web Essentials

Web Essentials extends Visual Studio 2013 with a lot of new features that web developers have been missing for years. If you ever write CSS, HTML, JavaScript,

Markdown, TypeScript, CoffeeScript or LESS, then you will find many useful features that make your life easier as a developer.

Link: http://vswebessentials.com/

Browser link

Pushes changes made in views out to all browsers and devices connected with the MVC application at run-time. Browser link ships with Visual Studio 2013.

Shortcut: **Ctrl+Alt+Enter**

SideWaffle

Is an extension for Visual Studio 2012/2013 which can make web developing much easier, richer and more productive. Adds useful snippets, project- and item templates to Visual Studio.

Link: http://www.sidewaffle.com/

Plunker

Plunker is an online community for creating, collaborating on and sharing your web development ideas.

- **Speed**: Despite its complexity, the Plunker editor is designed to load in under 2 seconds.
- **Ease of use**: Plunker's features should just work and not require additional explanation.
- **Collaboration**: From real-time collaboration to forking and commenting, Plunker seeks to encourage users to work together on their code.

Link: https://plnkr.co/

Visual Studio Code

An online code editor that runs everywhere, not only on PCs.

Go beyond syntax highlighting and autocomplete with IntelliSense, which provides smart completions based on variable types, function definitions, and imported modules.

Debug code right from the editor. Launch or attach to your running apps and debug with break points, call stacks, and an interactive console.

Working with Git has never been easier. Review diffs, stage files, and make commits right from the editor. Push and pull from any hosted Git service.

Install extensions to add new languages, themes, debuggers, and to connect to additional services. Extensions run in separate processes, ensuring they won't slow down your editor.

Link: https://code.visualstudio.com/

Atom

Atom is a text editor that's modern, approachable, yet hackable to the core—a tool you can customize to do anything but also use productively without ever touching a config file.

- Atom works across operating systems. You can use it on OS X, Windows, or Linux.
- Search for and install new packages or start creating your own—all from within Atom.
- Atom helps you write code faster with a smart, flexible autocomplete.
- Easily browse and open a single file, a whole project, or multiple projects in one window.
- Split your Atom interface into multiple panes to compare and edit code across files.
- Find, preview, and replace text as you type in a file or across all your projects.

Link: https://atom.io/

TypeScript

TypeScript enables JavaScript developers to use highly-productive development tools and practices like static checking and code refactoring when developing JavaScript applications.

TypeScript starts from the same syntax and semantics that millions of JavaScript developers know today. Use existing JavaScript code, incorporate popular JavaScript libraries, and call TypeScript code from JavaScript.

TypeScript compiles to clean, simple JavaScript code which runs on any browser, in Node.js, or in any JavaScript engine that supports ECMAScript 3 (or newer).

TypeScript offers support for the latest and evolving JavaScript features, including those from ECMAScript 2015 and future proposals, like async functions and decorators, to help build robust components.

Link: https://www.typescriptlang.org/

Angular

HTML is great for declaring static documents, but it falters when we try to use it for declaring dynamic views in web-applications. AngularJS lets you extend HTML vocabulary for your application. The resulting environment is extraordinarily expressive, readable, and quick to develop.

Other frameworks deal with HTML's shortcomings by either abstracting away HTML, CSS, and/or JavaScript or by providing an imperative way for manipulating the DOM. Neither of these address the root problem that HTML was not designed for dynamic views.

AngularJS is a toolset for building the framework most suited to your application development. It is fully extensible and works well with other libraries. Every feature can be modified or replaced to suit your unique development workflow and feature needs. Read on to find out how.

Link: https://angularjs.org/

Grunt

Is a JavaScript task runner. Why use a task runner? In one word: automation. The less work you have to do when performing repetitive tasks like minification, compilation, unit testing, linting, etc, the easier your job becomes. After you've configured it through a Gruntfile, a task runner can do most of that mundane work for you—and your team—with basically zero effort.

Why use Grunt? The Grunt ecosystem is huge and it's growing every day. With literally hundreds of plugins to choose from, you can use Grunt to automate just about anything with a minimum of effort. If someone hasn't already built what you need, authoring and publishing your own Grunt plugin to npm is a breeze.

Link: http://gruntjs.com/

Gulp

Use Gilp to automate and enhance your workflow. By preferring code over configuration, gulp keeps things simple and makes complex tasks manageable. Using the power of node streams, gulp gives you fast builds that don't write intermediary files to disk. By enforcing strict plugin guidelines, we ensure that plugins stay simple and work as expected. Using node best practices and maintaining a minimal API surface, your build works exactly as you would imagine.

Link: http://gulpjs.com/

ECMAScript 6 (JavaScript)

The next generation of JavaScript. ECMAScript 6, also known as ECMAScript 2015, is the latest version of the ECMAScript standard. ES6 is a significant update to the language, and the first update to the language since ES5 was standardized in 2009. Implementation of these features in major JavaScript engines is underway now.

Link (features): https://github.com/lukehoban/es6features

Link (language specification): http://www.ecma-international.org/ecma-262/6.0/

Entity Framework (EF Core)

Entity Framework is Microsoft's recommended data access technology for new applications in .NET.

Entity Framework Core (EF Core) provides a familiar developer experience to EF6.x, including LINQ, POCO, and Code First support. EF Core also enables access to data across relational and non-relational stores. EF Core is much more lightweight than previous versions and is built from the ground up to work great in the cloud (using ASP.NET vNext) on devices (i.e. in universal Windows apps) as well as in traditional .NET scenarios.

Link: https://github.com/aspnet/EntityFramework

Microsoft ASP.NET MVC Documentation

Link: http://www.asp.net/mvc